Promoting K-12 Civic Learning and Engagement Through Assessment

Promoting K-12 Civic Learning and Engagement Through Assessment is a comprehensive guide to the assessment of civic learning in primary and secondary education contexts. Today's schools have a responsibility to teach learners how to critically evaluate information, understand the rights and responsibilities of citizenship, and engage with people whose perspectives and experiences differ from their own. This book provides a vision for testing, measurement, and assessment efforts that support this broad vision of high-quality civic learning for all students.

The first section sets the stage for the rest of the volume by exploring historical, conceptual, and technological foundations of civic learning and assessment. The second section explores approaches to monitoring school-based civic learning opportunities and outcomes at the system level. It examines necessary innovations in large-scale assessment in order to generate high-quality data on a range of civic opportunities and outcomes. The third and final section presents work on assessment tools and strategies that directly support educators, students, and communities in cultivating meaningful civic engagement.

Scholars, teaching faculty, and graduate students of educational measurement, leadership, and policy, in addition to professionals in the assessment development field and other non-profits who are invested in fostering civic competencies among learners, will find an innovative resource to inform their work.

Laura S. Hamilton is a senior associate at the National Center for the Improvement of Educational Assessment.

Samuel H. Rikoon is a senior researcher at the American Institutes for Research.

David C. Kidd is Chief Assessment Scientist for the Democratic Knowledge Project in the Edmond & Lily Safra Center at Harvard University, U.S.A.

The NCME Applications of Educational Measurement
and Assessment Book Series
Editorial Board:

Kadriye Ercikan, ETS
Roy Levy, Arizona State University
Melissa Margolis, National Board of Medical Examiners
Willy Solano-Flores, Stanford University
Fritz Drasgow, University of Illinois at Urbana-Champaign
Henry Braun, Boston College
Rochelle Michel, Smarter Balanced

Fairness in Educational Assessment and Measurement
Edited by Neil J. Dorans and Linda L. Cook

Testing in the Professions: Credentialing Policies and Practice
Edited by Susan Davis-Becker and Chad W. Buckendahl

Validation of Score Meaning for the Next Generation of Assessments: The Use of Response Processes
Edited by Kadriye Ercikan and James W. Pellegrino

Preparing Students for College and Careers: Theory, Measurement, and Educational Practice
Edited by Katie Larsen McClarty, Krista D. Mattern, and Matthew N. Gaertner

Score Reporting Research and Applications
Edited by Diego Zapata-Rivera

Classroom Assessment and Educational Measurement
Edited by Susan M. Brookhart and James H. McMillan

Integrating Timing Considerations to Improve Testing Practices
Edited by Melissa J. Margolis and Richard A. Feinberg

Advancing Natural Language Processing in Educational Assessment
Edited by Victoria Yaneva and Matthias von Davier

Culturally Responsive Assessment in Classrooms and Large-Scale Contexts: Theory, Research, and Practice
Edited by Carla M. Evans and Catherine S. Taylor

Promoting K-12 Civic Learning and Engagement Through Assessment
Edited by Laura S. Hamilton, Samuel H. Rikoon, and David C. Kidd

For more information about this series, please visit: https://www.routledge.com/NCME-APPLICATIONS-OF-EDUCATIONAL-MEASUREMENT-AND-ASSESSMENT/book-series/NCME

Promoting K-12 Civic Learning and Engagement Through Assessment

Edited by Laura S. Hamilton,
Samuel H. Rikoon, and David C. Kidd

NEW YORK AND LONDON

Cover image: Shutterstock

First published 2026
by Routledge
605 Third Avenue, New York, NY 10158

and by Routledge
4 Park Square, Milton Park, Abingdon, Oxon, OX14 4RN

Routledge is an imprint of the Taylor & Francis Group, an informa business

© 2026 selection and editorial matter, Laura S. Hamilton, Samuel H. Rikoon, and David C. Kidd; individual chapters, the contributors

The right of Laura S. Hamilton, Samuel H. Rikoon, and David C. Kidd to be identified as the authors of the editorial material, and of the authors for their individual chapters, has been asserted in accordance with sections 77 and 78 of the Copyright, Designs and Patents Act 1988.

The Open Access version of this book, available at www.taylorfrancis.com, has been made available under a Creative Commons Attribution-Non Commercial-No Derivatives (CC-BY-NC-ND) 4.0 International license.

Any third party material in this book is not included in the OA Creative Commons license, unless indicated otherwise in a credit line to the material. Please direct any permissions enquiries to the original rightsholder.

For Product Safety Concerns and Information please contact our EU representative GPSR@taylorandfrancis.com. Taylor & Francis Verlag GmbH, Kaufingerstraße 24, 80331 München, Germany.

Trademark notice: Product or corporate names may be trademarks or registered trademarks, and are used only for identification and explanation without intent to infringe.

ISBN: 978-1-032-76050-6 (hbk)
ISBN: 978-1-032-75504-5 (pbk)
ISBN: 978-1-003-47682-5 (ebk)

DOI: 10.4324/9781003476825

Typeset in Minion Pro
by KnowledgeWorks Global Ltd.

Contents

Contributor Biographies — vii
Foreword — xiv
    DANIELLE ALLEN
Acknowledgments — xvi

1. The Role of Assessment in Advancing Civic Learning in K-12 Schools — 1
   LAURA S. HAMILTON, SAMUEL H. RIKOON, AND DAVID C. KIDD

Section 1: Setting the Stage: The Civic Assessment Landscape — 5

2. Cultures and Contexts of Civics Education and Assessment in the US — 7
   BENJAMIN M. JACOBS AND MICHAEL J. FEUER

3. Advancing the Future of Civic Learning and Engagement Through Assessment: How AI Might Power Innovation in What and How We Measure — 22
   ERIC M. TUCKER AND EVA L. BAKER

4. Mapping Civic Measurement: Assessing Readiness and Opportunities for an Engaged Citizenry — 41
   ANNA GALLOS, JESSICA SUTTER, MATT LEIGHNINGER, AND RAJIV VINNAKOTA

Section 2: Assessment for Large-Scale Monitoring of Civic Learning Outcomes and Opportunities — 63

5. Understanding Civic Learning and Engagement Through Large-Scale Assessments — 65
   MADELINE GOODMAN AND IRWIN KIRSCH

6. Measuring Civic and Citizenship Education Through Large-Scale Assessments: Insights from the International Civic and Citizenship Education Study (ICCS) — 80
   WOLFRAM SCHULZ AND VALERIA DAMIANI

7 Building the Backpack: Replicating State Standards Review
   and Assessment Processes in Civics Education   107
   BETH RATWAY AND PETER MABLI

8 Assessing Student Engagement in a U.S. History and Civics Curriculum   123
   LEAH BUESO, MARSHA ING, ABIGAIL DYM, AND JOSEPH KAHNE

9 Measuring Civic Values to Assess Civic Identity Development in Adolescents   137
   DAVID C. KIDD AND NICOLÁS RIVEROS MEDELIUS

10 Defining and Monitoring K-12 Civic Learning Opportunities in the
   United States   151
   MARGARITA OLIVERA-AGUILAR, LAURA S. HAMILTON, COREY SAVAGE,
   AND SAMUEL H. RIKOON

11 Can Discrete-Choice Measures and Situational-Judgment Tests Address
   Ongoing Questions about How to Quantify Global Citizenship?   168
   MICHAEL THIER

Section 3: Assessment to Foster Civic Learning Opportunities in the Classroom and Beyond   185

12 Assessing Digital Literacy as a Civic Skill in K-12 Classrooms   187
   MARK SMITH, JOEL BREAKSTONE, AND SAM WINEBURG

13 Reasoning with Content: Complex Scenarios as Performance Assessments 203
   JANE C. LO, SHEILA W. VALENCIA, AND WALTER C. PARKER

14 Developing Civic Competencies through Scenario-Based Learning
   and Assessment Tasks   220
   ALLI BRETTSCHNEIDER, GREG VAFIS, AND CAROLINE WYLIE

15 Exploring Implications of Transformative SEL for Civic Measurement
   in Diverse K-12 School Communities   238
   ROBERT J. JAGERS, BRITTNEY V. WILLIAMS, JOHARI HARRIS,
   AND BRIANA COLEMAN

16 CIRCLE's Civic Data Tool: Connecting Practitioners with Measures
   and Data for Impact   256
   ABBY KIESA AND ALBERTO MEDINA

Index   275

Contributor Biographies

Danielle Allen is James Bryant Conant University Professor at Harvard University. She is also Director of the Allen Lab for Democracy Renovation at the Harvard Kennedy School and Director of the Democratic Knowledge Project-Learn, a research lab focused on civic education at the Harvard Graduate School of Education. She is Professor of political philosophy, ethics, and public policy as well as a seasoned nonprofit leader, democracy advocate, tech ethicist, distinguished author, and mom. She is a contributing columnist at *The Atlantic* magazine and was the 2020 winner of the Library of Congress' Kluge Prize "for her internationally recognized scholarship in political theory and her commitment to improving democratic practice and civics education."

Eva L. Baker is Distinguished Professor Emerita at UCLA and Founding Director of CRESST, an R&D Center with a long history of research in assessment, evaluation, technology, learning, and policy. She conducted evaluations of AI-based games and systems supported by DARPA, ONR, and other Federal science-focused organizations. Her current work involves AI-based design for training assessments. She served as President of the American Educational Research Association and the World Education Research Association and as a co-chair of the NCME-AERA-APA Committee on Test Standards. Widely published, she is co-chair of a team designing an AI roadmap for the National Academy of Education.

Joel Breakstone is Cofounder and Executive Director of DIG. He previously directed the Stanford History Education Group. He leads DIG's efforts to research, develop, and disseminate free curriculum and assessments. He completed a Ph.D. at the Stanford Graduate School of Education. Before Stanford, he was a high school history teacher.

Alli Brettschneider is Director of English language arts curriculum (Grades 6–8) at Amplify. Before joining Amplify, she was a senior assessment specialist at the Educational Testing Service, where she led the development of the civics prototype described in the chapter. Her interests include the design of innovative K-12 assessments, curricula, and professional learning programs, with a focus on English language arts and social studies.

Leah Bueso is Assistant Professor of Urban Education at the University of Illinois, Springfield. Her research examines issues of racial and socioeconomic inequality in school law, policy, and pedagogy using interdisciplinary and mixed methods. In particular, Leah focuses on the subject areas of social studies, civics, special education, and education law. Leah received her Ph.D. in Urban Schooling from the University of California, Los Angeles and her J.D. from the University of Michigan Law School. She is also a credentialed special education teacher and reading specialist for children diagnosed with a language-based learning disability.

Briana Coleman is a researcher and evaluator who works within schools and nonprofit and community-based organizations to influence institutional and sectoral change. Briana largely uses participatory methods in partnership with young people and adults to disrupt racial injustice in their communities. She holds a Ph.D. in educational leadership and has an interdisciplinary educational and professional background.

Valeria Damiani is Associate Professor at LUMSA University in Rome (Italy). She was a member of the Joint Management Committee for the second and third cycles of the IEA International Civic and Citizenship Education Study (ICCS) 2016 and 2022. She has participated in several EU-funded projects on citizenship and inclusion since 2012. Currently, she is part of the working group on Quality Assurance for the European Space for Citizenship Education at the Council of Europe. Her research interests include civic and citizenship education, global citizenship education, education for sustainable development, and social inclusion.

Abigail Dym is Assistant Professor of Public and Community Service Studies at Providence College. She collaborates with schools, communities, and institutions to conduct rigorous scholarship on civic education, political participation, social studies curriculum and teaching, education policy, and policy feedback. Abigail received a joint-Ph.D. in Political Science and Education Policy from the University of Pennsylvania and is a former K-12 social studies teacher.

Michael J. Feuer is Professor of Education and International Affairs at the George Washington University, where he recently completed 15 years as Dean of the Graduate School of Education and Human Development. Previously, at the National Academy of Sciences, he was Founding Director of the Board on Testing and Assessment and later head of the behavioral and social sciences and education division. Feuer's work centers on the uses and misuses of standardized testing, the economics of education, the role of philanthropy in education research, international comparisons of education, and the revival of civics in American schools. He holds a Ph.D. in public policy from the University of Pennsylvania.

Anna Gallos is a Senior Project Manager at the National Constitution Center where she supports professional learning initiatives for educators in remote and rural communities. Previously, Anna spent eight years at the Institute for Citizens & Scholars developing and managing programs to equip young people with skills to be effective citizens. She also supported the Campuswide Immersion Initiative, which accelerates civic skill-building opportunities on college campuses. Earlier, she gained first-hand classroom experience serving as an interim Spanish teacher and previously worked in logistics management. Anna earned her BA in International Studies from American University.

Madeline Goodman is an independent researcher and writer who previously served as a senior researcher for the National Assessment of Educational Progress (NAEP) at ETS. Dr. Goodman has co-authored national and international assessment reports, including *Improving the Measurement of Civic Learning* (2023), *Opportunity across the States* (2021), *Too Big to Fail* (2018), and *America's Skills Challenge* (2015). Her scholarly work focuses on the intersection of large-scale assessment, civic and history education, and social equity. She holds a Ph.D. in U.S. history from Carnegie Mellon University and is Spencer Fellow and Fulbright Scholar. Dr. Goodman also earned an M.S. in Clinical Psychology and currently works as a psychotherapist in private practice.

Contributor Biographies • ix

Laura S. Hamilton is a senior associate at the National Center for the Improvement of Educational Assessment, where she collaborates with states, districts, and nonprofit organizations on the design and implementation of assessment policies and practices. Before joining the Center, Hamilton served as Senior Director at American Institutes for Research, Associate Vice President of the Research Centers at ETS, and distinguished chair in learning and assessment at RAND. She has also served on numerous expert committees, including the Joint Committee to revise the *Standards for Educational and Psychological Testing*. She is Fellow of the American Educational Research Association and received the Joseph A. Zins Distinguished Scholar Award from CASEL. Hamilton received a Ph.D. in educational psychology and an M.S. in statistics from Stanford University.

Johari Harris is Assistant Professor of educational psychology at Kennesaw State University in the Secondary and Middle Grades Department. Her research examines the development of transformative social-emotional competencies within secondary school contexts.

Marsha Ing is Associate Professor of educational psychology in the School of Education at the University of California, Riverside. Her research examines measures that support teacher and student learning. Marsha received her Ph.D. in Quantitative Research Methods from the University of California, Los Angeles.

Benjamin M. Jacobs, Research Associate Professor at the George Washington University, has spent most of his career preparing social studies teachers and Jewish educators for school and non-school settings, and consulting with various organizations on curriculum and research. His scholarship focuses on the history, theory, and practice of social education, history education, Jewish education, and teacher education on the American scene. Jacobs co-chairs the advisory board of the Collaborative for Applied Studies in Jewish Education (CASJE) and serves on the coordinating team of the Forum for Democracy and Education at GW. He holds a Ph.D. from Teachers College, Columbia University.

Robert J. Jagers is an independent senior researcher, focused on capacity building among local stakeholders to improve civic learning experiences and developmental outcomes for young people and adults in underserved school communities. Dr. Jagers previously served as Vice President of Research at Collaborative for Academic, Social, and Emotional Learning (CASEL). Prior to joining CASEL, he was a faculty member in the Combined Program in Education and Psychology at the University of Michigan, a Co-PI of the Center for the Study of Black Youth in Context (CSBYC), and Founding Director of Wolverine Pathways, a university-sponsored diversity pipeline program for qualified secondary school students.

Joseph Kahne is Dutton Presidential Professor of Education Policy and Politics at the University of California, Riverside. His research and school reform work focus on ways to identify and support equitable and impactful forms of civic and democratic education.

David C. Kidd is Chief Assessment Scientist at the Edmond & Lily Safra Center for Ethics (ELSCE) at Harvard, where he leads research projects related to civic education, civil discourse, and ethics education. David received a Ph.D. in Social Psychology from the New School for Social Research in 2015.

Abby Kiesa, M.A., was Deputy Director of the Center for Information & Research on Civic Learning and Engagement (CIRCLE), part of Tufts University's Tisch College of Civic Life, from 2020 to 2024. Prior to that she led CIRCLE's election research, launched the organization's research on youth and media, and led outreach and research translation efforts from 2005 to 2019.

Irwin Kirsch, who held the Ralph Tyler Chair in large-scale assessment and served as Director of the Center for Research on Human Capital and Education at ETS, is an elected member of the National Academy of Education. He oversaw several teams of research scientists, assessment designers, and platform engineers who were responsible for the development, management, and implementation of national and international large-scale assessments as well as the publication of policy reports focusing on the growing importance of literacy and its connection to life outcomes. Dr. Kirsch also serves on the board of a nonprofit literacy organization and as a reviewer for several journals. He has published numerous research articles and book chapters dealing with issues involved with developing and interpreting cognitive-based scales. Dr. Kirsch has been involved in projects using evidence-centered design principles to link learning and assessment in adult populations.

Matt Leighninger is the Vice President of the National Civic League, and directs the League's Center for Democracy Innovation. NCL was founded in 1894 by Teddy Roosevelt and Louis Brandeis; it maintains the Model City Charter, organizes the All-America City Awards, and supports communities in their work to renovate local democracy. Matt leads the Center's work in strengthening civic infrastructure, using technology to scale engagement, and measuring the quality of participation and democracy. Over the last 30 years, Matt has worked with democracy-building efforts in over 100 communities in 41 states. Matt's first book, *The Next Form of Democracy*, is a firsthand account of the wave of democratic innovation that emerged in the 1990s and 2000s. His second, *Public Participation for 21st Century Democracy*, with Tina Nabatchi, is a guide and textbook that surveys the role and potential of democratic engagement. The Center is currently leading two major projects: Better Public Meetings," which is helping communities change the typical (broken) format of their official interactions with residents; and the Healthy Democracy Ecosystem Map," a comprehensive dataset and visualization of all the organizations in America that are working to improve democracy.

Jane C. Lo is Associate Professor of Teacher Education at Michigan State University. She studies social studies education broadly, with a specific focus on the experiences of students in civic education. Her recent works can be found in *Democracy & Education* and *Educational Theory*. Her edited book on *Making Discussions Work in Social Studies Classrooms* can be found at Teachers College Press.

Peter Mabli is a senior technical assistance consultant at American Institutes for Research, bringing over 15 years of experience in social studies education. He leads and supports standards revision and professional development for state and local education agencies, specializing in history, civics, and social studies curriculum. Dr. Mabli recently aided social studies standards revisions in Pennsylvania, Kentucky, and Alaska, and curriculum development in the U.S. Virgin Islands. Previously, he directed online programs at the American Social History Project, managing projects for organizations like the NYCDOE and the NEH. He also teaches history at Fairleigh Dickinson University.

Nicolás Riveros Medelius is a Ph.D. student at the Harvard Graduate School of Education (HGSE). He has participated in a wide range of educational projects in Latin America, the Caribbean, and the United States. Before his doctoral studies, he worked as Technical Adviser for the Abdul Latif Jameel Poverty Action Lab (J-PAL), and in various leadership positions for the popular education movement Fe y Alegría. In his research, Nicolás uses a mixed-methods approach to study child and youth political socialization processes. He has a particular interest in describing and understanding the interpersonal and relational dynamics involved in civic and citizenship learning. Nicolás holds a B.A. and Master's in Political Science from Universidad de los Andes, as well as an Ed.M. in International Education Policy from HGSE.

Alberto Medina is the Communications Manager at the Center for Information & Research on Civic Learning and Engagement (CIRCLE), part of Tufts University's Tisch College of Civic Life. He oversees the editorial production and dissemination of CIRCLE's work and has more than a decade of experience in efforts to drive the public impact of civic engagement research.

Margarita Olivera-Aguilar is a senior researcher at the American Institutes for Research (AIR). Her work centers on the measurement and assessment of academic and nonacademic constructs, including social, emotional, and civic learning. She specializes in the design, analysis, and reporting of surveys and assessments in both cross-sectional and longitudinal studies, spanning populations from middle school to the workforce. Prior to joining AIR, she was Research Scientist at ETS and Assistant Professor at the National University Autonomous of Mexico. She holds a Ph.D. and M.A. in Quantitative Psychology from Arizona State University.

Walter C. Parker is Professor of Education and (by courtesy) Political Science Emeritus at the University of Washington, Seattle. He is a member of the National Academy of Education and Fellow of the American Educational Research Association. His research and other scholarship concern civic education in elementary and secondary schools, and his publications include *Teaching Democracy* (2003), *Social Studies Today* (2015), and *Education for Liberal Democracy* (2023).

Beth Ratway is a principal technical assistant consultant at American Institutes for Research with over 25 years in education. She leads a portfolio supporting state and local agencies in implementing standards revisions and providing evidence-based professional development. Ratway has facilitated standards development for multiple states, creating tools and guides for the process. Her previous experience includes roles as a social studies teacher and professional development coordinator. At the Wisconsin Department of Public Instruction, she developed a 21st-century social studies framework, created a task force for innovative high school systems, and guided the development of K-12 personal financial literacy standards.

Samuel H. Rikoon is a senior researcher at the American Institutes for Research. His work focuses on efforts to advance practical applications of measurement and assessment, including projects such as designing and generating validity evidence for survey instruments and scenario-based assessments, evaluating the efficacy of educational interventions, and examining how multiple indicators impact school accountability systems and designations. He recently co-edited the volume *Assessing Competencies for Social and Emotional Learning*. Prior to joining AIR, he was Senior Research Scientist at ETS. He holds a Ph.D. in policy research, evaluation, and measurement from the University of Pennsylvania.

Corey Savage is an associate professor of educational science at the University of Stavanger. He studies the effects of education systems on a broad range of outcomes, with an emphasis on students' civic learning outcomes. Prior to the University of Stavanger, he held positions at the University of Glasgow, AIR, Brown University, the University of Tübingen, and ETS. He earned his Ph.D. in educational policy from Michigan State University.

Wolfram Schulz is Principal Research Fellow at the Australian Council for Educational Research (ACER) and was Study Director for the first three cycles of IEA International Civic and Citizenship Education Study (ICCS 2009, 2016, and 2022). He was also coordinator for questionnaire development and analysis for PISA (2003, 2006) and the IEA International Computer and Information Literacy Study (ICILS 2013 and 2018), and he contributed as a senior advisor to a wide range of other large-scale assessments conducted by ACER. Dr Schulz is the author of many international and national research reports and is a well-known expert in the field of international comparative research and large-scale assessment methodology.

Mark Smith is Director of Research at the Digital Inquiry Group (DIG). He was formerly Director of Assessment for the Stanford History Education Group, DIG's predecessor organization. He holds a doctorate in education from Stanford University, and he has over 20 years of experience in education, both as a classroom teacher and researcher.

Jessica Sutter is President of EdPro Consulting, where she manages projects, crafts strategy, and authors research for organizations across the country. She served from 2019 to 2022 as the elected Ward 6 Representative on the D.C. State Board of Education, concluding her tenure as Board President. She began her career as a middle school civics teacher. Jessica holds a BA from Loyola College in Maryland and an MA and Ph.D. in Education Policy Studies from the University of Maryland, College Park. She currently volunteers on the Board of Trustees for Washington Yu Ying Public Charter School and the Gay Men's Chorus of Washington.

Michael Thier is Research Manager (Impact & Validity) for International Baccalaureate and an instructor of program evaluation at the University of Oregon. His research exceeds $2 million in funding, involves collaborators in more than 25 nations, and has generated about 80 publications and 130 presentations to scholarly and professional audiences. The American Educational Research Association awarded his work the outstanding dissertation for mixed methods. Previously, he worked for ten years in classroom and administrative roles in New York and North Carolina public schools. Most importantly, he is the proud father of two inquisitive, courageous, and strong daughters.

Eric M. Tucker is President and CEO of the Study Group. He has served as President of Equity by Design; Senior Research Scientist at the UCLA Center for Research on Evaluation, Standards, and Student Testing (CRESST); Superintendent and Executive Director of Brooklyn Laboratory Charter Schools; Cofounder of Educating All Learners Alliance; Cofounder and Executive Director of InnovateEDU; Director at the Federal Reserve Bank of New York; and Cofounder and Chief Academic Officer of the National Association for Urban Debate Leagues. He served as co-editor of the *Handbook for Assessment in the Service of Learning* (Vol. 1–3) and co-editor of the *SAGE Handbook of Measurement*.

Greg Vafis is Senior Director of Academic Content at ACT. Before joining ACT, he was Executive Director of Assessment Technology, Accessibility, and Innovation at Educational Testing Service, where the civics work described in this chapter was developed. His central interests include design and implementation of technology-enabled learning and assessment systems, providing meaningful and engaging assessment experiences that support learner agency and provide actionable feedback to participants and their teachers.

Sheila W. Valencia is Professor of Literacy Education Emerita at the University of Washington, Seattle. Her research focuses on K-12 reading and writing instruction, assessment, and policy. She consults with national and state educational organizations to develop both large-scale and classroom-based assessments. She is co-author of *An Exploration of Opportunity to Learn and Implications for NAEP* (2024) and *Putting Text Complexity in Context: Refocusing on Comprehension of Complex Text* (2014).

Rajiv Vinnakota is President of the Institute for Citizens & Scholars (formerly the Woodrow Wilson National Fellowship Foundation). Prior to joining C&S in July 2019, Raj served as an EVP at the Aspen Institute. For 18 years, Raj was the Cofounder and CEO of The SEED Foundation, a network of public, college-preparatory boarding schools for underserved children. Raj is Board Director for two public companies, Enovis Corporation and ESAB, in addition to being a former trustee and executive committee member for Princeton University, where he majored in molecular biology and also earned a certificate of studies from the School of Public & International Affairs.

Brittney V. Williams served as Assistant Director of Research-Practice Partnerships at CASEL. There she led the development of research agendas, focusing on the impact of transformative SEL on student experiences and outcomes. Dr. Williams collaborated closely with district leaders, providing continuous improvement technical assistance and translating research into actionable strategies. Her research centers on advancing educational equity by leveraging transformative SEL to foster inclusive learning environments that drive toward meaningful change in schools.

Sam Wineburg is Margaret Jacks Professor of Education, Emeritus, at Stanford University. Educated at Brown and Berkeley, he holds a doctorate in Psychological Studies in Education from Stanford. His book, *Historical Thinking and Other Unnatural Acts*, won the Frederic W. Ness Award for scholarship that contributes most to the "understanding and improvement of liberal education." Wineburg's public scholarship has appeared in *The New York Times*, *The Washington Post*, *The Boston Globe*, and *Slate*. His latest book, with co-author Mike Caulfield, is entitled *Verified: How to Think Straight, Get Duped Less, and Make Better Decisions about What to Believe Online*.

Caroline Wylie is a senior associate at the National Center for the Improvement of Educational Assessment. Her primary research interests include the design, implementation, and evaluation of balanced assessment systems, with a focus on the use of formative assessment to improve classroom teaching and learning. She has led studies related to the creation of effective, scalable, and sustainable teacher professional development, the formative use of diagnostic questions for classroom-based assessment, assessment literacy, and the role of learning progressions to support formative assessment in mathematics and science. She serves as a co-advisor for the CCSSO Balanced Assessment Systems Collaborative.

Foreword

After the Constitutional Convention in Philadelphia in 1788, Benjamin Franklin was famously asked, "Well, Doctor what have we got a republic or a monarchy?" His reply was, "A republic, if you can keep it."

The question of what the Convention had delivered was already very much debated. Like Franklin, the *Federalist Papers* would designate the new creation a "republic," while Alexander Hamilton in the New York ratifying convention described it as a "representative democracy." How the new creation was labeled didn't matter much, though. As a democracy, it was a new form, not a direct democracy but one relying on representation and constitutionalism. As a republic, it already had popular elements, especially in the form of the House of Representatives.

The real weight of Franklin's remark landed on a charge to the citizenry to do the work of sustaining the institutions of free self-government. Their new government would not run on its own, nor keep itself alive. All the way back in the 1650s, residents of Massachusetts Bay Colony understood that young people would need an education in the laws. This was for two reasons: so that the society might be stable and so that ordinary citizens not be taken advantage of by the powerful. This kind of civic education lay behind the emergence of free self-government among citizens prior to the emergence of the American nation. Such civic education was claimed equally as a foundation for liberation by figures like David Walker, Frederick Douglass, and Ida B. Wells, for whom civic education included also teaching the country how to be honest about the facts of lynching.

Now in the 21st century, we are watching a resurgence of interest in securing a solid infrastructure for civic learning. Starting in 2019, the Educating for American Democracy Initiative has forged a nationwide cross-ideological network to answer the question of what should be taught in K-12 history and civics classrooms. The 1619 and 1776 projects have each also tackled parts of the puzzle from different perspectives. Interest is running high.

But for all the efforts to develop new frameworks, curricula and resources, and pedagogic innovations, we cannot secure a durable infrastructure to deliver rich civic learning opportunities to students unless we are able to evaluate the impact of this teaching on their learning. The absence of strong tools of evaluation in the civic learning space has led many states to adopt the U.S. Naturalization test as a high school graduation requirement. While the effort to add an assessment is laudable, the use of this test in particular could be dangerous. It has already led some politicians to propose tying the right to vote to passing the exam, even for native-born citizens. This is to reintroduce literacy tests for voting.

The importance and sensitivity of assessing civic learning so that as a society we can do it well—without turning civic education into a politicized domain—requires that scholars dig deep and do the hard work of generating the standalone tools needed to assess civic learning.

That is why this volume is so exciting. For the first time in recent memory, scholars are pooling their knowledge to provide definition to the field of assessing civic learning.

There continues to be work to do to clarify our educational goals in the civic education space—our goals for growth in civic knowledge, civic skills, and civic dispositions and virtues. Yet with tools like the Educating for American Democracy Roadmap, we have come a long way in establishing those goals. Now, here in this volume, the assembled scholars are showing us how we can assess performance of our instructional efforts in relation to those goals.

Knowledge tests are an important part of assessment in civic learning, and they come in for some attention here. In addition, though, civic learning must also assess a range of competencies and dispositions, as well as higher order cognitive processes. The authors of this volume cover the whole gamut and collectively provide the resources we need for laying out a path to richer and more helpful assessment methodologies in the civic learning space. They bring new hope that we will build our way to the tools we need for strong civic education and thereby ensure that we can pass on our republic, our constitutional democracy, to many more generations.

Danielle Allen

Acknowledgments

This volume represents the collective efforts of innumerable individuals and organizations. The 40 authors whose work appears here come from a variety of roles and disciplinary backgrounds, but they share a deep commitment to improving opportunities for all young people to succeed and thrive. We are deeply grateful for their collaboration on this volume and for the work they are doing to advance civic goals.

We are also indebted to the National Council on Measurement in Education (NCME) for the opportunity to publish this volume as part of the NCME Educational Measurement and Assessment Book Series, and we are especially thankful to Editorial Board chair Kadriye Ercikan and to Editorial Board members Henry Braun and Guillermo Solano-Flores for their insightful reviews and guidance. We also appreciate the support we received from our current and past employers—the American Institutes for Research, the Center for Assessment, ETS, and the Edmond & Lily Safra Center for Ethics at Harvard.

We owe an enormous debt of gratitude to all the young people and educators who participated in the research and development efforts described in this book and whose contributions to building and sustaining a thriving democratic society are more important than ever. Finally, we thank our families and colleagues who provided essential encouragement and support for this work.

1

The Role of Assessment in Advancing Civic Learning in K-12 Schools

Laura S. Hamilton, Samuel H. Rikoon, and David C. Kidd

Schools that serve students in grades kindergarten through 12, in the U.S. and around the world, offer learning opportunities that address multiple aspects of students' development. Schools are responsible for preparing young people who can not only succeed in higher education and the workforce but who are equipped with the knowledge, skills, and dispositions needed to engage and thrive in their communities and in civil society (Aspen Institute, 2022; Barton & Coley, 2011; Hamilton & Martinez, 2024). Over the past few decades, events and trends, including the COVID-19 pandemic, an increasingly polarized news and information landscape, advances in artificial intelligence, and changing migration patterns have highlighted the importance of equipping young people with competencies they will need to evaluate information critically, to identify and address societal challenges, and to understand the nuanced perspectives of people whose views and background differ from their own (Lee et al., 2021; Vinnakota, 2019). The concept of *civic learning* has increasingly come to refer to this broad set of competencies, with a recognition that civic learning can happen in settings well beyond the history or social studies classroom. Initiatives such as Educating for American Democracy[1] have made substantial progress in supporting educators with instructional materials and professional learning tools.

To be successful, these instructional and professional learning resources must be accompanied by high-quality assessment tools and practices that generate information to support decision makers at all levels, from classrooms to school boards, statehouses, and the federal government (Marion et al., 2024; National Academies of Sciences, Engineering, and Medicine, 2019; Rupp & Pinsonneault, 2025; Wiliam, 2009). Although numerous assessment tools are available to educators and policymakers, the field lacks access to a comprehensive set of guiding examples of civic learning assessment for different purposes, and much of the existing work on assessment in this area occurs in silos within specific academic or practice fields such social studies or media literacy (Hamilton & Parsi, 2022). In this volume, we bring together a diverse set of leading scholars, practitioners, and developers to explore how assessment across a wide range of contexts and purposes can contribute to high-quality civic learning opportunities and outcomes for all students.

DOI: 10.4324/9781003476825-1
This chapter has been made available under a CC BY-NC-ND license.

Defining Civic Learning

The authors who contributed to this volume have explored a variety of competencies and learning opportunities related to preparing young people for effective civic and community engagement. Together, the constructs that the chapter authors explore are parts of a broad conceptualization of civic learning as the set of skills (e.g., digital information literacy, social perspective taking), knowledge (e.g., understanding of how government works, understanding of the rights and responsibilities of citizens), dispositions (e.g., concern for the welfare of others, commitment to preserving democratic institutions), and actions (e.g., registering to vote, participating in public debate) that contribute to effective civic engagement (National Council for the Social Studies, 2013; Vinnakota, 2019; Winthrop, 2020).

Schools in the U.S. and in many other nations have always embraced a civic mission, but there is often contention about the role of civics-related instruction in school curricula. Efforts to support K-12 schools in achieving their civic missions should recognize the nonpartisan nature of core civic competencies as well as the ways in which these competencies align with the skills and dispositions young people will need to demonstrate to achieve success in other areas of their lives (e.g., post-secondary education, careers, and personal relationships). Additionally, instruction to promote the broad conceptualization of civic learning described above cannot be limited to the social studies classroom. Instruction in other academic subjects, along with schoolwide and out-of-school learning opportunities, can also contribute to the cultivation of this broad set of civic outcomes (Gould et al., 2011; Rimm-Kaufman et al., 2021). The chapters in this volume illustrate the breadth of school settings where civic learning and assessment can occur.

Overview of the Volume

This volume brings together leading scholars and practitioners to examine how assessment can illuminate, strengthen, and expand civic learning in K-12 schools. Civic education has long been recognized as a cornerstone of democratic life, yet measuring its outcomes and opportunities remains complex. The chapters presented here approach that challenge from multiple angles, offering historical insights, large-scale monitoring strategies, and classroom-based tools to support students' development as informed and engaged participants in democracy.

The chapters are organized into three sections providing a wide-ranging view of the current landscape and future directions of civic assessment in K-12 education. Section 1 situates readers in the historical, technological, and conceptual foundations of civic assessment, offering the context needed to understand both its promise and its challenges. In Chapter 2, Jacobs and Feuer trace the historical evolution of civics education and its relationship to assessment, illuminating how measurement practices both reflect and shape democratic values. Chapter 3, by Tucker and Baker, explores how artificial intelligence could enhance the assessment of complex civic competencies, and it offers innovative approaches while also addressing equity, privacy, and ethical concerns. In Chapter 4, Gallos, Sutter, Leighninger, and Vinnakota present the Civic Measurement Maps, a framework that synthesizes existing measures of civic readiness and opportunity, highlighting gaps and identifying pathways to more coherent and actionable assessment efforts.

Section 2 explores tools, frameworks, and approaches for measuring civic learning at the system level to inform policy and practice. In Chapter 5, Goodman and Kirsch examine how large-scale national and international assessments, including the National Assessment of Educational Progress (NAEP) civics assessment and the International Civic and Citizenship Education Study (ICCS), capture multidimensional civic learning and inform our understanding of democratic preparedness. Chapter 6, by Schulz and Damiani, offers a more detailed look at ICCS, presenting its design, key findings from the 2022 cycle, and the ongoing challenges of cross-national measurement. Ratway and Mabli in Chapter 7 highlight how revising state social studies standards through processes grounded in civic principles can produce measurable indicators of civic learning, linking the design of state standards to assessment. Chapter 8, by Bueso, Ing, Dym, and Kahne, investigates how student engagement in social studies and civics can be assessed through surveys and observations, revealing variation across classrooms and curricula. In Chapter 9, Kidd and Medelius describe the development of the Civic Values Questionnaire and a broader assessment toolkit designed to measure civic readiness in alignment with curriculum and developmental theory. Chapter 10, by Olivera-Aguilar, Hamilton, Savage, and Rikoon, extends the concept of "opportunity to learn" to civic education, offering a framework and indicators to monitor access to civic learning experiences. Finally, in Chapter 11, Thier describes approaches to assessing global citizenship education using discrete-choice measures and situational-judgment tests, illustrating how newer methodologies could be applied to capture complex civic competencies on a large scale.

Section 3 focuses on tools and strategies that directly support educators, students, and communities in cultivating meaningful civic engagement. In Chapter 12, Smith, Breakstone, and Wineburg examine approaches to assessing digital literacy, highlighting methods for evaluating students' ability to discern credible online information – a critical 21st-century civic skill. Chapter 13, by Lo, Valencia, and Parker, introduces the Complex Scenario Test, offering validity evidence and attention to equity considerations with respect to a performance measure of students' ability to transfer civic reasoning to novel contexts. Chapter 14, by Brettschneider, Vafis, and Wylie, discusses another approach to performance assessment. The authors describe a scenario-based learning and assessment prototype for eighth-grade classrooms integrating formative feedback, multimedia resources, and teacher supports to strengthen civic reasoning and engagement. In Chapter 15, Jagers, Williams, Harris, and Coleman link transformative social-emotional learning (tSEL) with civic assessment, illustrating how participatory and process-oriented evaluation can build school-family-community partnerships that advance equity and democratic practices. Finally, Chapter 16, by Kiesa and Medina, showcases the CIRCLE Data Tool, which provides community-level data on youth civic engagement and the conditions that shape it, enabling educators, policymakers, and advocates to identify local levers for fostering youth participation in democracy.

Toward More Robust Systems of Assessment for Civic Learning

Together, the chapters in this volume illustrate how thoughtful, rigorously designed and implemented assessment of civic learning opportunities and outcomes can strengthen the role of schools in preparing young people for democratic participation. The authors describe examples of large-scale assessment tools for monitoring outcomes and opportunities as well as assessment tools and practices that can inform decision making at the school and classroom levels. One promising direction for future civics assessment work involves the development of *balanced assessment systems* (Marion et al., 2024) that include a coherent set of assessment approaches to address the needs of students, educators, and system leaders. A balanced system of assessments of civic learning opportunities and outcomes could have numerous benefits, including signaling the importance of civic development and providing data to support decision making at all levels of the education system. The research and development described throughout this volume lays important groundwork for this more comprehensive and coherent approach to assessment in civics.

This collection of chapters points to a few key themes that can guide future assessment research and development. First, collaboration among the measurement, research, and practice communities can foster the development of assessment tools and practices that meet the needs of educators and learners. Second, this work reinforces the many ways in which schools and other institutions can cultivate civic competencies, including through community involvement and instruction in a variety of academic disciplines. Social studies educators play an important role in supporting civic learning, but they should not be responsible for doing so in isolation. Third, despite the impressive body of work presented in this volume, numerous civic competencies remain challenging to measure, which creates a risk that educators and policymakers will be forced to rely on an insufficiently nuanced description of civic learning in schools. Finally, this work highlights the ways in which changes in information technology, assessment methodology, and broader societal trends can influence the adoption of civic assessment tools and practices. Because these changes will continue to affect the work of schools and those who support them, continued research and development to inform high-quality, innovative, and beneficial civic learning assessment systems will be crucial.

Note

1 https://www.educatingforamericandemocracy.org/

References

Aspen Institute. (2022). *We are what we teach: Re-envisioning public education for a just, free, and prosperous America.* Aspen Institute Education and Society Program.

Barton, P. E., & Coley, R. J. (2011). *The mission of the high school: A new consensus of the purposes of public education?* ETS. https://files.eric.ed.gov/fulltext/ED525305.pdf

Gould, J., Jamieson, K. H., Levine, P., McConnell, T., & Smith, D. B. (Eds.). (2011). *Guardian of democracy: The civic mission of schools.* Lenore Annenberg Institute for Civics of the Annenberg Public Policy Center and the Civic Mission of Schools. https://media.carnegie.org/filer_public/ab/dd/abdda62e-6e84-47a4-a043-348d2f2085ae/ccny_grantee_2011_guardian.pdf

Hamilton, L. S., & Martinez, J. F. (2024). Policy influences on ambitious classroom instruction, assessment, and learning. In S. F. Marion, J. W. Pellegrino, & A. I. Berman (Eds.), *Reimagining balanced assessment systems.* National Academy of Education.

Hamilton, L. S., & Parsi, A. (2022). *Monitoring civic learning opportunities and outcomes: Lessons from a symposium sponsored by ETS and educating for American democracy.* ETS. https://www.ets.org/Media/Research/pdf/Research_Notes_Hamilton_Parsi.pdf

Lee, C. D., White, G., & Dong, D. (Eds.). (2021). *Educating for civic reasoning and discourse.* National Academy of Education. https://naeducation.org/wp-content/uploads/2021/04/NAEd-Educating-for-Civic-Reasoning-and-Discourse.pdf

Marion, S. F., Pellegrino, J. W., & Berman, A. I. (Eds.). (2024). *Reimagining balanced assessment systems.* National Academy of Education. https://naeducation.org/wp-content/uploads/2024/04/Full-Report_Reimagining-Balanced-Assessment-Systems.pdf

National Academies of Sciences, Engineering, and Medicine. (2019). *Monitoring educational equity.* The National Academies Press. https://doi.org/10.17226/25389

National Council for the Social Studies. (2013). *Revitalizing civic learning in our schools.* https://www.socialstudies.org/position-statements/revitalizing-civic-learning-our-schools

Rimm-Kaufman, S. E., Merritt, E. G., Lapan, C., DeCoster, J., Hunt, A., & Bowers, N. (2021). Can service-learning boost science achievement, civic engagement, and social skills? A randomized controlled trial of connect science. *Journal of Applied Developmental Psychology, 74,* 101236. https://doi.org/10.1016/j.appdev.2020.101236

Rupp, A. A., & Pinsonneault, L. (2025). *Understanding student performance on state assessments: Leveraging multiple sources of state data for strategic guidance.* Center for Assessment. https://www.nciea.org/wp-content/uploads/2025/05/Leveraging-SEA-Data-for-Strategic-Insight-and-Guidance-FINAL.pdf

Vinnakota, R. (2019). *From civic education to a civic learning ecosystem: A landscape analysis and case for collaboration.* Red & Blue Works. https://citizensandscholars.org/wp-content/uploads/2022/12/Civic-Learning-White-Paper.pdf

Wiliam, D. (2009). *Assessment for learning: Why, what and how?* University of London. Institute of Education.

Winthrop, R. (2020). *The need for civic education in 21st-century schools.* Brookings. https://www.brookings.edu/articles/the-need-for-civic-education-in-21st-century-schools/

Section 1
Setting the Stage
The Civic Assessment Landscape

2
Cultures and Contexts of Civics Education and Assessment in the US

Benjamin M. Jacobs and Michael J. Feuer

A decisive and often daunting undertaking for immigrants seeking US citizenship is preparing for and passing the US Citizenship and Immigration Services' Naturalization Test, which includes written and oral questions on the Constitution, American history and culture, and civics. Since the founding of the republic, some modicum of English-language literacy and an expressed allegiance to American democracy has been expected of all naturalized citizens, on the assumption that good citizenship entails, among other things, facility in a common language, a shared set of values, and commitment to civic responsibility. This blend of knowledge, skills, and dispositions was typically assessed informally, haphazardly, and often arbitrarily by local judges who altered their lines of inquiry based on factors such as the examinee's length of time in the country, educational attainment, and language ability, as well as, in some cases, their ethnic, national, or religious background, political party affiliation, and other prejudicial factors (Schneider, 2001). It was not until the Immigration and Nationality Act of 1952 that aspiring citizens were explicitly required by federal law to demonstrate, through formal examination, knowledge of the fundamentals of US history and civics (US Citizenship and Immigration Services (USCIS), 2020). Subsequent modifications to the Naturalization Test adjusted the number, type, and emphasis of the questions, but idiosyncrasy remained. For example, a 1996 report by a watchdog group found that in Arlington, VA, examinees needed to score a 7 out of 12 questions, which could be written or oral; in Miami, FL, it was 7 out of 10 oral questions; and in Atlanta, GA, it was upward of 100 questions with no set passing score—it was entirely up to the discretion of the INS officer administering the exam (Kunnan, 2009).

Growing awareness that a pillar of American democracy—the concept of "citizenship"—was at risk from the inchoate and somewhat clumsy hodgepodge of metrics and methods used to assess whether newcomers were qualified, led to a Congressional request to the National Academy of Sciences to study the existing test and make recommendations for its overhaul. Although the project was aborted before the Academy committee could conclude its deliberations, the interim report issued in 2004 already offered a set of proposed guidelines on both the content of a revised exam and a process for assuring its adherence to rigorous standards of testing and assessment (National Research Council (NRC), 2004). Following further investigations

DOI: 10.4324/9781003476825-3
This chapter has been made available under a CC BY-NC-ND license.

and protestations of the inequity of the exam—for example, were aspiring citizens being treated in ways that actually controverted core values enshrined in the foundational documents they were supposed to have mastered?—the Naturalization Test was finally standardized in 2008. Today's version comprises 100 US history and civics study questions for examiners to choose from in the categories of principles of democracy, the American system of government, rights and responsibilities, and American history, geography, symbols, and holidays; some of the questions may require written responses in addition to oral responses; and examinees need to score a minimum of 6 out of 10 to pass (USCIS, 2022).

The good news for prospective US citizens is that, in 2022, over 92% passed the civics part of the Naturalization Test on the first try (USCIS, 2022). Yet, perhaps disconcertingly, a 2018 study found only 36% of US-born adult citizens could pass a multiple-choice exam comprising items from that same test (Institute for Citizens & Scholars (ICS), 2018). This paltry performance comports with results from a 2022 survey that found only 47% of American adults able to identify all three branches of government (Annenberg Public Policy Center, 2022). The apparent lack of basic civics knowledge among adults cannot be attributed solely to temporal distance from exposure to these concepts in school, however. The National Assessment of Educational Progress (NAEP) civics exam, also in 2022, demonstrated that only 22% of eighth-grade students performed at or above proficient on their knowledge of civics, even after having recently taken a course on the subject (for the US history assessment, the result was an abysmal 13%) (National Assessment of Educational Progress (NAEP), 2022). With alarms going off in statehouses about the apparent decline in civics knowledge among the rising generation of Americans, an all-too-predictable trend soon emerged: At least 17 states now require high school students to pass the US citizenship exam before graduation (Shapiro & Brown, 2018). Indeed, the revival of public interest in civics education, viewed as a godsend by people who believe that a goal of public schools is to prepare youth for active participation in a democracy, has been spurred both by evidence of major gaps in Americans' knowledge and by perceived threats to the system from decades of political polarization and partisan animosity (Feuer, 2023).

The aims, instruments, and outcomes of various methods for measuring civics knowledge raise vexing questions around civics education and assessment more broadly. These questions frame the discussion in this chapter:

1) What civics knowledge is of most worth, to whom, and for what purposes?
2) What forces determine what is included and excluded in the canon of US civics, and how does that canon become legitimated?
3) What are the anticipated outcomes of civics education, and what are the most appropriate forms of civics assessment?
4) How does civics knowledge expected of US residents by the US government (e.g., USCIS, NAEP) compare to the knowledge of the average US resident? If they are discrepant, what are the consequences?
5) How does civics knowledge relate to civic behaviors and dispositions?
6) What are the implications of civics education and assessment for the functioning of American democracy and society broadly?

These questions go to the heart of civics education and assessment, challenging common assumptions about the intrinsic and/or instrumental value of mastering principles of democracy, functions of government, responsibilities of citizens, and modes of civic participation, as well as the methods of gauging competencies in these areas.

This chapter provides a condensed history of the evolution of civics education and its links to the uses of assessment in US schools. Our premise is that assessment can be a tool to evaluate—and influence—the quality of civics curricula and instruction. The duality will be familiar to students of testing and assessment: We have abundant empirical evidence and experience showing that assessment can promote or impede the cultivation of valued educational outcomes (e.g., Koretz, 2017; NRC, 1999; Office of Technology Assessment (OTA), 1992). This dilemma is manifest in the context of efforts to assess civic and democratic values in classrooms, schools, individuals, and society. We delve into ideologies embedded in civics curricula, whose interests are served, what content and skills are emphasized in various types of assessments and why, and what the effects are. We will argue that, just as curriculum can be a powerful cultural and political device that can be wielded and/or manipulated for a variety of purposes, so too is it imperative to build into the future of civics assessment considerations of use and misuse.

Before we continue, a brief note on terminology. In this chapter, we use the term *civic education* to refer broadly to learning values, principles, and proclivities for active and intelligent participation in a healthy democracy. This kind of learning can happen in schools (e.g., citizenship education, social studies education) and in society at large (e.g., the workplace, museums, libraries, media, public spaces, and the family dinner table). We use the term *civics education* (note the "s" in civics) to refer more specifically to the formal school subject that covers the structures of American democracy, government, and civil society, along with the rights and responsibilities of citizens, and is typically evaluated through standardized exams and other forms of assessment (Feuer, 2023).

Foundations of Civic(s) Education and Assessment in the US

Benjamin Franklin's famous 1787 rejoinder regarding what kind of government was formed at the Constitutional Convention—"A republic, if you can keep it!" (National Park Service (NPS), n.d.)—was as much a warning about the effort needed to maintain a democracy as it was an admonition to uphold the shared civic values of the nascent state. In this spirit, common schools in the early republic were conceived as state-sponsored training grounds for "good American citizens" (meaning, in those days, propertied White Christian males) well-versed in democratic principles, virtuous character traits, and civil behaviors. The concern of prominent statesmen like Franklin, Thomas Jefferson, Benjamin Rush, and Noah Webster was that an uneducated and unrefined electorate would quickly undermine a wise and just representative government. To counteract these forces, an American curriculum thoroughly imbued with the values of freedom, liberty, and equality; focused on moral (Christian) training; and promoting the responsibilities of citizenship, would "convert men to republican machines," as Rush put it (cited in Kaestle, 1983, p. 7). Harsh realities in the schools made widespread adoption of the new American curriculum challenging and uneven, given inadequate resources, a meager teaching force (in quantity and quality), irregular student attendance, and local administrative control, among other constraints. Nonetheless, a consensus around using common schools as means for instilling knowledge of and allegiance to "American" ideals was born along with the new nation. Indeed, education—and specifically, the inculcation of civic virtue—became America's *paideia*, both a cultural touchstone and political linchpin for the grand American experiment (Herbst, 1991).

The first known textbook developed expressly for civics instruction in American schools was Elhanan Winchester's (1796) *A Plain Political Catechism*, which he described as "Intended for the use of Schools in the United States of America, wherein the great principles of Liberty and of the Federal Constitution are laid down and explained by way of Question and Answer, made level to the lowest Capacities" (Winchester, 1796, p. 1). In addition to patriotic queries (e.g., "What are the blessings which the inhabitants of the United States enjoy under the present excellent constitution?" [p. 12]), as well as straightforward probes about the functions of government (e.g., "What are the powers designated to the Congress of the United States?" [p. 19]), Winchester posed larger political and moral questions about "What makes government necessary?" (p. 5) and "Is the true love of liberty destructive to virtue, and subversive of the principles of genuine morality, as some would have us believe?" (p. 59). Not surprisingly, his responses to these questions strongly promoted fidelity to democratic principles, the Constitution, the US, and Christian ethics. An appendix also covered some basic dates, facts, and places of American history and geography, including "Which of the states have no slaves?" and "Which of the states has the most slaves?" (p. 96). Particularly noteworthy about the text, though, is that it established civics instruction and assessment in schools as a didactic and standardized endeavor, comprising mainly memorization and recitation of facts and predetermined conclusions about American government and society. That Winchester titled it a "catechism" lent further gravitas both to the text and to the teaching and learning of America's new civil religion.

With the emergence of the common school movement in the early- to mid-19th century came the proliferation of a number of other civics textbooks, each of which promised a unique version of the history and subject matter of the Constitution, and an explanation of the uses of political power, the rights and responsibilities of citizens, civil jurisprudence, the health and happiness of the nation, and, in one case, "'actually' how government is run—i.e., the 'real Facts'" (Kohlmeyer, 1925, p. 14). In keeping with the pedagogical times, instruction and evaluation mainly consisted of mimetic recitation, memorization, and regurgitation of facts from textbooks. Most assessments were oral, though written examinations evolved in this period, as well (Vinovskis, 2019). While in the aftermath of the Civil War, textbooks continued to focus almost entirely on the minutiae of civil government, particularly on the federal level, some also included considerations of state and local governments (perhaps a nod to the states' rights claims of mid-century) and others featured a new emphasis on critical analysis (perhaps a nod to the strife of mid-century). Still, according to one survey of textbooks of the time, "practically nothing was done to give the pupils knowledge of government in its practical workings, or to teach the duties of citizens, except in an abstract, formal way" (Kohlmeyer, 1925, p. 24).

The latter part of the 19th century brought about significant changes to the organization, delivery, and assessment of the civics curriculum, resulting from the professionalization of the social science disciplines, the extension of compulsory education on the secondary level, the progressive reform of education, and the expansion of schooling to include freed Blacks and new immigrants. For starters, the growth of political science and history as academic disciplines in colleges and universities in the 1880s meant that rising students were expected to have some exposure to the basics of those disciplines prior to pursuing post-secondary education (see, e.g., Schaper, 1905). Consequently, academicians (many of whom were once schoolteachers) began taking keen interest in what was being taught about history and civics in the lower schools, how, by whom, with what materials, and to what effect, as the universities now had stakes in the enterprise. Accordingly, the emerging professional disciplinary organizations (American Historical Association, American Political Science Association) formed commissions, wrote white papers, and developed instructional materials and assessments to promote more academic and scientific study of their subjects in schools. Whereas the teaching of American history and civics had once relied mostly on storytelling and catechisms, it would now focus increasingly on methodical critical inquiry that could pass muster with disciplinary experts (Hertzberg, 1988).

The 1892 Conference on History, Civil Government, and Political Economy—part of the National Education Association's (NEA) Committee of Ten, which was convened to provide recommendations for the formation of high school subjects—called for civil government to be taught in conjunction with American history in both 7th and 12th grade and to include seminar discussions along with didactic lectures; multiple sources of information (documents, maps, images, literature) in addition to textbooks; and hands-on investigation of real-world problems.

These innovative approaches to instruction and assessment were inspired, in part, by progressive pedagogy, which emerged concurrently with the social science disciplines and placed emphasis on learner-centered instruction, project-based activities, and participatory experiences. Whereas a century earlier the civics curriculum consisted entirely of normative questions and answers about America's history, politics, culture, and society, the Committee of Ten suggested adding direct observation of the workings of government (e.g., field trips to statehouses), in-class debates and mock town meetings, and student decision-making on contentious issues. "As to methods," concluded the Committee, "we have to suggest only the use of the methods which, in good schools, are now accustoming pupils to think for themselves" (National Education Association (NEA), 1892, pp. 200–201).

Alongside these developments of the late 19th and early 20th centuries, academicians, educators, and school stakeholders increasingly focused on orienting instruction toward "social efficiency," meaning practical application, occupational utility, and social responsibility, with an eye toward preparing future citizens for their functional roles in a more orderly, stable, and efficient industrial, diverse, and democratic society (Kliebard, 2004). Part of the motivation for social efficiency education was to assimilate large populations of freed Blacks, Native Americans, and new immigrants into the rapidly expanding school system in two ways: (1) by sorting them into anticipated occupational roles and differentiating instruction through college-preparatory or vocational tracks, and (2) by inculcating in them an appreciation of, and a desire to participate in, the industrial economy, democratic civic life, and the social status quo (Jacobs, 2014). Given these aims, many observers of social efficiency education have pointed out its sometimes racist and sexist objectives and nativist overtones, particularly considering that most non-Whites and women were pushed toward menial jobs within a manifestly hostile social and political environment in which Jim Crow laws and other crushing forms of discrimination were prevalent (Vaughan, 2018). At the same time, the pragmatic orientation toward schooling in the social efficiency framework meant that school subjects for everyone (college-bound and vocational students alike) would place greater emphasis on preparation for adult life by recreating real-world tasks in embryonic form. While traditional academic subjects would be preserved, they increasingly were expected to impart knowledge, skills, behaviors, and attitudes that were utilitarian in form and function.

It was in this context that social studies education emerged. The essential task of the social studies curriculum—of which civics education was a major constituent—was to prepare students for intelligent *and* active citizenship in American society. The 1916 Report of the NEA's Committee on Social Studies, which is credited with establishing and legitimating social studies as a core school subject, claimed that social studies generally "should have for their conscious and constant purpose the cultivation of good citizenship," the first step of which includes "a realization of national ideals, national efficiency, national loyalty, [and] national self-respect" (NEA, 1916, p. 9). Speaking of civics education in particular, the committee recommended that subject matter and instructional methods be "adapted to the pupil's immediate needs of social growth," by which they meant that it should address contemporary issues of interest and concern to the students themselves (NEA, 1916, p. 10). In this new scheme, civics would be taught mostly as a stand-alone subject, rather than in conjunction with American history, and it would comprise the 8th or 9th grade and part of the 12th grade of the social studies curriculum. Among the most significant departures from the way civics had been taught and assessed previously was a shift away from civics as the study of government, political rights, and civic responsibilities exclusively and toward the study of active and cooperative participation in local communities, known as "community civics" (Reuben, 1997). The implications of this change for the selection of civics subject matter, instructional methods, and assessment included more emphasis on promoting social welfare and engagement in community activities (e.g., at social service agencies), and a new capstone high school course, Problems of Democracy, focused on the integrated study of "actual [current] problems, or issues, or conditions, as they occur in life, and in their several aspects, political, economic, and sociological" (NEA, 1916, p. 50). The intended outcome of this program was the formation of intelligent public opinions and the propensity to act on them in the community.

"Cultivation of good citizenship" also meant renewed stress on developing good character generally, particularly when it came to training the increasingly larger and more racially, ethnically, linguistically, and religiously diverse social underclass in White, Christian, bourgeois values (Crocco, 2004). The NEA's *Cardinal Principles of Secondary Education* (1918) proposed an alternative model to the organization of the high school curriculum around seven social efficiency objectives—vocation, health, command of fundamental processes, worthy home membership, worthy use of leisure, ethical character, and citizenship—to be differentiated from the academic school subjects established earlier by the Committee of Ten. The *Cardinal Principles* furthermore put "the cultivation of personal and social interests" as the highest priority of education in a democracy and put civic education, or citizenship education (the report used the terms interchangeably), at the heart of the high school curriculum (NEA Commission on the Reorganization of Secondary Education, 1918, p. 10). Academically, civics emphasized socialization, democratic organization of the school and classroom, finding cooperative solutions to common problems, cultivation of social ideals, concern for the "informal activities of daily life that regard and seek the common good," and loyalty to American democracy, as well as "a wiser and more sympathetic approach to international problems" (NEA Commission on the Reorganization of Secondary Education, 1918, p. 14). Beyond the subject of civics, beginning in the 1920s, topics and activities as disparate as domestic science (especially for girls), health, physical education, temperance, disease prevention, and even fire drills (a lesson in civic responsibility), in addition to character education (i.e., morals and manners), were subsumed under the far-reaching aegis of civic education in schools (Makler, 2004). Taken together, social studies education, community civics, Problems of Democracy, and the new civic education broadly conceived "represented the idealized version of education for social betterment" (Evans, 2004, p. 26; McDonnell et al., 2000) at a time when concerns were heightened among social elites about the allegedly deleterious effects of unrefined Others within the American social fabric.

Early 20th-Century Challenges of Citizenship Education and Assessment

Supporting the new social efficiency model of academic and vocational sorting and differentiation, as well as the purported civilizing function of schools, was a system of standardized testing that emerged in the early 20th century to measure intelligence, aptitude, and sophistication. Psychologists and other educational scientists developed scales for determining abilities in rudimentary skills including arithmetic, reading, writing, spelling, drawing, and language facility, and soon enough, subject-specific tests on elementary and secondary school content as well as college entrance exams. The stated aim of these innovations in educational assessment was to provide scientific, evidence-based guidance for the efficient evaluation, classification, grouping, and tracking of children into academic or vocational programs based on their innate proclivities and aptitudes (Lagemann, 2000). All the same, it was hardly lost on observers of the time that the tests could be biased not only in their form but also in their function. One contemporaneous critic called intelligence testing "propaganda" that "seeks to demonstrate that the Negro is intellectually and physically incapable of assuming the dignities, rights and duties which devolve upon him as a member of modern society" (Bond, 1924, p. 61). Much the same was said with respect to the outcomes for new immigrants and young women. While, on the one hand, some would claim that success on intelligence, subject matter, and college-readiness exams would enable the social underclass to have access to a meritocracy that was previously denied to them, others recognized that testing often was used nefariously to weed out "unwelcome guests" for the sake of maintaining rigid racial, ethnic, class, and gender hierarchies (Wechsler & Diner, 2022).

Indeed, for the mass influx of new immigrants from around the world at the turn of the century, schools provided the prospect of assimilation and, thereby, the promise of fulfilment of the American Dream. The very notion of "Americanization" was fraught with definitional ambiguity, resolution of which was a challenge for assessment and testing designers tasked with evaluating just how "Americanized" newcomers were becoming. As noted at the outset, the Naturalization Test was one such means of determining, quite literally, who was in and who was out, based on the candidate's ability to memorize, recall, and relate orally—in adequate English—esoteric facts about civics, history, and the principles of the Constitution. Far from being a one-off exercise, for millions of new immigrants, the Naturalization Test was in effect a capstone exam that followed participation in a comprehensive Americanization program in schools. Adapting some of the earlier work of immigrant settlement houses and freedmen's industrial schools, Americanization programs in the 1910s and 1920s—serving *in loco parentis*—endeavored to adjust young immigrants to American society through intensive socialization efforts including instruction in English language and civics along with personal hygiene, industriousness, discipline, Anglo-Saxon/Christian norms, individual character, and social-mindedness (Fass, 1989). Some of these same approaches were applied to Bureau of Indian Affairs schools and majority Black schools and classrooms of the time, albeit under the banner of industrial education (Anderson, 1988). According to some critiques, disparagement of one's native heritage was essential to Americanization efforts, as the progressive civic ethos was about service to the general commonweal above all, so distinctive, "deviant" habits, practices, and mores needed to be sublimated for the sake of social efficiency, i.e., participation in a well-ordered, unified society (Olneck, 1989). Others have noted that unlike efforts in other societies toward "homogenization" of diverse immigrant populations, the American approach encouraged loyalty to one's ethnic and national heritage as compatible with adoption of the new "American" identity (Mirel, 2010).

More than any other school subject, social studies was rendered either the hero or scapegoat for the successful development of "American" character and good citizenship via the schools, providing (or failing to provide) the "essentials of civilization" as "antidotes" to supposed cultural deficiencies and backward ways (Crocco, 2004). It therefore became a lightning rod for public controversy and conflict, particularly with respect to broader culture wars in American society and politics. Americanization programs were supported by a powerful conglomerate of unlikely bedfellows that included social elites *and* social reformers; indigent welfare organizations *and* blue-blooded patriotic societies; nativist public officials *and* assimilationist immigrant advocates; and more. However, immigrants themselves sometimes resisted participation in these perceptibly paternalistic and patronizing programs, or they at least advocated for a more pluralistic and cosmopolitan vision for Americanization education—and American society at-large—in which immigrant contributions would be acknowledged if not celebrated (Mirel, 2010). Competing visions of the role of schools in acculturating non-natives and non-Whites, in addition to educating US-born White Christians, fell under two major rubrics: *citizenship (or civic) education*, with its emphasis on socialization into proper "American" character, attitudes, behaviors, dispositions, and practices, both at home (fitness, hygiene, sobriety) and in public (symbols, language, ways); and *civics education*, with its concern for academic knowledge of and commitment to democracy, pluralism, mutuality, civic participation, and a unified "American" life. While civics education was always considered elemental to citizenship education, the project of training "good citizens" was much greater than anything civics education could accomplish or assess on its own.

It is ironic then, and perhaps not surprising, that the Naturalization Test, intended to assess fitness for American *citizenship*, was (and remains) mostly composed of items meant to measure *civics* content knowledge. Large-scale assessments at best provide estimates of complex domains of skill, knowledge, and disposition, based on a limited number of items. In the present instance, there is intuitively a connection between civics content knowledge and citizenship, although no test is likely to capture all the subtleties and fragilities embedded in that connection. The Naturalization Test's items differed little from those that were commonly found on assessments in schoolrooms nationwide, where students were expected to recount textbook-based facts about federal and state governments and democratic principles on short-answer, multiple-choice, or short-essay exams (Mattson, 1925). Some classroom assessments focused more extensively on social studies disciplinary skills, such as reading comprehension, the use of primary sources, interpreting charts and graphs, summarizing and outlining data, making generalizations and inferences, and analyzing political cartoons, in addition to subject matter knowledge (Morse & McCune, 1971). But from the start, the field of social studies education generally—along with civics education specifically—was beset by challenges and constraints in developing standardized assessment measures.

One challenge, as already mentioned, was that testing for academic civics knowledge and skills is distinct from assessing real-world civic dispositions and behaviors (Hamilton & Parsi, 2022). One way educators eventually attempted to remedy this problem was by developing projects that practiced civic participatory skills, such as writing letters to the editor of a newspaper, crafting petitions to local councils, or doing service learning at community organizations—what we currently refer to as "authentic assessments" (Hahn, 1999). But these were highly localized and resource-intensive projects that could not be easily standardized or conducted on a large scale.

A second challenge, also discussed above, was that social studies education and civics education mean many things to many people, not to mention that the subject matter is prone to multiple interpretations and perspectives. The American Historical Association's 1934 Commission on the Social Studies in the Schools brought together statisticians and social scientists to explore a variety of measurement tools, including tests and exercises assessing history and civics concepts, skills, and evidence, in addition to character traits such as honesty, courtesy, fairness, loyalty to classmates, and regard for personal property. Yet, the project's ambitious goals were tempered by the fact that, as one of the report's authors concluded, "it became clear that the most 'objective' fact about social science was that it was so largely 'subjective'" (cited in Wilson, 1935, p. 146). This hampered efforts to determine exactly what standardized aims and outcomes should or could be assessed.

A third challenge was more conceptual and moral in nature: How could the American ethos of individual achievement, the progressive educational ethos of social efficiency, and the democratic ethos of equity be reconciled with the desire to use standardized tests as a measure of what civics and citizenship education were supposed to accomplish, especially when the tests could be biased and unfair? The stakes of the assessment enterprise may have been too high. No other school subject was as intimately tied to the American *paideia* as social studies and civics, so anything less than perfection was destined to be deemed a failure.

If formal assessment of citizenship and civics education proved to be challenging, informal means of demonstrating knowledge of and allegiance to American values were widespread in schools in the early 20th century, particularly in the context of Americanization efforts and the First World War. One lasting example is the recitation of the Pledge of Allegiance and its accompanying US flag salute. Composed in 1892 and first mandated by Washington State schools in 1919, the Pledge soon became a regular and required ritual in schoolrooms across the country. Modifications to the Pledge over time reflected the political contexts in which they were proposed, such as when "my Flag" was changed to "the flag of the United States of

America" in 1923 so that immigrants could not mistake it with loyalty to their native insignia, and when "under God" was added in 1954 as an ostensible bulwark to communism (Ellis, 2005). Advocates for the Pledge saw it as a quasi-religious catechism (much like the first US civics textbook discussed earlier) with the power to inspire faithfulness. As its composer Francis Bellamy, an ordained minister, put it, "this little formula has been pounding away on the impressionable minds of children for a generation, awakening a daily enthusiasm for the flag, driving in the idea of loyalty, giving them a notion of the great republic, reminding them of a liberty and justice for all,—*thinking those thoughts for them*" (cited in Ellis, 2005, p. 69; emphasis in original). Some critics of the Pledge have argued that its bald patriotism elides many people's perception that America is not "one nation," "under God," "indivisible," and "with liberty and justice for all," while others are concerned that the Pledge lulls children into thinking that merely reciting an oath is a sufficient form of civic engagement and participation. In any event, this visible, visceral, and demonstrable expression of American values and one's commitment to them—entrenched in classrooms for the past century—is an example of how a more informal mechanism, i.e., recitation of the Pledge, can serve as a performative indicator of civic competency that no paper-and-pencil exam could easily provide.

Culture Wars and Civics Assessment in the 20th and 21st Centuries

Few circumstances test the mettle of civic participation and the efficacy of citizenship education more than a nation at war. During the Second World War and the Cold War, there was widespread agreement that fending off totalitarian adversaries meant doubling-down on the defense of American democracy. This move, in turn, shifted the focus of American education (and American culture more broadly) from progressivism, with its emphasis on the Problems of Democracy, to consensus, with its celebration of longstanding American institutions and values. While schools had always been champions or scapegoats for everything right or wrong in society as a whole, it was during the 1940s–1950s that storms over the schoolhouse erupted in earnest, bringing the culture wars to bear on social studies education particularly (Evans, 2004; Zimmerman, 2002).

The first salvos were aimed at a widely used social studies textbook series by the education scholar and Frontier Thinker Harold Rugg, whose Progressive- and New Deal-era take on US history and civics was rather disparaging of the average American's living conditions under democracy and capitalism. With titles such as *An Introduction to Problems of American Culture* and an approach to pedagogy and assessment that explicitly encouraged critical inquiry and problem solving rather than retention and recitation of facts, Rugg's materials were deemed by patriotic groups (e.g., Daughters of the American Revolution) as "un-American" and subversive. A nationwide campaign against the textbooks, backed by the American Legion, culminated in 1940–1941 with book bans and bonfires across the country "strangely resembling the book-burning orgies now commonly associated with Nazi Germany," as one reporter wryly observed (Krane, 1940). A similar campaign was launched in the early years of the Cold War against political scientist Frank Magruder's popular *American Government* civics textbook, accusing it of promoting America's welfare state and therefore cleaving perilously close to collectivism if not communism. As with the Rugg series, the critical questions Magruder posed in the "Problems for Discussion" section were seen by right-wing detractors as miseducative, and demands were made to censor the text.

Equally, if not more troubling to wartime critics of social studies, education was their impression that America's youth were woefully ignorant of US history and government, a byproduct of decades of "diluted," "confused," "half-hearted," and "ineffective" school courses in the subject, to paraphrase one noteworthy screed (Nevins, 1942). Beyond the problems of "Problems" courses and textbooks, or the departure of citizenship education from the history and civics that was supposed to be at its heart, was the worry that too much instruction in world history would lead students to interests (e.g., socialism, Eastern religions, Russian literature, primitive civilizations) that diverged from the glories and spirit of the American story ("Topics," 1942). These concerns about the lack of sufficient attention in schools to American culture and tradition were exacerbated by results of an exam developed by the *New York Times* and published on the front page in 1943, showing that most college students were ignorant of even the basics of US history and government, despite having taken high school social studies classes. In addition to providing statistical findings from the exam demonstrating that only small percentages of students could identify American historical figures, geographic features, key events, and chronology, much of the report was dedicated to a litany of outlandish responses by students regarding the powers of Congress ("the right to veto bills that the President wishes to be passed") and the freedoms guaranteed by the Bill of Rights ("freedom from no jobs," "the right to get ahead") (Fine, 1943, p. 32). Not surprisingly, jingoistic pundits jumped at the opportunity to slam the schools for falling "so far short of their fundamental responsibility to the American people" (Evans, 2004, p. 91).

In this context, conditions were ripe for public calls to go back to basics in civics education. Conformity, consensus, and assiduous avoidance of controversy were the rules of the day in the 1950s, in direct contrast to the progressivism, critical analysis, and reconstructionist activism of decades prior. Textbooks and teachers sought to affirm the virtues of American cohesion, stability, prosperity, and optimism, and to play down warts-and-all approaches that once emphasized social tensions, racial segregation, and economic deprivation. Part of this trend included interest in intercultural education, a framework that highlighted the cultural contributions of diverse groups, emphasized tolerance and pluralism, and whitewashed the struggles between ethnic, religious, racial, and class groups in American society, thereby affording women, Black Americans, Asian Americans, and American Jews (among others) more prominence in the American curriculum than had been allowed before (Beadie et al., 2021). Contributing further to the consensus ambiance were sociological analyses of the US at mid-century, such as Gunnar Myrdal's "American Creed" (1940s) and Will Herberg's "American Way of Life" (1950s), positing that civil religion unified Americans based on their common faith in democracy, free enterprise, individualism, egalitarianism, humanitarianism, community responsibility, a Supreme Being, and, above all, idealism. In this vision, the back-to-basics role of the public schools was to provide children with a baptism into the American civil religion so that they could be adequately prepared for the ultimate American sacrament—participation in direct democracy—and the fight against the devilish forces of communism. Civics textbooks in this period, harkening back to those in the pre-progressive era, centered mostly on the proper legal roles and responsibilities of American citizens as well as their patriotic duties to advance American stability and supremacy on the world stage (Ngalande, 2024).

A second impetus for the back-to-basics campaign was the fear, precipitated by the Soviets' launch of Sputnik-1 in 1957, that the US was falling behind the USSR in science, technology, and education. The National Defense Education Act mandated the "'fullest development of the mental resources and technical skills' of American youth" (Evans, 2004, p. 116). Not long beforehand, the Council for Basic Education advocacy group formed to decry the allegedly anti-intellectual and overly vocational bent of progressive education and to return instead to the traditional academic approach to school subjects. In this scheme, social studies would be supplanted by disciplinary courses in history, government, and allied subjects, as originally proposed by the Committee of Ten more than half a century earlier. Massive funding from public and private sources poured into universities to develop disciplinary curriculum projects and materials for the lower schools. One renowned 1950s civics education initiative, the Carnegie Corporation-funded *Citizenship Education Project*, offered resources on the "Premises of American Liberty," which were mostly the opportunities and challenges of political citizenship and matched them with "Laboratory Practices in Citizenship" (à la, scientific experimentation) that encouraged students to observe and participate in government and civic agencies in situ. While ostensibly reminiscent of the hands-on, student-centered, inquiry-oriented Problems of Democracy course, the *Citizenship Education Project* hardly questioned whether democracy was problematic and instead inculcated and assessed conventional content knowledge and skills designed to represent the American system at its best (Streb, 1979). In the 1960s–1970s, the National Science Foundation and US Office of Education sponsored "New Social Studies" projects that emphasized not only learning *about* history and government (i.e., content coverage) but also, and especially, *how to do* history and civics (i.e., disciplinary skills). The *American Political Behavior* project, for example, focused foremost on political science concepts such as political culture, political behavior, and political socialization, and then gave students experience in formulating hypotheses, conducting research, and making decisions around public policy (Hahn, 2010). Assessments mainly consisted of short-answer and multiple-choice exams at the end of each unit, in addition to a general Political Knowledge Test, a Political Science Skills Test, and Political Attitude Scales (Mehlinger & Patrick, 1977). Rather than focusing broadly on civics or citizenship education, the project was mainly about political science disciplinary knowledge and skills.

A third back-to-basics effort that emerged in the latter days of the Cold War and has persisted in American schools ever since is the standards and accountability movement. In the early 1980s, amid a shifting political climate in which new concerns were raised about national security, economic efficiency, and international competitiveness, calls for reform of American education were built on the premise that the US was *A Nation at Risk* (1983) because the schools were not meeting society's needs adequately. Appalling results on standardized tests demonstrated not only that American children were woefully ignorant of mathematics, science, and history but also that the schools had slackened their academic standards considerably. Part of the backlash was against 1970s countercultural, neo-progressive forms of instruction such as the "Open Classroom" movement, which replaced wooden school desks and hardback textbooks with comfy chairs and cushy rugs on which children could freely explore their interests at their own pace (Cuban, 2022). Many critics demanded that the schools offer an intellectually rigorous, back-to-basics program that would guarantee more than minimum competence, but rather, educational excellence for all. Another concern stemmed from the 1960s–1970s expansion of "area studies" in universities and schools that brought racial, ethnic, gender, religious, and other nonhegemonic groups to the fore. Sidebars, illustrations, and short biographies in social studies textbooks increasingly included people of color, while theories and practices were developed for the incorporation of ethnic subject matter into the emerging multicultural curriculum (Thornton, 1994). Reform advocates began to agitate for schools to be used once again as proving grounds for a new social order in which diversity, justice, equity, and inclusion and the development of political action skills would lead to reduced prejudice and discrimination. Pushing against these trends were cultural conservatives who controlled the White House through the 1980s and thought America's status as a superpower depended on good, old-fashioned Americanism. If attention to multiculturalism meant that students were not able to answer correctly on an exam that George Washington commanded the American army during the Revolution, or that Abraham Lincoln wrote the Emancipation Proclamation, or that the Declaration of Independence marked the formal separation of the colonies from Britain, then the nation was at risk (Ravitch & Finn, 1987). Curriculum standards in the school subjects need to be developed and implemented reliably, they argued, and assessments of knowledge and skills need to be measured on standardized exams.

Over the ensuing decades, various standards and frameworks for civics education were created by organizations such as the National Council for the Social Studies (most recently, the *College, Career, and Civic Life (C3) Framework for Social Studies State Standards* (2013)) and the Center for Civic Education (*National Standards for Civics and Government* (1995)) gained widespread adaptation in school districts and classrooms. The College Board's *Advanced Placement in US Government and Politics* also set a standard for rigorous study of the US political system that includes not only multiple-choice and free response items on the exam but also a required research or applied civics project for the course (College Board, 2023). Perhaps the most influential standard-setter is NAEP, a/k/a "The Nation's Report Card," which since 1969 has been assessing 4th, 8th, and 12th graders' competencies in civics. As noted earlier, the NAEP assessment historically has shown that the rising generation of American citizens has little knowledge of the workings of American democracy or how to participate in it (NAEP, 2022). Rather than faulting the students for this deficit, most civics education advocates have claimed that the exam proves, better than anything, the major gap between America's professed interest in inculcating civics knowledge, values, virtues, and skills (the American *paideia*) and what actually goes on in schools, where attention to achievement in literacy and STEM subjects far outweighs concern for American history, politics, and culture, among other areas (e.g., arts, languages, physical education). As one commentator put it, a school district in which 50% of its graduates cannot read would fire its superintendent, but no superintendent has been held similarly accountable for the fact that fewer than 50% of Americans regularly vote (Johanek, 2012).

If we take the NAEP results at face value, they demonstrate that students who study the US Constitution as a primary source in courses that focus exclusively on civics perform significantly higher than students who do not have adequate civics education (Strauss, 2023). [In 2025, 36 states and DC required a stand-alone high school civics course; 29 states required a civics assessment, most often in the form of a knowledge-based exam, as a graduation requirement; 39 states and DC provided credit for service-learning projects (Benites, 2025).] What is more, students perform better on this written, content-based exam when they have had some participatory experience with practicing civics skills, such as in mock trials and debates, and when they engage in civic activity outside the classroom, such as following current events and volunteering at community agencies. All of this suggests the value of a mutual minds-on *and* hands-on approach to civics education that encourages formal instruction in the classroom and assesses its application in real-world situations. (For specific suggestions on civics instruction that includes attention to principles of political economy and social choice, see Feuer, 2023.)

The Civic Consequences of Jaywalking

"Jaywalking," a recurrent and beloved routine on *The Tonight Show with Jay Leno* (1992–2014), consisted of the comedian doing "person-on-the street" interviews with everyday people who notoriously were unable to name the sitting vice president, the original 13 colonies, the color of the White House, and other basic facts about American history and government. That some of these individuals were engaged at the time in the illegal act of jaywalking added to the sketch's humor, further demonstrating how oblivious average Americans are about both the fundamentals of civics and the responsibilities of citizenship. Far less humorous—and far more troubling with respect to civic knowledge and participation—are occasions such as the January 6, 2021 insurrection at the US Capitol, where mass confusion and ignorance were on full display (among the powerful and populists alike) around how presidential elections are certified, what constitutes protected speech and the right to assembly, and, perhaps above all, what American democracy and values are all about.

Looking back over the history of civics education and assessment in the US through the lens of these real-world examples, we are compelled to reflect on whether the basic premise of the enterprise holds true: Does civic knowledge affect civic action and if so, how can we tell? The Naturalization Test, for example, is an efficient way to check if newcomers have "jaywalking-style" information purportedly suitable or necessary for productive participation in American democracy. But does a passing score really predict or guarantee civic engagement, let alone "good citizenship"? What would happen if those who got their citizenship by birth were also tested? When only 22% of eighth graders earn a passing grade on the Nation's Report Card assessment of civic knowledge, does it mean American civic life is on the verge of collapse?

When the late Senator Ted Kennedy opened a hearing on the Naturalization Test in the early 2000s, he told a story that brought gales of laughter in the chamber, as recalled by the second author. Paraphrasing the senator, "I had a constituent who told me why he kept failing the oral citizenship test: asked if he favored the toppling of the American government using *force* or *violence*, he said he never knew which one to choose." Yes, there will always be limits to the validity and utility of tests, whether for measuring citizenship, civics, or any valued knowledge, skill, and disposition. But on balance we are better off approaching these complexities with tools that, though imperfect, move us in the direction of more coherent and equitable decision-making, especially when the consequences of those decisions can have powerful impacts on individuals and society. It is unlikely that any single assessment will solve all the problems of civics and citizenship, but it is even more unlikely that a return to wholly subjective impressions and narratives, unburdened by logic and evidence, will move us in the right direction. We conclude with cautious optimism that the assessment research and development community will continue to contribute to what is, indeed, a civic goal: the reinforcement and preservation of our democratic way of life.

References

Anderson, J. D. (1988). *The education of Blacks in the South, 1860-1935*. UNC Press.
Annenberg Public Policy Center. (2022, September 13). *2022 Annenberg Constitution Day civics survey*. https://www.annenbergpublicpolicycenter.org/americans-civics-knowledge-drops-on-first-amendment-and-branches-of-government
Beadie, N., Burkholder, Z., Anderson, J. D., Hartman, A., Parker, W. C., & Steineker, R. (2021). From the diffusion of knowledge to the cultivation of agency: A short history of civic education policy and practice in the United States. In C. D. Lee, G. White, & D. Dong (Eds.), *Educating for civic reasoning and discourse* (pp. 109–155). National Academy of Education.
Benites, A. (2025, August 25). 2025 state policy scan provides updated insight into civic learning policies, state by state. *iCivics CivxNow*. https://civxnow.org/2025-state-policy-scan/
Bond, H. M. (1924). Intelligence tests and propaganda. *The Crisis, 28*(2), 61–64.
College Board (2023). *Most popular AP courses and exams*. https://apcentral.collegeboard.org/about-ap/start-expand-ap-program/build/most-popular-ap-courses
Crocco, M. S. (2004). Dealing with difference in the social studies: A historical perspective. *International Journal of Social Education, 18*(2), 106–120.
Cuban, L. (2022, January 10). Whatever happened to open education? *National Education Policy Center*. https://nepc.colorado.edu/blog/open-education
Ellis, R. J. (2005). *To the flag: The unlikely history of the Pledge of Allegiance*. University Press of Kansas.
Evans, R. (2004). *The social studies wars: What should we teach the children?* Teachers College Press.
Fass, P. S. (1989). *Outside in: Minorities and the transformation of American education*. Oxford University Press.
Feuer, M. (2023). *Can schools save democracy? Civic education and the common good*. JHU Press.
Fine, B. (1943, April 4). Ignorance of US history shown by college freshmen. *The New York Times, 1*, 32–33.
Hahn, C. L. (1999). Challenges to civic education in the United States. In J. Torney-Purta, J Schwille, & J. Amadeo (Eds.), *Civic education across countries: Twenty-four national case studies from the IEA civic education project* (pp. 583–607). International Association for the Evaluation of Educational Achievement.
Hahn, C. L. (2010). American Political Behavior: The project and the people. In B. Slater Stern (Ed.), *The New Social Studies: People, projects and perspectives* (pp. 261–284). Information Age Publishing.
Hamilton, L., & Parsi, A. (2022). *Monitoring civic learning opportunities and outcomes: Lessons from a symposium sponsored by ETS and Educating for American Democracy* (ETS Research Notes). ETS.
Herbst, J. (1991). Cremin's American *paideia*. *The American Scholar, 60*(1), 128–140.

Hertzberg, H. W. (1988). Are method and content enemies? In B. R. Gifford (Ed.), *History in the schools: What shall we teach?* (pp. 13–40). Macmillan.

Institute for Citizens & Scholars (ICS). (2018, October 3). *National survey finds just 1 in 3 Americans would pass citizenship test.* https://citizensandscholars.org/resource/national-survey-finds-just-1-in-3-americans-would-pass-citizenship-test/

Jacobs, B. M. (2014). Social studies as a means for the preparation of teachers: A look back at the foundations of social foundations courses. *Curriculum Inquiry, 44*(2), 249–275.

Johanek, M. C. (2012). Preparing *pluribus* for *unum*: Historical perspectives on civic education. In D. E. Campbell, M. Levinson, & F. M. Hess (Eds.), *Making civics count: Citizenship education for a new generation* (pp. 57–88). Harvard Education Press.

Kaestle, C. F. (1983). *Pillars of the republic: Common schools and American society, 1780-1860.* Macmillan.

Kliebard, H. (2004). *The struggle for the American curriculum, 1893-1958* (3rd ed.) Routledge.

Kohlmeyer, H. F. (1925). *The history of the development of the aims of teaching civics in the secondary schools of the United States.* Indiana University.

Koretz, D. (2017). *The testing charade: Pretending to make schools better.* University of Chicago Press.

Krane, J. B. (1940, October 3). Rugg's books under fire: T.C. professor's social science texts burned in Ohio, banned in ten states. *Columbia Spectator*, 1A.

Kunnan, A. J. (2009). Testing for citizenship: The U.S. Naturalization Test. *Language Assessment Quarterly, 6*(1), 89–97.

Lagemann, E. C. (2000). *An elusive science: The troubling history of education research.* University of Chicago Press.

Makler, A. (2004). Problems of democracy and the social studies curriculum during the long armistice. In C. Woyshner, J. Watras, & M. S. Crocco (Eds.), *Social education in the twentieth century: Curriculum and context for citizenship* (pp. 20–41). Peter Lang.

Mattson, O. F. (1925). *A course of instruction for naturalization.* University of Wisconsin–Madison.

McDonnell, L., Timpane, M., & Benjamin, R. (Eds.). (2000). *Rediscovering the democratic purposes of education.* University of Kansas Press.

Mehlinger, H. D., & Patrick, J. J. (1977). *American political behavior, revised edition: Teacher's guide.* Ginn & Co.

Mirel, J. E. (2010). *Patriotic pluralism: Americanization education and European immigrants.* Harvard University Press.

Morse, H. T., & McCune, G. H. (1971). *Selected items for the testing of study skills and critical thinking.* Bulletin 15. National Council for the Social Studies.

National Assessment of Educational Progress (NAEP). (2022). *The nation's report card: Civics.* https://www.nationsreportcard.gov/civics

National Education Association (NEA). (1892; reprint 1969). *Report of the [Committee of Ten] committee on secondary social studies.* Arno Press & The New York Times.

National Education Association (NEA). (1916; reprint 1994). *The social studies in secondary education.* US Government Printing Office & ERIC.

National Education Association (NEA) Commission on the Reorganization of Secondary Education. (1918). *Cardinal principles of secondary education* (no. 35). US Government Printing Office & ERIC.

National Park Service (NPS). (n.d.). *September 17, 1787: A republic, if you can keep it.* https://www.nps.gov/articles/000/constitutionalconvention-september17.htm

National Research Council (NRC). (1999). *High stakes: Testing for tracking, promotion, and graduation.* Committee on Appropriate Test Use. The National Academies Press.

National Research Council (NRC). (2004). *Redesigning the U.S. naturalization tests: Interim report.* Committee on the U.S. Naturalization Test Redesign. Board on Testing and Assessment, Center for Education, Division of Behavioral and Social Sciences and Education. The National Academies Press.

Nevins, A. (1942, May 3). American history for Americans. *The New York Times Magazine*, 6, 28.

Ngalande, J. (2024). *A century-plus of civic education: What the textbooks show.* Hoover Institution.

Office of Technology Assessment (OTA). (1992). *Testing in American schools: Asking the right questions.* Government Printing Office.

Olneck, M. R. (1989). Americanization and the education of immigrants, 1900-1925: An analysis of symbolic action. *American Journal of Education, 97*(4), 398–423.

Ravitch, D., & Finn, C. (1987). *What do our 17-year-olds know?* Harper & Row.

Reuben, J. A. (1997). Beyond politics: Community civics and the redefinition of citizenship in the Progressive Era. *History of Education Quarterly, 37*(4), 399–420.

Schaper, W. A. (1905). What do students know about American government, before taking college courses in political science? A report to the section on instruction in political science. *Proceedings of the American Political Science Association, 2*, 207–228.

Schneider, D. (2001). Naturalization and United States citizenship in two periods of mass migration: 1894-1930, 1965-2000. *Journal of American Ethnic History, 21*(1), 50–82.

Shapiro, S., & Brown, C. (2018, February 21). *The state of civics education.* Center for American Progress.

Strauss, V. (2023, May 11). What new civics test scores show us, besides the obvious. *The Washington Post.* May 11, https://www.washingtonpost.com/education/2023/05/11/naep-civics-test-scores/

Streb, R. W. (1979). *A history of the Citizenship Education Project: A model curricular study.* Teachers College, Columbia University.

Thornton, S. J. (1994). The social studies near century's end: Reconsidering patterns of curriculum and instruction. *Review of Research in Education, 20*(1), 223–254.

Topics of the times. (1942, May 3). *The New York Times*, E8.

US Citizenship and Immigration Services (USCIS) (2020). *Origins of the naturalization civics test.* https://www.uscis.gov/about-us/our-history/stories-from-the-archives/origins-of-the-naturalization-civics-test

US Citizenship and Immigration Services (USCIS) (2022). *Naturalization test performance.* https://www.uscis.gov/citizenship-resource-center/naturalization-related-data-and-statistics/naturalization-test-performance

Vaughan, K. (2018). Progressive education and racial justice: Examining the work of John Dewey. *Education and Culture, 34*(2), 39–68.

Vinovskis, M. A. (2019). History of testing in the United States: PK–12 education. *The Annals of the American Academy of Political and Social Science, 683*(1), 22–37.

Wechsler, H. S., & Diner, S. J. (2022). *Unwelcome guests: A history of access to American higher education.* JHU Press.

Wilson, W. R. (1935). [Review of the book *Tests and measurements in the social sciences*, by T. L. Kelley & A. C. Krey]. *The Washington Historical Quarterly, 26*(2), 146–148.

Winchester, E. (1796). *A plain political catechism.* T. Dickman Press.

Zimmerman, J. (2002). *Whose America? Culture wars in the public schools.* Harvard University Press.

3
Advancing the Future of Civic Learning and Engagement Through Assessment
How AI Might Power Innovation in What and How We Measure

Eric M. Tucker and Eva L. Baker

Artificial intelligence (AI) is rapidly transforming how digital-first learning experiences are developed, significantly accelerating the pace and enhancing the quality of educational content design and creation. Duolingo, for instance, recently leveraged generative AI to launch 148 new courses in roughly a year—surpassing the 100 courses previously developed over a span of 12 years—demonstrating unprecedented scalability in educational technology (Malik, 2025). These developments suggest profound implications for assessing civic learning, as AI's affordances might begin to open new avenues for creating adaptive, interactive, and personalized assessment tasks, potentially reshaping both what competencies we measure and how effectively we measure them. The analogy to Duolingo is imperfect, but it suggests the importance of exploring how rapidly developing affordances of AI might influence this critical domain (Agrawal et al., 2022).

Applied researchers, measurement scientists, and designers of educational technologies leveraging AI[1] have the potential to transform assessment practices concerning civic learning and engagement. The rapid advancement in general-purpose, multimodal AI technologies potentially opens significant opportunities for measuring critical civic competencies—such as digital information literacy, AI literacy, critical thinking, communication, and collaborative problem-solving. This chapter explores how AI-enabled systems can operationalize these traditionally "difficult-to-measure" competencies, aiming to improve the scientific soundness, efficacy, and scalability of civic assessment solutions.

We begin by describing civic competencies increasingly demanded in educational and professional spaces shaped by AI. Next, we examine some innovative methods emerging to assess these complex civic learning and engagement skills, including how AI technologies might influence the entire assessment value chain, from domain ontology mapping, task generation, quality control, piloting, refinement, validation, scoring, analysis, and reporting. Although the pace and trajectory of innovations in AI remain challenging to predict, safe, accountable, fair, and effective application of these tools holds promise for enhancing the productivity, validity, and transparency of civic assessments.

We then consider working examples that illustrate practical applications of AI-driven assessment, including a civic advocacy simulation, a Global AI Debates initiative, and a scenario for

DOI: 10.4324/9781003476825-4
This chapter has been made available under a CC BY-NC-ND license.

early learner engagement. These early-stage exemplars aim to illustrate how AI-based assessments can authentically capture evidence of civic skills in contextually relevant ways, enhancing learner engagement and personalization (Baker & Gordon, 2014; Bennett, 2014; Bryk et al., 2015; Gordon, 2020, Gordon et al., 2012; Gordon & Rajagopalan, 2015).

The integration of AI into educational assessment raises important challenges. The widespread use of AI raises significant concerns around fairness, particularly due to algorithmic bias, unequal access to technological resources, and issues related to privacy and data security (AERA et al., 1990, 2014; Association of Test Publishers, 2022). Grounded in the principles of fair, accountable, transparent, and ethical (FATE) use, we propose directions that promote both quality and efficacy. As a result of the rapid pace of AI's evolution and growth, there is a pressing need to ensure that AI-driven assessments are developed responsibly with appropriate safeguards.

Understanding Assessment and Its Value Proposition

Robert Mislevy proposes shifting our conception from viewing the validity of assessment as primarily a measurement requirement toward "seeing it as an evidentiary argument, situated in social contexts, shaped by purposes, and centered on students' developing capabilities for valued activities" (2019, p. 164). This approach emphasizes the importance of intentional evidence gathering, guided by human judgment, to support inferences about learning and development that ultimately enhance teaching and learning practices (Mislevy, 2018).

Technological advances and AI can support maximizing the relevance and precision of feedback, moving beyond traditional assessment to better meet the needs of all stakeholders. The innovative assessment systems proposed by Foster and Piacentini (2023) aim to assess complex skills like critical thinking, problem-solving, and collaboration. This shift toward "measuring what matters" aims to align assessment with key competencies for modern life rather than just those easiest to quantify (Tucker, Armour-Thomas et al., 2025; Tucker, Everson et al., 2025).

Traditional methods of measuring complex skills—e.g., self-reports and peer evaluations—are often affected by biases such as response format (He et al., 2014), halo effects (Cooper, 1981), and reference bias (Lira et al., 2022). Thus, more potentially accurate approaches, including personalized, interactive tasks and simulations, and analyzing process data (e.g., keystrokes, response times), have emerged as promising ways to evaluate complex skills (Liu, Kell, et al., 2023C).

Studies in AI and education confirm that continuous, actionable feedback, rather than single-point snapshots, is essential for development (Koedinger et al., 2023; Zapata-Rivera & Hu, 2022). For test-takers, assessments hopefully not only reflect current skill levels but also deliver actionable feedback for targeted improvement.

Defining Essential Civic Learning Skills

To assess civic learning effectively, there must be clarity regarding what skills constitute relevant competencies. Historically, educational assessment efforts have emphasized traditional curricular skills, such as those described in curriculum standards and classroom texts and typically ask students to know and "understand" particular domain knowledge. However, there is now an increasing need to focus more explicitly on complex, multidimensional competencies increasingly considered critical to civic and professional success. These competencies include critical thinking, communication, collaboration, and problem-solving. Such skills are no longer peripheral; rather, they have become foundational elements required for meaningful civic participation and future workforce readiness (Autor et al., 2024; Eloundou et al., 2023).

Andreas Schleicher of the OECD emphasizes that "skills are becoming more like currency" (Kyllonen et al., 2024). Civic education increasingly prioritizes competencies like critical thinking, media literacy, and collaborative problem-solving, which support informed participation in society and contribute to resilience in communities. Moreover, as the pace of societal and economic change accelerates, skills once acquired and maintained over a lifetime now require continuous updating. Lifelong learning is therefore not just advantageous but essential (OECD, 2023). Civic education thus is asked to prepare learners to navigate societal complexities, such as misinformation and polarization. The civic skills related to collaboration, analysis and problem-solving approaches may be applied to current as well as unanticipated future domains of knowledge. Applying them in a social context is paramount to improving and adapting civics learning.

Civic Skills for the Future: Navigating Technology's Impact on Society

Technological advancements, particularly the rise of AI, are reshaping the civic landscape, demanding that education systems respond proactively. Much of civics discourse takes place in technological environments, online in podcasts, chats, and posts on social networks. Detecting inaccuracies, identifying recurrent (and probably bot-like contributions), and understanding how AI can both enhance and complicate civic engagement represent new applications of existing cognitive skills. Future civic competencies must include adaptability and a commitment to lifelong learning, including a focus on "learning how to learn." Students are well-advised to consistently update their skills, integrating technical knowledge with durable skills. Cultivating critical engagement with emerging technologies enables individuals to leverage new tools ethically and responsibly. Educators hold a critical role in ensuring learners who are not only technologically proficient but also socially responsible citizens capable of navigating rapid technological shifts.

Understanding Demand for Key Competencies

To further clarify what skills need assessing, we turn to competencies increasingly prioritized by stakeholders in workforce development, higher education, and K-12 systems. Analyses drawn from employer surveys, labor market trends, and educational frameworks highlight crucial competencies, underscoring the importance of aligning civic assessment with broader societal and economic demands (Kyllonen et al., 2024).

The ETS Human Progress Report (ETS, 2024) identifies several competencies as critical for both career readiness and lifelong success. Among these are communication, creativity, digital literacy, problem-solving, and resilience. This array of competencies encompasses cognitive skills (e.g., analytical reasoning), interpersonal abilities (e.g., collaboration), and intrapersonal traits (e.g., self-direction). These competencies enable individuals to effectively engage a range of perspectives, adapt to change, and tackle multifaceted challenges. Although technical skills continue to be valued, competencies such as critical thinking and adaptability increasingly define readiness in both professional and civic contexts.

High-demand Skills According to Employers, Higher Education, and K-12

Employer surveys and job ads consistently identify communication (especially listening), analytical thinking, problem-solving, teamwork, social intelligence, and self-motivation as top skills. Indeed, employers increasingly prioritize cultural competence, adaptability, and digital literacy over traditional metrics like GPA (National Association of Colleges and Employers (NACE), 2022). Studies, such as those by Rios et al. (2020) and Burning Glass (2019), suggest the importance of communication, collaboration, and self-direction, highlighting how versatile technical and foundational skills are in the labor market. Civil society and volunteer organizations also value these competencies for effective participation.

In higher education, resilience, time management, adaptability, and continuous learning are essential for both academic and career success. The National Academies (Hilton & Herman, 2017) emphasize interpersonal and intrapersonal skills, such as growth mindset and self-efficacy, as crucial for student success. These competencies also support civic learning, promoting skills for active democratic participation, yet are often assessed through self-reports.

As demand for assessment rebalances to reflect the importance of competencies beyond traditional academics, for instance, a focus on cognitive, social, and practical skills essential for professional and civic engagement is emerging through portrait of graduate frameworks (Patrick, 2021). Portrait-aligned assessments—enabled by digital platforms and AI to capture complex problem-solving and collaborative skills—have the potential to align with civic learning goals by focusing on communication, critical reasoning, and social intelligence. Such competencies are foundational for active citizenship, equipping learners for roles that require adaptability, digital literacy, and empathy within a democratic society (OECD, 2019, 2021).

Demand for Complex, Difficult-to-Measure Civic Skills

Technological advances shift the demand from routine tasks toward non-routine cognitive and interpersonal skills, essential for navigating complex social environments. Studies like Autor et al. (2003) demonstrate that as automation replaces routine tasks, critical thinking, adaptability, and social intelligence become central to workforce success and civic participation. The rise of communication technologies, as Deming (2017) notes, emphasizes the need for strong social skills, crucial for roles involving community and collaborative problem-solving. As technology reshapes society, education must focus on developing cognitive, social, and technical skills that prepare individuals for both professional success and meaningful civic engagement.

Civic Skills and the Artificial Intelligence Era

Predictive AI, Generative AI, AI Literacy, and Jobs for the Future

Digital and AI literacy are now foundational skills for both civic life and workforce demands. Digital literacy enables critical assessment and responsible information management in online spaces, supporting informed decision-making and civic participation. Building on this, AI literacy helps individuals understand AI's capabilities, limitations, and potential biases, promoting ethical interactions with AI tools. With AI influencing areas from news to policy, these literacies prepare citizens for informed personal and community choices. Beyond career readiness, these skills align with civic goals of reducing knowledge gaps and promoting technology access. An ETS report underscores the importance of digital and AI literacy in cultivating resilient, adaptable citizens prepared for roles requiring both professional and civic competence (Sparks et al., 2025). Embedding these literacies into civic learning equips students to navigate AI-rich environments responsibly, fostering citizens capable of critical information evaluation and addressing technological challenges in their communities.

A well-defined research agenda is critical to developing accurate tools for tracking civic learning skills at scale. Certain methods of obtaining respondents' knowledge, such as self-reports, cannot fully capture competencies like digital literacy, critical thinking, and adaptability. Advancing tools to actually demonstrate ability to distinguish accurate from inaccurate arguments, or to apply or transfer problem-solving skills to civics domains can be simulated and captured online (Chung et al., 2002) and such will support the vital work of cultivating civic-minded, adaptable individuals prepared to navigate an evolving world.

Emerging Approaches to Measuring Difficult-to-Measure Civic Skills and Predispositions

Emerging approaches hold promise for assessing complex civic skills accurately. Performance-based approaches offer more dynamic and authentic measures of abilities, aligning with Foster and Piacentini's (2023) emphasis on authentic contexts for learning experiences.

In coming years, AI has the potential to play a pivotal role in refining these assessment methods. AI-powered learning tools claim to analyze student data, providing feedback that identifies strengths and areas for improvement (EdTech Insiders, n.d.). Computer-adaptive testing, which adjusts in real time to student responses in large-scale assessment environments, claims to help advance fairer and more accurate measures of developing competencies. AI-powered tools applying similar methods to alternative response modes, including writing and performance, have provided insights into how this might unfold over a period of time (Chung et al., 2002; Grover & Pea, 2013; Guo et al., 2022, 2024). These advances suggest how technology might inform civic learning beyond knowledge acquisition to foster active engagement with learning. Performance-based tasks, simulations, and AI-driven personalization potentially support this goal, offering a practical approach to measuring critical civic skills such as critical thinking, collaboration, empathy, and decision-making.

Performance Measures in Civic Learning

Performance measures for civic skills such as critical thinking and problem-solving are essential and have the potential to support the development of informed citizenship (Liu et al., 2016; Weiss et al., 2021). Future assessments might leverage such innovations within civic contexts. For example, adaptive learning approaches, such as Duolingo's Birdbrain, dynamically adjust the difficulty and content of questions based on real-time user responses by applying statistical models such as item response theory (IRT), aiming to tailor the learning process to individual strengths and weaknesses (Bicknell et al., 2023). Applying similar adaptive methods to civic learning might involve customizing assessments of media literacy and argumentation by presenting learners with scenarios tailored to their current understanding, progressively challenging them with potentially more complex media sources and nuanced arguments as their skills develop. Due to their subjective and dynamic nature, skills like teamwork, leadership, and cultural sensitivity are challenging to assess through traditional methods.

Game-Based Approaches and Simulations

Game-based approaches in civic learning can engage learners while measuring skills like problem-solving and decision-making (Gee, forthcoming; Landers & Sanchez, 2022). iCivics, founded by Justice Sandra Day O'Connor, offers games like "Do I Have a Right?" and "Win the White House" to teach students about constitutional rights and the electoral process. Gamified assessments add game elements (e.g., scoreboards or badging) to existing assessments, while game-designed assessments create immersive experiences to measure civic skills. These methods are valuable for evaluating leadership roles in community projects and encouraging democratic participation (Thomas & Seely Brown, 2011). They are potentially useful in assessing skills like curiosity about civic issues and social preferences that influence community involvement (Tang & Kirman, 2023). In low-stakes settings, game-based assessments can boost engagement, leading to more accurate measures of civic skills (Buckley et al., 2021). Their design needs to become more sophisticated, particularly concerning how player performances on (or, interactions with) game-based assessments might be comparable across learners, and by focusing on not only whether answers are correct but also to other factors like learner engagement, decision-making processes, and demonstrated curiosity.

Ratings and Related Methods

Self-reports are commonly used but often biased by response style, social desirability, and faking (Geiger et al., 2021; van de Vijver & He, 2016). These biases are particularly problematic in high-stakes situations (Niessen et al., 2017). Informant ratings from peers or educators can help reduce these biases and predict future behavior better than self-ratings (Oh et al., 2011). These ratings may provide a more reliable assessment of behaviors and traits by leveraging observations from others. Advances in scoring these methods have improved their reliability and predictive power (Cao et al., 2015). Anchoring methods were designed to address response biases in rating scales. Anchoring vignettes (King & Wand, 2007) prompt responses by asking respondents to rate themselves to a vignette, making self-assessments more comparable. Stankov et al. (2017) provide an example of potential drawbacks associated with anchoring vignette methods, noting concerns such as spurious correlations, questionable reliability, and limited evidence for validity.

Situational Judgment Tests

Situational judgment tests (SJTs) present scenarios and ask respondents how they would react, either to behavioral scenarios or to the substance of responses (for a more extensive description of SJTs, see Thier, this volume). They effectively assess domains like interpersonal skills and decision-making (Christian et al., 2010). SJTs use written or video scenarios and are commonly used for employee selection and admissions decisions (Sternberg et al., 2000). SJTs assess competencies like empathy, adaptability, and ethical reasoning. An example is Acuity Insights' Casper, which assesses competencies like empathy, professionalism, and cultural awareness (Acuity Insights, 2023). These tools evaluate how individuals handle real-world challenges. Compared to rating scales, SJTs are less reliable per minute of testing, requiring longer testing times to achieve reliable scores (Schmitt et al., 2009). Their ability to simulate real-world situations makes them well-suited for assessing practical competencies. Ongoing research aims to improve the reliability of SJTs for efficiently assessing multiple dimensions (Kepes et al., 2024).

Ratings of behavior, predispositions, and SJTs are potentially valuable for assessing civic competencies like empathy, teamwork, cultural awareness, and decision-making. Peer or educator ratings provide insights into civic behaviors such as collaboration and ethical decision-making, capturing aspects that tests of academic achievement or knowledge often overlook. SJTs might simulate real-world civic challenges, requiring respondents to demonstrate critical thinking, empathy, and ethical judgment—skills essential for civic participation. For example, an SJT might present a scenario involving a community dispute and ask respondents to choose a course of action, helping evaluate how students apply civic knowledge in practical situations.

Multimodal Measures of Civic Learning

Multimodal measures involve collecting data from multiple sources, such as physiological signals, behavioral logs, and audio or video recordings analyzed by human evaluators or automated systems (Molenaar et al., 2023). Integrating these measures into civic learning assessments has the potential to provide a more comprehensive understanding of students' skills. By analyzing diverse data, educators can gain valuable insights into student engagement, communication, and collaboration, for example—key components of civic learning. In civic learning, reporting of activities may allow the evaluation of community service and activism behaviors. Administrative, social media, and mobile data availability have made life-data collection easier, providing insights into students' civic behaviors (Kautz & Zanoni, 2014). Multimodal AI models have the potential to enhance civic learning assessments by efficiently analyzing complex combinations of text, audio, visual, and behavioral data, providing insights into nuanced student competencies such as collaboration, empathy, and civic engagement.

One example (which is directionally intriguing) is an ETS project conducted by Chen et al. (2014), which examined public speaking skills using audio, video, and 3D capturing devices to extract features through natural language processing (NLP), speech analysis, and multimodal sensing. This approach captured verbal and non-verbal communication. The scoring models developed from this data showed strong correlations with human evaluations, highlighting the potential of multimodal measures in assessing complex communication skills. Similarly, Martin-Raugh et al. (2020) investigated negotiation and collaborative problem-solving using NLP to classify different parts of conversations. Multimodal assessments might enable richer data collection, providing a more nuanced understanding of students' knowledge and skills, particularly in the context of civic learning.

How AI Might Amplify Emerging Assessment Approaches

AI can potentially enhance measurement methods by providing adaptive, personalized assessments with person-specific feedback. AI-driven tools can analyze responses in real time, offering suggestions for improvement and helping learners refine their civic skills. For example, AI could provide feedback on a student's response to an SJT scenario, highlighting areas for improvement. Such personalized feedback might spur development civic competencies, while measuring attainment.

Innovative Measures for Civic Learning: Conclusions

Assessment of civic learning and engagement can benefit from the use of performance-based measures, such as interactive tasks, game experiences, or simulations that replicate real-world scenarios such as collaborative problem-solving, as explored in Chapter 14. By placing learners in realistic contexts, these assessments offer more nuanced evaluations of civic competencies, such as leadership, teamwork, and cultural sensitivity.

Multimodal and performance-based assessments offer promising pathways for effectively evaluating civic learning competencies. Moving forward, such measures will likely be enhanced through data mining and process analysis, reducing the reliance on traditional ratings and tests. As these methods develop, they may contribute to more effective educational strategies and outcomes in civic learning, better-preparing students to become informed and active citizens.

By combining innovative data collection methods with real-world scenarios, educators can create richer, more meaningful assessments. These advancements can contribute to deepening understanding of students' civic learning and help cultivate a generation of learners equipped to participate actively in democratic society.

Operations Breakthroughs: AI and Technology-Enabled Advances

As the Duolingo example suggests, generative and predictive AI has potential to transform aspects of measurement and assessment operations. Advanced technologies may increasingly play a crucial role in various stages, including domain ontology mapping, task generation, piloting, refinement, validation, secure delivery, scoring, analysis, and results reporting. Additionally, AI has the potential to enhance test assembly and quality control, addressing the significant challenges of making assessments valid, reliable, fair, and valuable to learners, educators, and other stakeholders. Although the pace and direction of specific innovations is difficult to predict, AI is increasingly likely to drive adjustments regarding the efficiency, quality, and security of test operations, ensuring that assessments provide meaningful value to all examinees and that the inferences drawn from scores are transparent and sound.

AI and Related Technology Are Beginning to Transform Assessment

Test administration efficiencies can yield benefits to both learners and the precision of results. Combining assessments with instructional benefits can also increase engagement. Game-based assessments may make testing experiences more engaging than paper and pencil, as seen in DARPA's Warrior Simulation program, which used games for training (O'Neil et al., 2004). AI's affordances enable anytime, anywhere testing, which has accelerated in the wake of the COVID-19 pandemic. Remote testing offers convenience and cost benefits but presents security challenges, especially in high-stakes scenarios (Burstein et al., 2024). For civic learning, remote testing platforms offer flexible assessment opportunities, accommodating functional learning differences and increasing accessibility. Privacy-enhancing technologies also have the potential to improve test securing and thus may help ensure assessment scores more accurately reflect students' abilities.

Advances in Automated Task Generation and Contextualization

Generative AI is already powering some task- and item-generation. Traditionally, item development has relied on human experts, making it costly and time-consuming (Lane et al., 2016). Automatic item generation (AIG) offers a more efficient alternative. Early AIG approaches focused on creating detailed item models to generate variants (Irvine & Kyllonen, 2013). Today, generative AI tools are beginning to address these challenges by producing varied item types across multiple formats and specifications (Attali et al., 2022). A blend of item modeling and large language models (LLMs) shows significant promise for automating item development.

Incorporating civic learning competencies into AIG operations can enhance assessments by including items that evaluate civic knowledge and engagement. Most AIG methods focus on initial task drafting or "generation." Innovations throughout the item development cycle—including review, calibration, and test assembly—are necessary for addressing bottlenecks and achieving efficiency and scalability.

Modeling item difficulty is essential for assembling test forms and determining scores. Traditionally, the difficulty is estimated using responses from large groups of test-takers, which is impractical for an effective AIG system producing numerous new items rapidly. ETS researchers have also developed techniques to manage uncertainty in predicted difficulty (Mislevy et al., 1993). Leveraging the emerging affordances of LLM-powered tools to model item difficulty has the potential for assessments to be more appropriately challenging, enabling sound inferences about civic learning and engagement.

AI can help to enable cost-effective contextualization (e.g., translation or other adaptation) and personalization of assessments at scale. Large-scale assessments, such as OECD's PISA, require cultural adaptation to ensure comparability across countries and languages (cApStAn & Halleux, 2019). These adaptations minimize cultural differences that could affect evidence supporting the valid use of such assessments. Adaptation is also crucial for subgroups within a country, as biases in cross-cultural assessments can occur even within subcultures of a single language group. LLMs are well-suited to enable scaled contextualization of assessments of civic learning and engagement when learners reflect a range of home languages, cultural backgrounds, learning differences, and functional needs. Tailoring content to linguistic or cultural emphasis of tasks has the potential to produce assessments that are meaningful to a wider range of learners. Careful oversight and quality control are needed to prevent any biases reflected in LLM training models from perpetuating existing concerns about fairness.

The use of LLMs in testing introduces new challenges for cheating detection, including sophisticated deception methods such as deepfakes—realistic but fabricated audio, images, or videos—and voice cloning, where someone's voice is artificially replicated to impersonate them. Potential solutions include monitoring test-takers via cameras to verify their identity and detect unauthorized assistance and redesigning assessments to include tasks less susceptible to LLM-generated responses, such as critical thinking and performance-based items. Detection measures can flag potentially AI-generated responses, though false positives remain a major concern. Adequate detectors must consider metrics like false positives, true negatives, and resilience against human modifications (Liu, Zhang, et al., 2023).

AI Scoring of Tasks and Essays

AI scoring can be used in adaptive testing as well as for open-ended essays and other performance tasks. Scoring for traditional multiple-choice tests is well-established using IRT and other model-based methods (Ostini & Nering, 2006). One AIG approach factors affecting task difficulty and, as well as "non-influential elements," which are surface-level features that vary the item's context or presentation without altering its fundamental cognitive demands. This approach works by constructing item templates containing "slots" that can be filled with interchangeable values, which aims to efficiently generate numerous, unique test items, which is especially valuable in content areas such as math and physics, where structured variations of similar problems are common (Bejar et al., 2002). AI can provide scoring models and execution for complex, open-ended behaviors. Within the context of civic learning, AI can assess open-ended responses on civic topics, such as analyzing policies, proposing community initiatives, and encouraging civic engagement and critical thinking. Automated essay scoring with LLMs can provide increasingly human-level accuracy while reducing rater biases (Williamson et al., 2012). However, AI bias in scoring remains an area of ongoing research for open-ended tasks (Burstein et al., 2024).

Analysis and Results Reporting

Integrating multimodal, generative AI into assessment systems can enable analysis and reporting by enabling natural language interactions. Educators, administrators, and learners can increasingly access insights by asking questions in plain language or using voice commands, removing the constraints of specialized technical skills or extensive training. This capacity has the potential to begin to democratize access to insights, increasingly allowing users to generate customized reports and dashboards tailored to their needs. AI-driven interfaces can adapt based on user interactions, highlighting key data, suggesting relevant findings, and uncovering trends that might go unnoticed. By automating data analysis and report generation, these systems can provide real-time, actionable insights, empowering educators to respond quickly to students' needs and optimize educational outcomes.

Fairness in Testing

Fairness means striving for valid score interpretation by measuring domains equivalently for all test-takers, regardless of background (AERA et al., 2014). Item writing guidelines help eliminate offensive content and ensure comparable group performance (Millsap, 2011). Culturally responsive assessments (CRAs) reflect a range of learner backgrounds, potentially enhancing engagement and fairness (Bennett, 2023). Those integrating civic learning competencies into AI-powered assessment development should make efforts to evaluate and mitigate biases, ensure representative training data, and embed fairness into design and architecture.

Working Examples of Performance Tasks with AI Enhancements

Of key importance to new AI-supported approaches is adopting a clear logic model for the design, data collection, and interpretation of data to discern the quality and trustworthiness of the approach. Among such models, Evidence Centered Design (ECD) (Mislevy et al., 1999) is a well-known assessment development framework that systematically investigates the interpretation of student performance data with explicitly defined claims and supporting evidence (Mislevy & Haertel, 2006). To implement ECD or other appropriate models and examples, it is necessary to identify the types of knowledge and skills expected of the learner in a civics setting. There is a set of content based on the domains of civics typically found in the curriculum. These may involve knowledge of government and quasi-governmental agencies' levels, types, and functions. Examples of relevant knowledge include understanding who has authority over the local police department or which public offices are appointed or elected. Knowledge will need to be appropriately bounded. For instance, the types of level and oversight would all be made explicit for the designer of assessments. Appropriate cognitive demands delimiting the desired behaviors or products would be made explicit. Consider, for instance, problem-solving and collaboration or the two together. Problem-solving, in a civics context, requires recognizing a target issue, difficulty, or obstruction, one that potentially could be solved by civic action. Knowledge of roles, authority, and limits of action for relevant offices or personnel will further refine the problem and solution spaces. The learner would need to formulate a plan, either singly or in concert with others, and plan for its implementation and means to predict or evaluate the success or failure. Good problem-solvers can also generate alternatives if their original solution fails. Collaboration is a second generalizable skill that comes into play in the civics domain. Because group action is often required, the learner needs to be able to communicate clearly the goals and steps of the solution to develop support. These may be done by enlisting the support of one or more colleagues to conceive, design, and "execute" the plan. Collaboration may require different roles, including direct and less formal leadership, where ownership of ideas is shared or may be developed by others. Persistence and adaptability are other characteristics of civics problem-solving and collaboration, as most problems are not solved in a single try.

With elements identified for assessment including domain knowledge, problem-solving, collaboration, and leadership dimensions, the following models and examples are offered for potential use by users who are interested in employing AI-based assessment but who are relatively unsophisticated in the technology. We assume they have knowledge of civics, and the cognitive demands needed to enact solutions. The models we propose may be used with suitable complexity for learners of different ages. While these assessments may be adapted to large-scale environments by using technology administration and monitoring systems, they focus on uses that are closely linked to specific outcomes and defined situations (rather than more expansive constructs). They also focus on assessing complex learning displayed in open-ended environments. Let's illustrate the vast range of civics learning and engagement topics with several examples.

Mock Civic Advocacy

One set of examples used for learners from upper elementary to university involves the analysis of communications made in the broad civics context. They may be speeches, video clips, written documents outlining policy, or practical positions for school, community, or governmental decisions. Two or more perspectives may be given. In our experience, choosing examples with varying or even opposing views allows learners to structure their responses. No matter the behavior desired, written or oral presentation for instance, the learner is expected to generate an analysis of what is being described in writing or speech. One example could be concerns for divided elements in society about a local problem, such as the price of housing.

In this approach, learners or teams select a pressing social issue, conduct applied research, and propose solutions requiring private and public coordination. Students complete an individual research-based essay integrating source materials, independent inquiry, and a multimedia presentation on their topic. They then participate in an oral defense, responding to community member- or teacher-posed questions about their research process and argumentation. The goal is to develop research, analysis, argumentation, collaboration, writing, and presentation skills, fostering critical thinking and evidence-based civic advocacy. A housing policy project serves as an example.

Generative AI tools could serve as aids in this process, supporting the search for credible sources, clarifying complex data, and offering writing assistance for grammar or tone. With housing as an example, AI might help identify data on cost distributions or affordability challenges. AI agents aside, students remain responsible for reading and interpreting source material firsthand, considering the accuracy and credibility of materials, ensuring an authentic, original analysis. Educators would review and validate drafts or checkpoints to confirm that learners engage deeply with credible sources and consider diverse perspectives.

Scoring criteria emphasize using significant principles or concepts, accurate and relevant content knowledge, and a coherent organizational structure. While previously established rubrics (e.g., AP Seminar and Capstone) can inform these standards, local confirmation by knowledgeable adults may also be employed. In some contexts, performance could be measured by comparing students' arguments to those offered by experts, gauging the alignment between professional perspectives and student work. Educators or advanced learners would need sufficient training in prompt development and data interpretation for design or assessment tasks that utilize AI prompts.

Additionally, the production of quality civic texts—aligned with desired complexity and rigor—can be guided by AI research assistants, ensuring personalized reading levels and well-structured outputs for texts such as speeches or Op-Eds. Yet the essence of mock civic advocacy lies in structured disagreements and public presentations. By placing an emphasis on turn-taking, listening, and structured disagreement, instructors can cultivate a classroom environment where evidence and reasoning guide discussions, even when viewpoints differ significantly.

Ultimately, mock civic advocacy projects have the potential to help students internalize norms for productive civil discourse. Teachers are critical in establishing evidence standards, directing refutation requirements, and clarifying speech burdens. When norms are explicit and upheld, structured controversy can focus on facts and their deeper meanings. In this way, mock civic advocacy—amplified by carefully integrated AI tools— may enable students to hone their research and communication abilities, preparing them to engage thoughtfully in civic life (Bauschard et al., 2023).

The Global AI Debates

The Global AI Debates[2] initiative represents a distinctive approach to fostering civic learning and engagement in the age of AI. Designed to cultivate critical thinking, persuasive communication, perspective-taking, and ethical awareness, the competition challenges learners aged 8–22 to grapple with complex AI-related issues. Structured as a multi-stage competition, the debates begin with essay submissions on a range of topics tailored to different age groups, encouraging in-depth research and nuanced argumentation. Essay prompts, such as "Students should be able to use generative AI in school" or "AI developments will reduce global poverty," prompt students to explore the societal implications of AI from a range of perspectives.

The competition then transitions to online debates, where participants engage in real-time argument and counter-argument, refining their ability to defend claims, counter opponent warrants, and adapt to new lines of reasoning. This format simulates real-world civic case-making, where applied research, effective communication, and critical thinking are essential for navigating complex issues and contributing meaningfully to public discourse. The debates are judged according to argumentation, evidence evaluation, communication skills, and ethical considerations, ensuring a comprehensive assessment of civic competencies.

The initiative provides all participants with free access to the AI-powered platform BoodleBox. This suite of tools enables participating learners to leverage LLMs for research, collaboration, and content creation, fostering digital literacy and responsible technology use. BoodleBox's features—such as AI assistants, "GroupChat" functionality, and knowledge integration—support students in exploring diverse perspectives, organizing their thoughts, and refining their arguments. Notably, the competition places no restrictions on using generative AI tools, encouraging students to explore their potential while emphasizing ethical considerations and academic integrity.

In the Global AI Debates, AI will evaluate both written and verbal submissions, offering instant, data-driven insights that supplement human judges' expert assessments. By working in tandem with human judges with extensive experience, AI can highlight strengths, pinpoint areas for improvement, and help ensure consistent, transparent evaluations. As technology and competition evolve, AI's capacity to critique and provide feedback on research, argumentation, and communication will expand, deepening participants' learning experiences.

By combining iterative written submissions, real-time debates, and public speaking challenges, the Global AI Debates platform not only cultivates students' argumentative skills but also serves as a dynamic site for measuring their civic readiness. Specifically, the competition's design incentivizes learners to engage with evolving controversies around AI, encouraging them to examine evidence, scrutinize contrasting perspectives, and articulate informed stances on pressing technological and ethical questions. In doing so, it models how AI-related discourse can function as a microcosm of broader civic engagement, illustrating the potential for well-structured competitions to sharpen critical thinking, nurture empathetic perspective-taking, and instill habits of democratic deliberation among emerging generations.

The AI Debates build on research showing that urban debate leagues (UDLs) not only bolster academic performance but also serve as engines for civic engagement and learning. Numerous studies affirm that the structured practice of argumentation fosters critical thinking, community awareness, and democratic participation. In Boston, Schueler and Larned

(2023a, 2023b) found that debate participants achieved English language arts gains equivalent to two-thirds of a standard ninth-grade year. Meanwhile, Ko and Mezuk (2021), examining a debate-focused initiative in the Houston Independent School District, noted improvements in GPAs and SAT scores, as well as a growing ability among students to critically evaluate societal issues.

Shackelford's (2019) study of the Baltimore UDL linked debate involvement to improved attendance and more engaged academic trajectories. In Chicago, a decade-long study demonstrated that students who debated were over three times likelier to graduate from high school and outperformed their peers in core subject benchmarks on the ACT (Mezuk, 2009; Mezuk et al., 2011). Collectively, these findings illustrate the potential of UDLs to nurture essential civic competencies—such as critical reflection, respectful discourse, and community participation—thereby positioning students in certain contexts for meaningful contributions to civil society.

The Global AI Debates initiative aims to provide an engaging platform for cultivating civic learning and engagement in the digital age. It aims to empower students to become informed, critical thinkers, effective communicators, and ethical decision-makers, well-equipped to navigate the complexities of an AI-driven world and contribute meaningfully to shaping its future.

Engaged Early

A third example (Baker et al., 2005) involves four-year-olds trying to earn money to give to an associated school. The children suggested what they wanted to do (sell something to the rest of the school), identified what to sell (smoothies), and planned to acquire needed equipment, e.g., blenders and fruit. They planned the publicity (signs and announcements in visits to all classrooms), cost to cover supplies and generate profit, and the tasks needed to succeed such as making and transporting to the serving area the smoothies, making change, and cleaning up. AI technology could be applied to such a situation by creating a model simulation (complete with avatars that look like students) to help children plan. AI characters might simulate and guide projects. Given a different flow of potential customers, AI might identify how many students would be needed in each duty station. AI could help students consider how to expend various amounts of profit on items needed for the associated school, such as paints or outside balls to play with. Through off-the-shelf sensors or self-reporting, AI could help evaluate the extent to which the plan of action results in the desired performance.

These examples show how critical civic skills could be paired with interactive data collection to provide a comprehensive picture of civic learning. Future systems may leverage AI to analyze varied data—such as written submissions, oral presentations, and collaborative work—capturing authentic evidence of problem-solving, collaboration, and critical thinking. By identifying patterns in student outputs, AI could enable educators to draw meaningful inferences about civic learning and engagement in varying and authentic settings.

Conclusion

Advances in technology, particularly AI, are set to transform assessments—changing what skills we measure, how results are delivered, and how they are used to foster learning and engagement. Civic skills like teamwork, adaptability, creativity, and critical thinking are becoming increasingly vital in education, work, and life. While traditional assessments have primarily focused on technical competencies (e.g., math and reading), frameworks such as the World Economic Forum's Education 4.0 highlight the growing importance of lifelong learning, global citizenship, and technology skills (World Economic Forum, 2022, 2023). These priorities suggest demand for more sophisticated assessment systems that measure complex, hard-to-quantify skills (Cantor et al., 2021; Cantor & Osher, 2021)

This chapter explored promising approaches for assessing difficult-to-measure civic skills and examined directional reflections on how AI might enhance processes such as domain development, feedback, and personalized learning experiences. Current assessments often rely on subjective methods, such as self-reports, which present limitations in accuracy and reliability. The integration of AI offers an opportunity to develop rigorous, scalable, and actionable assessments that better capture these vital competencies. To realize this potential, assessments must deliver AI-powered feedback that is timely, personalized, and actionable, enabling learners to refine their skills in meaningful ways (Hattie, 2011, 2023; Hattie & Clarke, 2018; Hattie & Zierer, 2017).

AI-powered assessments introduce risks that must be responsibly managed. Issues of fairness and bias require continuous vigilance (ETS, 2025). Privacy and security are paramount, as robust safeguards must protect sensitive student data from unauthorized access and misuse. (Additionally, transparency, explainability, and accountability are vital for stakeholders to trust AI-driven decisions, while educational integrity demands evidence-based models, international cooperation, and constant adaptation through feedback-driven continuous improvement processes (ETS, 2025). Furthermore, the advent of generative AI technologies amplifies existing risks by increasing the speed and scale of potential threats, such as cyber-attacks and the dissemination of synthetic media, which can erode public trust. These technologies may also empower less-sophisticated actors, underscoring the need for proactive risk management strategies (Department for Science, Innovation & Technology, 2025).

We introduced three working examples to illustrate the potential of AI-powered civic learning and assessment. The **mock civic advocacy project** engages learners in research, argumentation, and presentation tasks focused on real-world issues like housing policy, fostering critical thinking and evidence-based advocacy. The **Global AI Debates** competition connects learners worldwide, using AI tools to support their research, argumentation, and communication on complex ethical and social issues tied to AI's societal impact. Finally, the **engaged early example** demonstrated how even young children can engage in civic problem-solving, potentially supported by AI to simulate planning, resource allocation, and decision-making in projects like fundraising for a community cause.

Our predictions about the future of civic assessments come with limitations. We focused on areas likely to see the most significant change due to technological advances and opportunities to make civic assessments more valuable. Testing processes—including task development, contextualization, automated scoring, and reporting—are evolving rapidly due to the integration of LLMs into test operations workflows.

This chapter explored the transformative potential of predictive and generative AI to enhance the quality, benchmarking, and overall value of civic learning assessments. Well-designed systems can provide learners with actionable insights while supporting lifelong learning and informed decision-making. Within this context, it is essential to establish benchmarks, evaluate quality, and address unique challenges AI presents for civic learning, particularly around safety, accountability, fairness, and efficacy.

As generative AI technologies become central to civic learning and engagement, advances in both theoretical frameworks and practical applications are necessary to ensure responsible AI use. This includes fostering fairness, accountability, transparency, ethics, privacy, and security, especially for young children and learners growing up far from opportunity. Responsible AI implementation must embed ethical practices at every stage of research and development, ensuring transparency, addressing biases, and amplifying efficacy through broad stakeholder input.

In conclusion, we suggest a bright future for assessment and its role in advancing civic learning and engagement. Predictive and generative AI hold tremendous potential to improve quality and cost-efficiency. However, their FATE application is essential to maximize the benefits of learning in this critical domain, ensuring that all learners are equipped to participate thoughtfully and effectively in civic life.

Note

1 Artificial intelligence is defined in 15 U.S.C. 9401(3) as follows: "a machine-based system that can, for a given set of human-defined objectives, make predictions, recommendations, or decisions influencing real or virtual environments. Artificial intelligence systems use machine- and human-based inputs to perceive real and virtual environments; abstract such perceptions into models through analysis in an automated manner; and use model inference to formulate options for information or action."
2 https://globalaidebates.org/

References

Acuity Insights. (2023). *Casper technical manual.* https://acuityinsights.com/casper-technical-manual/

Agrawal, A., Gans, J., & Goldfarb, A. (2022). *Power and prediction: The disruptive economics of intelligence.* Harvard Business Review Press.

American Educational Research Association, American Psychological Association, & National Council on Measurement in Education (2014). *Standards for educational and psychological testing.* American Educational Research Association.

Association of Test Publishers (2022). *Guidelines for technology-based assessment.* https://www.testpublishers.org/assets/TBA%20Guidelines%203-14-2022%20draft%20numbered.pdf

Attali, Y., Runge, A., LaFlair, G. T., Yancey, K., Goodwin, S., Park, Y., & von Davier, A. A. (2022). The interactive reading task: Transformer-based automatic item generation. *Frontiers in Artificial Intelligence, 5,* Article 903077. https://doi.org/10.3389/frai.2022.903077

Autor, D. H., Chin, C., Salomons, A., & Seegmiller, B. (2024). New frontiers: The origins and content of new work, 1940–2018. *The Quarterly Journal of Economics.* Advance online publication. https://doi.org/10.1093/qje/qjae008

Autor, D. H., Levy, F., & Murnane, R. J. (2003). The skill content of recent technological change: An empirical exploration. *The Quarterly Journal of Economics, 118*(4), 1279–1333. https://doi.org/10.1162/003355303322552801

Baker, E. L., Avetisian, H., Huang, D., Eisenberg, N., & Marshall, A. (2005, April). *Converting problem-based learning to standards-based assessment* [Conference presentation]. Annual Meeting of the American Educational Research Association.

Baker, E. L., & Gordon, E. W. (2014). From the assessment of education to the assessment for education: Policy and futures. *Teachers College Record, 116*(11), 1–24. https://doi.org/10.1177/016146811411601107

Bauschard, S., Coverstone, A., Rao, P. A., & Rao, S. (2023). *Beyond algorithmic solutions: The significance of academic debate for learning assessment and skill cultivation in the AI world.* DebateUS. https://papers.ssrn.com/sol3/papers.cfm?abstract_id=4567346

Bejar, I. I., Lawless, R. R., Morley, M. E., Wagner, M. E., Bennett, R. E., & Revuelta, J. (2002). *A feasibility study of on-the-fly item generation in adaptive testing* (Research Report No. RR-02-03). Educational Testing Service.

Bennett, R. E. (2014). Preparing for the future: What educational assessment must do. *Teachers College Record, 116*(11), 1–18. https://doi.org/10.1177/016146811411601109

Bennett, R. E. (2023). Toward a theory of socioculturally responsive assessment. *Educational Assessment, 28*(2), 83–104. https://doi.org/10.1080/10627197.2023.2202312

Bicknell, K., Brust, C., & Settles, B. (2023, February 5). How Duolingo's AI learns what you need to learn. *IEEE Spectrum.* https://spectrum.ieee.org/duolingo

Bryk, A. S., Gomez, L. M., Grunow, A., & LeMahieu, P. G. (2015). *Learning to improve: How America's schools can get better at getting better.* Harvard Education Press.

Buckley, J., Colosimo, L., Kantar, R., McCall, M., & Snow, E. (2021). Game-based assessment for education. In *OECD digital education outlook 2021: Pushing the frontiers with artificial intelligence, blockchain and robots* (pp. 195–208). OECD.

Burning Glass Technologies. (2019). *Mapping the genome of jobs: The Burning Glass skills taxonomy* [White paper]. https://www.voced.edu.au/content/ngv:84406

Burstein, J., LaFlair, G. T., Yancey, K., von Davier, A. A., & Dotan, R. (2024). *Responsible AI for test equity and quality: The Duolingo English Test as a case study* (arXiv preprint). https://doi.org/10.48550/arXiv.2409.07476

Cantor, P., Lerner, R., Pittman, K., Chase, P., & Gomperts, N. (2021). *Whole-child development, learning, and thriving: A dynamic systems approach* (Elements in Child Development). Cambridge University Press. https://doi.org/10.1017/9781108954600

Cantor, P., & Osher, D. (2021). *The science of learning and development* (1st ed.). Routledge.

Cao, M., Drasgow, F., & Cho, S. (2015). Developing ideal intermediate personality items for the ideal point model. *Organizational Research Methods, 18*(2), 252–275. https://doi.org/10.1177/1094428114555993

Chen, L., Feng, G., Joe, J., Leong, C. W., Kitchen, C., & Lee, C. M. (2014). Towards automated assessment of public speaking skills using multimodal cues. In *Proceedings of the 16th International Conference on Multimodal Interaction (ICMI '14)* (pp. 200–203). ACM. https://doi.org/10.1145/2663204.2663265

Christian, M. S., Edwards, B. D., & Bradley, J. C. (2010). Situational judgment tests: Constructs assessed and a meta-analysis of their criterion-related validities. *Personnel Psychology, 63*(1), 83–117. https://doi.org/10.1111/j.1744-6570.2009.01163.x

Chung, G. K. W. K., de Vries, L. F., Cheak, A. M., Stevens, R. H., & Bewley, W. L. (2002). Cognitive process validation of an online problem solving assessment. *Computers in Human Behavior, 18*, 669–684.

Cooper, W. H. (1981). Ubiquitous halo. *Psychological Bulletin, 90*(2), 218–244. https://doi.org/10.1037/0033-2909.90.2.218

Deming, D. J. (2017). The growing importance of social skills in the labor market. *The Quarterly Journal of Economics, 132*(4), 1593–1640. https://doi.org/10.1093/qje/qjx022

Department for Science, Innovation & Technology. (2025). *Safety and security risks of generative artificial intelligence to 2025 (Annex B)*. [Report].

EdTech Insiders. (n.d.). *AI in education landscape map*. https://www.edtechinsiders.ai/

Eloundou, T., Manning, S., Mishkin, P., & Rock, D. (2023). *GPTs are GPTs: An early look at the labor market impact potential of large language models*. arXiv. https://arxiv.org/abs/2303.10130v4

ETS (2025). *Responsible use of AI in assessment: ETS principles*. Educational Testing Service.

Foster, N., & Piacentini, M. (Eds.). (2023). *Innovating assessments to measure and support complex skills*. OECD Publishing. https://doi.org/10.1787/e5f3e341-en

Gee, J. (2025). Games, learning, and assessment. In S. Sireci, E. Tucker, & E. W. Gordon, (Eds.), *The handbook for assessment in the service of learning* (Vol. II, 2025). University of Massachusetts Libraries.

Geiger, M., Bärwaldt, R., & Wilhelm, O. (2021). The good, the bad, and the clever: Faking ability as a socio-emotional ability? *Journal of Intelligence, 9*(1), 1–22. https://doi.org/10.3390/jintelligence9010013

Gordon, E. W. (2020). Toward assessment in the service of learning. *Educational Measurement: Issues and Practice, 39*(3), 72–78. https://doi.org/10.1111/emip.12370

Gordon, E. W., Gordon, E. W., Aber, L., & Berliner, D. (2012). *Changing paradigms for education: From filling buckets to lighting fires to cultivation of intellective competence* (The Gordon Commission on the Future of Assessment in Education). Educational Testing Service. Https://Www.Ets.Org/Media/Research/Pdf/Gordon_gordon_berliner_aber_changing_paradigms_education.Pdf

Gordon, E. W., & Rajagopalan, K. (2015). *The testing and learning revolution: The future of assessment in education*. Palgrave Macmillan New York. https://doi.org/10.1057/9781137519962

Grover, S., & Pea, R. (2013). Computational thinking in K–12: A review of the state of the field. *Educational Researcher, 42*(1), 38–43. https://doi.org/10.3102/0013189X12463051

Guo, H., Johnson, M., Saldivia, L., Worthington, M., & Ercikan, K. (2024). Human-centered AI for discovering student engagement profiles on large-scale educational assessments. *Journal of Measurement and Evaluation in Education and Psychology, 15*(Special Issue), 282–301. *https://doi.org/10.21031/epod.1532846*

Guo, K., Wang, J., & Chu, S. K. W. (2022). Using chatbots to scaffold EFL students' argumentative writing. *Assessing Writing, 54*, Article 100666. https://doi.org/10.1016/j.asw.2022.100666

cApStAn & Halleux, B. (2019). *PISA 2021 translation and adaptation guidelines*. OECD. https://www.oecd.org/pisa/pisaproducts/PISA%202022-Translation-and-Adaptation-Guidelines.pdf

Hattie, J. (2011). *Visible learning for teachers: Maximizing impact on learning* (1st ed.). Routledge. https://doi.org/10.4324/9780203181522

Hattie, J. (2023). *Visible learning: The sequel: A synthesis of over 2,100 meta-analyses relating to achievement* (1st ed.). Routledge. https://doi.org/10.4324/9781003380542

Hattie, J., & Clarke, S. (2018). *Visible learning: Feedback* (1st ed.). Routledge. https://doi.org/10.4324/9780429485480

Hattie, J., & Zierer, K. (2017). *10 Mindframes for visible learning: Teaching for success* (1st ed.). Routledge. https://doi.org/10.4324/9781315206387

He, J., Bartram, D., Inceoglu, I., & van de Vijver, F. J. R. (2014). Response styles and personality traits: A multilevel analysis. *Journal of Cross-Cultural Psychology, 45*(7), 1028–1045. https://doi.org/10.1177/0022022114534773

Hilton, M., & Herman, J. (Eds.). (2017). *Supporting students' college success: The role of assessment of intrapersonal and interpersonal competencies*. National Academies Press.

Irvine, S. H., & Kyllonen, P. C. (Eds.). (2013). *Item generation for test development*. Routledge.

Kautz, T., & Zanoni, W. (2014). *Measuring and fostering non-cognitive skills in adolescence: Evidence from Chicago Public Schools and the OneGoal Program*. University of Chicago.

Kepes, S., Keener, S. K., Lievens, F., & McDaniel, M. A. (2024). An integrative, systematic review of the situational judgment test literature. *Journal of Management*. https://doi.org/10.1177/01492063241288545

King, G., & Wand, J. (2007). Comparing incomparable survey responses: Evaluating and selecting anchoring vignettes. *Political Analysis, 15*(1), 46–66. https://doi.org/10.1093/pan/mpl011

Ko, T., & Mezuk, B. (2021). Debate participation and academic achievement among high School students in the Houston Independent School District: 2012–2015. *Educational Research and Reviews, 16*(6), 219–225. https://academicjournals.org/journal/ERR/article-full-text/BF2278466879

Koedinger, K. R., Carvalho, P. F., Liu, R., & McLaughlin, E. A. (2023). An astonishing regularity in student learning rate. *Proceedings of the National Academy of Sciences, 120*(13), Article e2221311120. https://doi.org/10.1073/pnas.2221311120

Kyllonen, P. C., Sevak, A., Ober, T., Choi, I., Sparks, J., & Fishtein, D. (2024). *Charting the future of assessments*. ETS Research Institute. https://www.de.ets.org/research/charting-the-future-of-assessments.html

Landers, R. N., & Sanchez, D. R. (2022). Game-based, gamified, and gamefully designed assessments for employee selection: Definitions, distinctions, design, and validation. *International Journal of Selection and Assessment, 30*(1), 1–13. https://doi.org/10.1111/ijsa.12376

Lane, S., Raymond, M. R., & Haladyna, T. M. (Eds.). (2016). *Handbook of test development* (Vol. 2, pp. 3–18). Routledge.

Lira, B., O'Brien, J. M., Peña, P. A., Galla, B. M., D'Mello, S., Yeager, D. S., ... & Duckworth, A. L. (2022). Large studies reveal how reference bias limits policy applications of self-report measures. *Scientific Reports, 12*, Article 19189. https://doi.org/10.1038/s41598-022-23373-9

Liu, O. L., Kell, H. J., Liu, L., Ling, G., Wang, Y., Wylie, C., ... & Knowles, T. (2023). *A new vision for skills-based assessment*. Educational Testing Service. https://ets.org/pdfs/rd/new-vision-skills-based-assessment.pdf

Liu, O. L., Mao, L., Frankel, L., & Xu, J. (2016). Assessing critical thinking in higher education: The HEIghten approach and preliminary validity evidence. *Assessment & Evaluation in Higher Education, 41*(5), 677–694. https://doi.org/10.1080/02602938.2016.1168358

Liu, X., Zhang, Z., Wang, Y., Pu, H., Lan, Y., & Shen, C. (2023). COCO: Coherence-enhanced machine-generated text detection under low-resource conditions with contrastive learning. In H. Bouamor, J. Pino, & K. Bali (Eds.), *Proceedings of the 2023 Conference on Empirical Methods in Natural Language Processing* (pp. 16167–16188). Association for Computational Linguistics. https://doi.org/10.18653/v1/2023.emnlp-main.1005

Malik, A. (2025, April 30). Duolingo launches 148 courses created with AI after sharing plans to replace contractors with AI. *TechCrunch*. https://techcrunch.com/2025/04/30/duolingo-launches-148-courses-created-with-ai-after-sharing-plans-to-replace-contractors-with-ai/

Martin-Raugh, M. P., Kyllonen, P. C., Hao, J., Bacall, A., Becker, D., Kurzum, C., ... & Barnwell, P. (2020). Negotiation as an interpersonal skill: Generalizability of negotiation outcomes and tactics across contexts at the individual and collective levels. *Computers in Human Behavior, 104*, Article 105966. https://doi.org/10.1016/j.chb.2019.03.030

Mezuk, B. (2009). Urban Debate and high school educational outcomes for African American males: The case of the Chicago Debate League. *The Journal of Negro Education, 78*(3), 290–304.

Mezuk, B., Bondarenko, I., Smith, S., & Tucker, E. (2011). Impact of participating in a policy debate program on academic achievement. *Educational Research and Reviews, 6*(9), 622–635.

Millsap, R. E. (2011). *Statistical approaches to measurement invariance*. Routledge.

Mislevy, R. J. (2018). *Sociocognitive foundations of educational measurement* (1st ed.). Routledge. https://doi.org/10.4324/9781315871691

Mislevy, R. J. (2019). Advances in measurement and cognition. *The Annals of the American Academy of Political and Social Science, 683*(1), 164–182. https://doi.org/10.1177/0002716219843816

Mislevy, R. J., & Haertel, G. D. (2006). Implications of evidence-centered design for educational testing. *Educational Measurement: Issues and Practice, 25*(4), 6–20. https://doi.org/10.1111/j.1745-3992.2006.00075.x

Mislevy, R. J., Sheehan, K. M., & Wingersky, M. (1993). How to equate tests with little or no data. *Journal of Educational Measurement, 30*(1), 55–78. https://doi.org/10.1111/j.1745-3984.1993.tb00422.x

Mislevy, R. J., Steinberg, L. S., & Almond, R. G. (1999). *On the roles of task model variables in assessment design* (CSE Technical Report 500). National Center for Research on Evaluation, Standards, and Student Testing (CRESST). University of California. https://cresst.org/wp-content/uploads/TECH500.pdf

Molenaar, I., de Mooij, S., Azevedo, R., Bannert, M., Järvelä, S., & Gašević, D. (2023). Measuring self-regulated learning and the role of AI: Five years of research using multimodal multichannel data. *Computers in Human Behavior, 139*, Article 107540. https://doi.org/10.1016/j.chb.2022.107540

National Association of Colleges and Employers (NACE). (2022). *NACE Job Outlook 2022*. https://www.naceweb.org/uploadedfiles/files/2022/resources/nace-job-outlook-2022.pdf

Niessen, A. S. M., Meijer, R. R., & Tendeiro, J. N. (2017). Measuring non-cognitive predictors in high-stakes contexts: The effect of self-presentation on self-report instruments used in admission to higher education. *Personality and Individual Differences, 106*, 183–189. https://doi.org/10.1016/j.paid.2016.11.014

O'Neil, H., Baker, E. L., Wainess, R., Chen, C., Mislevy, R. J., & Kyllonen, P. (2004). *Final report on plan for the assessment and evaluation of individual and team proficiencies developed by the DARWARS environments.* Office of Naval Research; Defense Advanced Research Projects Agency. https://apps.dtic.mil/sti/pdfs/ADA432802.pdf

OECD (2019). An OECD learning framework 2030. In G. Bast, E. G. Carayannis, & D. F. J. Campbell (Eds.), *The future of education and labor* (Arts, Research, Innovation and Society series, pp. 23–35). Springer. https://doi.org/10.1007/978-3-030-26068-2_3

OECD (2021). *AI and the future of skills, volume 1: Capabilities and assessments.* OECD Publishing. https://doi.org/10.1787/5ee71f34-en

OECD (2023). *OECD skills outlook 2023: skills for a resilient green and digital transition.* OECD Publishing. https://doi.org/10.1787/27452f29-en

Oh, I.-S., Wang, G., & Mount, M. K. (2011). Validity of observer ratings of the five-factor model of personality traits: A meta-analysis. *Journal of Applied Psychology, 96*(4), 762–773. https://doi.org/10.1037/a0021832

Ostini, R., & Nering, M. L. (2006). *Polytomous item response theory.* Sage.

Patrick, S. (2021). Transforming learning through competency-based education. *State Education Standard, 21*(2), 23–29.

Rios, J. A., Ling, G., Pugh, R., Becker, D., & Bacall, A. (2020). Identifying critical 21st-century skills for workplace success: A content analysis of job advertisements. *Educational Researcher, 49*(2), 80–89. https://doi.org/10.3102/0013189X19890600

Schmitt, N., Keeney, J., Oswald, F. L., Pleskac, T. J., Billington, A. Q., Sinha, R., & Zorzie, M. (2009). Prediction of 4-year college student performance using cognitive and noncognitive predictors and the impact on demographic status of admitted students. *Journal of Applied Psychology, 94*(6), 1479–1497. https://doi.org/10.1037/a0016810

Schueler, B. E., & Larned, K. E. (2023a). Interscholastic policy debate promotes critical thinking and college-going: Evidence from Boston Public Schools. *Educational Evaluation and Policy Analysis.* Advance online publication. https://doi.org/10.3102/01623737231200234

Schueler, B. E., & Larned, K. E. (2023b). *Interscholastic policy debate promotes critical thinking and college-going: Evidence from Boston Public Schools. (EdWorkingPaper: 23-825).* Annenberg Institute at Brown University. https://doi.org/10.26300/e8at-8836

Shackelford, A. (2019). The BUDL effect: Examining academic engagement outcomes of preadolescent Baltimore Urban Debate League participants. *Educational Researcher, 48*(3), 172–184. https://journals.sagepub.com/doi/10.3102/0013189X19830998

Sparks, J. R., Ober, T. M., Tenison, C., Arslan, B., Roll, I., Deane, P., Zapata-Rivera, D., Gooch, R. M., & O'Reilly, T. (2025). *Opportunities and challenges for assessing digital and AI literacies.* ETS Research Institute. https://www.ets.org/research/opportunities-and-challenges-for-assessing-digital-and-ai-literacies.html

Stankov, L., Lee, J., & von Davier, M. (2017). A note on construct validity of the anchoring method in PISA 2012. *Journal of Psychoeducational Assessment, 36*(7), 709–724. https://doi.org/10.1177/0734282917702270

Sternberg, R. J., Forsythe, G. B., Hedlund, J., Horvath, J. A., Wagner, R. K., Williams, W. M., Snook, S. A., & Grigorenko, E. L. (2000). *Practical intelligence in everyday life.* Cambridge University Press.

Tang, Z., & Kirman, B. (2023). Exploring curiosity in games: A framework and questionnaire study of player perspectives. *International Journal of Human-Computer Interaction.* Advance online publication. https://doi.org/10.1080/10447318.2024.2325171

Thomas, D., & Seely Brown, J. (2011, April 28). *Multiplayer high: How games help learning. Boing.* https://boingboing.net/2011/04/28/flux.html

Tucker, E., Armour-Thomas, E., & Gordon, E. W. (Eds.). (2025). *The handbook for assessment in the service of learning* (Vol. I). University of Massachusetts–Amherst Libraries Press.

Tucker, E., Everson, H., Baker, E., & Gordon, E. W. (Eds.). (2025). *The handbook for assessment in the service of learning* (Vol. III). University of Massachusetts–Amherst Libraries Press.

van de Vijver, F. J. R., & He, J. (2016). Bias assessment and prevention in noncognitive outcome measures in context assessments. In S. Kuger, E. Klieme, N. Jude, & D. Kaplan (Eds.), *Assessing contexts of learning: International perspectives* (pp. 229–253). Springer. https://doi.org/10.1007/978-3-319-45357-6_9

Weiss, S., Wilhelm, O., & Kyllonen, P. (2021). An improved taxonomy of creativity measures based on salient task attributes. *Psychology of Aesthetics, Creativity, and the Arts.* Advance online publication. https://doi.org/10.1037/aca0000434

Williamson, D. M., Xi, X., & Breyer, F. J. (2012). A framework for evaluation and use of automated scoring. *Educational Measurement: Issues and Practice, 31*(1), 2–13. https://doi.org/10.1111/j.1745-3992.2011.00223.x

World Economic Forum (2022). *Catalysing Education 4.0: Investing in the future of learning for a human-centric recovery* (Insight Report). https://www3.weforum.org/docs/WEF_Catalysing_Education_4.0_2022.pdf

World Economic Forum (2023). *Defining Education 4.0: A taxonomy for the future of learning.* https://www3.weforum.org/docs/WEF_Defining_Education_4.0_2023.pdf

Zapata-Rivera, D., & Hu, X. (2022). Assessment in intelligent tutoring systems SWOT analysis. In A. M. Sinatra, A. C. Graesser, X. Hu, G. Goodwin, & V. Rus (Eds.), *Design recommendations for intelligent tutoring systems: Vol. 10. strengths, weaknesses, opportunities and threats (SWOT) analysis of intelligent tutoring systems* (pp. 83–90). U.S. Army Combat Capabilities Development Command – Soldier Center.

4

Mapping Civic Measurement

Assessing Readiness and Opportunities for an Engaged Citizenry

Anna Gallos, Jessica Sutter, Matt Leighninger, and Rajiv Vinnakota

Questions about the strength and efficacy of our constitutional democracy are currently front and center for many Americans (Annenberg Public Policy Center, 2021; Atwell et al., 2021). Given the complexity of the problem, how do we measure whether and how we are making progress? Are various efforts helping, hurting, or neither? What kinds of activities have a positive impact, and do we even agree on what it means to have a positive impact?

Measurement is a core piece of the answer. Knowing whether our society has equipped our citizens to engage in democracy is critical to understanding what needs to be strengthened. Understanding, in turn, whether we are providing the opportunities to develop those capabilities is important in ascertaining what interventions to prioritize (Voelkel et al., 2023).

In late 2022 and early 2023, the Institute for Citizens & Scholars set out to create a landscape scan of the state of civic measurement. We defined "civic measurement" as the attempt to answer two key questions: how ready are people to contribute effectively to civic life ("civic readiness")? And how well does our civic infrastructure (Groth, 2023; Kaufman et al., 2022) support, enable, and inspire those contributions ("civic opportunities")?

Our goal with this project was to identify what tools exist to measure both civic opportunities and civic readiness. Civic opportunities are systems, platforms, programs, laws, and processes for individuals and groups to practice and build civic understanding, participation, connection, and beliefs. Civic readiness is an individual's preparation to be an effective citizen through what individuals understand, what or how they participate, how they connect with organizations and others, and what they believe that influences their engagement as citizens.

Our expectation was that the landscape scan might help us get closer to understanding how we will know if our efforts to improve our constitutional democracy are working. The results of our project, and of subsequent work emerging from the initial scan, are captured in this chapter.

While this study provides a significant contribution to understanding the realm of civic measurement, it should be understood as an exploratory analysis rather than a comprehensive review of the literature and field. We have welcomed feedback and critique from researchers on gaps in our framework and hope that this chapter serves as an opportunity to continue the

DOI: 10.4324/9781003476825-5

This chapter has been made available under a CC BY-NC-ND license.

conversation with the field. While our focus was to provide a framework and identify tools for researchers, we have learned that the measurement maps have also resonated with practitioners and other leaders. This realization led us to build out additional resources to support use of the framework by a wide array of leaders.

We begin with an overview of the landscape scan and the conceptual framework that emerged from our study. We then discuss how we employed the framework to better understand the availability of civic measurement tools and the findings we think are relevant for the field of civic learning and measurement. We share responses to the initial study and the small suite of studies that helped us further build out our emerging knowledge of civic measurement. We conclude with a discussion of the implications of equity and lingering questions facing the field of civic measurement.

Methodology

To begin our survey of the terrain of civic measurement, we interviewed 72 people who were conducting or curating research and data in what might broadly be described as the "civic field," including some who do not necessarily describe their work as "civic." Our interview subjects comprised professionals from many different sectors, including education, business, philanthropy, community institutions, media, government, and civil society. Interviews were semi-structured, beginning with several open-ended questions asked of all respondents. Interviews lasted between 30 and 60 minutes on average and were a mix of one-on-one conversations and small group discussions with multiple researchers and multiple respondents.

The interviews focused on these guiding questions:

1) What do you think of the state of measurement in the space?
2) What is measured well and what isn't?
3) Who are the key players in this space (in addition to you) that we should learn about or include in our process?
4) What do you think when I say "measures for civic knowledge, capacities, skills, and dispositions/attitudes"?

Researchers then probed on a variety of themes, including individuals, institutions, and civic infrastructure; equity; levels of government; modes of citizenship; and impacts of technology.

We did not make a systematic attempt to cover the full terrain of civic measurement applications, nor did we begin with a systematic review of the literature in the field. Instead, we used what we learned in the 72 interviews to begin to construct a framework for how we might present a way to think about readiness and opportunities for preparing people to be citizens.

Based on these interviews and our resource and tool collection (described below), we developed a framework for organizing the ways that people across different sectors define and measure different aspects of civic readiness (the skills, capacities, and beliefs of individuals) and civic opportunities (the arenas within institutions and communities where people can practice and hone those skills, capacities, and beliefs). This framework is presented as the civic measurement maps, explored in greater detail below.

As part of the interviews, we also collected as many suggestions for approaches to civic measurement as we could, as well as studies that addressed civic measurement. Our original list included research resources of varying types, including both qualitative and quantitative studies, as well as meta-analyses, from which we identified 160 tools. We defined a *tool* as a discreet method for capturing and reporting qualitative or quantitative data. The tools we identified included rubrics, assessments, surveys, observational checklists, and other kinds of data collection instruments. The tools reflect a variety of use cases, including assessing knowledge of U.S. history and government, understanding the state of civic engagement in the general population, evaluating civic interventions, observing group collaboration dynamics, gauging public opinion, and more.

We reviewed the descriptions of each tool to identify what the tools were measuring. We did not review the tools themselves. Oftentimes, a summary or description indicated that the tool was designed to measure multiple constructs; in such cases, all those constructs were captured.

We then took the tools and the information about their measurement purpose to "plot" them onto the maps as an analog for the distribution of research intensity for civic measurement. The map segments—the dimensions, elements, coordinates, and building blocks—allowed us to plot the measurement tools where we thought they best fit. In cases where a tool was described as measuring multiple constructs, the tool was plotted to each of the appropriate segments of the maps. This process was simple, yet it revealed patterns and findings that may be of general interest and have wide application.

The final plot allowed us to visually display a landscape of civic measurement. We observed places where multiple—or in some cases, many—tools are available to measure a construct. We also observed gaps in the availability of tools; the existence of these gaps is a call to action for the field to create new tools or to seek tools from other fields that deal with the same constructs.

We acknowledge that our approach has significant limitations. First, since we did not begin with a systematic review of the existing literature, we may have missed or underrepresented some constructs important to understanding the full landscape of civic measurement applications. By seeking first to identify tools, we may have missed or underrepresented constructs in the initial framework—the measurement maps—and any such missed items could have implications on the use of the maps as an accurate visual representation of measurement efforts in the field. Additionally, in our effort to provide a broad scan of information, we may have missed the chance to specify the kinds of tools that are more important to particular arenas of civic life, such as both K-12 and higher education settings.

As with the process of constructing the measurement maps, there are some limitations to the way we approached this plotting. We did not review the current state of availability of the tools in our inventory before we plotted them. As a result, some of the tools included in the landscape maps are no longer in circulation or available for general public use. Additionally, our approach to plotting the tools may also be considered a limitation. We chose this approach because analogs of mapping and plotting proved helpful to identify patterns and themes for the overall field. However, we acknowledge that our decisions about where to place the tools on the framework may differ from where the tool authors themselves might have placed them. This may lead to debate and discussion about how the tools are classified in the map framework, but we welcome and encourage such discussion and hope that it may contribute to further understanding of the complexity of civic measurement.

Conceptual Framework: Civic Measurement Maps

As briefly described above, we used the insights from our interviews to develop a framework for organizing the ways that people across different sectors define and measure different aspects of civic readiness and civic opportunities. We observed that there are two distinct but highly interrelated ecosystems at work in civic measurement: the factors we measure to understand individual civic readiness and the set of opportunities citizens have to express that readiness. As a result, our framework took the form of two maps: (1) civic readiness and (2) civic opportunities. We named the framework the civic measurement maps.

The maps are an attempt to illustrate the depth and breadth of the field of civic measurement. We began with a study and reconciliation of key terms and definitions to help create a common language to undergird the maps. Since our interviews sourced information from professionals in different fields, with nuanced differences in language, we found this to be an essential first step in creating the conceptual framework.

Here are some key concepts we defined as part of creating the maps:

Civic learning is the development of the civic knowledge, skills, and dispositions of people, resulting in citizens who are civically well-informed, productively engaged, and hopeful about democracy (Vinnakota, 2019). Civic learning is a broader conception of civic education that recognizes the long-term, multidimensional approach to cultivating effective citizens inside and outside the classroom, at the workplace, within the community, and online.

Civic measurement is the attempt to answer these two questions:

1) How ready are people to contribute effectively to civic life?
2) How well does our civic infrastructure support, enable, and inspire those contributions?

Both questions contribute to the overarching goal of understanding if we are making ongoing progress as a healthy democracy.

Civic readiness is an individual's preparation to be an effective citizen through four overarching civic dimensions: what individuals *understand*, how they *participate*, how they *connect* with organizations and others, and what they *believe* that influences their engagement as citizens.

Civic opportunities are the systems, platforms, programs, laws, and processes for individuals and groups to practice and build the civic dimensions of *understand*, *participate*, *connect*, and *believe*.

These maps are *not* meant to suggest a prescription for what we think citizens should know and be able to do. Nor are the maps intended to provide an exhaustive set of the aspects of civic readiness and opportunities. The maps are a conceptual framework, sourced from insights of practitioners, that we hope will help frame ongoing dialogue within the field about what constitutes essential civic readiness and civic opportunities for Americans.

The Civic Readiness Map

The civic readiness map shows efforts to measure the civic knowledge, skills, and dispositions of individuals. The map consists of three rings: dimensions, elements, and coordinates (Figure 4.1).

The innermost ring of the map is made up of the four overarching **dimensions** that people are trying to measure: what individuals *understand* or know, how they *participate* in American democracy, how they *connect* with others, and what they *believe* that influences their engagement. We started with *understand*, *believe*, and *participate* because they are commonly understood within the field as aspects of civic preparedness. We then added *connect* because many of the subjects we spoke with in interviews suggested it was an essential dimension that warranted its own quadrant of the map—as opposed to being considered an element of *understand*, *believe*, or *participate*.

The middle ring of the map lists the main **elements** of those **dimensions**. For example:

- *Government and political systems* is an **element** of *understand* that includes several different areas of knowledge.
- *Public decision-making* is an **element** of *participate* that contains a number of skills that can be assessed.
- *Civic identity* is an **element** of *connect* that is concerned with how people feel about being part of groups and communities.
- *Trust and hope* is an **element** that encompasses measures of what individuals *believe* about institutions and democracy.

Mapping Civic Measurement • 45

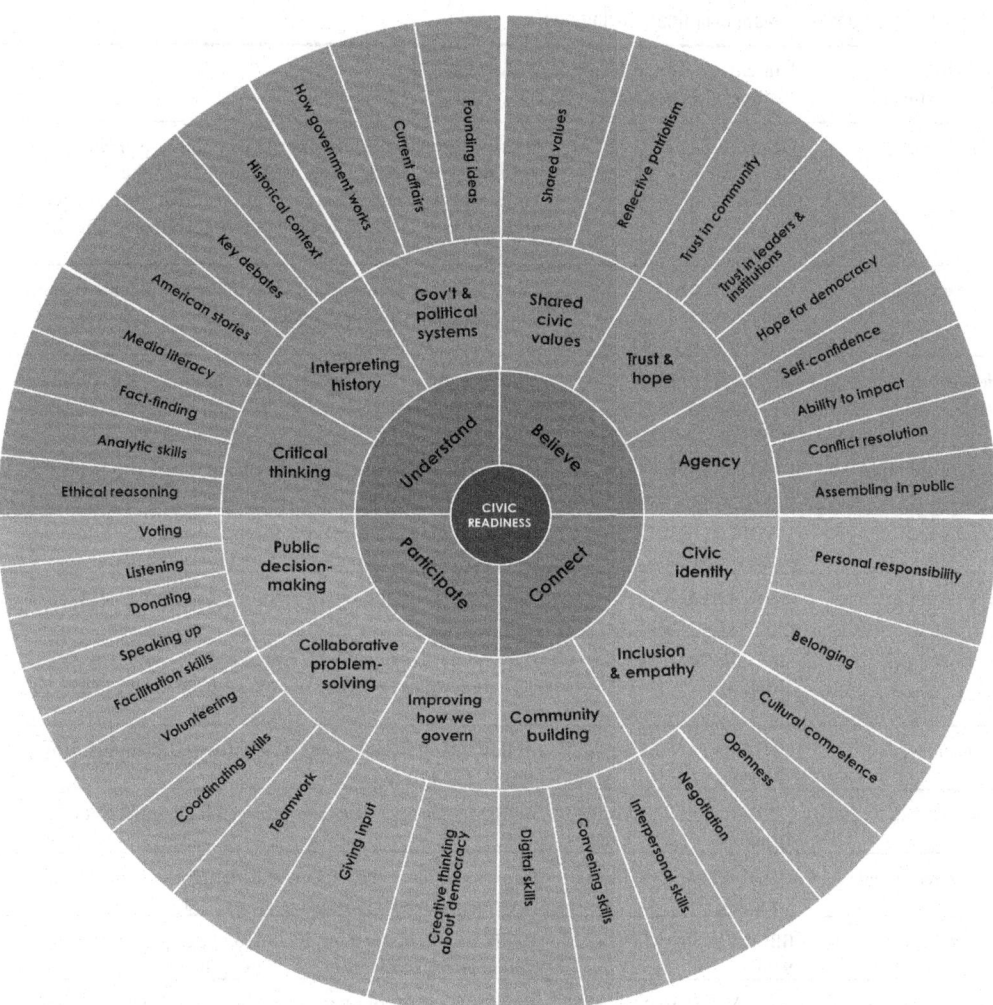

Figure 4.1 Civic Readiness Map.

The outermost ring of the map provides specific **coordinates.** Just as coordinates on a geographic map help you know where you are in the world, coordinates on the civic readiness map help users identify specific components for measuring civic readiness. For example:

Within *government and political systems*, some of the measures we found are assessing knowledge of *current events*.

- Within *public decision-making*, there are many measures of *voting*.
- Feelings of *belonging* are measured within the category of *civic identity*.
- *Hope for democracy* measures are part of *trust and hope (Table 4.1)*.

We decided upon the inclusion of elements and coordinates based on any evidence we were able to find that someone was measuring the concept and whether it seemed reasonable as a worthwhile aspect of civic readiness or civic opportunity. For us, "reasonable" was a judgment as to whether people working in and researching civic learning might have these elements and coordinates on their radar.

Table 4.1 Civic Readiness Map: Coordinate Definitions

Coordinate (Outer Ring)	Dimension (Inner Ring); Element (Middle Ring)	Definition
Founding ideas	UNDERSTAND; Government & Political Systems	Understanding of philosophical and political principles underlying the Declaration of Independence, the Constitution, and our system of government, such as checks and balances, the three branches, self-governance, and the Bill of Rights
Current affairs	UNDERSTAND; Government & Political Systems	Knowledge about important local, state, and federal policy questions, and why they matter
How government works	UNDERSTAND; Government & Political Systems	Understanding the structure, roles, and limits of government, and how public decisions are made at the federal, state, and local levels
Historical context	UNDERSTAND; Interpreting History	Familiarity with historically significant decisions, conflicts, victories and failures
Key debates	UNDERSTAND; Interpreting History	Understanding of the major concepts, debates, and different perspectives that informed what America is today
American stories	UNDERSTAND; Interpreting History	Appreciation for the experiences, cultures, and traditions of Americans
Media literacy	UNDERSTAND; Critical Thinking	Capacity to access, analyze, evaluate, create, and participate with messages in a variety of forms—from print to video to the Internet
Fact-finding	UNDERSTAND; Critical Thinking	Ability to find reliable sources, identify mis/disinformation, and sort fact from fiction
Analytic skills	UNDERSTAND; Critical Thinking	Ability to consider problems and weigh potential solutions
Ethical reasoning	UNDERSTAND; Critical Thinking	Capacity to reach individual, well-thought-out conclusions about issues where judgments are needed
Shared values	BELIEVE; Shared Civic Values	Dedication to understanding different perspectives, finding shared goals, and working to achieve them
Reflective patriotism	BELIEVE; Shared Civic Values	Commitment to country and an ability to both uphold and critique American institutions and ideals
Trust in community	BELIEVE; Trust & Hope	Earned trust in neighbors, fellow community members, and Americans as a whole
Trust in leaders and institutions	BELIEVE; Trust & Hope	Earned trust in government, business, faith, education, and other institutions and leaders
Hope for democracy	BELIEVE; Trust & Hope	Confidence in the strength and potential of citizenship and democracy
Self-confidence	BELIEVE; Agency	Confidence that you have the ability to effectively express your interests and concerns
Ability to impact	BELIEVE; Agency	Belief that you can contribute to solving community problems and making public decisions
Conflict resolutions	BELIEVE; Agency	Confidence that you can engage in difficult issues and resolve conflicts with others
Assembling in public	BELIEVE; Agency	Taking part in public events, marches, or peaceful forms of protest to show your support for a particular idea or cause
Voting	PARTICIPATE; Public decision-making	Commitment to vote, including the willingness to seek information about candidates and issues

(Continued)

Table 4.1 Civic Readiness Map: Coordinate Definitions *(Continued)*

Coordinate (Outer Ring)	Dimension (Inner Ring); Element (Middle Ring)	Definition
Listening	PARTICIPATE; Public decision-making	Willingness to listen to differing perspectives, even on controversial issues, and appreciate that a range of solutions might exist
Donating	PARTICIPATE; Public decision-making	Making financial contributions to candidates, parties, and political priorities
Speaking up	PARTICIPATE; Public decision-making	Making presentations, writing letters to the editor, or posting on social media
Facilitation skills	PARTICIPATE; Public decision-making	Ability to support discussions and deliberations among other people
Volunteering	PARTICIPATE; Collaborative Problem-solving	Ability to devote time, energy, skills, and connections on behalf of others, and to solve shared problems
Coordinating skills	PARTICIPATE; Collaborative Problem-solving	Ability to organize logistics, develop plans, and recruit other people
Teamwork	PARTICIPATE; Collaborative Problem-solving	Ability to help build and sustain teams, identify assets, and help assign roles
Giving input	PARTICIPATE; Improving how we govern	Ability to rate public services, report problems, and rank priorities
Creative thinking about democracy	PARTICIPATE; Improving how we govern	Willingness to think creatively about how democracy should work and help redesign systems, services, and processes
Interpersonal skills	CONNECT; Community Building	Self-regulation, self-awareness, and positive and clear communication
Convening skills	CONNECT; Community Building	Ability to bring people together around things they value
Digital skills	CONNECT; Community Building	Ability to use social media and other digital tools responsibly and well
Cultural competence	CONNECT; Inclusion & Empathy	Ability to understand and interact effectively with people from a range of backgrounds
Openness	CONNECT; Inclusion & Empathy	Tolerance and appreciation for different backgrounds, identities, and perspectives
Negotiation	CONNECT; Inclusion & Empathy	Skills for resolving conflicts across divides
Personal responsibility	CONNECT; Civic Identity	Belief that you are part of a social contract and have both rights and obligations in a pluralistic society
Belonging	CONNECT; Civic Identity	Belief that you matter to people in your family, neighborhood, school, workplace, and your community as a whole

In summary, the civic readiness map captures, both at a high level and in detail, efforts to measure the civic knowledge, skills, and dispositions of individuals. However, while citizens may be well-informed, believe they can make a difference, and be ready to participate, they may fail to find or be provided with opportunities to do so (Olivera-Aguilar et al., this volume). For this reason, a second map, the civic opportunities map, is also necessary for understanding civic measurement.

48 • Promoting K-12 Civic Learning and Engagement Through Assessment

The Civic Opportunities Map

The civic opportunities map portrays the ways that institutions and organizations allow citizens to build and use their civic skills and knowledge. This map ensures that the various channels through which citizens engage in civic opportunities, such as public decision-making, can be more quickly identified and understood. We included opportunities that we knew existed even though—as far as we were aware—their outcomes were not being measured. This was important to better demonstrate the ways in which the two maps correspond to and interact with one another, which we discuss in a subsequent section (Figure 4.2).

The innermost ring of the map repeats the four overarching **dimensions** of civic readiness: what individuals *understand*, how they *participate* in American democracy, how they *connect* with others, and what they *believe* that influences their engagement. It also follows the same breakdown of **elements** in each of those **dimensions**.

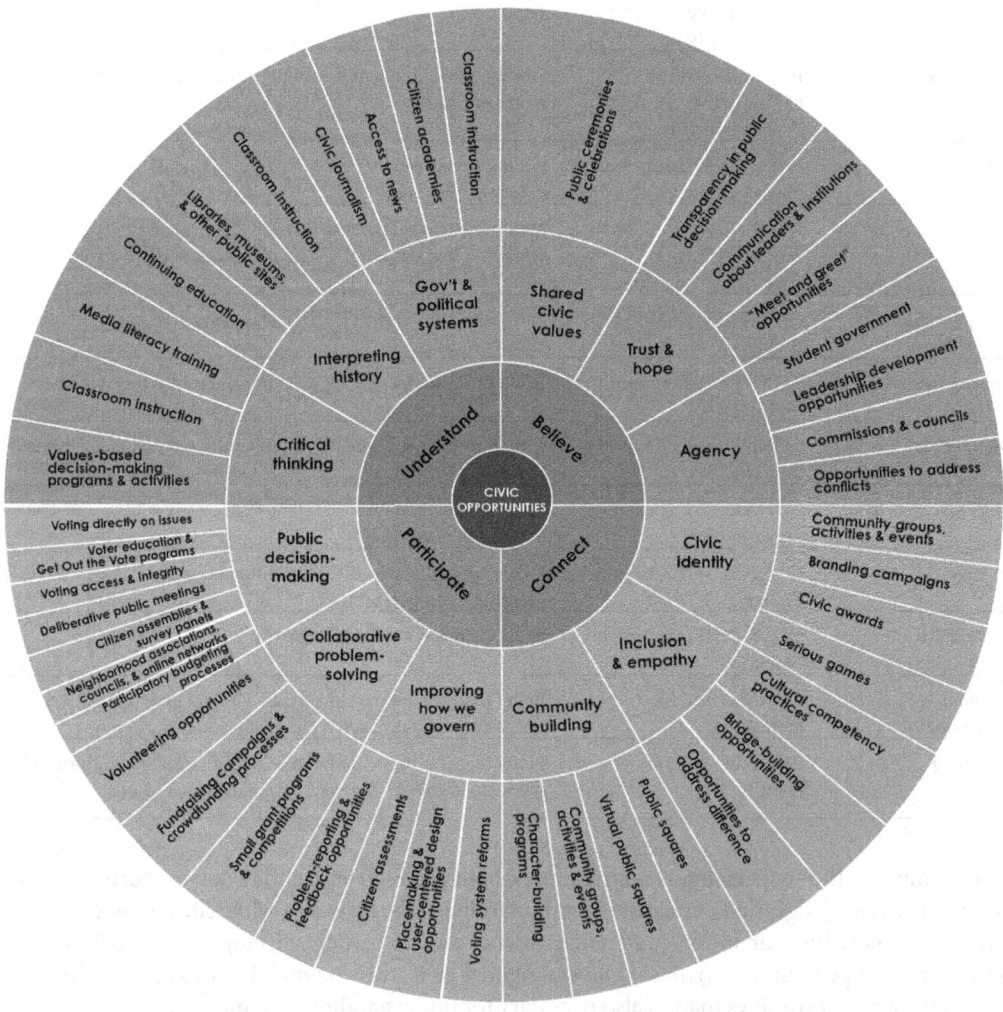

Figure 4.2 Civic Opportunities Map.

But the outermost ring of the civic opportunities map lists **building blocks** that can support those **elements** of citizenship and the tools that are being used to evaluate them. For example:

- *Classroom instruction* is a building block for increasing knowledge of *government and political systems*.
- *Deliberative public meetings* can give citizens a meaningful role in *public decision-making*.
- *Community groups, activities, and events* influence an individual's *civic identity*.
- *Communication about leaders and institutions* is measured to correlate to an individual's *trust and hope* in democracy (Table 4.2).

Table 4.2 Civic Opportunities Map: Building Block Definitions

Building Block (Outer Ring)	Dimension (Inner Ring); Element (Middle Ring)	Definition
Classroom instruction	UNDERSTAND; Government & Political Systems	Curricula and teaching practices that help students learn about government and our system and include discussions of current affairs
Citizen academies	UNDERSTAND; Government & Political Systems	Programs that teach citizens about their local government and how they can engage
Access to news	UNDERSTAND; Government & Political Systems	Objective, accessible coverage of public issues and decisions, especially at the local level
Civic journalism	UNDERSTAND; Government & Political Systems	Programs and practices that encourage interaction between journalists and their audiences around topics, editorials, and how to use the news
Classroom instruction	UNDERSTAND; Interpreting History	Curricula and teaching practices that help students learn about history and civics
Libraries, museums, and other public sites	UNDERSTAND; Interpreting History	Publicly available locations for people to learn about American history
Continuing education	UNDERSTAND; Interpreting History	Public programs provided by libraries, museums, universities, clubs, and other institutions
Classroom instruction	UNDERSTAND; Critical Thinking	Curricula and teaching practices that help people learn how to analyze information, solve problems, and engage in ethical reasoning
Media literacy training	UNDERSTAND; Critical Thinking	Programs that help people apply critical thinking to media messages and use media to create their own messages
Values-based decision-making programs and activities	UNDERSTAND; Critical Thinking	Community and civil society programs that help people build character and self-awareness
Public ceremonies and celebrations	BELIEVE; Shared Civic Values	Civic holidays, the national anthem, Pledge of Allegiance, citizenship ceremonies, and other events and practices that honor our country and communities
Transparency in public decision-making	BELIEVE; Trust & Hope	Laws and practices that ensure that public business is conducted in public, including televised meetings and easily accessible and searchable public records

(Continued)

Table 4.2 Civic Opportunities Map: Building Block Definitions *(Continued)*

Building Block (Outer Ring)	Dimension (Inner Ring); Element (Middle Ring)	Definition
Communication about leaders and institutions	BELIEVE; Trust & Hope	Making leaders and institutions accessible and available to the citizens they serve
"Meet and greet" opportunities	BELIEVE; Trust & Hope	Activities that allow public servants to build relationships with the people they serve
Student government	BELIEVE; Agency	At high schools and universities, it includes clubs and other student organizations
Leadership development opportunities	BELIEVE; Agency	Programs for young people and adults that help them make connections, find their voices, and learn and hone leadership skills
Commissions and councils	BELIEVE; Agency	Standing bodies of appointed citizens, including youth commissions, who represent and directly engage their peers on important issues
Opportunities to address conflicts	BELIEVE; Agency	Real-world or simulated activities that bring people together to negotiate conflicts and help them learn and hone dispute resolution skills
Voting directly on issues	PARTICIPATE; Public decision-making	Opportunities to vote directly on decisions and policies, such as ballot initiatives and referenda, in addition to voting for representatives
Voter education and get-out-the-vote programs	PARTICIPATE; Public decision-making	Efforts to inform voters and encourage them to participate in elections for candidates and on issues
Voting access and inetrity	PARTICIPATE; Public decision-making	Efforts to ensure that people are able to vote, such as early voting or voting by mail, and that elections are fair, such as voter identification laws or election monitoring
Deliberative public meetings	PARTICIPATE; Public decision-making	Regular meetings and hearings that include officials, staff, citizens, and other stakeholders and allow people to share experiences, learn together, consider options, and decide on solutions
Citizen assemblies and survey panels	PARTICIPATE; Public decision-making	Groups of citizens who have been randomly selected to give input, either by answering surveys on public issues or by deliberating intensively on an issue and then issuing recommendations to officials
Neighborhood associations, councils, and online networks	PARTICIPATE; Public decision-making	Ongoing opportunities for neighbors to meet (in-person, online, or both) to share information, give input on public decisions, and solve local problems
Participatory budgeting processes	PARTICIPATE; Public decision-making	Regular processes at the school, neighborhood, or local level that allow people to allocate money from a dedicated fund to worthwhile projects and ideas, and in some cases to give input on the overall organizational budget
Volunteering opportunities	PARTICIPATE; Collaborative Problem-solving	Projects and programs that encourage people to devote their time and energy to helping other people and their communities, including school- and university-based programs
Fundraising campaigns and crowdfunding processes	PARTICIPATE; Collaborative Problem-solving	Platforms and programs that allow people to donate money and services to ideas and community improvement efforts
Small grant programs and competitions	PARTICIPATE; Collaborative Problem-solving	Programs run by governments, foundations, and other institutions that offer small amounts of money for problem-solving and community improvement efforts powered by volunteers

(Continued)

Table 4.2 Civic Opportunities Map: Building Block Definitions *(Continued)*

Building Block (Outer Ring)	Dimension (Inner Ring); Element (Middle Ring)	Definition
Problem-reporting and feedback opportunities	PARTICIPATE; Improving how we govern	Digital platforms and other opportunities for people to report problems like potholes or graffiti or give feedback on a public service like bus routes or health clinics
Citizen assessments	PARTICIPATE; Improving how we govern	Citizen audits and ratings systems that allow people to assess the overall performance of institutions
Placemaking and user-centered design opportunities	PARTICIPATE; Improving how we govern	Exercises that encourage people to co-design buildings or public spaces, or how a service is administered, according to the needs and goals of the users
Voting system reforms	PARTICIPATE; Improving how we govern	Changes in voting that try to ensure that the will of the people is accurately reflected in elections, such as runoffs, proportional representation, or ranked choice voting
Public squares	CONNECT; Community Building	Public buildings and outdoor spaces, including libraries, city halls, community centers, plazas, and parks, that are welcoming and useful to all kinds of people
Virtual public squares	CONNECT; Community Building	Online platforms and networks that allow neighbors to share information, build relationships, and identify problems and priorities
Community groups, activities, and events	CONNECT; Community Building	Clubs, associations, teams, concerts, festivals, sporting events, and other opportunities to build relationships with neighbors, leaders, officials, and public servants
Character-building programs	CONNECT; Community Building	Opportunities for young people and adults to become emotionally stronger, more independent, and better at dealing with problems
Cultural competency practices	CONNECT; Inclusion & Empathy	Workshops, trainings, and exercises that help people understand differences, biases, and debates around equity and opportunity
Bridge-building opportunities	CONNECT; Inclusion & Empathy	Programs and practices designed to build relationships between people of different backgrounds and beliefs
Opportunities to address difference	CONNECT; Inclusion & Empathy	Regular opportunities for people to productively discuss issues of ideology, race, gender, religion, and other differences
Community groups, activities and events	CONNECT; Civic Identity	Clubs, associations, teams, concerts, festivals, sporting events, and other opportunities that bring people together as part of a community
Branding campaigns	CONNECT; Civic Identity	Public art, signs, sporting events, celebrations, and other efforts to communicate the distinct qualities of a community or institution
Civic awards	CONNECT; Civic Identity	Awards, honors, and titles that recognize the contributions of neighborhood, school, and local leaders
Serious games	CONNECT; Civic Identity	Fun exercises that help people learn, understand different perspectives, strengthen relationships, and generate creative solutions to shared problems

Map Interactions

Individuals and institutions interact and have multidimensional relationships. This means that the civic readiness map and the civic opportunities map must also interact with each other. To reflect the interactions and multidimensional relationships that individuals and institutions have with one another, the maps are designed to "spin" to help people think more deeply about how these relationships between readiness and opportunities are related.

For example, a researcher interested in citizens' knowledge of *how government works* might start with the civics-related courses available to high school students. The researcher could examine evaluations of those courses, or the students' aggregate grades, or other measures of their success. In this case, the *classroom instruction* **building block** on the civic opportunities map lines up with the *how government works* **coordinate** on the civic readiness map. But it may also be that when adults get involved in some sort of public process—such as *participatory budgeting*—that they become much more knowledgeable about planning, zoning, and the budget process of local governments. By spinning the map to line up *participatory budgeting* with *how government works*, researchers can use the framework to explore interactions between a civic opportunity and a specific aspect of civic readiness.

This relationship can go both ways. Communities with excellent *classroom instruction* may produce graduates who have deep understanding of *how government works*; they are therefore more confident about getting involved in their *participatory budgeting* process, and it is more effective overall (Johnson et al., 2021).

Indeed, the interactions of the maps demonstrate the multidimensional and non-linear nature among the different items and the potential for multiple approaches to develop a specific element or coordinate. Alternatively, multiple elements or coordinates can be learned through one civic opportunity. The practical implications of this are many, including the potential to leverage a few critical civic opportunities to address multiple civic readiness coordinates as part of civic preparation for young people.

Key Findings: Civic Measurement Themes

As we reviewed the framework and the plotted tools, a few themes emerged. Most of the tools we identified for the civic readiness map are being used to assess middle school, high school, and college students. A few of the measures included on that map gauge what Americans of all ages think and feel about democracy and civic life. While most civic measurement tools in our collection of 160 focus on the individual, there are also clearly efforts to assess the state of civic infrastructure—all the systems, platforms, programs, laws, and processes that help people to solve problems, make decisions, and build community. Nearly all of this smaller set of tools are surveys, indexes, and audits (National Civic League, 2019).

We also identified four key findings about the landscape of civic measurement.

#1 Civic Readiness Is Being Measured Much More than Civic Opportunities

The civic readiness of individuals—such as *analytical skills* or understanding *how government functions*—is measured far more frequently than civic opportunities—such as *bridge-building activities* or *media literacy training*. As a reminder, many of the identified tools measured multiple coordinates on the maps. For instance, if a tool aimed to measure voting, volunteering, and donating, one dot was placed in each of those coordinates.

Mapping Civic Measurement • 53

We repeated this plotting process for each of the 160 measurement tools and reports identified through our research, ultimately allowing us to identify 339 instances of measuring civic readiness of individuals and 61 instances of measuring the outcomes of civic opportunities. These instances are shown as plot points on the corresponding maps, as seen in Figures 4.3 and 4.4.

We found that measurement tools are typically focused on individual civic readiness *or* civic opportunities, but rarely both. For example, tools that measure an individual's ability to deal with misinformation (*fact-finding*) do not correspond to assessments of the quality of local journalism (*access to news*). This singularity of purpose makes it difficult, therefore, to understand how civic opportunities affect civic readiness, and vice versa. Several respondents pointed out the need for both short- and long-term longitudinal studies to explore relationships between coordinates of readiness and building blocks of opportunity.

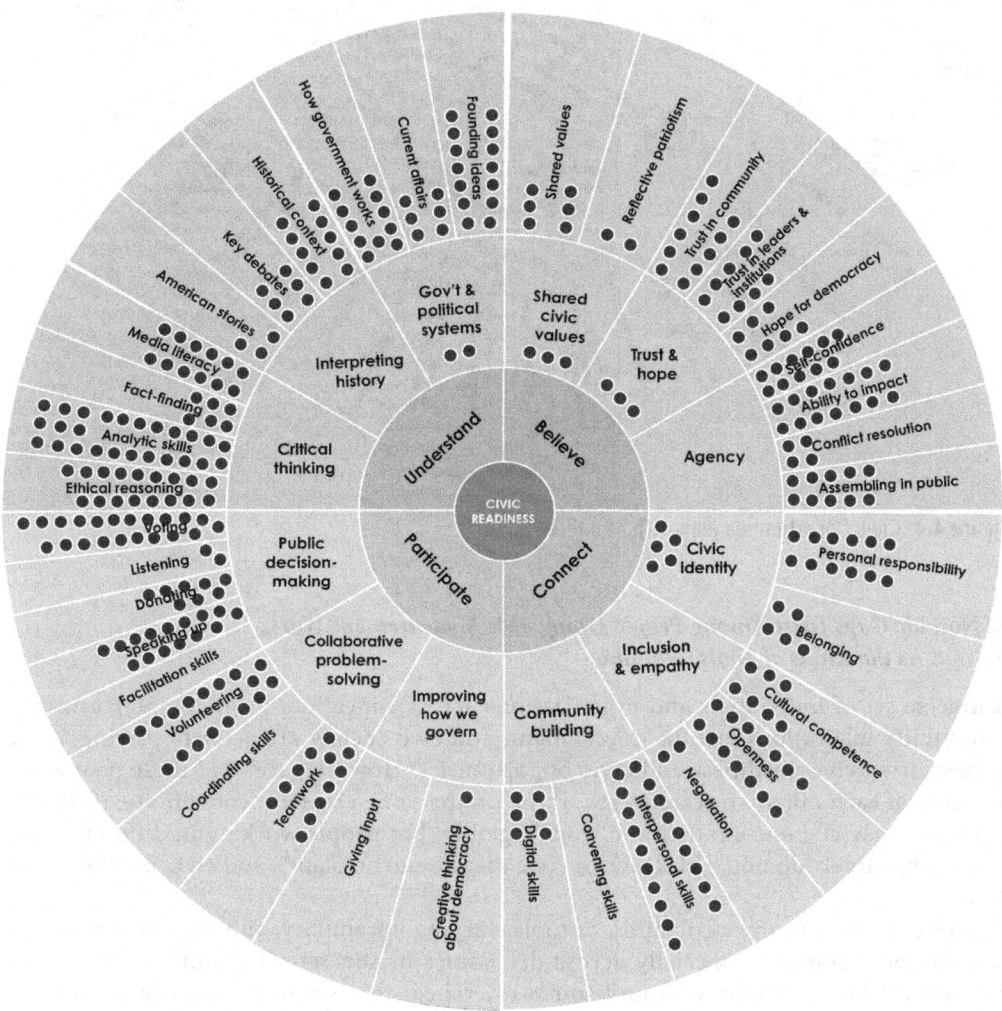

Figure 4.3 Civic Readiness Map with Tool Plot Points.

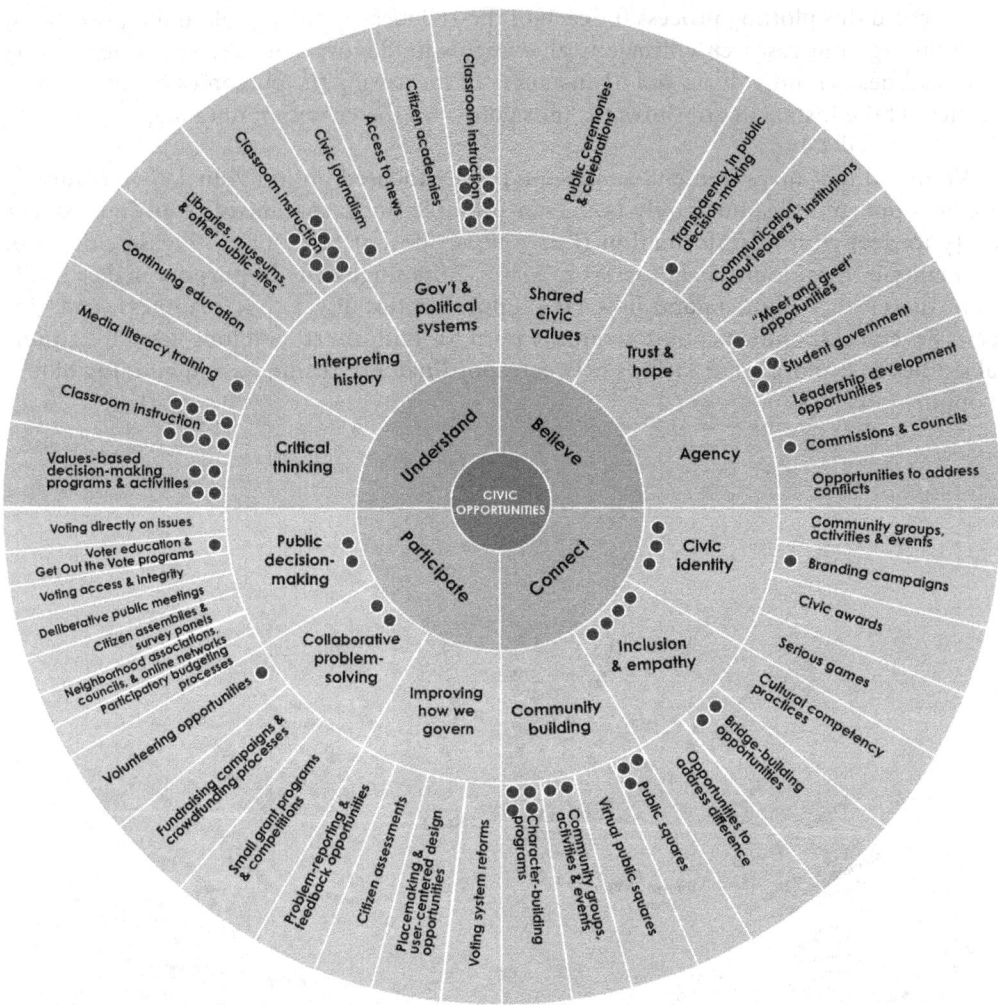

Figure 4.4 Civic Opportunities Map with Tool Plot Points.

#2 Notable Gaps Exist Among People Doing This Measurement Work, As Well As the Kinds of Tools Available

A diverse set of individuals and organizations across education, business, philanthropy, community institutions, media, government, and civil society are actively playing a role in measuring civic readiness and civic opportunities. However, some of these people are unaware of each other—researchers working on the same **element**, **coordinate**, or **building block** may cite one another and work together, but people working in different parts of the map largely do not. This leads to civic measurement islands and civic measurement deserts.

There are gaps in the availability of tools, varying vocabulary, and missed opportunities for collaboration—especially across disciplines or sectors—that hinder a true read on civic readiness. While we found some differences that seemed rooted in ideological divides, these were not as common as might be expected in today's partisan political environment.

We also identified two generalized patterns as we examined these gaps: civic measurement islands and civic measurement deserts.

Civic measurement islands are found in common civic **elements**. For example, there is an island of measures assessing the effectiveness of classroom instruction in understanding America's founding ideas. The researchers on this island may be connected to one another, but it appeared to us that, based on the measures we identified, they work independently from the island of media literacy researchers and their work on the role of social media in knowledge of the founding ideas.

Furthermore, our analysis found that measurement tools in one civic **dimension,** like *connect*, are distinct from those in another **dimension**, like *participate*. For example, researchers assessing participation in *public decision-making* processes are not using tools to explore the strength of *civic identity* in that place.

Plotting the tools on the civic measurement maps also surfaces important areas that are understudied, or at least under-measured. These include understanding the capacity of K-12 graduates to learn about and navigate across different cultures or assessing the role of public institutions to offer meaningful civic engagement opportunities for adults.

#3 Voting Dominates Civic Measurement

Our research found that there are many civic measurement tools designed to assess voter participation. Based on our interviews, we confirmed a hunch that researchers repeatedly turn to voting for political and methodological reasons. *Voting is relatively easy to measure and quantify, and it is the civic* **coordinate** *that is easiest to validate at scale.* Additional conversations after the release of the original report suggest one important difference from most (but not all) other areas of measurement: the significant financial opportunity to develop valid and predictive tools for voting propensity and which candidate voters would choose. Unlike many areas of civic measurement that rely on the interest of researchers or philanthropy to garner attention and resources, electoral cycles generate predictable capital to invest in measuring voting, voter behaviors, and voter motivation. Since measuring voting is comparatively easy and well-resourced when compared to other civic elements, it should perhaps not be surprising that it is measured often (Figure 4.5).

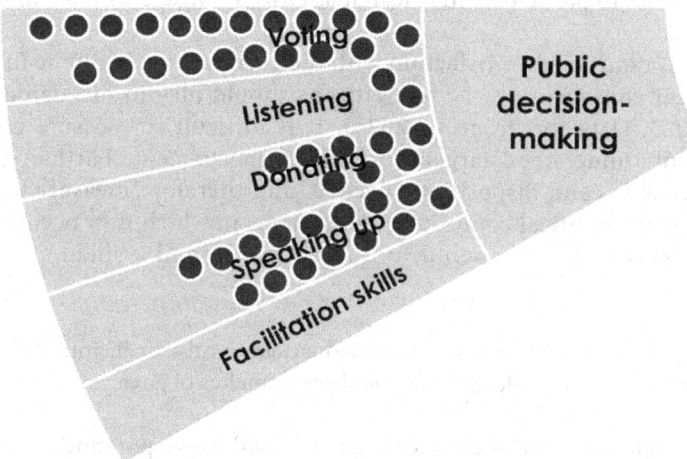

Figure 4.5 Voting Cluster.

The gravitational pull to assess voting as a singular action that an individual does or does not take may oversimplify and confuse attempts to measure civic readiness more holistically. Ironically, the narrow focus on voting—at the expense of other elements of civic readiness—may make it more difficult to assess voting in the larger context of trust in institutions and connection to community (Cox, 2022). Many studies suggest that people's willingness to vote is highly dependent on their connections with other people they trust, such as family, friends, colleagues, or other networks (Krebs, 2008). If researchers knew more about the status and influence of those connections, practitioners could strengthen voter education and civic opportunities.

#4 There Are Varying Definitions for What Good Citizenship Means, All of Which Need Examining as Our World is Changing

There have always been many different definitions of citizenship. This question has become even more uncertain in our era of dramatic social, technological, and political changes, which are changing what it takes to be a good citizen.

First, traditional measures may be out of step with current civic realities. For example, when researchers look more closely at how citizens are getting things done in their neighborhoods and communities, they often find people using skills and knowledge that haven't traditionally been taught in schools or incorporated in conventional definitions of civic readiness. One example of this is the work we see being done by youth civic activists to use social media to organize their peers to take action. Digital and social media skills are not included in most states' high school civics standards, but they are being used to significant effect by high school-age students (Hamilton et al., 2020).

Second, and connected to the example above, technology continues to be a powerful and transformative force affecting democracy and civil society. Fast-changing technology advances the skills citizens need to engage in democracy and their awareness of how they see their role in society. Researchers are just beginning to understand how to measure the influence of technology on civic readiness and citizenship. As a result, there is a need for research to keep pace with the changing environment in which civic activity takes place. This might look like more rapid-cycle research, measurement that takes advantage of new technologies to allow people to rate civic opportunities, and more community-embedded research to understand changing citizen behaviors and beliefs over time. It may also look like changes in who is sought after to participate in research as citizens engage with technology at varied rates of uptake.

Finally, there is rampant dissatisfaction with the current state of public life and institutions, but no clear consensus on the role citizens should play in our democracy (Angelucci & Prat, 2023; Data for Progress, 2025). It is difficult to measure civic readiness without commonly understood targets for citizen engagement. Further, the necessary civic knowledge, skills, and dispositions needed, and therefore measured, are informed and influenced by the political conditions and systems in which they occur. These conditions present numerous decision points for those studying and evaluating civic readiness, such as these:

The ability to successfully identify a social media post as mis- or disinformation may be more important than being able to name the three branches of government.

The awareness that democracies change over time—with corresponding impacts on how rights and responsibilities are viewed—could be considered an extremely valuable civic disposition.

In a polarized era, conflict resolution skills may be more important for citizens than knowing how to contact your member of Congress.

The fact that citizenship is a moving target means that attempts to measure civic readiness require more discussion, connection, and coordination than exist today. Practitioners and researchers are unlikely to achieve consensus on what citizens should know and be able to do, but there is an opportunity to identify shared assumptions and areas of agreement. This process can foster an environment where innovative measurement tools and studies complement and build on one another to drive to a common understanding.

Implications for Assessment and Equity

Since the release of the *Mapping Civic Measurement* report in February 2023, Citizens & Scholars has had the chance to share our research with a variety of audiences. At the time of publishing, we presented the maps and report findings to more than 600 individuals interested in civic measurement. In the process of sharing the measurement maps and the landscape of civic measurement tools, we have received considerable feedback on the measurement maps and some thoughtful suggestions on additional tools for consideration.

Reflections on Civic Measurement Tools

At the end of *Mapping Civic Measurement*, Citizens & Scholars outlined a series of follow-up projects it would undertake to address open questions that emerged from the research. One of those projects was an effort to review the 160 tools pinned onto the civic measurement maps in greater detail.

Initial work on this project surfaced challenges. For instance, not all tools are readily—or freely—available. Nor was it easy for us to identify evidence of validity and reliability. Additionally, we encountered difficulties in how to communicate validity and reliability evidence to the diverse set of civic field practitioners interested in our work. For instance, when we found evidence of validity and reliability because the tool has a specific use case—a civic knowledge test of Massachusetts eighth graders, for example—we then grappled with how to explain the relevance and importance of this validity and reliability to a user disconnected from that use case, such as a community organizer seeking to understand the level of civic knowledge in their neighborhood. While we strongly believe that using measures with validity evidence is a good idea for all who would seek to measure civic readiness and opportunities, we are also cognizant that simply providing information about the validity and reliability of measures may be insufficient for the diverse field of practitioners with whom we work. Educating civic practitioners on available tools, tools with evidence of validity, and advisable use cases for various tools is a complex and time-consuming endeavor.

Based on early feedback on and takeaways from this work, we continue to believe that there is significant value to the field in collecting additional information about these tools and reporting those findings in a centralized place. However, the work to do so will be resource intensive and remains a challenge to the field.

Reflections on the Civic Measurement Maps

As described in the "Methodology" section, our approach in creating the maps necessarily had limitations. Colleagues have pointed out the underrepresentation of some constructs or elements that are considered essential to civic readiness or opportunities but do not appear on the maps—such as political tolerance, civil discourse, and attitudes toward authoritarianism.

We believe this is a valid criticism. However, in order to provide a visual representation of the civic measurement efforts, we had to establish broad, inclusive categories that best represented our understanding of the civic measurement landscape and inevitably missed some opportunities to capture more specific constructs.

These ongoing conversations about missing constructs or underrepresented elements underscore that the maps themselves should not be considered static. We should consider how the maps—and the individuals and organizations using them—evolve as democracy evolves. To offer one obvious example: Had the maps been created in 2001, there would have been no call for including opportunities such as "virtual town squares" nor civic readiness elements specific to "digital skills."

In fact, the way in which Citizens & Scholars talks about agency and engagement with democracy has evolved since the report was first published. While we originally described civic learning as the development of individuals who are civically well-informed, productively engaged, and hopeful about democracy, the organization now refers, instead, to *commitment to democracy*. This shift was a result of greater input from the field, which described the need for more active representation of how people engage with democracy. Being *committed to* democracy, as a prerequisite for agency and active participation in our democratic system, suggests a more active level of *belief* than the feeling of hope.

We have also received some pushback about the report's third finding: *voting dominates civic measurement*. In some instances, this has been interpreted as a too-broad generalization about a field with diverse measurement interests; in others, it has been interpreted as a suggestion that no new research or refinement about measuring voting is necessary. While these critiques are both valid, we believe it is important not to lose sight of the need to deepen our understanding of how voting relates to other kinds of activities found in the *Participate* quadrant of the map, as well as the relationship between voting and skills, dispositions, and knowledge in the three other quadrants of the map.

The feedback and conversations that the maps have sparked have been illuminating, and we continue to evolve our thinking on the maps. What will they look like in 2030? In 2050?

Using the Maps

Just as we have received feedback on ways to amend the maps, we have also heard from the field that the maps are being used.

The maps are being utilized by colleagues in higher education within Citizens & Scholars' College Presidents for Civic Preparedness initiative. The Measurement Working Group, consisting of over 30 senior leaders and faculty members across 12 universities, has used the maps to guide decisions on the specific areas of civic readiness and opportunities the group will assess and measure on each of their campuses. Some members have taken an additional step and incorporated the maps into courses focused on student-led civic engagement research.

The maps are also being used and referenced by organizations seeking to better understand their impact and how to measure it. In this case, we have observed that in addition to serving as a conceptual framework, the maps have proven useful as a practical tool for understanding strategy and measurement.

Finally, some groups have used the maps in a way we didn't intend: to illustrate all the potential civic opportunities (and forms of civic readiness they build up and build on) that a community or institution might provide. While this is a more normative approach than we anticipated, it seems helpful for people who are trying to illustrate, in more concrete terms, what civic life can be like.

In October 2024, Citizens & Scholars, in partnership with the National Civic League, released the *Guide to Civic Measurement: Using* Mapping Civic Measurement *in your Community*.

As a companion to *Mapping Civic Measurement*, the guide was designed as a workbook-style resource with sections designed to help the user:

1) deepen their understanding of the various aspects of readiness and opportunities that could be measured in each quadrant of the map;
2) reflect on why sections of the map are important to them or their work and what they are already doing in those areas; and/or
3) prioritize what they want to measure and what resources they might need to do so.

At the time of writing, we have only just begun to receive feedback on the Guide and have connected with other nonprofit organizations, city governments, and representatives from college campuses about facilitating workshops with the guide.

Implications for Equity

The implications for promoting equity in civic measurement are many and significant. One such implication is the core question of definition: How are we defining equity? Is it equal access to civic opportunities? Or equal outcomes on measures of civic preparedness? Clarity about this definitional question is itself central to further pursuit of questions of equity.

Another key question might be: What is the role of measurement in promoting any societal value? It is widely understood that opportunities of all sorts are not distributed equally. The same would then be assumed to hold true for access to civic opportunities. However, without robust measures for assessing the state of civic opportunities, we cannot understand whether and how civic opportunities mirror or diverge from that typical pattern (Olivera-Aguilar, this volume). Are some populations, say urban dwellers, afforded greater access to civic opportunities than their rural counterparts? Or are civic opportunities designed differently across geographies but overall equally accessible? These questions require robust measures to help the field develop a fuller understanding of civic opportunities across multiple dimensions of access.

While our analysis showed greater numbers of tools for measuring civic readiness, our collective understanding of civic readiness outcomes is still lacking. Growing the field's knowledge of civic readiness outcomes across population segments, age cohorts, and geography can help inform efforts to ensure equity—whichever definition is being used—in civic readiness.

Equity considerations are significant for civic measurement. Often, the people most affected by policy and institutional decisions are also the most marginalized politically and electorally; frequently, they have the least supportive civic infrastructure (Groth, 2023; Kaufman et al., 2022) or access to opportunities (Kahne & Middaugh, 2008). Applying an equity lens to civic measurement could help us to better understand what kinds of civic infrastructure communities have access to, how well it addresses civic readiness, and how it helps people affect policy and institutional decisions in their civic lives.

Conclusion

How do we know if we are making progress as a democracy? That is the big question we sought to answer when we set out to explore the landscape of civic measurement. What we suspected—and what this work confirmed—is that many more people are dedicated to civic measurement than might be apparent.

Any number of skills—critical thinking, interpersonal skills, and ethical reasoning, to name only three—are important and necessary not only for their *civic* implications but also across multiple facets of an individual's life. In many cases, questions related to skills that we identify as civic skills are being studied by individuals in fields traditionally not considered part of the "civic learning ecosystem." Their findings are being presented using different terminology, based on different assumptions. Yet our work on the maps has demonstrated that, by drawing in researchers and practitioners from fields traditionally outside of the "civic" ecosystem, we can collectively strengthen our measurement efforts.

We also believe that this mapping work supports a crucial idea: Despite the ideological differences that so often overshadow and derail good-faith conversations about effective citizens and civic education, the field actually has some shared understandings on which we can build. The evidence is in the maps. When identifying terms and definitions for the maps, we sought to avoid contentious politics and instead identify underlying constructs for potentially "hot button" terms. Ultimately, we believe we succeeded in identifying the core knowledge, skills, and dispositions that most individuals—across political and ideological divides—consider instrumental to being an effective citizen.

Given the unique challenges that face the civic learning field—hyperpolarized environments (Hawkins et al., 2018), scattered efforts in various disciplines, rampant dissatisfaction with the current state of public life, and rapid technological advances that influence how citizens think about their role in society—civic measurement can be a unifying force.

The maps themselves provide a unifying framework that we believe has already demonstrated its appeal across ideological divides. This is a step in the right direction to strengthen fieldwide measures. We have already found broad agreement that the maps successfully capture *most* (though certainly not all) aspects of readiness and opportunities that contribute to an effective citizenry and healthy democracy—even where good measures of that effectiveness and health have yet to be identified. With that as a starting point, the field can continue to assess where there is consistent measurement with agreed-upon methodology, better understand where gaps in measurement are, better assess readiness and opportunities, and establish more mechanisms to share tools and measurement methodologies.

To achieve all this, the field must invest in itself. Researchers and practitioners must hold knowledge-sharing convenings focused on measurement to help encourage field-building within and across civic learning. We must establish cross-disciplinary working groups to enable cross-pollination of measurement approaches, accelerating progress for all. And finally, it is essential to identify and build partnerships with funders who will not only support but in fact champion this type of work.

Every day, academics, young people, scholars, community leaders, practitioners, funders, and many others engage in ways that contribute to our country's civic health. Civic measurement is how we make sure those contributions are being captured so that we can continue to make progress as a democracy.

References

Angelucci, C., & Prat, A. (2023). Is journalistic truth dead? Measuring how informed voters are about political news. *SSRN*. https://ssrn.com/abstract=3593002 or http://dx.doi.org/10.2139/ssrn.3593002

Annenberg Public Policy Center. (2021). *Americans' civic knowledge increases during a stress-filled year*. https://www.annenbergpublicpolicycenter.org/2021-annenberg-constitution-day-civics-survey/

Atwell, M. N., Stillerman, B., & Bridgeland, J. M. (2021). *Civic health index 2021: Citizenship during crisis*. https://ncoc.org/civic-health-index-2021-citizenship-during-crisis/

Cox, D. (2022, August 24). *Gen Z is the most mistrustful generation*. Business Insider.

Data for Progress. (2025). *A slim majority of voters think U.S. democracy is currently working well*. https://www.dataforprogress.org/blog/2025/3/3/a-slim-majority-of-voters-think-us-democracy-is-currently-working-well

Groth, C. (2023). *What is this civic infrastructure?* Strive Together. https://www.strivetogether.org/what-is-this-civic-infrastructure/

Hamilton, L. S., Kaufman, J. H., & Hu, L. (2020). *Preparing children and youth for civic life in the era of truth decay: Insights from the American Teacher Panel*. RAND Corporation.

Hawkins, S., Yudkin, D., Juan-Torres, M., & Dixon, T. (2018). *Hidden tribes: A study of America's polarized landscape*. More in Common.

Johnson, C., Carlson, H. J., & Reynolds, S. (2021). Testing the participation hypothesis: Evidence from participatory budgeting. *Political Behavior, 45*(1), 3–32.

Kahne, J., & Middaugh, E. (2008). *Democracy for some: The civic opportunity gap in high school*. CIRCLE Working Paper 59. Center for Information & Research on Civic Learning & Engagement.

Kaufman, J. H., Diliberti, M. K., Yeung, D., & Kavanagh, J. (2022). *Defining and measuring civic infrastructure*. RAND Corporation. https://doi.org/10.1007/s11109-021-09679-w

Krebs, V. (2008). It's the conversations, stupid! The link between social interaction and political choice. In J. Lebkowsky & M. Ratcliff (Eds.), *Extreme democracy* (1st ed., pp. 102–112). Lulu.com.

National Civic League. (2019). *Civic index – 4th edition*. https://www.nationalcivicleague.org/resources/civicindex/

Vinnakota, R. (2019). *From civic education to a civic learning ecosystem: A landscape analysis and case for collaboration*. Red & Blue Works.

Voelkel, J., Stagnaro, M., Chu, J., Pink, S., Mernyk, J., Redekopp, C., Ghezae, I., Cashman, M., Adjodah, D., Allen, L., Allis, V., Baleria, G., Ballantyne, N., Bavel, J., Blunden, H., Braley, A., Bryan, C., Celniker, J., Cikara, M., & Willer, R. (2023). *Megastudy identifying effective interventions to strengthen Americans' democratic attitudes*. https://www.ipr.northwestern.edu/our-work/working-papers/2022/wp-22-38.html

Section 2
Assessment for Large-Scale Monitoring of Civic Learning Outcomes and Opportunities

5
Understanding Civic Learning and Engagement Through Large-Scale Assessments

Madeline Goodman and Irwin Kirsch

In October 1963, during a year of upheaval in U.S. race relations, James Baldwin spoke to a group of educators about what he deemed a fundamental "paradox of education" (Baldwin, 1985, para. 2). "The whole process of education occurs within a social framework and is designed to perpetuate the aims of society," he explained; yet "the purpose of education, finally, is to create in a person the ability to look at the world for himself, to make his own decisions" (Baldwin, 1985, para. 2), and to provide individuals with an understanding that they have "the right and the necessity to examine everything" (Baldwin, 1985, para. 19). This paradox is at the very heart of civic learning. How can we ensure that students are acquiring the knowledge and honing the skills and dispositions necessary to both sustain democracy and challenge democratic societies to live up to their ideals? What role can large-scale assessments (LSAs) play in the critical process of educating young people about citizenship? This chapter examines these questions by exploring the history and contributions of LSAs, assessments designed to measure and compare the skills, knowledge, and dispositions demonstrated by student or adult populations (Tierney et al., 2022). We explore how the construct of civic learning has been articulated in the civics frameworks for two prominent LSAs, the National Assessment of Educational Progress (NAEP) and the International Civic and Citizenship Education Study (ICCS), providing more detail regarding the former than the latter, which is described in detail in Chapter 5. We then compare these frameworks with an eye toward improving the measurement of civic learning, provide recommendations for next steps, and review challenges that confront large-scale measurement of civic learning at the present moment.

Admittedly, when considering the need to advance U.S. civic education, LSAs may not readily come to mind. Yet, these assessments reflect current theory about how the domain of civics is conceived. It is rare to find a policy report or article about civic education in the U.S. that does not rely on LSA data to ground its claims. For just a few examples, a 2018 report from The Brown Center on Educational Policy at the Brookings Institute (Hansen et al., 2018) relied on data from the NAEP's civics, mathematics, and reading assessments to explore how well American students are learning as well as deficiencies in civic learning. On Constitution Day (September 17, 2023), the *San Diego Union-Tribune* published an article (Dinkin, 2023)

DOI: 10.4324/9781003476825-7

This chapter has been made available under a CC BY-NC-ND license.

decrying the state of civic education in the U.S., similarly citing NAEP civics (and U.S. history) to bolster their claims. More profoundly, NAEP reading scores have been used in numerous high-level court cases around the country that have addressed the responsibilities of states to adequately (and fairly) provide equal access to quality of education (DFER Connecticut, 2022; Marsal Family School of Education, 2020).

Despite how frequently LSA data are referenced and used in educational policy research and in the popular media, the assessments themselves are often viewed with skepticism, criticism, or outright derision (Emler et al., 2019; Nichols & Berliner, 2007). Many see them (implicitly or explicitly) as irrelevant to—or detached from—the learning process (McCluskey, 2023). Ultimately, however, high-quality assessments at any level—formative, summative, or large scale—can and should meaningfully inform teaching and policy that aims to improve student and societal outcomes (Hamilton & Parsi, 2022).

In all assessments, but perhaps particularly in highly formal and organized LSAs that are specifically designed to inform educational policy, one should be careful not to let the tail wag the dog. In the words of Gert Biesta (2010), we need to "question whether we are indeed measuring what we value, or whether we are just measuring what we can easily measure and thus end up valuing what we (can) measure" (p. 35). It is our belief that given the complexity and multidisciplinary nature of civic learning (see Chapter 2), LSAs have a key role to play in helping us better understand the construct of civic learning and support educational reform in this multifaceted domain.

Defining Large-Scale Assessments

Since the 1980s, researchers have shown an increasing interest in the development and use of both national and international LSAs. This growth reflects not only the expanded importance of education and skills for both economic advancement and societal well-being but also the value of benchmarking performance within and across national boundaries (Kirsch et al., 2013). For the purposes of this chapter, LSAs are assessments designed to measure and compare the skills, knowledge, and dispositions demonstrated by student or adult populations, often within or across states or countries (Tierney et al., 2022). These types of assessments are generally supported and overseen by government agencies or key national or international nongovernmental organizations. A crucial characteristic of LSAs is that they utilize designs and analytical methodologies that optimize reporting results at the *group* rather than the *individual* level (Clarke & Luna-Bazaldua, 2021). In addition, LSAs are generally designed for "low-stakes" monitoring purposes rather than to provide data at the individual level that can be used to impact a person's grades, eligibility for graduation, or certification for licensure or employment (Klein & Hamilton, 1999).

Another key feature of LSAs at the national and international level is that, in addition to the cognitive domains measured, students, teachers, and school administrators answer questionnaires that can be related to group performance within and across schools, states, and even nations. These data enable researchers and policymakers to explore and compare how performance of specific groups or populations is correlated to other factors (e.g., students' demographic features, learning opportunities, school policy, or classroom practices). This supports an exploration of "opportunity to learn" (OTL) and equity factors to assist policymakers and educators in their efforts to decrease disparities in access to high-quality educational opportunities (Hamilton & Kaufman, 2022; National Academies of Sciences, Engineering, and Medicine, 2019).

Operationalizing an LSA at the national or international level requires careful and systematic articulation of the construct being measured. This may sound simple, even commonsensical, but judiciously designing any type of assessment aligned to a clearly delineated set of knowledge and skills is a step in the assessment-development process that is often less scrutinized than it should be (see, for example, Monte-Sano, 2012). The utility of the data derived from assessments is directly related to how well the construct being assessed is understood and instantiated in the assessment itself (Kirsch & Braun, 2020). Before turning to an in-depth exploration of existing LSA frameworks in civic learning, we will provide a brief history of the two major LSA efforts in this domain.

Construct Frameworks in Large-Scale Assessments

While several framework documents have been developed in recent years to address the conceptualization of the domain of civics, these have largely been aimed at defining the field for the purposes of teaching rather than measurement (see, for example, Croddy & Levine, 2014; Gallos et al., 2023; Lo, 2021). Naomi Chudowsky and James Pellegrino, who have written widely about measurement and learning sciences, assert that one of the most critical ways LSAs advance learning in a particular domain is by providing "clarity about the underlying construct to be assessed" (Chudowsky & Pellegrino, 2003, p. 76). Understanding a particular domain in such a way that it can be instantiated in assessment tasks and questions is no small feat; they concede it requires "a sustained, collaborative effort among specialists in academic content, learning, and assessment" (Chudowsky & Pellegrino, 2003, p. 76) as well as a commitment to understanding and delineating key aspects of a particular domain, including the student behaviors, knowledge, and skills that provide evidence of novice, competent, and expert proficiency. Such work generally culminates in a published framework/test specification document that outlines the underlying construct for assessment designers to devise questions/tasks that can be mapped back to the construct as it has been defined and operationalized in the framework.

The production of the assessment framework should proceed by examining and describing the central conceptual aspects of the domain that students must grasp to successfully move on to higher levels of understanding (Chudowsky & Pellegrino, 2003; Goldman et al., 2016). Those involved in writing the framework should have a deep understanding of the theoretical and epistemic features of the domain under consideration; that is, how knowledge is organized, understood, and applied in these domains. As Goldman et al. (2016) noted in their study on the relationship of literacy skills to specific domains of knowledge, "disciplinary core knowledge constructs capture not only the conventions negotiated by the disciplinary discourse community for what constitutes legitimate knowledge claims and how they are made but also the accepted means by which evidence is developed and related to knowledge claims" (Goldman et al., 2016, p. 3).

As part of the assessment design process, national entities or nongovernmental agencies responsible for overseeing the assessments coordinate a consensus-building process to produce the assessment framework. For several reasons, the frameworks and accompanying test specifications provide enormous potential value to practitioners and policymakers. First, they are the result of an organized (and often costly) effort to bring together content experts, cognitive and measurement scientists, policymakers, and assessment designers to critically examine existing theoretical and research literature about a construct like civic learning and come to consensus on the core attributes of the domain to target for assessment purposes—a useful exercise in and of itself. Second, defining and operationalizing a construct for assessment purposes requires a level of precision that makes the frameworks useful beyond the administration of a particular assessment. The purpose of such documents is to concretize what are otherwise often abstract ideas of "knowing" and "doing" in a domain such as civic learning so that, taken as a whole, the assessment best mirrors the knowledge, skills, and underlying epistemologies—that is, how knowledge is constructed—in the domain. This process of formulating framework documents, in turn, helps ensure that the data derived from the assessment can be best utilized by practitioners, policymakers, and the public (Kirsch & Braun, 2020). We will return to the issue of utility of data later in the chapter.

This chapter will next examine the two major LSA frameworks related to civic learning: NAEP's civics assessment framework and the latest revised framework for the ICCS. Our purpose here will be to examine commonalities and differences between these frameworks in relation to current theoretical and data research in this domain and to suggest how LSAs can improve the measurement of this critical domain.

NAEP

The NAEP Content Framework

As with all NAEP assessment frameworks, the 1996 civics framework development was directed by the National Assessment Governing Board, an independent entity that sets policy for the NAEP assessments (https://www.nagb.gov/naep/the-naep-law.html). The civics framework, which has governed the NAEP civics assessment since the 1998 administration and outlines the assessment at Grades 4, 8, and 12, was built upon the *National Standards for Civics and Government*, published in 1994 by the Center for Civic Education (National Assessment Governing Board [NAGB], 1996). While a similar effort to develop national standards in U.S. history earlier in the decade had caused lively debate and backlash in the national media (see, for example, Nash, 1997, an essay documenting the U.S. history standards process in 1997), the civics standards document met notably less resistance. In fact, the NAEP civics framework explicitly states that the "widespread favorable reception of the [Standards document] and their general approval by the public, professional educational institutions, and schools" (NAGB, n.d., p. ix) made the standards document a key reference point in composing the framework (see de Witt, 1994).

The NAEP civics framework identifies three interrelated domain components: knowledge, skills, and civic dispositions. The first component, knowledge, is organized around five questions: (a) What are civic life, politics, and government? (b) What are the foundations of the American political system? (c) How does the government established by the Constitution embody the purpose, values, and principles of American democracy? (d) What is the relationship of the U.S. to other nations and to world affairs? (e) What is the role of citizens in American democracy? This formulation of overarching content questions is somewhat unusual for NAEP frameworks and an explicit carryover from the national standards document (Center for Civic Education (Calif.), 1994; Weiss et al., 2001). The framework committee defined the second component of civics as "intellectual and participatory skills" that "involve the use of knowledge to think and act effectively and in a reasoned manner in response to the challenges of a life in a constitutional democracy" (NAGB, 2018, p. xv). The intellectual skills noted in the framework are identifying and describing; explaining and analyzing; and evaluating, taking, and defending positions, while the participatory component is defined in the skills of interacting, monitoring, and influencing. Finally, the third component of the domain, civic dispositions, is described as "traits of private and public character essential to the preservation and improvement of American constitutional democracy" (NAGB, 2018, p. 33). The framework defines these traits as those that relate to the notion of a "civic character" (a term that has largely fallen out of use) that embodies "moral responsibility, self-discipline, and respect of individual worth and human dignity" (NAGB, 2018, p. 34). This last component of the NAEP framework has been particularly challenging to measure in an LSA environment (Goodman et al., 2023; O'Malley & Norton, 2022). While the NAEP civics framework outlines these three core areas of civic learning (knowledge, skills, and dispositions), NAEP uses a unidimensional item response theory (IRT) model for scaling student responses in this domain; therefore, only one score is used in reporting and available for secondary analyses. The 2022 NAEP civics scale ranges from 0 to 300 with a mean of 150 and standard deviation of 34.

In addition to outlining *core content* (skills and dispositions to be measured in what is referred to as the "cognitive" component of the assessment), the NAEP frameworks provide achievement level descriptors for each subject, that is, explanations of what students should know and be able to do at three levels of competency: *NAEP Basic*, *NAEP Proficient*, and *NAEP Advanced* (see https://nces.ed.gov/nationsreportcard/civics/achieve.aspx/ for details on NAEP civic achievement level descriptors for Grades 4, 8, and 12). The percentages of students who fall Below *NAEP Basic* are also reported to the public; however, Below *NAEP Basic* is not considered an achievement level, per se, and it is generally understood that students who perform Below *NAEP Basic* do not have the knowledge or skills of those students at the *NAEP Basic* level. Across all NAEP subjects, these achievement levels have come under fire over the past decades, with detractors accusing NAGB of using them to inflate the challenges confronting education in the U.S. and often mistakenly assuming *NAEP Proficient* translates to grade-level performance (Loveless, 2016). Despite the confusion and controversy that surrounds the interpretation of NAEP achievement levels, the levels are intended to help guide a reader's interpretation of the results by indicating the types of knowledge and skills that students at different ranges on the IRT scale are expected to be able to know and to do, as well as where students at some levels will likely struggle (National Academies of Sciences, Engineering, and Medicine, 2017). For example, NAEP reported in 2022 that 79% of Grade 8 students perform at or below the NAEP *Basic level* (Nation's Report Card, undated a). This means that a little over three quarters of eighth graders are likely to struggle to analyze or infer meaning from a variety of civic sources, analyze the responsibilities and purposes of government, and recognize the need to balance the rights and responsibilities of citizens (see NAEP achievement level descriptions at https://nces.ed.gov/nationsreportcard/civics/achieve.aspx). In addition, NAEP also creates "item maps" that display the distribution of task difficulties along the IRT scale as another way to guide the interpretation of the data (see the 2022 NAEP civics item map at https://www.nationsreportcard.gov/itemmaps/?subj=CIV&grade=8&year=2022).

NAEP Survey Questionnaires

As mentioned previously, along with data gathered from student performance on cognitive assessments, NAEP collects information from students, teachers, and school administrators regarding learning attitudes, background information of students, classroom practices related to subject domains, and school environments. These data are linked to students who took the NAEP assessment in the respective subject area, allowing for analyses regarding the relationship of student group performance to various factors in and outside of school.

The NAEP survey questionnaires (SQs) undergo a development process that is wholly separate from that of the NAEP cognitive assessments; therefore, the NAEP civics assessment framework and test specifications documents do not cover the content that is measured in the survey portion of the assessment. Members of the committee of experts that oversee the cognitive portion of the assessment do, however, review the survey questions at a later stage of their development.[1] Student SQs contain a "general" section to elicit data on students' gender, home SES, and other demographic information, and a "subject" section that probes students' attitudes toward learning in a particular domain in and out of the classroom. Despite the need for trend and the time limitations for the NAEP SQ, which are intended to take students about 15 minutes to complete, in recent years new questions have been added to target domain-specific classroom experience, students' attitudes toward the subjects, teacher practices and training in these domains, and school resources (see, for example, https://www.nagb.gov/content/dam/nagb/en/documents/publications/frameworks/contextual-information/contextual-information-framework.pdf).

The International Civics and Citizenship Study

The ICCS is designed to measure "students' conceptual knowledge and understandings of aspects related to civic and citizenship education" and collect data about "student attitudes and engagement relevant to the area of civic and citizenship education" (Schulz et al., 2023, p. 1). In this section, we briefly describe the ICCS 2022 assessment framework. In Chapter 5, Schulz and Damiani presented a more detailed discussion of ICCS, including the framework.

The ICCS 2022 Framework

The most recent ICCS framework extends and builds upon previous frameworks written for two prior ICCS international assessments in 2009 and 2016. In each assessment cycle a new focus area is introduced. Approximately 68% of the cognitive item pool is readministered in each assessment cycle to facilitate country-level trend comparisons. The ICCS assesses students enrolled in the eighth grade, provided that the average age of students at this level is 13.5 years or above. In countries where the average age of students in Grade 8 is less than 13.5 years, Grade 9 is defined as the target population (Schulz et al., 2023).

These two core areas are very intentionally and explicitly addressed in the framework document. The first—students' knowledge/skills—is measured through a cognitive assessment. The second—gaining insight into students' civic attitudes around civic engagement—is measured through an extensive SQ taken by students. A third area of focus involves understanding the role of the school in civic learning. A comprehensive questionnaire is given to teachers and school administrators to obtain data related to learning contexts surrounding civics—in other words, how schools, home, and communities influence students' acquisition and exercising of their civic knowledge and skills. It is worth noting that while the 2022 framework regarding students' knowledge and skills is distinct from the framework on students' attitudes/behaviors toward engagement, these frameworks appear to have been developed in a tandem process (Schulz et al., 2023).

The 2022 ICCS administration was also designed to extend "the scope of ICCS 2016 to explore further content and themes associated with global citizenship, sustainable development, migration, changes to traditional political systems, and the use of digital technologies for civic engagement" (Schulz et al., 2023, p. 2) through new content and survey questions related to these themes developed for the 2022 administration. Finally, for the first time in 2022, countries participating in the assessment were given the option for administering the assessment in a digital rather than paper-based format.

ICCS Cognitive Framework

The cognitive component of the ICCS framework focuses on four key areas: (a) civic institutions and systems, (b) civic principles, (c) civic participation, and (d) civic roles and identities. As with NAEP civics, there are no separate reporting scales for knowledge, skills, or dispositions, and there is a single scale for reporting a student's performance in this domain. Nonetheless, ICCS framework authors make a clear distinction between skills related to *knowing* (defining, describing, and illustrating with examples) and skills related to *reasoning and applying* (interpreting, relating and justifying, integrating, evaluating, suggesting solutions, and predicting), which generally aligns with the work of cognitive scientists who differentiate between lower and higher order thinking skills (Lewis & Smith, 1993). As in the NAEP civics framework, there is a clear effort to measure knowledge and skills in this domain beyond the ability of students to simply recall information (i.e., lower order thinking skills). In addition, item types are similar across the two frameworks, with both selected-response (including traditional multiple-choice questions) and constructed-response questions. In both NAEP civics and ICCS, open-ended or constructed-response questions are human scored. It is worth noting that NAEP appears to devote a larger percentage of assessment time to CR questions than does the ICCS (Schulz et al., 2023), which may suggest a deeper focus on some of the civic learning skills in the latter. While these can be measured in selected-response format, there are likely limitations on the type and depth of skills that can be probed through this response type.[2]

The commitment to update the ICCS framework for each new assessment cycle provides an opportunity to not only address recent topics relevant to this domain but also introduce novel assessment technologies—such as digital assessments—and how they can be used to measure certain facets of the domain more effectively than traditional paper-based questions. For example, the 2022 framework calls for the explicit development of what they label "large-task items." These are tasks that provide students with a relatively complex assignment (for example, putting together a web page for a specific purpose) where students receive some form of dynamic feedback based on selections made as they move through the task. One such task has been developed for the ICCS 2022 assessment cycle. Although similar tasks have been developed in several NAEP subjects (e.g., science), they have not been operationalized for the NAEP social science subjects (for an example of such tasks, see https://www.nationsreportcard.gov/science/sample-questions/?grade=4).

ICCS Affective Behavioral Framework

Along with the cognitive aspect of the domain described above, the ICCS framework delineates how to measure the affective behavioral component of civics learning, which is analogous to what is termed "civic dispositions" in the NAEP framework. In NAEP, civic dispositions are measured (albeit with a good deal of constraints) in the cognitive part of the assessment; however, in ICCS, the attitudes and behaviors associated with good citizenship are probed through a comprehensive series of Likert questions related to students' level of agreement or disagreement with specific statements. At nearly 40 minutes in length, the ICCS allots students nearly three times the amount of time to complete the student survey (or SQ) than NAEP allows. The ICCS SQ is organized into two clusters and is common across all participating countries to allow for cross-country: (a) attitudes (e.g., judgments in relation to ideas, people, objects, events, or situations; trust in national and supranational entities) and (b) affective behaviors in relation to engagement (e.g., interest in, expectations of, and experience of civic engagement through civic action and future political participation).

ICCS Learning Context Framework

The final framework component that completes the ICCS instrument addresses contexts (both in and outside of school) that influence student learning in this domain, providing policymakers and researchers with an ability to explore how factors related to OTL, as well as local and national political issues, are related to student achievement in civics. This component is specific to the participating country.

Comparison of NAEP and ICCS Frameworks

This section describes some relevant comparisons between key features of the NAEP and ICCS large-scale frameworks with an eye toward better understanding how quality LSAs can improve policy and research in civic learning. Both frameworks provide a relatively consistent understanding of civics as a body of knowledge and a set of skills and dispositions that allow that knowledge to be put into practice. The delineation of three core areas that comprise civic learning—a knowledge base, a set of cognitive skills, and attitudinal (or socioemotional) dispositions to engage with that knowledge—is consistent with how the field has been defined at a meta-level for roughly the last 30 or 40 years (Chapter 2). The knowledge dimensions of the two frameworks do differ in substantive ways given the distinct aims to capture national-level understandings of democratic traditions and practices versus more global and universal democratic concepts, traditions, and instantiations of democracy in diverse political institutions. The ICCS framework also outlines a broader scope for understanding the role of schools and other societal institutions in the inculcation of democratic attitudes and behaviors. In addition, ICCS is a much lengthier assessment than NAEP (nearly 2 hours of student assessment time versus NAEP's 60 minutes of assessment time). The ICCS framework also provides a more comprehensive, theoretical foundation than the older NAEP framework, in part because its aim is to explore citizenship both in and across several national entities, while the NAEP framework is focused on assessing students' knowledge of U.S. democracy and government.

Another contrast between the two framework approaches involves the more frequent update of the ICCS framework to measure students' understanding of emerging issues and skills necessary in this domain. Given that the knowledge base on which this domain rests is in part responsive to immediate, emerging topics (often referred to in K-12 education in the U.S. as "current events"), such as the impact of climate change, the rise of new forms of totalitarianism and authoritarianism, and new demands on digital literacy, it may be particularly important for a national LSA of civics in the U.S. to consider having more frequent (for example, every ten years) content framework updates. Note that while NAEP does at times release 15%–20% of the item pool and write replacement questions, these are not written to specifically address new topics that may have arisen in the civics domain but rather to fill content holes left by the release of some portion of the assessment to the public.[3] At present, the NAEP civics (and U.S. history) framework, the latter of which also touches on many of the aspects of knowledge and skills of civic learning, is slated to be updated for the NAEP 2030 operational assessment in these two subject areas (O'Malley & Norton, 2022).

The two LSAs also take a different methodological approach to measuring the dispositional aspects of the domain—the affective attitudes, behaviors, and dispositions associated with civic learning and civic engagement. The NAEP framework outlines these as part of the cognitive framework, though operationalizing these in assessment questions and tasks has proven difficult since the assessment was first administered in 1998 (Goodman et al., 2023). Designers of the ICCS assessment framework, in contrast, explicitly seek to measure dispositional attitudes and behaviors through student responses to survey questions regarding their attitudes toward government and citizenship (local, national, and supranational) and engagement—that is, interest in, and expectations of, civic engagement through civic action and future political participation. In particular, the theoretical focus of the ICCS framework on social cohesion and social capital—with identification of agreed upon indicators of these constructs—differentiates it from the current scope of the NAEP civics framework. Having a more coherent or robust set of indicators derived from the student surveys—and being able to connect these to student group performance that reflects knowledge and skills—could potentially enhance the utility of the NAEP data.

Recommendations and Opportunities to Support Large-Scale Assessments in Civic Learning

Having investigated some of the commonalities and differences between the NAEP civics and ICCS frameworks, this section explores opportunities to advance the measurement of this domain in LSAs.

Measurement Opportunities in Civic Learning

Both the NAEP and ICCS civics framework authors acknowledge that while it is necessary to separate knowledge and skills to assure domain coverage, in practice, skills and knowledge are inextricably intertwined. It is precisely here that the rubber meets the road: In other words, where the (often abstract) ideas articulated in assessment frameworks must be instantiated in tasks that elicit evidence of students' ability to demonstrate higher level cognitive capabilities (Mislevy & Riconscente, 2011).

Practitioners in civics and U.S. history, fields of study that are closely aligned at the K-12 level in the U.S., have, over the past 30 years, contributed a good deal of solid scholarship to defining the skills that are embedded in civic learning (Goodman et al., 2023). Authors of key conceptual frameworks in social science education that have emerged in recent years have also heavily relied on this research in their framing documents (Educating for American Democracy, 2021; National Council for the Social Studies, 2013). However, these documents generally focus on pedagogy in terms of what to teach and how to focus instruction, rather than on measurement of knowledge and skills in these domains.

Although traditional question types such as multiple choice/selected response and constructed response can be designed to measure some of the skill components in domains such as civics and U.S. history, the complexity of the critical thinking and dispositional skills embedded in the domains will likely require the development of new questions/item types (Goodman et al., 2023; O'Malley & Norton, 2022). Borrowing from advancements in measurement science and question development work in other assessments, as well as advancements provided by digital delivery of LSAs, researchers have begun to explore the merits of designing new kinds of tasks and tools to enhance the measurement of cognitive skills and reasoning processes in civic learning (Deane & Sparks, 2019; O'Reilly, et al., 2018). As mentioned previously, the ICCS 2022 framework states that one such task has been developed for the most recent administration.[4]

By using simulated versions of authentic, disciplinary contexts, these types of assessment tasks can potentially provide more valid evidence of what it looks like when students engage in the work of a discipline, thereby making the data collected in LSAs more meaningful to educators, policymakers, and the general public (Deane & Sparks, 2019). Digital tools also can simulate disciplinary contexts that range from the simple to the complex and can be used in standalone items, in sets of items, or within a larger task design. Another benefit of digital tools is that they can produce rich process data—digital records of the sequence and timing of all test taker actions—that can yield evidence of students' moment-by-moment thinking and reasoning as they unfold while completing the task (Bergner & von Davier, 2018; Keehner et al., 2016). Tasks using digital tools can be designed with process data in mind and can thus provide additional insights into students' skills and possible problem-solving strategies. This information can then be leveraged to improve pedagogy and future assessments.

The following description of a simulated search tool (more fully illustrated with actual questions and screen shots in Goodman et al., 2023) demonstrates how a task and a series of questions related to that task can yield evidence of students' capacity to gather and evaluate relevant information using electronic sources. Given the ubiquitous nature of digital information, it has become clear that a core skill in this domain is media literacy, that is, the ability to find and select relevant, useful, and trustworthy information within online environments (Coiro et al., 2018; Sparks & Deane, 2015). A simulation that could provide features such as a search tool and an underlying, constrained search engine would allow students to demonstrate several skills central to media literacy. The simulated search engine would allow test takers to enter search terms in natural language and receive a set of search results or hits related to the terms used, similar to a typical Google search in appearance but far more constrained in its actual implementation in order to control the presentation of information and to support measurement goals (Coiro et al., 2018; Leu et al., 2012).[5] The search results would include website titles, brief descriptions of the website contents, and URLs (which for security reasons would not link to actual live websites). Test takers could then select the most appropriate website(s) for the assigned task. Websites presented within the simulated web browser tool can have graphics, hyperlinks, and subpages, much like typical websites, and students would be able to freely navigate among these different elements as they read and explore the websites. Using this part of the tool, students could be presented with a series of questions targeting skills such as navigating among the site's pages to locate, gather, and analyze information; understanding and assessing the positions and viewpoints of others; and developing and defending their own positions, using evidence to support them.

Overall, we believe that more attention should be paid to LSAs of civic learning to measure the complex, critical thinking skills associated with this domain. Advances in measurement science—as well as technology—provide a wealth of opportunities to do so.

Civics Assessments Across the Age-Span

One key area for improving our understanding of/measurement of civics is to develop and administer civics assessments that span K-16. At present, both NAEP and ICCS have administered their assessments only at Grade 8 (or age 13). As with all domains, civic knowledge, skills, and dispositions are acquired over time in relation to other developmental changes that children and young adults undergo over their years of schooling. Moreover, as many have pointed out, the dispositional skills so central to civic learning are also necessary workplace skills that young adults and adults need to continue to learn, practice, and cultivate in nearly all labor contexts (see, for example, Carney, 2023; Eddy, 2023; Torney-Purta et al., 2015).

Given the attention to the social and emotional learning (SEL) component that aligns with civic learning in the dispositional components of the domain (see Chapter 15 for a more detailed discussion of this overlap), it seems particularly relevant to use a developmental lens to better understand how students and young adults acquire the critical skills and knowledge in this domain. Administering both the NAEP civics and U.S. history assessments at Grades 4, 8, and 12 would be a key step in providing data to inform policy to improve SEL through these domains. In addition, there have also been several calls to extend the assessment of civic learning to postsecondary education, particularly on the areas of civic/political engagement. In fact, some scholars have argued that "the goal for universities should be to contribute *significantly* to developing and sustaining democratic schools, communities, and societies" (Harkavy, 2006, p. 5).

Utilize LSAs to Support and Improve Teaching

Another area of civic learning that merits attentional focus is teacher preparation and professional development, as this is so closely aligned to many of the student competencies LSAs measure. Insofar as schools provide one (of several) key places where civic knowledge and attitudes are gained, it stands to reason that we need better information about whether we are adequately preparing teachers to teach core civic knowledge, skills, and dispositions.

A relatively recent report from the Brown Center for American Education (Hansen et al., 2018) noted the dearth of research (and solid data) pertaining to the training of social science educators, particularly compared to teacher preparation in mathematics, reading, and science-related subjects (Hansen et al., 2018). The extant research on teacher preparation in civics and other social science subjects indicates that teachers may not be receiving the necessary training and professional development they need in this subject area (Goodman et al., 2023; Hamilton et al., 2020). A recent report using nationally representative data from RAND's American Teacher Panel found that on a scale of "not prepared at all" to "very well prepared," a little over 60% of teachers indicated that they were "somewhat prepared" to teach aspects of civic learning within their classes. In addition, only 19% of teachers overall reported that they felt "very well prepared" (Hamilton et al., 2020). Hamilton et al. noted that this contrasts markedly from responses from teachers about their preparation to teach English language arts and mathematics, with nearly 50% of teachers responding that they were well prepared to teach those subjects (Hamilton et al., 2020). LSAs that specifically target obtaining information about teacher background, classroom practices, and attitudes toward this domain provide an opportunity to investigate this area more deeply and provide analyses to support effective teacher preparation and instruction in civics and related fields.

Better Educate Media and Public on Interpreting LSA Data

As researcher Henry Braun asserted in a chapter discussing the prospects for international LSAs, "volumes can be written concerning both the proper use of [I]LSA results and decrying the misuse of those same results" (Braun, 2013, p. 155). The kind of "league charts" and comparisons that are made between countries, in the case of international assessments, or states, in the case of national assessments in the U.S., can be misleading and confusing. This is a serious problem, since the impetus for LSAs often rests on their utility to policymakers, parents, and others concerned with the state of education. If this outcome data from the LSAs is misinterpreted by the very audience it is trying to inform to create more sound and evidence-based policy, then the LSAs have not fulfilled a key purpose they purport to serve.

The overreliance on tables of ranks necessitates a clearer communication about the underlying complexities of LSAs and what they can and cannot tell us about student or adult competencies in certain domains. In the realm of international assessments, or NAEP assessments with state-level results, there is a tendency to focus on cross-national and cross-state comparisons and deemphasize within-state or national data (Braun, 2013). Moreover, reports of LSA data should make it easier to compare like with like and attempt to disentangle factors that confound surface-level comparisons of scale scores across geographic entities. Recent attention to issues subsumed under OTL factors seems to support the creation of a set of indicators related to resources available to certain communities, districts, states, and schools that might help explain the relationship of place to achievement (Guiton & Oakes, 1995; National Academies of Sciences, Engineering, and Medicine, 2019). For example, the Urban Institute released a tool that allows users to compare NAEP district results in mathematics and reading while accounting for various factors such as socioeconomic status and race/ethnicity (Chingos, 2015). Similarly, the National Center for Educational Statistics agency has released an NAEP achievement-gap tool to compare score differences between selected racial/ethnic groups while accounting for factors related to SES, academic preparation, and students' attitudes toward learning (Nation's Report Card, undated b). These are two examples of ways in which public release of data from LSAs can improve the communication of results to aid policymakers and other consumers of NAEP data.

U.S. Participation in ICCS

On the international front, U.S. participation in the ICCS could enrich the data available that allow for a deeper understanding of how well we are preparing students in the U.S. to participate in democracy and how U.S. students compare to those of other nations in terms of their competencies in this domain. At the very least, the next civics framework process could examine how participation in ICCS could supplement and enhance NAEP data.

Challenges and Conclusion

Providing recommendations for improving LSAs in civic learning is obviously an important aim of this chapter; nonetheless, it is necessary to acknowledge the myriad obstacles that will make these recommendations challenging to implement. First and foremost is the difficulty of currently gaining consensus on how we define and operationalize civic learning in a precise and detailed enough manner to support an LSA. It is notable that while several overarching frameworks have been written to bolster the field, they have often shied away from specifics, noting that teaching and learning in civics "has become dominated by certain ideological viewpoints with specific agendas" (Gallos et al., 2023, p. 31). In terms of assessing the civic knowledge, skills, and dispositions that form the core of this domain, the devil will be in the details. For assessments in this domain to provide meaningful data, they must specifically define the construct in a way that it can be operationalized across tasks or questions and reported to the public in ways that have utility for policymakers, researchers, and other stakeholders. Moreover, agencies responsible for these LSAs need to communicate results so that key knowledge and skills in the domain can be mapped to the questions, tasks, and construct definitions outlined in the assessment framework. Given the polarized political climate in the U.S. surrounding the teaching and learning of material related to U.S. politics and history (Rogers et al., 2022; Weingarten, 2023), this will be no simple task.

In terms of the former, it will not be easy for those with different theoretical perspectives on the role of government in American democracy to come to consensus about core knowledge that students should possess. Projects such as Educating for American Democracy (EAD) have provided a model for how such consensus regarding content can occur. Yet even with broad representation across the political divide on the committee that worked on this project, the publication of their roadmap resulted in a fierce backlash (Pondiscio, 2023; Riley & Polikoff, 2021). In terms of the skills and dispositional aspects of civics learning, discussions about teaching aspects of SEL have also been targeted in what one publication calls the "education wars" (Field, 2022, headline) suggesting that measuring this aspect of the domain will also meet resistance in some quarters.

Notwithstanding the outcries across the political spectrum regarding the state of our democracy (which, one must mention, is run by adults, many of whom were educated between the 1950s and the 1990s), the current school systems in the U.S. alone cannot and should not bear the brunt of the blame for the problems of our democracy or be the sole source of its cure. Baldwin's identification of the paradox of education serves as a reminder that education and democracy—democracy that involves the ability and responsibility of citizens to scrutinize and continually challenge our country to live up to its ideals—are simultaneously perfect partners and strange bedfellows. For democracy to survive, we must inculcate the values and principles of engaged citizenship. This includes educating students about the rights *and* responsibilities of citizenship and civic engagement—that is, the need to engage civilly with one another and acknowledge that democracy is always in flux. Over many centuries, political philosophers and observers have reminded us that democracy is a state of becoming, not a stagnant condition to achieve and maintain. As Walt Whitman wrote in an essay during another volatile moment for

American democracy in 1871, "I cannot too often repeat that [democracy] is a word the real gist of which still sleeps, quite unawaken'd, notwithstanding the resonance and the many angry tempests out of which its syllables have come, from pen or tongue. It is a great word, whose history, I suppose, remains unwritten, because that history has yet to be enacted" (Whitman, 2000, para. 3).

Notes

1 Per conversation of authors with NAEP Survey Development Team member at ETS.
2 NAEP reports percentage of *time* for CR items as 60%; the ICCS framework reports that 90% of assessment items are multiple choice, so an exact comparison is difficult.
3 For publicly released NAEP questions, please see the NAEP Questions Tool: https://www.nationsreportcard.gov/nqt/.
4 For an example of such a task in the ISSC framework, see Schulz et al. (2023, p. 133).
5 This constrained design is consistent with simulated search tools developed in previous assessments.

References

Baldwin, J. (1985). *A talk to teachers* [Speech: transcript]. https://richgibson.com/talktoteachers.htm
Bergner, Y., & von Davier, A. A. (2018). Process data in NAEP: Past, present, and future. *Journal of Educational and Behavioral Statistics*, *44*(6), 706–732. https://doi.org/10.3102/1076998618784700
Biesta, G. J. J. (2010). *Good education in an age of measurement: Ethics, politics, democracy*. Paradigm.
Braun, H. (2013). Prospects for the future: A framework and discussion of directions for the next generation of international large-scale assessments. In M. von Davier, E. Gonzalez, I. Kirsch, & K. Yamamoto (Eds.), *The role of international large-scale assessments: Perspectives from technology, economy, and educational research* (pp. 149–160). Springer. https://doi.org/10.1007/978-94-007-4629-9_8
Carney, M. (2023, May 15). *Unlocking our future: Why we all need to learn about civics*. U.S. Chamber of Commerce Foundation. https://www.uschamberfoundation.org/civics/unlocking-our-future-why-we-all-need-learn-about-civics
Center for Civic Education (Calif.) (1994). https://www.civiced.org/resource-materials/national-standards-for-civics-and-government
Chingos, M. M. (2015). *Breaking the curve: Promises and pitfalls of using NAEP data to assess the state role in student achievement*. Urban Institute. https://www.urban.org/sites/default/files/publication/72411/2000484-breaking-the-curve-promises-and-pitfalls-of-using-naep-data-to-assess-the-state-role-in-student-achievement_1.pdf
Chudowsky, N., & Pellegrino, J. W. (2003). Large-scale assessments that support learning: What will it take? *Theory Into Practice*, *42*(1), 75–83. https://doi.org/10.1353/tip.2003.0002
Clarke, M., & Luna-Bazaldua, D. (2021). *Primer on large-scale assessments of educational achievement*. World Bank. https://doi.org/10.1596/978-1-4648-1659-8
Coiro, J., Sparks, J. R., & Kulikowich, J. M. (2018). Assessing online collaborative inquiry and social deliberation skills as learners navigate multiple sources and perspectives. In J. L. G. Braasch, I. Bråten, & M. T. McCrudden (Eds.), *Handbook of multiple source use* (pp. 485–501). Routledge. https://doi.org/10.4324/9781315627496-27
Croddy, M., & Levine, P. (2014). The C3 framework: A powerful tool for preparing future generations for informed and engaged civic life. *Social Education*, *78*(6), 282–285.
Deane, P., & Sparks, J. R. (2019). Scenario-based formative assessment of key practices in the English language arts. In H. L. Andrade, R. E. Bennett, & G. J. Cizek (Eds.), *Handbook of formative assessment in the disciplines* (pp. 68–96). Routledge. https://doi.org/10.4324/9781315166933-4
de Witt, K. (1994, November 16). Guidelines for classes on civics are issued. *The New York Times*. https://www.nytimes.com/1994/11/16/us/guidelines-for-classes-on-civics-are-issued.html
DFER Connecticut. (2022, December 7). About last night: Right to read and literacy in New Haven. *Wednesday Weekly*. https://www.dferct.org/post/ww-12-07-22
Dinkin, S. P. (2023, September 17). Declining interest in civic education hurts our democracy. *San Diego Union-Tribune*. https://www.sandiegouniontribune.com/a-path-forward/story/2023-09-17/declining-interest-in-civic-education-hurts-our-democracy
Eddy, M. (2023, October 29). A new place to learn civics: The workplace. *The New York Times*. https://www.nytimes.com/2023/10/29/world/europe/businesses-civics-education.html
Educating for American Democracy. (2021). *The roadmap to educating for American democracy*. https://www.educatingforamericandemocracy.org/the-roadmap/
Emler, T. E., Zhao, Y., Deng, J., Yin, D., & Wang, Y. (2019). Side effects of large-scale assessments in education. *ECNU Review of Education*, *2*(3), 279–296. https://doi.org/10.1177/2096531119878964

Field, K. (2022, February, 21). *Social and emotional learning is the latest flashpoint in the education wars.* Hechinger Report. https://hechingerreport.org/social-and-emotional-learning-is-the-latest-flashpoint-in-the-education-wars/

Gallos, A., Geneske, J., Ghate, D., Leighninger, M., & Vinnakota, R. (2023). *Mapping civic measurement: How are we assessing readiness and opportunities for an engaged citizenry?* Institute for Citizens & Scholars. https://citizensandscholars.org/wp-content/uploads/2023/02/Citizens-Scholars-Mapping-Civic-Measurement-1.pdf

Goldman, S. R., Britt, M. A., Brown, W., Cribb, G., George, M., Greenleaf, C., Lee, C. D., Shanahan, C., & Project READI. (2016). Disciplinary literacies and learning to read for understanding: A conceptual framework for disciplinary literacy. *Educational Psychologist, 51*(2), 219–246. https://doi.org/10.1080/00461520.2016.1168741

Goodman, M. J., Weiss, A. R., Sparks, J. R., & Dreier, K. D. (2023). *Improving the measurement of civic learning.* ETS. https://www.ets.org/pdfs/rd/improving-measurement-civic-learning.pdf

Guiton, G., & Oakes, J. (1995). Opportunity to learn and conceptions of educational equality. *Educational Evaluation and Policy Analysis, 17*(3), 323–336. https://doi.org/10.3102/01623737017003323

Hamilton, L. S., & Kaufman, J. H. (2022). Indicators of equitable civic learning in US public schools. *Educational Assessment, 27*(2), 187–196. https://doi.org/10.1080/10627197.2022.2087623

Hamilton, L. S., Kaufman, J. H., & Hu, L. (2020). *Preparing children and youth for civic life in the era of truth decay: Insights from the American Teacher Panel.* RAND. https://www.rand.org/content/dam/rand/pubs/research_reports/RRA100/RRA112-6/RAND_RRA112-6.pdf

Hamilton, L. S., & Parsi, A. (2022). *Monitoring civic learning opportunities and outcomes: Lessons from a symposium sponsored by ETS and Educating for American Democracy* (Research Notes). ETS. https://www.ets.org/Media/Research/pdf/Research_Notes_Hamilton_Parsi.pdf

Hansen, M., Levesque, E., Valant, J., & Quintero, D. (2018). *The 2018 Brown Center report on American education: How well are American students learning.* Brookings Institution.

Harkavy, I. (2006). The role of universities in advancing citizenship and social justice in the 21st century. *Education, Citizenship and Social Justice, 1*(1), 5–37. https://doi.org/10.1177/1746197906060711

Keehner, M., Gorin, J. S., Feng, G., & Katz, I. R. (2016). Developing and validating cognitive models in assessment. In A. A. Rupp and J. P. Leighton (Eds.), *The Wiley handbook of cognition and assessment: Frameworks, methodologies, and applications* (pp. 75–101). Wiley Blackwell. https://doi.org/10.1002/9781118956588.ch4

Kirsch, I., & Braun, H. (2020). Changing times, changing needs: Enhancing the utility of international large-scale assessments. *Large-Scale Assessments in Education, 8*, Article 10. https://doi.org/10.1186/s40536-020-00088-9

Kirsch, I. S., Lennon, M. L., von Davier, M., Gonzalez, E. J., & Yamamoto, K. (2013). On the growing importance of international large-scale assessments. In M. von Davier, E. Gonzalez, I. Kirsch, & K. Yamamoto (Eds.), *The role of international large-scale assessments: Perspectives from technology, economy, and educational research* (pp. 1–11). Springer. https://doi.org/10.1007/978-94-007-4629-9_1

Klein, S. P., & Hamilton, L. S. (1999). *Large-scale testing: Current practices and new directions.* RAND. https://doi.org/10.7249/IP182

Leu, D. J., Coiro, J., Kulikowich, J., & Cui, W. (2012, November 28–December 1). *Using the psychometric characteristics of multiple choice, open internet, and closed (simulated) internet formats to refine the development of online research and comprehension assessments in science: Year three of the ORCA project* [Paper presentation]. Literacy Research Association 62nd Annual Meeting.

Lewis, A., & Smith, D. (1993). Defining higher order thinking. *Theory Into Practice, 32*(3), 131–137. https://doi.org/10.1080/00405849309543588

Lo, J. C. (2021). A roadmap to E Pluribus Unum: The educating for American Democracy Project. *Social Education, 85*(3), 139–142.

Loveless, T. (2016). *The NAEP proficiency myth.* Brookings Institution. https://www.brookings.edu/articles/the-naep-proficiency-myth/

Marsal Family School of Education. (2020, April 25). *University of Michigan School of Education helps lead efforts to ensure the Right to Literacy for all children.* University of Michigan. https://marsal.umich.edu/news/university-michigan-school-education-helps-lead-efforts-ensure-right-literacy-all-children

McCluskey, N. (2023, May 3). Why lower civics and U.S. history scores? Maybe just less emphasis on testing. *CATO at Liberty.* https://www.cato.org/blog/why-lower-civics-us-history-scores-maybe-just-less-emphasis-testing

Mislevy, R. J., & Riconscente, M. M. (2011). Evidence-centered assessment design. In *Handbook of test development* (pp. 75–104). Routledge. https://padi.sri.com/downloads/TR9_ECD.pdf

Monte-Sano, C. (2012). What makes a good history essay? Assessing historical aspects of argumentative writing. *Social Education, 76*(6), 294–298. https://www.socialstudies.org/system/files/publications/articles/se_7606294.pdf

Nash, G., (1997). Reflections on the national history standards. *National Forum.* https://public.websites.umich.edu/~mlassite/discussions261/nash.html

National Academies of Sciences, Engineering, and Medicine. (2017). *Evaluation of the achievement levels for mathematics and Reading on the national assessment of educational progress.* National Academies Press. https://doi.org/10.17226/23409

National Academies of Sciences, Engineering, and Medicine. (2019). *Monitoring educational equity*. National Academies Press.

National Assessment Governing Board (NAGB). (n.d.). *Civics framework for the 2010 National Assessment of Educational Progress*. U.S. Department of Education. https://www.nagb.gov/assets/documents/publications/frameworks/civics/2010-civics-framework.doc

National Assessment Governing Board (NAGB). (1996). *National Assessment of Educational Progress (NAEP) in civics*. U.S. Department of Education. https://www.nagb.org/content/dam/nagb/en/documents/publications/frameworks/civics/2010-civics-specification.pdf

National Assessment Governing Board (NAGB). (2018). *Civics framework for the 2018 national assessment of educational progress*. U.S. Department of Education. https://www.nagb.gov/content/dam/nagb/en/documents/publications/frameworks/civics/2018-civics-framework.pdf

National Council for the Social Studies. (2013). *The college, career, & civic life (C3) framework for social studies state standards: Guidance for enhancing the rigor of K–12 civics, economics, geography, and history*.

Nation's Report Card (undated, b). *Racial-ethnic score gap tool*. Retrieved May 5, 2024. https://www.nationsreportcard.gov/dashboards/regression/default.aspx

Nation's Report Card (undated, a). *Achievement-level results*. Retrieved March 13, 2024. https://www.nationsreportcard.gov/civics/results/achievement/

Nichols, S. L., & Berliner, D. C. (2007). *Collateral damage: How high-stakes testing corrupts America's schools*. Harvard Education Press.

O'Malley, F., & Norton, S. (2022). *Maintaining the validity of the NAEP frameworks and assessments in civics and US history*. American Institutes for Research.

O'Reilly, T., Sabatini, J., Wang, Z., & Dreier, K. (2018). Using scenario-based assessments to measure deep learning. In K. Millis, D. L. Long, J. P. Magliano, & K. Wiemer (Eds.), *Deep comprehension: Multi-disciplinary approaches to understanding, enhancing, and measuring comprehension* (pp. 197–208). Routledge. https://doi.org/10.4324/9781315109503-16

Pondiscio, R. (2023, April 27). Stiff headwinds for civic education. *Flypaper*. https://fordhaminstitute.org/national/commentary/stiff-headwinds-civic-education

Riley, B., & Polikoff, M. (2021, May 28). Opinion: *The wrong roadmap for teaching American history*. Hechinger Report. https://hechingerreport.org/opinion-the-wrong-roadmap-for-teaching-american-history/

Rogers, J., Kahne, J., with Ishimoto, M., Kwako, A., Stern, S. C., Bingener, C., Raphael, L., Alkam, S., & Conde, Y. (2022). *Educating for a diverse democracy: The chilling role of political conflict in blue, purple, and red communities*. UCLA IDEA; Civic Engagement Research Group. https://idea.gseis.ucla.edu/publications/educating-for-a-diverse-democracy/publications/files/diverse-democracy-report

Schulz, W., Fraillon, J., Losito, B., Agrusti, G., Ainley, J., Damiani, V., & Friedman, T. (2023). *IEA International Civic and Citizenship Education Study 2022 assessment framework*. Springer Nature. https://doi.org/10.1007/978-3-031-20113-4

Sparks, J. R., & Deane, P. (2015). *Cognitively based assessment of research and inquiry skills: Defining a key practice in the English language arts* (Research Report No. RR-15-35). ETS. https://doi.org/10.1002/ets2.12082

Tierney, R. J., Rizvi, F., & Ercikan, K. (Eds.). (2022). *International encyclopedia of education* (4th ed.). Elsevier Science. https://shop.elsevier.com/books/international-encyclopedia-of-education/tierney/978-0-12-818629-9

Torney-Purta, J., Cabrera, J. C., Crotts Roohr, K., Liu, O. L., & Rios, J. A. (2015). *Assessing civic competency and engagement in higher education: Research background, frameworks, and directions for next-generation assessment* (Research Report No. RR-15-34). ETS. https://doi.org/10.1002/ets2.12081

Weingarten, R. (2023, May 21). *Culture wars harm education*. American Federation of Teachers. https://www.aft.org/column/culture-wars-harm-education

Weiss, A. R., Lutkus, A. D., Grigg, W. S., Niemi, R. G., with Kulick, E., Swinton, S., & Jerry, L. (2001). *The next generation of citizens: NAEP Civics Assessments, 1988 and 1998* (NCES 2001-452). U.S. Department of Education. https://www.nces.ed.gov/nationsreportcard/pdf/main1998/2001452.pdf

Whitman, W. (2000). *Prose works*. Bartleby. (Original work published 1892). https://www.bartleby.com/lit-hub/prose-works/2-democratic-vistas-paras-6089/

6
Measuring Civic and Citizenship Education Through Large-Scale Assessments
Insights from the International Civic and Citizenship Education Study (ICCS)

Wolfram Schulz and Valeria Damiani

International Large-Scale Assessments on Civic and Citizenship Education

The International Association for the Evaluation of Educational Achievement (IEA) has been conducting international large-scale assessments (ILSAs) for about 60 years and since then, these surveys have provided data and analyses to better understand the characteristics of educational systems across a wide range of countries. Data are collected with instruments developed according to conceptual frameworks grounded in educational research theory as well as scaled and analyzed using advanced psychometric methods.

Since its establishment, IEA has conducted more than 30 international comparative studies, starting with the Pilot Twelve-Country Study, implemented between 1959 and 1962 (Foshay et al., 1962). Among these surveys, civic and citizenship education (CCE) represented a field of particular relevance for the Association. This importance is well exemplified by its inclusion in the second study conducted by the IEA in the late 1960s, the Six Subject Survey, aimed at measuring civic education among other curricular areas (Science, Reading, Literature, English as a Foreign Language, French as a Foreign Language) (Walker, 1976).

The first IEA survey on civic education, carried out between 1967 and 1971 within the Six Subject Survey, presented some of the features that recurrently characterized the IEA studies in this field, namely, the need of measuring civic knowledge and attitudes, of considering the processes that occur inside and outside schools, and the status of civic education in school curricula. The dual objective of measuring both cognitive and attitudinal aspects adopted in the first Study of Civic Education and in all the following IEA studies in this field has been a distinguishing feature of CCE surveys (Torney et al., 1975).

Nearly two decades after the Six Subject Survey, the IEA decided to carry out another survey on civic education: the second IEA study on Civic Education (known as CIVED) (Amadeo et al., 2002; Torney-Purta et al., 1999; Torney-Purta et al., 2001). The theoretical model underpinning this study, called the "Octagon," reflects the complexity of the conceptualization of civic learning that underpinned CIVED and is based upon the theories of ecological development (Bronfenbrenner, 2004), situated cognition (Lave & Wenger, 1991; Wenger, 1998) and political socialization (Flanagan & Sherrod, 1998; Niemi & Hepburn, 1995). In this model, the

DOI: 10.4324/9781003476825-8
This chapter has been made available under a CC BY-NC-ND license.

student is at the center of different "nested" contexts (family, peer group, school, neighbors and broader society) and is influenced by them, considered as "agents" of socialization. The Octagon model also includes other broader factors, i.e. the society (institutions, mass media, processes and values in different domains such as economics, religion, education, politics) and national contextual factors. All these elements and contexts affect citizenship learning, which is therefore the result of students' interactions with them and not limited to school instruction. Learning about citizenship also implies the involvement of the political community, which influences the development of political understanding (Torney-Purta et al., 2001; Wenger, 1998).

The International Civic and Citizenship Education Study (ICCS) was first conducted in 2009. Since then, ICCS has become the IEA study on CCE, with a second cycle implemented in 2016 and a third cycle in 2022. In measuring how educational systems prepare young people to undertake their role as citizens, ICCS considers those developments and challenges that characterize contemporary societies that have implications for CCE. In ICCS 2009 those were related to the external threats to civil societies (e.g., terrorist attacks), international migration, new forms of participation (through, for example, non-governmental groups) and social inequalities (Schulz et al., 2008).

The study acknowledged the broadening of the traditional conceptualization of citizenship due to new interpretations of concepts and practices related to rights, responsibilities, access and belonging (Banks, 2008; White & Openshaw, 2005). As the acronym suggests, the research adopted the broader term "civic and citizenship education" (rather than civic education) and considered civic education in relation to "knowledge and understanding of formal institutions and processes of civic life (such as voting in elections). Citizenship education focuses on knowledge and understanding, as well as on opportunities for participation and engagement in both civic and civil society. It is concerned with the wider range of ways that citizens use to interact with and shape their communities (including schools) and societies" (Schulz et al., 2010, p. 22).

While ICCS had strong links to CIVED in terms of conceptual background and construct operationalization (through the inclusion of CIVED item material including cognitive and attitudinal items), it presented major differences concerning the study design and the assessment tools. In the assessment framework of the study, broader contents were included, with a stronger focus on different forms of young peoples' civic participation. Another significant change was related to the wider collection of data from larger and more representative samples of teachers in each school teaching all subjects at the target grade level – grade 8 (about 15 teachers for each sampled school) (Schulz et al., 2010).

Moreover, ICCS was (and still is) characterized by specific research instruments such as the National Context Survey (a questionnaire completed by each of the national research centers and aimed at collecting information on CCE at the country level), and regional instruments that are developed in reference to civic-related education topics deemed relevant in the context of geographic regions. In ICCS 2009 there were three regional components of the study for Europe, (East) Asia and Latin America. Regional instruments were administered to students at the target grade in participating countries from each region and the corresponding data provided a basis for the writing of additional regional reports (Fraillon et al., 2012; Kerr et al., 2010; Schulz et al., 2011). ICCS 2009 also published an encyclopedia that collected information on national curricula and policies on CCE in the countries involved in the study. The encyclopedia included chapters about most of the participating countries with information provided by center experts and aimed at describing the specific national contexts for CCE.

The second and third implementations of the study (in 2016 and in 2022) measured changes over time concerning students' civic knowledge, attitudes and engagement and at the same time investigated new emerging issues that characterize contemporary societies and were relevant for this learning area. In ICCS 2016 the new focus areas of the study comprised environmental sustainability in CCE, social interaction at school (including aspects related to bullying) and the use of new social media for civic engagement, while for the 2022 cycle of the study the new areas of assessment concerned global citizenship, sustainability, diversity, young people's views of the political system and the use of digital technologies for civic engagement (Schulz et al., 2016, 2022).

As in the first cycle, ICCS 2016 and 2022 gathered and analyzed data from students, teachers, school principals and education systems to understand how student achievement is related to the contexts where students learn about CCE (e.g., the family, peers, schools, classrooms and the local community). In addition to the civic knowledge test, the ICCS 2016 and 2022 instruments included the student questionnaire, the school and the teacher questionnaires and the National Context Survey (Schulz et al., 2018b, 2025).

The second and third cycle of ICCS also included regional student questionnaires for the European and Latin American regions; however, due to low country participation of Latin American countries, in 2022 there was only a regional report based on the European regional data (Damiani et al., 2025; Losito et al., 2018; Schulz et al., 2018).

ICCS 2009 results illustrated the heterogeneity of how civic learning is organized across education systems, and it showed great variation in civic knowledge of lower-secondary students both within and across participating countries. Majorities among young people also tended to endorse equal rights for gender groups, immigrants and members of all ethnic groups in society (Schulz et al., 2010). Results from ICCS 2016 recorded statistically significant increases in civic knowledge in many countries that participated in both cycles, as well as increases in endorsement of gender equality and equal rights for ethnic groups (Schulz et al., 2018). Both cycles highlighted associations between family background (SES, parental interest) and school-related factors (such as student report on an open classroom for discussions about political and social issues) with civic knowledge and expected civic engagement.

A publication describing influence of ICCS on practice, policy and research in participating countries and including chapters reflecting national perspectives (Malak-Minkiewicz & Torney-Purta, 2021) has highlighted some of the ways in which the study has had an impact within national contexts: participation in studies such as CIVED and ICCS provides reliable information for monitoring outcomes of civic learning over time, may serve as an opportunity to increase public interest in this area, can potentially be used to assist with the construction and implementation of in-service teacher training, and its results can be used to support student learning by focusing on specific aspects where weaknesses have been identified. Generally, CIVED and ICCS have led to the creation of a sizable research community that has contributed an impressive array of secondary research studies based on the publicly available data from IEA studies about civic learning aspects.

Framing the Assessment of ICCS 2022

As previously described, the study design of the third cycle of ICCS was consistent with previous ICCS rounds. ICCS 2022 assessed students at eighth grade, with an average age of 13.5 years or above. Grade 9 was defined as the target population only in countries where the average age of students in Grade 8 was less than 13.5 years. Following the practice of other IEA studies, in each sampled school intact classrooms were selected, and all students in a class were assessed.

Following prior ICCS cycles, ICCS 2022 surveyed all teachers teaching students in Grade 8 at each sampled school, during the testing period and employed at the school since the beginning of the school year. Fifteen teachers were randomly sampled in each participating school. In schools with less than 20 teachers, all of them were selected (Cortés & Atasever, 2024).

The instruments developed for ICCS 2022 are summarized in Table 6.1.

Table 6.1 Instruments Used in ICCS 2022

Instrument	Respondent	Purpose
International civic knowledge test	Student	Measuring students' civic knowledge and ability to analyze and reason
International student questionnaire	Student	Providing information about student background, school contexts, attitudes and engagement
Regional questionnaire	Student	Capturing students' attitudes and engagement in civic-related issues in a geographic region. Administered only to students from participating countries in the region
Teacher questionnaire	Teacher	Gauging teacher background variables, their perceptions and activities related to the context of civic and citizenship education in their schools
School questionnaire	Principal	Collecting data about school characteristics and school-level activities related to the learning area
National Contexts Survey	National Research Coordinator or designate	Gathering information about participating countries' education systems, the status of civic and citizenship education in the national curricula (including recent developments)

The measurement of student civic knowledge encompasses four content domains (civic institutions and systems; civic principles; civic participation; civic roles and identities) and two cognitive domains (knowing and reasoning; applying) related to the cognitive processes adopted by students in responding to test items. Each content domain in turn comprised subdomains, each concerning specific civic-related aspects (e.g., the content domain "civic institution and systems" has the subdomain "state institutions," related to more specific aspects such as, governments, and law enforcement bodies). The cognitive domains imply different cognitive processes (e.g., the cognitive domain "knowing" refers to processes related to defining, describing and illustrating with examples).

ICCS, in line with the other IEA studies on civic education, considered affective-behavioral aspects as a relevant outcome of students' civic learning. ICCS 2022 measures students' civic-related attitudes, views and behaviors within two affective-behavioral areas: (1) attitudes (i.e. "judgements or evaluations regarding ideas, persons, objects, events, situations and/or relationships", Schulz et al. 2022, p. 36) and (2) engagement (e.g., students' interest and ability to engage, students' expectations in their participation once they become adults, their preparedness to participate in forms of civic protest, their use of social media for civic action).

The contextual framework of ICCS 2022, as in previous ICCS studies, includes four levels: (1) the wider community, ranging from local to global levels, is related to the broader context of schools and home backgrounds; (2) school and classrooms contexts comprise factors related to the school/classroom environment and activities, teaching and the school culture and organization; (3) home and peer backgrounds include factors related to students' home background and the out-of-school environment (for example, peer-group activities); (4) the individual context refers to the individual characteristics of the student (e.g., gender).

It is important to note that the ICCS teacher questionnaire included two sections: the first collected data from all teachers teaching the target grade in sampled schools, independently from the subject taught (as the contexts of CCE cannot be limited to the teaching of the subject itself and also encompass engagement and relations at the school and classroom levels); the second (the international option) was addressed to teachers who teach CCE at the target grade level (as defined by national centers) and aimed at gathering information on the teaching of CCE (Losito et al., 2021).

Measuring Civic-Related Student Learning Outcomes and Contexts: Key Results from ICCS 2022

Students' Civic Knowledge and Citizenship Self-Efficacy

Political science research has always viewed citizens' knowledge about political institutions, processes and systems as a central measure of political sophistication (Converse, 2006; Luskin, 1987), and surveys have asked adults questions about factual political knowledge since the inception of quantitative research in this field (Berelson et al., 1954). Regular assessments of adults' political knowledge have formed part of US National Electoral Surveys (NES) (Delli Carpini & Keeter, 1993) as well as of European surveys (De Vreese & Boomgaarden, 2006). Given the aim of education systems to provide students with knowledge and understanding as a basis for their emerging roles as citizens in society, there have been a growing number of examples of national evaluations in this learning area over recent decades (Australian Curriculum, Assessment and Reporting Authority, 2020; Lutkus et al., 1999; Niemi & Junn, 1998; Torney-Purta, 2000).

The data collected in ICCS 2009 provided the initial basis for the establishment of a described ICCS civic knowledge proficiency scale, which considered the contents of test items in combination with their scaled difficulties (Schulz et al., 2013). Analysis of the item content and relative difficulty allowed the identification of common themes of content and processes to characterize ranges of civic knowledge (levels) on this scale (see a description in Schulz et al., 2025). Through the use of link items, it was possible to equate results from ICCS 2016 as well as ICCS 2022 with those from ICCS 2009 and derive comparable scale scores (where 500 reflects the ICCS 2009 average and 100 the standard deviation for equally weighted countries) that allow comparisons over time (see more details in Schulz & Macaskill, 2024).

The concept of self-efficacy constitutes an important element of Bandura's social cognitive theory about the learning process, in which learners direct their own learning (Bandura, 1997). Bandura (1986, p. 391) suggests that individuals' "judgments of their capabilities to organize and execute courses of action required to attain designated types of performances" denote self-efficacy. Within the context of civic learning, students' sense of citizenship self-efficacy may be considered an essential part of personal engagement with political and social issues. Being an active and engaged citizen requires not only knowledge but also confidence in applying it in order to participate in society.

ICCS defined students' sense of citizenship self-efficacy as their self-confidence in undertaking specific behaviors in the area of civic participation and measured it using questions where students were asked to rate their ability ("very well", "quite well", "not so well" or "not at all well") to undertake different tasks. The resulting scale had an average reliability[1] of 0.87 across participating countries and was equated so that scores were comparable across all three cycles on a metric where 50 reflects the average and 10 the standard deviation of equally weighted countries in ICCS 2009 (see further details in Schulz & Friedman, 2024).

Table 6.2 shows national and average results for students' civic knowledge and citizenship self-efficacy across the three cycles (2009, 2016, 2022) as well as the correlations between the two scales.[2] Brazil and Denmark did not meet the IEA sampling participation requirements, and their results are reported separately from those for other countries as well as those from the two German benchmarking participants (North Rhine-Westphalia and Schleswig-Holstein). Countries that did participate in previous cycles but not in 2022 are not included in this table.

Civic knowledge results varied considerably across countries, with Chinese Taipei, Sweden and Poland having average results of more than 50 points (roughly equivalent to half a standard deviation) above the ICCS 2022 average, and Bulgaria and Colombia recording results that were more than 50 points below. When comparing results across the three ICCS cycles, there

Table 6.2 Average Scores of Students' Civic Knowledge and Citizenship Self-Efficacy 2009–2022

Country	Civic Knowledge			Citizenship Self-Efficacy			Correlation Between Scales in 2022
	2022	2016	2009	2022	2016	2009	
Chinese Taipei	583 (2.3)	581 (3.0)	◄ 559 (2.4)	54 (0.2)	52 (0.2) ◄	48 (0.2)	−0.08 (0.02)
Sweden¹	565 (3.5) ▷	579 (2.8)	◄ 537 (3.1)	51 (0.3)	52 (0.2)	49 (0.3)	0.08 (0.03)
Poland	554 (2.5)	–	–	51 (0.2)	–	51 (0.2)	0.17 (0.02)
Estonia	545 (5.5)	546 (3.1)	◄ 525 (4.5)	49 (0.3)	49 (0.2)	48 (0.2)	0.18 (0.02)
Croatia¹	531 (2.6)	531 (2.5)	–	52 (0.2)	54 (0.2) ▷	–	0.23 (0.02)
Norway (9)¹	529 (2.8) ▷	564 (2.2)	◄ 538 (4.0)	50 (0.2)	51 (0.2)	49 (0.3)	0.13 (0.02)
Italy	523 (3.6)	524 (2.4)	◄ 531 (3.3)	52 (0.2)	52 (0.2) ◄	51 (0.3)	0.20 (0.02)
Spain	510 (3.3)	–	–	51 (0.2)	–	49 (0.2)	0.07 (0.02)
Lithuania	509 (4.0)	518 (3.0)	◄ 505 (2.8)	50 (0.2)	51 (0.2) ▷	50 (0.2)	0.06 (0.02)
Netherlands†	508 (4.1) ▷	523 (4.5)	–	48 (0.3)	48 (0.2)	–	0.05 (0.03)
France	508 (3.3)	–	–	49 (0.2)	–	–	0.11 (0.02)
Slovenia	504 (2.3) ▷	532 (2.5)	◄ 516 (2.7)	50 (0.2)	50 (0.2)	50 (0.3)	0.10 (0.02)
Slovak Republic	501 (3.3)	–	–	48 (0.2)	–	48 (0.2)	0.04 (0.02)
Latvia¹	490 (2.8)	492 (3.1)	◄ 482 (4.0)	49 (0.3)	48 (0.2) ◄	49 (0.2) ▷	0.11 (0.02)
Malta	490 (7.4)	491 (2.7)	◄ 490 (4.5)	50 (0.4)	50 (0.2)	47 (0.3)	0.05 (0.02)
Romania	470 (9.1)	–	–	54 (0.4)	–	–	0.09 (0.03)
Serbia	464 (3.4)	–	–	49 (0.4)	–	–	0.10 (0.02)
Cyprus	459 (2.5)	–	–	53 (0.3)	–	51 (0.3)	0.19 (0.02)
Bulgaria	456 (4.6) ▷	485 (5.3)	◄ 466 (5.0)	52 (0.3)	52 (0.3)	50 (0.3)	0.12 (0.02)
Colombia	452 (3.8) ▷	482 (3.4)	◄ 462 (2.9)	51 (0.3)	53 (0.2) ◄	53 (0.3)	−0.05 (0.02)
Average ICCS 2022	508 (0.9)	–	–	51 (0.1)	51 (0.1)	–	0.10 (0.01)

(Continued)

Table 6.2 Average Scores of Students' Civic Knowledge and Citizenship Self-Efficacy 2009–2022 (Continued)

Country	Civic Knowledge						Citizenship Self-Efficacy						Correlation Between Scales in 2022	
	2022		2016		2009		2022		2016		2009			
Average common countries ICCS 2009–2022	516	(1.0)	541	(0.7) ▽	520	(0.6) ▲	51	(0.1)	51	(0.0)	50	(0.1)	**0.07**	(0.01)
Countries not meeting sample participation requirements														
Brazil	457	(3.3)	–		–		55	(0.2)	–		–		0.01	(0.02)
Denmark	556	(3.5)	–		–		50	(0.2)	–		–		**0.19**	(0.02)
German benchmarking participant meeting sample participation requirements														
North Rhine-Westphalia	524	(2.6)	–		–		49	(0.2)	–		–		**0.18**	(0.02)
German benchmarking participant not meeting sample participation requirements														
Schleswig-Holstein	544	(4.4)	–		–		49	(0.3)	–		–		0.07	(0.04)

In comparison with the previous survey national results were:
Significantly (p < 0.05) higher ▲
Significantly (p < 0.05) lower ▽
( ) Standard errors appear in parentheses. Statistically significant correlation coefficients (p < 0.05) are displayed in bold.
(9) Country deviated from international defined population and surveyed adjacent upper grade.
– No comparable data available.
† Nearly met guidelines for sampling participation rates only after replacement schools were included.
[1] National Defined Population covers 90%–95% of National Target Population.

were statistically significant increases between 2009 and 2016 in 9 out of 11 countries with comparable data, on average across countries participating in all three cycles of 21 score points. However, between 2016 and 2022 students' civic knowledge decreased significantly in 6 out of 13 countries with comparable data, and on average for countries participating all three cycles there was a decrease of 25 score points.

Results for students' citizenship self-efficacy showed somewhat less variation across countries compared to that for civic knowledge: the highest averages in Chinese Taipei and Romania (both 54 score points) were about three points (roughly equivalent to a third of a standard deviation) higher than the ICCS 2022 average, while the lowest averages in the Netherlands and Slovak Republic (both 48) were about three points below. While between 2009 and 2016 in most countries there were statistically significant increases (in 9 out of 11 countries with comparable data) and a decrease in one country, between 2016 and 2022 there were three significant increases and three significant decreases in scale score averages. In six of the nine ICCS 2016 countries with statistically significant increases in civic knowledge there were also significant increases in scale score averages for citizenship self-efficacy. However, there was no association between changes in civic knowledge and those in citizenship self-efficacy between 2016 and 2022.

Table 6.2 also illustrates the correlations (Pearson's r) between civic knowledge and citizenship self-efficacy at the level of students within each participating country. Weak but statistically significant positive correlations were found in 16 out of 20 ICCS 2022 countries as well as in the German state of North Rhine-Westphalia, however, also (weak) significant negative correlations were found in Chinese Taipei and Colombia. At the level of countries, we also did not find any clear association between the levels of civic knowledge and citizenship self-efficacy.

To review associations with other variables, civic knowledge and citizenship self-efficacy scores were correlated with the following background indicators:

- Gender (female =1, male = 0);
- Socio-economic background derived as nationally z-standardized composite index (averages of 0 and standard deviations of 1 within each participating country) based on highest parental occupation, highest parental educational attainment and the number of books at home;
- Students' perceptions of an open classroom climate for discussion (IRT scale, nationally standardized scores).

Table 6.3 illustrates the associations of students' civic knowledge and citizenship self-efficacy with these three variables. The highest correlations were observed for civic knowledge and socio-economic background, and in all countries students who perceived an open classroom climate for civic-related discussion tended to have higher civic knowledge scores. Further, statistically significant albeit relatively weak correlations with (female) gender were apparent in almost all countries. While associations between (female) gender and citizenship self-efficacy tended to be inconsistent across countries, there were consistently positive and significant correlations between perceptions of an open classroom climate and students' citizenship self-efficacy.

Students' Perceptions of and Engagement in Environmental Sustainability

This section presents selected key findings regarding the ICCS 2022 focus area *sustainability*. To illustrate findings from ICCS 2022, we selected one scale reflecting attitudes and another

Table 6.3 Correlations of Students' Civic Knowledge and Citizenship Self-Efficacy with Female Gender, Socio-Economic Background and Perceptions of an Open Classroom Climate for Civic-Related Discussions

Country	Correlation of Civic Knowledge with...						Correlation of Citizenship Self-Efficacy with...					
	Gender (Female)		Socio-Economic Background		Open Classroom Climate		Gender (Female)		Socio-Economic Background		Open Classroom Climate	
Bulgaria	**0.18**	(0.03)	**0.48**	(0.02)	**0.29**	(0.02)	**0.05**	(0.02)	**0.07**	(0.02)	**0.15**	(0.03)
Chinese Taipei	**0.12**	(0.02)	**0.36**	(0.02)	**0.21**	(0.02)	**−0.08**	(0.02)	0.02	(0.02)	**0.18**	(0.02)
Colombia	0.04	(0.03)	**0.30**	(0.03)	**0.26**	(0.03)	0.01	(0.02)	**0.06**	(0.02)	**0.15**	(0.02)
Croatia[1]	**0.19**	(0.03)	**0.34**	(0.02)	**0.26**	(0.03)	**0.09**	(0.02)	**0.11**	(0.02)	**0.21**	(0.03)
Cyprus	**0.17**	(0.02)	**0.42**	(0.02)	**0.20**	(0.02)	**0.06**	(0.02)	**0.08**	(0.02)	**0.21**	(0.03)
Estonia	**0.13**	(0.02)	**0.38**	(0.03)	**0.21**	(0.02)	−0.01	(0.02)	**0.13**	(0.02)	**0.20**	(0.02)
France	**0.07**	(0.02)	**0.43**	(0.02)	**0.20**	(0.02)	**−0.11**	(0.02)	**0.08**	(0.02)	**0.14**	(0.02)
Italy	**0.15**	(0.02)	**0.39**	(0.02)	**0.25**	(0.03)	**0.07**	(0.02)	**0.17**	(0.02)	**0.21**	(0.02)
Latvia[1]	**0.19**	(0.02)	**0.38**	(0.02)	**0.26**	(0.02)	0.02	(0.02)	**0.12**	(0.02)	**0.13**	(0.03)
Lithuania	**0.18**	(0.02)	**0.46**	(0.03)	**0.11**	(0.03)	0.02	(0.02)	**0.08**	(0.02)	**0.14**	(0.03)
Malta	**0.13**	(0.04)	**0.38**	(0.03)	**0.27**	(0.02)	−0.02	(0.01)	**0.05**	(0.02)	**0.17**	(0.03)
Netherlands†	0.05	(0.03)	**0.39**	(0.03)	**0.28**	(0.03)	−0.04	(0.02)	**0.05**	(0.02)	**0.18**	(0.03)
Norway (9)[1]	**0.17**	(0.02)	**0.40**	(0.01)	**0.26**	(0.02)	−0.03	(0.01)	**0.12**	(0.02)	**0.14**	(0.02)
Poland	**0.14**	(0.02)	**0.42**	(0.02)	**0.23**	(0.02)	**0.09**	(0.02)	**0.13**	(0.02)	**0.20**	(0.02)
Romania	**0.17**	(0.02)	**0.40**	(0.05)	**0.14**	(0.03)	**0.13**	(0.02)	**0.08**	(0.03)	**0.10**	(0.05)
Serbia	**0.14**	(0.02)	**0.40**	(0.02)	**0.23**	(0.03)	**0.06**	(0.02)	0.04	(0.02)	**0.18**	(0.02)
Slovak Republic	**0.10**	(0.02)	**0.55**	(0.02)	**0.20**	(0.02)	−0.02	(0.02)	0.04	(0.02)	**0.14**	(0.03)
Slovenia	**0.17**	(0.02)	**0.35**	(0.02)	**0.24**	(0.02)	−0.02	(0.02)	**0.06**	(0.02)	**0.15**	(0.02)
Spain	**0.09**	(0.02)	**0.36**	(0.02)	**0.21**	(0.02)	0.03	(0.02)	**0.06**	(0.02)	**0.12**	(0.02)
Sweden[1]	**0.17**	(0.02)	**0.43**	(0.02)	**0.18**	(0.03)	**−0.05**	(0.02)	**0.07**	(0.02)	**0.17**	(0.02)
Average ICCS 2022	**0.14**	(0.01)	**0.40**	(0.01)	**0.22**	(0.01)	0.01	(0.00)	**0.08**	(0.00)	**0.16**	(0.01)
Countries not meeting sample participation requirements												
Brazil	**0.11**	(0.02)	**0.41**	(0.02)	**0.28**	(0.03)	0.00	(0.02)	**0.06**	(0.02)	**0.14**	(0.02)
Denmark	**0.16**	(0.02)	**0.33**	(0.02)	**0.32**	(0.02)	0.02	(0.02)	**0.16**	(0.02)	**0.22**	(0.02)
German benchmarking participant meeting sample participation requirements												
North Rhine-Westphalia	0.01	(0.02)	**0.43**	(0.02)	**0.22**	(0.03)	0.00	(0.02)	**0.11**	(0.02)	**0.21**	(0.03)
German benchmarking participant not meeting sample participation requirements												
Schleswig-Holstein	0.03	(0.04)	**0.40**	(0.03)	**0.19**	(0.03)	0.02	(0.04)	**0.08**	(0.03)	**0.19**	(0.04)

() Standard errors appear in parentheses. Statistically significant correlation coefficients (p < 0.05) are displayed in **bold**.
(9) Country deviated from international defined population and surveyed adjacent upper grade
† Nearly met guidelines for sampling participation rates only after replacement schools were included.
[1] National Defined Population covers 90%–95% of National Target Population.

one reflecting expected engagement.³ The following two scales were chosen as related to environmental sustainability:

- *Students' positive attitudes toward environmental protection*: Students rated their agreement ("strongly agree", "agree", "disagree", "strongly disagree") with five statements regarding environmental protection: "[Country]⁴ should contribute to protecting the environment in other countries" (average percentage of students strongly agreeing or agreeing: 73%); "governments should focus more on protecting the environment than on supporting economic growth" (79%); "every citizen needs to contribute to the reduction of pollution" (90%); "all human beings should take responsibility for preserving the natural world" (90%); and "countries need to work together to preserve the world's natural resources" (92%). Positive scores reflected student endorsement of environmental protection, and the scale had an average reliability of 0.77 across countries.
- *Students' expected participation in environmental protection activities*: Students rated their expectations ("I would certainly do this", "I would probably do this", "I would probably not do this", "I would certainly not do this") to participate in the following activities to protect the environment: "Refuse to buy products that are harmful for the environment" (average percentage of students expecting to certainly or probably participate: 66%); "tell someone to stop causing damage to the environment" (72%); "participate in an organized protest to demand more action to protect our environment" (57%); and "encourage other people to make personal efforts to help the environment (e.g., through saving water)" (72%). Positive scale scores indicated higher expectations to participate in environmental protection activities, and the scale had an average reliability of 0.83 across countries.

The results for students' attitudes toward environmental protection show some variation in scale score averages across countries, ranging from 53 score points (about one-third of standard deviation above the ICCS 2022 average) in Chinese Taipei, France and Spain to 47 (about one-third of a standard deviation below average) in Latvia, the Netherlands, Poland and the Slovak Republic (Table 6.4). Similar ranges across national scale score averages were apparent for students' expected participation in environmental protection activities that ranged from 54 score points in Colombia and Romania to 44 in the Netherlands. The fact that all national averages for both scales appear on the lighter colored background indicates that on average students tended to express agreement with the statements measuring attitudes toward environmental protection, or that they indicated an expected participation in activities to protect the environment.⁵

In all countries there were moderately high (and statistically significant) positive correlations between the two scales (0.41 on average). When reviewing the association at the level of countries, national averages for the two scales were correlated at 0.52, indicating that in countries where students expressed more positive attitudes toward environmental protection there were also higher levels of expectations to participate in environmental protection activities.

Table 6.5 presents the average scale scores of students' positive attitudes toward environmental protection and expected participation in environmental protection activities by levels of their civic knowledge. Gray bars indicate the size of statistically significant differences in favor of students with civic knowledge at level B or above,⁶ while black bars record significant differences in favor of those with civic knowledge below level B. Bars displayed in white depict differences that were not statistically significant.

The results suggest that students with higher levels of civic knowledge (level B or above) tended to have more positive attitudes toward environmental protection and were also more

Table 6.4 Average Scale Scores for Students' Positive Attitudes Toward Environmental Protection and Expected Participation in Environmental Protection Activities

Country	Positive attitudes toward environmental protection – Average scores in 2022	Expected participation in environmental protection activities – Average scores in 2022	Correlation between scales
Bulgaria	49 (0.3) ▽	50 (0.2)	**0.38** (0.02)
Chinese Taipei	53 (0.2) ▲	53 (0.2) △	**0.37** (0.02)
Colombia	52 (0.3) △	54 (0.3) ▲	**0.35** (0.02)
Croatia[1]	51 (0.2) △	51 (0.2)	**0.42** (0.02)
Cyprus	50 (0.3)	51 (0.3) △	**0.39** (0.02)
Estonia	49 (0.3) ▽	47 (0.3) ▼	**0.40** (0.02)
France	53 (0.2) ▲	51 (0.2) △	**0.40** (0.02)
Italy	52 (0.2) △	53 (0.2) △	**0.43** (0.02)
Latvia[1]	47 (0.2) ▽	46 (0.3) ▼	**0.39** (0.02)
Lithuania	50 (0.2)	51 (0.2) △	**0.41** (0.02)
Malta	51 (0.5) △	50 (0.3)	**0.37** (0.04)
Netherlands†	47 (0.3) ▼	44 (0.3) ▼	**0.45** (0.02)
Norway (9)[1]	50 (0.2)	46 (0.2) ▼	**0.45** (0.02)
Poland	47 (0.2) ▽	51 (0.2) △	**0.47** (0.02)
Romania	49 (0.3) ▽	54 (0.3) ▲	**0.38** (0.02)
Serbia	50 (0.3)	50 (0.3)	**0.38** (0.02)
Slovak Republic	47 (0.2) ▼	51 (0.3) △	**0.42** (0.02)
Slovenia	49 (0.2) ▽	49 (0.2) ▽	**0.38** (0.02)
Spain	53 (0.2) △	52 (0.2) △	**0.40** (0.02)
Sweden[1]	50 (0.2)	47 (0.2) ▽	**0.48** (0.02)
ICCS 2022 average	50 (0.1)	50 (0.1)	**0.41** (0.00)
Countries not meeting sample participation requirements			
Brazil	53 (0.2)	53 (0.2)	**0.37** (0.02)
Denmark	48 (0.2)	47 (0.2)	**0.49** (0.02)
German benchmarking participant meeting sample participation requirements			
North Rhine-Westphalia	48 (0.2) ▽	47 (0.3) △	**0.43** (0.02)
German benchmarking participant not meeting sample participation requirements			
Schleswig-Holstein	49 (0.3)	48 (0.3)	**0.46** (0.02)

National ICCS 2022 results
More than 3 score points above ICCS 2022 average ▲
Significantly above ICCS 2022 average △
Significantly below ICCS 2022 average ▽
More than 3 score points below ICCS 2022 average ▼

Average score for expected legal activities +/- confidence interval
Average score for expected illegal activities +/- confidence interval

On average across items, students with a score in the range with this color have more than 50% probability to indicate:
Disagreement or expected non-participation
Agreement or expected participation

Notes:
() Standard errors appear in parentheses. Statistically significant correlation coefficients (p < 0.05) are displayed in **bold**.
(9) Country deviated from international defined population and surveyed adjacent upper grade.
† Nearly met guidelines for sampling participation rates only after replacement schools were included.
[1] National defined population covers 90% to 95% of national target population

likely to expect engagement in activities to protect the environment. On average across ICCS 2022 countries, for both scales there was a score point difference of about three points (equivalent to about one-third of standard deviation for each scale) between students with civic knowledge below or at or above level B.

Young People's Views of the Political System

This section presents selected key findings regarding the ICCS 2022 focus area *young people's view of political systems*. As in the previous section, we selected one scale reflecting attitudes

Table 6.5 Average Scores for Students' Positive Attitudes toward Environmental Protection and Expected Participation in Environmental Protection Activities by Their Level of Civic Knowledge

Country	Positive attitudes toward environmental protection			Expected participation in environmental protection activities		
	Civic knowledge below Level B (below 479)		Civic knowledge at or above Level B (479 and above)	Civic knowledge below Level B (below 479)		Civic knowledge at or above Level B (479 and above)
Bulgaria	47 (0.3)		**51** (0.3)	48 (0.3)		**52** (0.3)
Chinese Taipei	51 (0.8)		**54** (0.2)	52 (0.8)		53 (0.2)
Colombia	51 (0.4)		**54** (0.3)	52 (0.3)		**56** (0.3)
Croatia[1]	50 (0.4)		**52** (0.3)	50 (0.5)		51 (0.2)
Cyprus	48 (0.4)		**53** (0.3)	49 (0.3)		**53** (0.4)
Estonia	46 (0.5)		**50** (0.3)	44 (0.4)		**48** (0.3)
France	52 (0.5)		**54** (0.3)	48 (0.4)		**52** (0.3)
Italy	50 (0.4)		**53** (0.2)	50 (0.5)		**54** (0.3)
Latvia[1]	45 (0.3)		**48** (0.3)	44 (0.4)		**48** (0.3)
Lithuania	48 (0.4)		**52** (0.2)	48 (0.4)		**52** (0.3)
Malta	49 (0.9)		**53** (0.2)	48 (0.5)		**52** (0.3)
Netherlands†	44 (0.6)		**48** (0.3)	42 (0.4)		**45** (0.3)
Norway (9)[1]	47 (0.5)		**51** (0.2)	45 (0.4)		46 (0.2)
Poland	46 (0.4)		**48** (0.2)	50 (0.4)		**52** (0.2)
Romania	47 (0.4)		**51** (0.4)	53 (0.4)		**56** (0.4)
Serbia	50 (0.4)		**52** (0.4)	49 (0.4)		**52** (0.3)
Slovak Republic	45 (0.3)		**48** (0.3)	49 (0.4)		**52** (0.3)
Slovenia	47 (0.3)		**50** (0.2)	47 (0.4)		**50** (0.2)
Spain	51 (0.5)		**54** (0.2)	50 (0.4)		**53** (0.2)
Sweden[1]	47 (0.8)		**51** (0.2)	46 (0.6)		47 (0.2)
ICCS 2022 average	48 (0.1)		**51** (0.1)	48 (0.1)		**51** (0.1)
Countries not meeting sample participation requirements						
Brazil	51 (0.3)		**55** (0.3)	51 (0.3)		**54** (0.3)
Denmark	45 (0.4)		**49** (0.2)	45 (0.4)		**47** (0.2)
German benchmarking participant meeting sample participation requirements						
North Rhine-Westphalia	46 (0.4)		**49** (0.3)	46 (0.4)		47 (0.3)
German benchmarking participant not meeting sample participation requirements						
Schleswig-Holstein	46 (0.7)		**50** (0.4)	46 (0.7)		**48** (0.4)

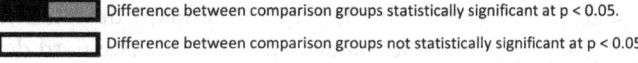

■ Difference between comparison groups statistically significant at p < 0.05.
□ Difference between comparison groups not statistically significant at p < 0.05.

Notes:

Score averages which are Significantly larger (p < 0.05) than those in the comparison group are displayed in bold.

(9) Country deviated from international defined population and surveyed adjacent upper grade.

† Nearly met guidelines for sampling paticipation rates only after replacement schools were included.

[1] National defined population covers 90% to 95% of national target population

and another one reflecting expected engagement. The following two scales were chosen as related to young people's views of the political system:

Students' satisfaction with the political system: Students rated their agreement ("strongly agree", "agree", "disagree", "strongly disagree") with the following four statements about the political system of their country of residence: "The political system of [country of test] works well" (average percentage of students strongly agreeing or agreeing: 55%); "members of [parliament/congress] are good at representing the interests of young people" (44%); "members of [parliament/congress] generally represent the interests of people in their country well" (55%); and "members of [parliament/congress] treat all people in society fairly" (45%). Positive scale scores reflected student satisfaction with their political system, and the scale had an average reliability of 0.78 across countries.

Students' expected active political participation: Students rated their expectations ("I would certainly do this", "I would probably do this", "I would probably not do this", "I would certainly not do this") to participate in the following active political activities: "join a political party" (25%), "join a trade union" (27%), "stand as a candidate in local elections" (24%) and "join an organization for a political or social cause" (31%). Positive scale scores indicated higher expectations to become actively involved in politics, and the scale had an average reliability of 0.86 across countries.

Table 6.6 shows the average scale scores for students' satisfaction with their political system and expected active political participation. There was considerable variation across countries in students' satisfaction with their political system, ranging from 57 score points (more than two-thirds of a standard deviation above the ICCS 2022 average) in Norway, followed by also relatively high averages in Chinese Taipei (55), Sweden (54) and the Netherlands (53) to 45 in the Slovak Republic, with also relatively low averages recorded for Croatia, Poland and Romania (46, more than a third of a standard deviation below the ICCS 2022 average). There was somewhat less variation across countries for scale scores reflecting expected active political participation: the highest scale scores were observed in Colombia (53 score points), and the lowest in Serbia (46). All national averages for expected active political participation are located on a darker colored background, indicating that on average students did not expect to undertake these activities.

There were consistently significant positive correlations between students' perceptions of the political system and their expectations to become actively involved in politics (0.38 on average across countries). However, there was no association at the level of countries between national averages for the two scales with a correlation coefficient of −0.02. This suggests that higher levels of satisfaction with the political system in a country are not associated with higher levels of expected active political engagement.

When analyzing the average scores for both scales across levels of civic knowledge (below level B vs. at or above level B), results show significant differences in most countries (Table 6.7). On average, students with a higher level of civic knowledge had about three points lower scale scores (about one-third of a standard deviation) for satisfaction with the political system and two points (about one-fifth of a standard deviation) for expected active political participation. For students' satisfaction with the political system, there were also significantly albeit only slightly higher scales scores among student with higher levels of civic knowledge in the Netherlands and Norway, two countries where we also found the highest proportions of students expressing satisfaction with their political system.

These results suggest that students with higher levels of civic knowledge tend to be more informed and also more critical about shortcomings in their political systems and institutions, which make them less inclined to express higher levels of satisfaction and also less inclined to expect conventional political participation (see Schulz, 2024). It is likely that these findings are related to young people's trust in civic institutions. Research has shown trust to be negatively

Table 6.6 Average Scale Scores for Students' Satisfaction with the Political System and Expected Active Political Participation

Country	Satisfaction with the political system — Average scores in 2022	Expected active political participation — Average scores in 2022	Correlation between scales
Bulgaria	47 (0.4) ▽	50 (0.3) △	**0.37** (0.02)
Chinese Taipei	55 (0.2) ▲	50 (0.2)	**0.41** (0.02)
Colombia	52 (0.4) △	53 (0.3) ▲	**0.38** (0.02)
Croatia[1]	46 (0.2) ▼	47 (0.2) ▽	**0.34** (0.02)
Cyprus	48 (0.2) ▽	51 (0.3) △	**0.39** (0.02)
Estonia	52 (0.2) △	48 (0.2) ▽	**0.40** (0.03)
France	51 (0.2) △	52 (0.2) △	**0.34** (0.02)
Italy	49 (0.2) ▽	51 (0.2) △	**0.44** (0.03)
Latvia[1]	48 (0.2) ▽	49 (0.2) ▽	**0.35** (0.03)
Lithuania	49 (0.2) ▽	50 (0.2) △	**0.33** (0.02)
Malta	52 (0.4) △	50 (0.2)	**0.43** (0.02)
Netherlands†	53 (0.3) ▲	47 (0.2) ▽	**0.33** (0.03)
Norway (9)[1]	57 (0.2) ▲	49 (0.2) ▽	**0.40** (0.02)
Poland	46 (0.2) ▼	49 (0.1) ▽	**0.36** (0.02)
Romania	46 (0.5) ▼	52 (0.5) △	**0.44** (0.03)
Serbia	50 (0.3)	46 (0.3) ▼	**0.35** (0.02)
Slovak Republic	45 (0.3) ▼	48 (0.3) ▽	**0.31** (0.02)
Slovenia	50 (0.2)	49 (0.2) ▽	**0.42** (0.02)
Spain	50 (0.2)	51 (0.2) △	**0.41** (0.02)
Sweden[1]	54 (0.3) ▲	50 (0.2) △	**0.36** (0.02)
ICCS 2022 average	50 (0.1)	50 (0.1)	**0.38** (0.01)
Countries not meeting sample participation requirements			
Brazil	50 (0.2)	53 (0.2)	**0.41** (0.02)
Denmark	54 (0.2)	50 (0.2)	**0.38** (0.02)
German benchmarking participant meeting sample participation requirements			
North Rhine-Westphalia	53 (0.2) △	49 (0.2) △	**0.35** (0.02)
German benchmarking participant not meeting sample participation requirements			
Schleswig-Holstein	52 (0.3)	49 (0.3)	**0.38** (0.03)

National ICCS 2022 results
More than 3 score points above ICCS 2022 average ▲
Significantly above ICCS 2022 average △
Significantly below ICCS 2022 average ▽
More than 3 score points below ICCS 2022 average ▼

Average score for expected legal activities +/- confidence interval
Average score for expected illegal activities +/- confidence interval

On average across items, students with a score in the range with this color have more than 50% probablity to indicate:
Disagreement or expected non-participation
Agreement or expected participation

Notes:
() Standard errors appear in parentheses. Statistically significant correlation coefficients (p < 0.05) are displayed in **bold**.
(9) Country deviated from international defined population and surveyed adjacent upper grade.
† Nearly met guidelines for sampling paticipation rates only after replacement schools were included.
[1] National defined population covers 90% to 95% of national target population

correlated with civic knowledge in countries with higher indices of perceived corruption, while in countries with higher levels of transparency more knowledgeable students expressed more trust in their institutions (Lauglo, 2013). The observation that more knowledgeable young people are less likely to consider traditional channels of engagement, which continue to be fundamental in a democracy, is quite concerning, especially in societies where trust in institutions has been eroded by perceptions of dysfunctionality.

School and Classroom Contexts

To fully evaluate CCE, it is important to not only look at cognitive and affective-behavioral learning outcomes but also to consider the contexts in which civic learning takes place.

Table 6.7 Average Scores for Students' Satisfaction with the Political System and Expected Active Political Participation by Their Level of Civic Knowledge

Country	Satisfaction with the political system		Expected active political participation	
	Civic knowledge below Level B (below 479)	Civic knowledge at or above Level B (479 and above)	Civic knowledge below Level B (below 479)	Civic knowledge at or above Level B (479 and above)
Bulgaria	**50** (0.6)	43 (0.3)	**53** (0.4)	47 (0.3)
Chinese Taipei	**58** (0.7)	54 (0.2)	54 (0.8)	49 (0.2)
Colombia	**55** (0.4)	47 (0.4)	**56** (0.3)	50 (0.3)
Croatia[1]	**48** (0.5)	46 (0.2)	48 (0.5)	47 (0.3)
Cyprus	49 (0.4)	47 (0.4)	**52** (0.3)	50 (0.4)
Estonia	52 (0.4)	51 (0.2)	49 (0.4)	48 (0.2)
France	52 (0.4)	50 (0.3)	52 (0.4)	52 (0.2)
Italy	**53** (0.5)	47 (0.3)	51 (0.4)	51 (0.3)
Latvia[1]	48 (0.3)	48 (0.3)	50 (0.4)	48 (0.3)
Lithuania	**51** (0.4)	48 (0.3)	**52** (0.3)	49 (0.2)
Malta	**54** (0.5)	50 (0.5)	52 (0.4)	48 (0.3)
Netherlands†	52 (0.5)	54 (0.3)	48 (0.4)	46 (0.3)
Norway (9)[1]	56 (0.3)	57 (0.2)	**51** (0.5)	48 (0.2)
Poland	**49** (0.5)	45 (0.2)	51 (0.4)	49 (0.2)
Romania	**49** (0.6)	44 (0.5)	**54** (0.4)	50 (0.5)
Serbia	**51** (0.4)	48 (0.4)	**48** (0.4)	45 (0.4)
Slovak Republic	**48** (0.5)	44 (0.3)	**51** (0.5)	46 (0.3)
Slovenia	**51** (0.4)	49 (0.3)	**51** (0.4)	48 (0.3)
Spain	**52** (0.4)	49 (0.2)	52 (0.4)	50 (0.3)
Sweden[1]	53 (0.7)	54 (0.2)	52 (0.6)	50 (0.2)
ICCS 2022 average	**52** (0.1)	49 (0.1)	**51** (0.1)	49 (0.1)
Countries not meeting sample participation requirements				
Brazil	**53** (0.3)	47 (0.4)	**56** (0.3)	50 (0.3)
Denmark	53 (0.5)	55 (0.2)	51 (0.4)	50 (0.2)
German benchmarking participant meeting sample participation requirements				
North Rhine-Westphalia	54 (0.3)	53 (0.2)	50 (0.4)	48 (0.3)
German benchmarking participant not meeting sample participation requirements				
Schleswig-Holstein	53 (0.5)	52 (0.3)	51 (0.8)	48 (0.3)

Difference between comparison groups statistically significant at p < 0.05.
Difference between comparison groups not statistically significant at p < 0.05.

Notes:
Score averages which are Significantly larger (p < 0.05) than those in the comparison group are displayed in bold.
(9) Country deviated from international defined population and surveyed adjacent upper grade.
† Nearly met guidelines for sampling paticipation rates only after replacement schools were included.
[1] National defined population covers 90% to 95% of national target population

While there is ample evidence about the influence of home background factors such as socio-economic status (especially on cognitive learning outcomes), schools and classrooms are contexts in which both formal (such as aspects embedded in the curriculum) and informal (such as aspects related to civic experiences at school) learning as well as political socialization takes place. Research has further highlighted the importance of providing "democratic learning environments" during school education so that students may practice a democratic lifestyle, influence what happens at school and develop a sense of their ability to influence their community (Mosher et al., 1994; Pasek et al., 2008).

To look at school contexts for students' perceptions of environmental sustainability and their political system, Table 6.8 displays the percentages of students at schools where principals viewed promoting respect for and safeguard of the environment and promoting knowledge about social, political and civic institutions as the most important aims of CCE.[7] On average more than a third of principals (36%) viewed promoting learning about environment protection, and about a quarter (26%) learning about social, political and civic institutions as among the most important goals. However, there was considerable variation across countries, and in some countries learning about institutions was rated as more important than learning about environmental protection (as for example, in Estonia, France and Norway).

We also reviewed the percentages of students at schools where principals reported that most, nearly all or all students participated in activities related to environmental sustainability, and in visits to political institutions.[8] While participation in environment-related activities was reportedly quite widespread across countries with more than two-thirds of students (68%) enrolled at schools where this is common (ranging from 36% in the Netherlands to 95% in Poland), visiting political institutions appeared less common, with fewer than one-fifth of students enrolled at schools where this was reported as frequent (ranging from 4% to 44%). It is important to note that activities such as visits to institutions may be constrained through factors like school location and resources.

Table 6.8 further displays the percentages of students who reported to have learned to a large or moderate extent about how to protect the environment and how laws are introduced and changed in their country.[9] While on average about four-fifths of students (81%, ranging from 67% in the Netherlands to 91% in Italy) reported learning about environmental protection, only about half of them indicated learning about how laws are made in their country (53%, ranging from 32% in the Netherlands to 87% in Chinese Taipei). It is noteworthy that reported learning about legislation appeared to vary much more considerably than learning about environmental protection, given that the former could be considered a traditional central aspect of civic learning.

ICCS 2022 also collected teacher data[10] about school and classroom contexts in general from all educators at the target grade, as well as specific data about teaching and learning from those that were teaching civic-related subjects. Table 6.9 focuses on teacher reports on their pre- and in-service training, their feelings of preparedness for teaching, and their perceptions of students' opportunities to learn about the environment and environmental sustainability, and the constitution and political systems.

The results show that for aspects related to the environment and sustainability on average about half of the teachers (51%, ranging from 30% in Croatia to 89% in Chinese Taipei) reported to have attended pre- or in-service training. Large majorities among teachers (84% on average, ranging from 72% in Romania to 91% in Italy and Malta) felt well or quite well prepared to teach about this area, and most teachers (87% on average, ranging from 74% in Chinese Taipei to 98% in Italy) indicated that students had to a large or moderate extent opportunities to learn about environmental sustainability.

When asked about pre- or in-service training about the constitution and political systems, there was considerable variation across countries (ranging from 19% in Croatia to 89% in

96 • Promoting K-12 Civic Learning and Engagement Through Assessment

Table 6.8 Educational Goals, School Activities and Student Reports on Civic Learning Regarding Topics Related to Environmental Sustainability and Learning About Civic Institutions

Country	Percentages of Students at Schools Where Principals Considered as an Important Aim of Civic and Citizenship Education:		Percentages of Students at Schools Where Principals Reported that All, Nearly All, or Most of the Students…		Percentages of Students Who Report to Have Learned to Moderate or Large Extent…	
	Promoting Respect for and Safeguard of the Environment	Promoting Knowledge of Social, Political and Civic Institutions	Participate in Activities Related to Environmental Sustainability (e.g., Energy and Water Saving, Recycling)	Visits to Political Institutions (e.g., Parliament House, Prime Minister's/President's Official Residence)	How to Protect the Environment (e.g., Through Energy-Saving or Recycling)	How Laws Are Introduced and Changed in Country of Test
Bulgaria	38 (4.0)	35 (4.2) ◁	67 (4.3)	11 (2.5) ▷	81 (1.0)	50 (1.2) ▷
Chinese Taipei	33 (3.6)	17 (3.2) ▷	84 (3.2)	30 (3.6)	88 (0.7) ◀	87 (0.7) ◀
Colombia	41 (5.1)	20 (4.0)	58 (4.7)	11 (2.7) ▷	88 (0.8) ◁	60 (1.0) ◁
Croatia[1]	38 (4.5)	28 (3.9)	82 (3.4) ◀	11 (2.7) ▷	89 (0.8) ◁	42 (1.4) ▶
Cyprus	47 (0.3) ◀	25 (0.2)	60 (0.3) ▶	11 (0.1) ▷	81 (0.8)	39 (1.0) ▶
Estonia	22 (3.8) ▶	30 (5.9)	68 (5.4) ▷	44 (5.1) ◀	70 (1.1) ▶	41 (2.0)
France	31 (4.9)	49 (5.0) ◀	59 (4.9)	6 (2.4) ▶	66 (1.2) ▶	53 (1.2)
Italy	49 (4.7) ◀	28 (3.9)	80 (3.9) ▷	13 (2.7)	91 (0.7) ◀	61 (1.6) ◁
Latvia[1]	26 (3.9) ▷	20 (3.6)	60 (3.9) ▷	17 (3.1)	76 (0.9) ▷	39 (1.2) ▶
Lithuania	58 (4.8) ◀	13 (2.9) ▶	79 (3.4) ◀	27 (4.1) ◀	85 (0.7) ◁	45 (1.1) ▷
Malta	37 (7.6)	26 (9.4)	57 (12.2) ▷	4 (3.1) ▷	81 (1.7)	44 (1.5) ▶
Netherlands‡	24 (4.6) ▶	29 (5.9)	36 (5.6) ▶	17 (4.7) ▶	67 (1.5) ▶	32 (1.6) ▶
Norway (9)[1]	19 (3.5) ▶	44 (4.7) ◀	61 (5.1)	19 (3.5)	86 (0.7) ◁	54 (1.0) ◁
Poland	35 (3.5)	11 (2.5) ▶	95 (1.5) ◀	9 (2.6) ▷	79 (0.9) ▷	48 (1.2) ▷
Romania	38 (7.0)	27 (8.6)	66 (6.7)	36 (8.2) ◀	85 (1.1) ◀	62 (1.7) ◁
Serbia	28 (3.7)	26 (4.1) ▷	66 (3.8)	5 (1.8) ▶	83 (0.8) ▶	40 (1.5) ▶
Slovak Republic	43 (4.5)	30 (4.0)	83 (3.2) ◀	19 (3.1)	84 (0.9) ◁	63 (1.4) ◀
Slovenia	37 (4.2)	31 (3.7)	79 (3.5) ◀	7 (2.2) ▷	79 (0.8) ▷	74 (0.9) ◀
Spain	49 (4.1) ◀	9 (2.5) ◀	73 (4.1) ▶	22 (3.6)	81 (1.0)	34 (1.0) ▶
Sweden[1]	30 (4.5)	17 (5.1)	51 (5.4) ▶	16 (3.6)	83 (1.1)	83 (1.5) ◀

ICCS 2022 average	36	(1.0)	26	(1.1)	68	(1.1)	17	(0.8)	81	(0.2)	53	(0.3)

Countries not meeting sample participation requirements

Denmark	17	(3.4)	38	(5.1)	64	(4.9)	56	(4.6)	74	(1.1)	68	(1.4)

German benchmarking participant meeting sample participation requirements

North Rhine-Westphalia	31	(3.7)	22	(4.0)	47	(3.9) ▼	16	(3.4)	78	(1.0)	58 △	(1.7)

German benchmarking participant not meeting sample participation requirements

Schleswig-Holstein	28	(5.6)	23	(5.6)	55	(6.8)	22	(4.9)	74	(1.5)	43	(2.0)

National ICCS 2022 results are as follows:

More than 10 percentage points above ICCS 2022 average ▲
Significantly above ICCS 2022 average △
Significantly below ICCS 2022 average ▽
More than 10 percentage points below ICCS 2022 average ▼

Notes:

Statistically significant changes ($p < 0.05$) between 2009 and 2016 are displayed in **bold**.
() Standard errors appear in parentheses. Because results are rounded to the nearest whole number, some aggregate statistics may appear inconsistent.
(9) Country deviated from international defined population and surveyed adjacent upper grade.
- No comparable data available.
‡ Nearly met guidelines for sampling participation rates only after replacement schools were included.
[1] National Defined Population covers 90%–95% of National Target Population.

Table 6.9 Teachers' Participation in Training Courses, Their Preparedness for Teaching and Teachers' Reports on Students' Opportunities to Learn About Civic Topic and Skills

Percentages of Teachers of Civic-Related Subjects Who Reported Regarding the Topics:

	The Environment and Environmental Sustainability			The Constitution and Political Systems		
	To Have Attended Courses in Pre- or In-Service Training	To Feel Well or Quite Well Prepared to Teaching This Topic	That Students Have to a Large or Moderate Extent Opportunities to Learn About This Topic	To Have Attended Courses in Pre- or In-Service Training	To Feel Well or Quite Well Prepared to Teaching This Topic	That Students Have to a Large or Moderate Extent Opportunities to Learn About This Topic
Bulgaria†	58 (3.7)	85 (4.9)	81 (3.1)	58 (4.7)	85 (4.3)	71 (4.7)
Chinese Taipei	89 (2.2)	89 (2.6)	74 (3.4)	89 (2.3)	92 (2.6)	95 (2.2)
Croatia	30 (1.7)	81 (1.2)	83 (1.4)	19 (1.1)	50 (1.5)	46 (2.0)
Italy	54 (1.2)	91 (1.1)	98 (0.4)	24 (0.9)	68 (1.6)	82 (1.1)
Lithuania	53 (3.4)	80 (1.7)	91 (1.1)	44 (2.3)	68 (2.4)	77 (2.1)
Malta	48 (4.3)	91 (3.7)	80 (4.6)	23 (4.7)	53 (7.4)	54 (6.7)
Norway (9)	28 (3.1)	89 (2.1)	98 (0.6)	29 (2.8)	90 (1.7)	98 (0.9)
Poland	57 (4.9)	81 (3.7)	85 (3.5)	82 (3.9)	98 (1.1)	97 (1.1)
Romania	52 (3.3)	72 (2.9)	85 (3.5)	48 (3.6)	62 (4.0)	70 (4.2)
Serbia	47 (4.2)	88 (3.6)	90 (3.9)	26 (4.3)	55 (7.4)	53 (8.9)
Slovak Republic	47 (2.4)	87 (1.5)	91 (1.5)	39 (3.2)	72 (2.5)	83 (2.5)
Slovenia	55 (2.1)	77 (1.8)	92 (1.1)	65 (2.1)	69 (1.7)	77 (1.8)
Spain	46 (3.3)	84 (2.3)	88 (1.6)	25 (3.1)	69 (3.3)	64 (2.6)
ICCS 2022 average	51 (0.9)	84 (0.8)	87 (0.7)	44 (0.9)	72 (1.1)	74 (1.1)
Countries not meeting sample participation requirements						
Brazil	75 (4.5)	80 (4.6)	94 (1.7)	69 (3.1)	73 (3.4)	82 (3.0)
Colombia	61 (5.1)	83 (3.5)	89 (3.8)	41 (5.2)	71 (3.7)	88 (2.5)
Cyprus	53 (2.7)	80 (2.0)	89 (1.4)	16 (1.9)	42 (2.3)	41 (2.5)

Denmark	38	(5.8)	77	(4.8)	90	(3.1)	74	(5.5)	97	(2.1)	99	(1.4)
Estonia	57	(3.2)	79	(3.0)	84	(2.7)	45	(3.0)	70	(2.7)	74	(2.9)
France	43	(4.0)	87	(2.2)	86	(3.4)	40	(4.1)	88	(2.3)	61	(4.2)
Latvia	61	(5.0)	85	(2.9)	86	(3.5)	60	(5.1)	90	(2.3)	80	(3.9)
Netherlands	79	(3.8)	81	(2.5)	73	(4.9)	73	(5.0)	64	(4.6)	54	(2.4)
Sweden	72	(4.1)	92	(2.2)	98	(1.1)	73	(3.3)	94	(1.7)	97	(1.2)
German benchmarking participant not meeting sample participation requirements												
North Rhine-Westphalia	36	(1.9) ▼	83	(1.4)	86	(1.5)	40	(1.6) ▽	68	(1.4)	78	(1.8)

National ICCS 2022 results are as follows:

More than 10 percentage points above ICCS 2022 average ▲
Significantly above ICCS 2022 average △
Significantly below ICCS 2022 average ▽
More than 10 percentage points below ICCS 2022 average ▼

Notes:

( ) Standard errors appear in parentheses. Because results are rounded to the nearest whole number, some aggregate statistics may appear inconsistent.
(9) Country deviated from international defined population and surveyed adjacent upper grade.
† Met guidelines for sampling participation rates only after replacement schools were included.
[1] National Defined Population covers 90%–95% of National Target Population.

Chinese Taipei) with 44% on average indicating to have received training in this area. However, most teachers (72% on average, ranging from 50% in Croatia to 98% in Poland) felt quite well or well prepared to teach about this area and also perceived to a large or moderate extent opportunities for students to learn about it (74% on average, ranging from 46% in Croatia to 98% in Norway).

Assessing Civic and Citizenship Education Cross-nationally

The ICCS 2022 findings concerning education for sustainable development and young people's views of the political system indicate strong associations between civic knowledge and different attitudinal and behavioral aspects as well as considerable variation across countries regarding findings about school and classroom contexts for civic learning (aims and activities, teachers' preparedness in teaching civic-related topics and skills, their participation in training activities and students' opportunities to learn).

These results, together with the general overview of the ICCS 2022 study design provided at the start of this chapter, outline the complexity of measuring a multifaceted learning area such as CCE in a comparative study, considering cross-national variation in students' cognitive and affective-behavioral aspects, and their related background contexts (from the national to the individual level).

Assessing CCE presents many challenges, both long-standing and related to more recent developments. It needs to be highlighted that civic learning should not be limited to the acquisition of civic knowledge but also encompasses students' attitudes and behaviors inside and outside the school. This conceptualization of what CCE should comprise requires determining how instruction should be conceived and delivered (considering the different dimensions of this learning area) and which role contexts (related to formal, non-formal and informal learning [11]) should play in promoting civic and citizenship knowledge, attitudes and behaviors.

Open and democratic school and classroom environments, where students can actively be engaged in meaningful opportunities (from classroom discussion of civic-related issues to decision-making processes at the school and classroom level, for instance) represent key features for experiencing citizenship first-hand and, as shown by ICCS results, also have implications for civic learning outcomes, as illustrated by associations with civic knowledge and expected engagement. In addition, the links between the school and the local community can provide further opportunities to practice citizenship in real-life contexts, involving experts and organizations that deal with contemporary civic-related topics. The ICCS framework and assessment design consider this complexity using a broad range of research instruments (the student test, the student questionnaire, the school and teacher questionnaires) that aim at gauging, from different levels and perspectives, multiple dimensions of civic learning.

Further, the cross-national nature of the study leads to additional challenges due to the considerable diversity in this learning area across different educational systems, starting from how civic learning is implemented in the curriculum. Many studies have shown the heterogeneity of curricular approaches to the teaching of CCE transnationally: CCE can be taught as a separate subject, as integrated in subjects related to human and social sciences, can be taught in all school subjects and can also be intended as a cross-curricular area (Birzea et al., 2004; European Commission/EACEA/Eurydice, 2005, 2012, 2017). The results from the three cycles of ICCS have highlighted that these different approaches may coexist within the same schools (Schulz et al., 2010, 2018, 2025).

The gap found between national regulations on how CCE should be delivered and how it is actually implemented in schools is another recurrent finding from ICCS as well as in other research studies (Birzea et al., 2004; European Commission/EACEA/Eurydice, 2005, 2012, 2017; Schulz et al., 2010, 2018, 2025). Addressing these issues, in a cross-national study, entails the need to gather and compare, once again, data from different sources. Combining information from the National Context Survey (that allows us to measure civic-related dimensions at the national level in terms of civic-related guidelines and recommendations) with data from the contextual questionnaires has the potential of contributing further insights into the varying characteristics of education systems and how these have an impact on school and classroom practices.

The evolving "object" of measurement represents another critical issue that needs to be addressed when designing a comparative large-scale assessment concerned with this learning area. CCE may be regarded as a "moving target" due to the strong connections of civic-related topics with contemporary developments at local and global levels (Malak-Minkiewicz & Torney-Purta, 2021). Research has shown the broad scope of civic-related content and learning objectives (e.g., ranging from teaching a country's constitution to environmental sustainability, from acting responsibly to effective cooperation and communication with others) that can be addressed, prioritized and included at different levels of each educational system (Council of Europe, 2018; European Commission/EACEA [The European Education and Culture Executive Agency]/Eurydice, 2017).

Another aspect interconnected to this is the emergence of cross-curricular areas (such as education for sustainable development and global citizenship education) that are expanding the notion of civic learning over and beyond the foundational topics in this field (such as learning about topics related to the functioning of the political systems) and are characterized by multidimensional curriculum content (comprising knowledge and affective and behavioral dimensions) and whole-school approaches for their implementation.

The adoption of new focus areas in each cycle of ICCS mirrors this evolving nature of CCE: every new cycle presented both core contents related to the foundations of the learning area as well as other additional focus areas, strongly connected to contemporary issues and development. Moreover, data from the National Context Survey and the contextual questionnaires allow us to measure which civic-related learning objectives are included in the curriculum from a national perspective (i.e. which learning objectives are encompassed in regulations at the country level) and related perceptions of school principals and teachers.

Conclusion

The crucial role of schools for preparing young people to undertake their roles as citizens in society has been emphasized since the beginnings of research in education (see Dewey, 1916). Though not always established as a specific subject, national curricula tend to include civic learning as an important objective of education (e.g., Ainley et al., 2013; European Commission/EACEA [The European Education and Culture Executive Agency]/Eurydice, 2017).

The history of IEA's studies of CCE shows the complexity of assessing such a diverse and cross-curricular learning area. Evaluation as part of an international perspective requires the development of different instruments that measure a broad range of aspects (e.g., cognitive test, student questionnaire, contextual questionnaires) while at the same time considering cross-national differences and finding common ground that transcends national curricula and learning objectives.

The successful implementation of five international studies in 1971, 1999, 2009, 2016 and 2022 confirms that this is possible and can provide invaluable insights into the state of and developments in civic learning as well as factors that influence it. The success of developing these studies has always required a high degree of collaboration between international and national research staff and experts in the field. It further warrants a considerable amount of flexibility when developing appropriate instruments that can be administered across national contexts but are also appropriate for capturing new relevant civic-related topics across different study cycles (Schulz, 2021).

There have been recent developments that raise concerns about a global "democratic recession" (Diamond, 2015, 2021), which is exemplified in the rise of authoritarian government practices as well as the electoral successes of extreme political movements causing instability even in long-established democratic systems (Boogards, 2017; Mair, 2002). At the same time, societies are also feeling the impact of climate change that challenges the sustainability of human development and poses a serious threat to its future. Both developments have implications for civic learning and ICCS 2022 results provide important insights regarding the perceptions of lower-secondary students on environmental sustainability and their political systems.

After statistically significant increases in students' civic knowledge across many countries participating in both ICCS 2009 and 2016, the results from ICCS 2022 showed no increases but decreasing levels in civic knowledge. While these findings should be considered within the wider context of recent disruptions of education caused by the COVID-19 pandemic, the exact nature or magnitude cannot be determined. The results from 2022 also confirmed associations of civic knowledge with gender, socio-economic background and open classroom climate perceptions. Levels of students' citizenship self-efficacy had also increased in most countries from 2009 to 2016, but they did not change much between 2016 and 2022. Correlations between civic knowledge and citizenship self-efficacy tended to be weakly positive across countries and illustrate that students' confidence in their ability to engage were only marginally related to their levels of civic knowledge.

ICCS 2022 data further show that positive attitudes toward and expected engagement with environmental protection tend to be positively associated with civic knowledge. However, the data also suggest that perceptions of the political system and intentions to become involved in conventional active participation tend to be negatively related to civic knowledge, which suggests that having more insights into the workings of the political system does not necessarily translate to its acceptance but can also be associated with critical views. Further, comparisons of students' civic knowledge across the first cycles suggest that there remains considerable variation across countries, and that there have been recent decreases in many countries.

Associations with measures of open classroom climate further indicate the importance of school and classroom contexts for civic learning that go beyond the influence of background factors. ICCS 2022 results show that schools provide many opportunities for learning about environmental sustainability and are widely regarded as crucial aspects of civic learning. However, there is also considerable variation across education systems. When it comes to learning about political systems and institutions, we found relatively low proportions of teachers who reported having received training and were lower than those for training about topics related to environmental sustainability. This finding might suggest that "traditional" goals of CCE are becoming less central for this learning area in a time where the stability of political system even in long-established democracies becomes increasingly challenged.

While ICCS and its predecessors have contributed rich data and provided deeper insights into this important learning area, it is also imperative to point out the limitations of these kinds of studies that are related to their cross-sectional design, which does not permit inferences about causality (Rutkowski & Delandshere, 2016). Therefore, ICCS results (and those of any other international large-scale assessments) should be interpreted primarily in terms of associations between variables (e.g., civic knowledge and students' expected participation) and other relevant background variables (e.g., students' gender or socio-economic status). Findings from this study may suggest the possibility of causal relationships but observed statistically significant effects do not easily translate into firm conclusions about causality.

Studies of CCE continue to constitute important elements of educational evaluation, both at the national and international levels. It is crucial to be mindful of how civic learning has changed over the past decades and will continue to change, not least in the face of the ongoing digitalization of communication and information, which has already changed the ways in which (especially) young people interact with others and society at large (Kahne & Bowyer, 2019; Middaugh et al., 2016). Therefore, studies of civic learning need to adapt to such new challenges and be mindful of how these may impact their results in the future.

Notes

1 To report on the reliability of questionnaire scales, in this chapter we refer to Cronbach's alpha coefficient.
2 Given the nature of the cluster sampling design used in ICCS, where students are nested within classrooms/schools, all standard errors of population parameters (such as percentages, averages or correlations) were calculated using jack-knife repeated replication (JRR) (see Schulz et al., 2018a).
3 All scales were set to a reporting metric where 50 is equal to the average of scale scores and 10 the standard deviation for a pooled dataset with weights that assigned equal weight to each participating country in the ICCS cycles where the scale was first introduced. Linking procedures were applied to make scale scores comparable across cycles for those item sets (such as citizenship self-efficacy or expected active political participation) that were used to measure changes over time (see Schulz & Friedman, 2024).
4 Text in square brackets was adapted by national centers to be appropriate for the respective national context.
5 As item sets were scaled with the Rasch Partial Credit Model, it is possible to relate average scale scores back to the expected on-average responses to all items in a set. Item maps can be used to describe which item responses can be expected given different scales scores (see Schulz & Friedman, 2024).
6 The ICCS proficiency levels represent a hierarchy of civic knowledge in terms of increasing sophistication of content knowledge and cognitive process. Increasing levels on the scale typically represent more complex content and cognitive processes as they are demonstrated through student performance. ICCS distinguishes four levels of civic knowledge ranging from A (highest level) to D (lowest level). Detailed information about the levels can be found in Schulz et al. (2022, 2024).
7 The question included a total of 13 possible goals, of which three had to be selected by principals of schools sampled for ICCS 2022 (see Schulz et al., 2024, pp. 31–32).
8 The question included a total of ten activities for which school principals reported how many students ("all or nearly all", "most", "some of them", "none or hardly any", "not offered at school") participated in them (see Schulz et al., 2024, pp. 182–183).
9 This question required students to rate how much they had learned ("to a large extent", "to a moderate extent", "to a small extent", "not at all") about nine different issues or topics (see Schulz et al., 2024, pp. 187–188).
10 As it was much more difficult to obtain higher levels of teacher participation, there were more countries where the teacher survey did not meet IEA sample participation requirements and for which data were reported outside the main reporting table (see Atasever & Cortés, 2024). Only country data meeting sample participation requirements were included in the calculation of the ICCS 2022 average and interpretations of results.
11 Non-formal learning takes place outside formal learning environments and provides selected types of learning to particular subgroups (Coombs & Ahmed, 1974), while informal learning is the learning that people experience everyday throughout their lives. It is involuntary and is related to the learner's involvement in activities that are not undertaken with a learning purpose in mind (Johnson, & Majewska, 2022).

References

Ainley, J., Schulz, W., and Friedman, T. (eds.) (2013). ICCS 2009 Encyclopedia. *Approaches to civic and citizenship education around the world*. International Association for the Evaluation of Educational Achievement.
Amadeo, J., Torney-Purta, J., Lehmann, R., Husfeldt, V., & Nikolova, R. (2002). *Civic knowledge and engagement: An IEA study of upper secondary students in sixteen countries*. International Association for the Evaluation of Educational Achievement (IEA.

Atasever, U., & Cortés, D. (2024). Weighting procedures. In: *ICCS 2022 technical report* (pp. 128–143). IEA.

Australian Curriculum, Assessment and Reporting Authority (2020). *National Assessment Program-Civics and Citizenship Years 6 and 10 Report 2019*. Australian Curriculum, Assessment and Reporting Authority.

Bandura, A. (1986). *Social foundations of thought and action: A social cognitive theory*. Prentice-Hall.

Bandura, A. (1997). *Self-efficacy: The exercise of control*. W. H. Freeman and Company.

Banks, J. (2008). Diversity and citizenship education in global times. In J. Arthur, I. Davies, & C. Hahn (Eds.), *Education for citizenship and democracy* (pp. 57–70). Sage Publications.

Berelson, B. R., Lazarsfeld, P. F., & McPhee, W. N. (1954). *Voting: A study of opinion formation in a presidential campaign*. University of Chicago Press. [Database]

Birzea, C., Kerr, D., Mikkelsen, R., Pol, M., Froumin, I., Losito, B., & Sardoc, M. (2004). *All-European study on education for democratic citizenship policies*. Council of Europe. https://book.coe.int/en/human-rights-democratic-citizenship-and-interculturalism/3009-all-european-study-on-education-for-democratic-citizenship-policies.html

Boogards, M. (2017). Lessons from Brexit and Trump: Populism is what happens when political parties lose control. *Zeitschrift für Vergleichende Politikwissenschaft, 11*(4), 513–518. https://doi.org/10.1007/s12286-017-0352-y

Bronfenbrenner, U. (2004). *Making human beings human: Bioecological perspectives on human development*. SAGE Publications. https://us.sagepub.com/en-us/nam/making-human-beings-human/book225589

Converse, P. E. (2006). The nature of belief systems in mass publics (1964). *Critical Review, 18*(1–3), 1–74, https://doi.org/10.1080/08913810608443650

Coombs, P. H., & Ahmed, M. (1974). *Attacking rural poverty: How nonformal education can help. A research report for the World Bank prepared by the International Council for Educational Development*. International Council for Educational Development.

Cortés, D., & Atasever, U. (2024). Sampling design and implementation. In: *ICCS 2022 technical report* (pp. 73–82). IEA.

Council of Europe (2018). *Reference framework of competences for democratic culture*. Council of Europe Publishing. https://www.coe.int/en/web/campaign-free-to-speak-safe-to-learn/reference-framework-of-competences-for-democratic-culture

Damiani, V., Losito, B., Agrusti, G., & Schulz, W. (2025). *Young Citizens' views and engagement in a changing Europe. IEA International Civic and Citizenship Education Study 2022* European Report. Springer.

Delli Carpini, M. X., & Keeter, S. (1993). Measuring political knowledge: Putting first things first. *American Journal of Political Science, 37*(4), 1179–1206.

De Vreese, C. H., & Boomgaarden, H. (2006). News, political knowledge and participation: The differential effects of news media exposure on political knowledge and participation. *Acta Politica, 41*, 317–341.

Dewey, J. (1916). *Democracy and education: An introduction to the philosophy of education*. Macmillan.

Diamond, L. (2015). Facing up to democratic recession. *Journal of Democracy, 26*(1), 141–155.

Diamond, L. (2021). Democratic regression in comparative perspective: Scope, methods, and causes. *Democratization, 28*(1), 22–42. https://doi.org/10.1080/13510347.2020.1807517

European Commission/EACEA/Eurydice. (2005). *Citizenship education at school in Europe*. Publications Office of the European Union.

European Commission/EACEA/Eurydice. (2012). *Citizenship education in Europe*. Publications Office of the European Union. https://ec.europa.eu/citizenship/pdf/citizenship_education_in_europe_en.pdf

European Commission/EACEA/Eurydice. (2017). *Citizenship education at school in Europe – 2017*. Eurydice Report. Publications Office of the European Union. https://data.europa.eu/doi/10.2797/818387

Flanagan, C. A., & Sherrod, L. R. (1998). Youth political development: An introduction. *Journal of Social Issues, 54*(3), 447–456. https://doi.org/10.1111/0022-4537.761998076

Foshay, A. W., Thorndike, R. L., Hotyat, F., Pidgeon, D. A., & Walker, D. A. (1962). *Educational achievements of 13-year-olds in twelve countries*. UNESCO Institute for Education.

Fraillon, J., Schulz, W., & Ainley, J. (2012). *ICCS 2009 Asian Report. Civic knowledge and attitudes among lower secondary students in five Asian countries*. International Association for the Evaluation of Educational Achievement (IEA).

Johnson, M., & Majewska, D. (2022). *Formal, non-formal, and informal learning: What are they, and how can we research them?* Cambridge University Press & Assessment Research Report.

Kahne, J., & Bowyer, B. (2019). Can media literacy education increase digital engagement in politics? *Learning, Media and Technology, 44*(2), 211–224. https://doi.org/10.1080/17439884.2019.1601108

Kerr, D., Sturman, L., Schulz, W., & Bethan, B. (2010). *ICCS 2009 European report. Civic knowledge, attitudes and engagement among lower secondary school students in twenty-four European countries*. International Association for the Evaluation of Educational Achievement (IEA).

Lauglo, J. (2013). Do more knowledgeable adolescents have more rationally based civic attitudes? Analysis of 38 countries. *Educational Psychology, 33*(3), 262–282. https://ilsa-gateway.org/papers/do-more-knowledgeable-adolescents-have-more-rationally-based-civic-attitudes

Lave, J., & Wenger, E. (1991). *Situated learning: Legitimate peripheral participation*. Cambridge University Press. https://doi.org/10.1017/CBO9780511815355

Losito, B., Agrusti, G., Damiani, V., Schulz, W., Ainley, J., Fraillon, J., & Friedman, G. (2018). *Young People's perceptions of Europe in a time of change. The International Civic and Citizenship Education Study 2016 European Report*. International Association for the Evaluation of Educational Achievement (IEA).

Losito, B., Agrusti, G., & Damiani, V. (2021). Understanding school and classroom contexts for civic and citizenship education: The importance of teacher data in the IEA studies. In B. Malak-Minkiewicz & J. Torney-Purta (Eds.) *Influences of the IEA civic and citizenship education studies* (pp. 247–259). IEA. https://doi.org/10.1007/978-3-030-71102-3_21

Luskin, R. C. (1987). Measuring political sophistication. *American Journal of Political Science*, 31(4), 856–899. https://doi.org/10.2307/2111227

Lutkus, A. D., Weiss, A. R., Campbell, J. R., Mazzeo, J., & Lazer, S. (1999). *The NAEP civics report card for the nation*. National Center for Education Statistics.

Mair, P. (2002). Populist democracy vs party democracy. In: Y. Mény, & Y. Surel (Eds.), *Democracies and the populist challenge* (pp. 81–98). Palgrave Macmillan. https://doi.org/10.1057/9781403920072_5

Malak-Minkiewicz, B., & Torney-Purta, J. (2021). *Contributions of IEA civic and citizenship studies to educational discourse: Practice, policy, and research across countries and regions*. Springer.

Middaugh, E., Bowyer, B., & Kahne, J. (2016). U suk! Participatory media and youth experiences with political discourse. *Youth & Society*, 49(7), 902–922. https://doi.org/10.1177/0044118X16655246

Mosher, R., Kenny, R. A., & Garrod, A. (1994). *Preparing for citizenship: Teaching youth to live democratically*. Praeger.

Niemi, R., & Junn, J. (1998). *Civic education: What makes students learn?* Yale University Press.

Niemi, R. G., & Hepburn, M. A. (1995). The rebirth of political socialization. *Perspectives on Political Science*, 24(1), 7–16. https://doi.org/10.1080/10457097.1995.9941860

Pasek, J., Feldman, L., Romer, D., & Jamieson, K. (2008). Schools as incubators of democratic participation: Building long-term political efficacy with civic education. *Applied Developmental Science*, 12(1), 236–237.

Rutkowski, D., & Delandshere, G. (2016). Causal inferences with large scale assessment data: Using a validity framework. *Large-Scale Assessments in Education*, 4(6). doi.org/10.1186/s40536-016-0019-1.

Schulz, W. (2021). Reflections on the development of the IEA civic and citizenship education studies. In B. Malak-Minkiewicz & J. Torney-Purta (Eds.). *Contributions of IEA civic and citizenship studies to educational discourse: Practice, policy, and research across countries and regions* (pp. 277–289). Springer.

Schulz, W. (2024). Young people's trust in institutions, civic knowledge and their dispositions toward civic engagement. *Large-Scale Assessments in Education 12*, 23. https://doi.org/10.1186/s40536-024-00210-1

Schulz, W., Ainley, J., Cox, C., & Friedman, T. (2018a). *Young people's views of government, peaceful coexistence and diversity in five Latin American countries. The International Civic and Citizenship Education Study 2016 Latin American Report*. International Association for the Evaluation of Educational Achievement (IEA).

Schulz, W., Ainley, J., Fraillon, J., Kerr, D., & Losito, B. (2010). *ICCS 2009 international report: Civic knowledge, attitudes and engagement among lower secondary school students in thirty-eight countries*. International Association for the Evaluation of Educational Achievement (IEA.

Schulz, W., Ainley, J., Fraillon, J., Losito, B., & Agrusti, G. (2016). *IEA international civic and citizenship education study 2016: Assessment framework*. International Association for the Evaluation of Educational Achievement (IEA).

Schulz, W., Ainley, J., Fraillon, J., Losito, B., Agrusti, G., & Friedman, T. (2018b). *Becoming citizens in a changing world. The International Civic and Citizenship Education Study 2016 International Report*. Springer.

Schulz, W., Ainley, J., Fraillon, J., Losito, B., Agrusti, G., Friedman, T., & Damiani, V. (2025). *Education for citizenship in times of global challenge. IEA International Civic and Citizenship Education Study 2022 International Report*. Springer.

Schulz, W., Ainley, J., Friedman, T., & Lietz, P. (2011). *ICCS 2009 Latin American Report: Civic knowledge and attitudes among lower secondary students in six Latin American countries*. International Association for the Evaluation of Educational Achievement (IEA).

Schulz, W., Fraillon, J., Ainley, J., Losito, B., & Kerr, D. (2008). *International Civic and Citizenship Education Study: Assessment framework*. International Association for the Evaluation of Educational Achievement (IEA).

Schulz, W., Fraillon, J., & Ainley, J. (2013). Measuring young people's understanding of civics and citizenship in a cross-national study. *Educational Psychology: An International Journal of Experimental Educational Psychology*, 33(3), 327–349.

Schulz, W., Fraillon, J., Losito, B., Agrusti, G., Ainley, J., Damiani, V., & Friedman, T. (2022). *IEA International Civic and Citizenship Education Study 2022. Assessment framework*. Springer.

Schulz, W., & Friedman, T. (2024). Scaling procedures for ICCS 2022 questionnaire items. In: *ICCS 2022 technical report* (pp. 173–282). IEA.

Schulz, W., & Macaskill, G. (2024). Scaling procedures for ICCS 2022 test items. In: *ICCS 2022 technical report* (pp. 144–172). IEA.

Torney, J., Oppenheim, A. N., & Farnen, R. F. (1975). *Civic education in ten countries: An empirical study*. John Wiley and Sons.

Torney-Purta, J. (2000). An international perspective on the NAEP Civics Report Card. *The Social Studies, 94,* 148–150.
Torney-Purta, J., Lehmann, R., Oswald, H., & Schulz, W. (2001). *Citizenship and education in twenty-eight countries.* International Association for the Evaluation of Educational Achievement (IEA).
Torney-Purta, J., Schwille, J., & Amadeo, J. A. (1999). *Civic Education across countries: Twenty-four case studies from the IEA Civic Education Project.* International Association for the Evaluation of Educational Achievement (IEA).
Walker, D. A. (1976). *The IEA Six Subject Study: An empirical study of education in twenty-one countries.* Almqvist and Wiksell International/John Wiley and Sons.
Wenger, E. (1998). *Communities of practice: Learning, meaning, and identity.* Cambridge University Press. https://doi.org/10.1017/CBO9780511803932
White, C., & Openshaw, R. (2005). *Democracy at the crossroads: International perspectives on critical global citizenship education.* Lexington Books.

7
Building the Backpack
Replicating State Standards Review and Assessment Processes in Civics Education

Beth Ratway and Peter Mabli

Introduction

This chapter explores how using civic principles when designing, revising, and implementing civics standards and assessment indicators can help ensure that these standards and assessments are designed to promote democratic values, encourage active and informed participation, and uphold fairness and inclusivity. Civic principles are fundamental values that underpin a healthy and functioning democratic society. The application of civic principles to the development of civics standards and assessment indicators is intended to contribute to indicators that reflect the rights, responsibilities, and diverse perspectives of all community members, thereby fostering a more engaged, equitable, and well-informed society. In this chapter, we outline our process of revising and implementing civics standards across the country, detail the civic principles utilized throughout the process, and review assessment indicators and lessons learned. It is important to acknowledge that this work does not involve conducting research. Instead, our primary goal is to describe an approach to standards and assessment development that is informed by civic principles and to share lessons learned that could be applicable to other standards and assessment development efforts.

According to the National Council for the Social Studies, "The primary purpose of Social Studies is to help young people develop the ability to make informed and reasoned decisions for the public good as citizens of a culturally diverse, democratic society in an interdependent world" (National Council for the Social Studies, 1994). Social studies classrooms are the ideal locations to foster civic virtue, apply inquiry practices, consider current issues, engage in civil discourse, and build a civic identity and an awareness of international issues. They are laboratories of democracy where the diversity among learners embodies our democratic goals. In effective social studies classrooms, students are taught to cherish freedom and accept responsibility for preserving and extending it, finding their own best practices for free, independent thinking. These skills, habits, and qualities of character prepare students to accept responsibility for preserving and defending their liberties and empower them to think critically, reason, and solve problems. At the heart of this process is the development and implementation of robust, viable, and effective social studies standards that emphasize and incorporate such civic principles throughout.

DOI: 10.4324/9781003476825-9
This chapter has been made available under a CC BY-NC-ND license.

However, social studies education—and the standards required to teach the material—has increasingly been at the center of combative local, state, and national discourse, and civics practices have unfortunately decreased in importance and influence as a result. Some of these debates center on prevailing concerns regarding the content and skills presented in civics education. An example of this is the influence of critical race theory (CRT) presented in K-12 education. This concern has led some states to restrict concepts believed to represent CRT in the classroom. For example, restrictions have been imposed not only on what can be taught but on what materials educators can use for instruction, such as the 1619 Project. In Florida in 2022, criteria or guidelines for state-approved social studies textbooks were added that prohibit the inclusion of CRT, social justice, culturally responsive teaching, and social and emotional learning. In addition, Florida passed the Parental Rights in Education Act that year, which prohibits instruction on sexual orientation and gender identity before Grade 4 and developmentally appropriate materials in subsequent grades.

At the national level, the National Assessment of Educational Progress (NAEP) 2022 U.S. History and Civics results have placed a spotlight on social studies. When viewed alongside 2014 and 2018 NAEP assessments, the average 2022 U.S. history score for eighth-grade students decreased by 5 points compared to 2018 and by 9 points compared to 2014. Eighth-grade students' performance in NAEP Civics also decreased for the first time since 1998, by 2 points, sparking numerous conversations related to the marginalization of the field as well as the quality of social studies education (The National Assessment of Educational Progress, 2023). Furthermore, the Fordham Institute report *The State of State Standards for Civics and U.S. History* evaluated the quality of the state standards based on their content, rigor, clarity, and organization. Results presented in the report highlighted gaps in state civics and U.S. history standards, subsequently influencing the standards revision process undertaken by states.

Regardless of such complications (or perhaps because of them), numerous states have recently undertaken reviews and revisions of their civics social studies standards. Ohio revamped their social studies standards in 2018 for more specific K-12 standards (Ohio Department of Education and Workforce, 2018). In 2019, Nebraska and Kentucky adopted new state standards, while Utah in 2022 underwent public comments for revised K-6 social studies standards. Kentucky continues to support the standards implementation as they introduced significant changes, such as more inquiry practices and disciplinary standards, along with major transitions at the middle school level (e.g., sixth-grade geography became ancient and classical studies) (Levy, 2021). For Nebraska, the state council, state department, and service units are looking to support educators by developing inquiry-based lessons and high-quality professional development (PD), including methods for addressing controversial issues. Texas is also starting their standards rewrite process, and Alabama recently completed their revision of state social studies standards (Alabama State Department of Education, 2024). And numerous other states continue to revisit their social studies and civics standards.

Most states require students to complete social studies coursework in order to graduate; there are numerous states with assessment systems that include civics, citizenship, or social studies education (American Institutes for Research, 2024). Various states—including Arizona, Idaho, Minnesota, Missouri, North Dakota, Tennessee, and Utah—require students to take a portion of the naturalization test used by the U.S. Citizenship and Immigration Services department to fulfill graduation requirements. In some states, students may have to pass a portion of the exam, but many states specified that students would not be inhibited from graduating or passing a course if they did not pass the naturalization exam. Additionally, multiple states assess social studies topics at different grades, which includes state-level assessments and end-of-course assessments in social studies. It also included that South Carolina administers end-of-course assessments but does not have K-12 state social studies assessment

(South Carolina Code, 2024). Furthermore, recent efforts with multiple representatives from the Texas Education Administration and local community partners have attempted to draft research-based instructional strategies for social studies, including a strategy dedicated to promoting civic discourse in all classrooms (Morrow et al., 2024).

Indeed, the current landscape of social studies is rife with division and complications that impact the presentation of civics content in the classroom. But the inherent importance of a strong civics education remains a priority for State Education Agencies (SEAs), teachers, community organizations, and families across the U.S. From our experience in this field, we believe that a robust revision process of social studies standards that is grounded in civic principles is an essential component of the development of measurable civics assessment indicators. These civic principles ground both the process of revising standards and the development of standards content and are a strong example of theory in action being practiced in the standards revision process.

Background and Focus of Our Social Studies Team

Our social studies team is housed at the American Institutes for Research (AIR), a behavioral and social science research and evaluation institution. AIR has experience working with states and organizations on systems aligned with social studies standards. Our specific team is involved in standards revision and implementation, developing processes for standards revision, supporting implementation of the standards, equipping educators to teach those standards, supporting effective measurement of students' ability to meet the standards, and conducting research to keep current on the demands of our students to support the next iteration of standards. Currently, our social studies team partners with multiple states and the U.S. Virgin Islands (USVI) to facilitate and support their standards development and implementation processes (American Institutes for Research, 2025).

Civics Standards Revision Process

The social studies team starts the standards revision process with a landscape scan. Subject matter experts at AIR conduct national and international landscape scans of standards and assessments to provide current context that informs the developing, updating, or revising of standards. The scans may include overviews of key national and international frameworks, current frameworks for national and international assessments, and analyses of other states' standards and assessment policies. Landscape scans are also used to engage constituent voices in each state.

Next, we use an established set of protocols and processes, based on research and evidence-based practices, to plan and facilitate the development and revision of standards and assessment frameworks. These engagement strategies are informed by resources developed using research and best practices from the field and deep experience in technical assistance (Learning Policy Institute, 2022). For instance, AIR created evidence-informed guides that offer techniques to encourage brainstorming and implement effective constituent engagement strategies such as developing key messages and creating two-way feedback loops.

The team also lays the groundwork for successful implementation of the civics standards through a variety of educator supports. Supports are mapped out with various levers and roles well defined, including notably PD modules built to assist educators in integrating new content/skills represented in their revised standards. Examples include our team's recent work in New Mexico with PD topics such as "culturally and linguistically responsive teaching and learning," "utilizing best practices in discourse to discuss difficult topics," and "creating collaborative civic spaces." Finally, numerous performance-based and localized assessment strategies are incorporated into the process to ensure that social studies standards are implemented consistently and effectively throughout the state.

We have identified three core components of civics standards revision process: prepare, revise, and implement. At each step of this process, civic ideals are deeply and purposely integrated. The subsequent standards generated from this process benefit from such integration, as the content of the standards themselves prioritizes civic ideals in both theory and practice. In the following section, we will review each step in the process in detail and provide examples of civic concept integration.

Step 1: Prepare

The preparation phase of standards work focuses on analyzing the contextual factors and critical issues that impact standards development and implementation. From the outset, SEAs must pay close attention to issues and community partner groups that may support or threaten the development and implementation of civics standards. Doing so allows SEAs to plan and act in ways that mobilize support while countering threats, while simultaneously integrating civic principles and procedures into the process.

Part of the work associated with preparing for the development or revision of civics standards includes bringing together a cross-section of critical community partners to engage in an analysis of the current context that impacts standards development, revision, and implementation. Key community partners might include SEA staff, regional service agencies, representatives from state content organizations, local administrators, teachers, parents, representatives from postsecondary institutions, as well as community, union, and business leaders. Key community partners should also include representatives from diverse groups who will play a role in approving standards (e.g., state board, legislature), and whose participation may reduce possible threats as the process shifts to the adoption phase.

An example of the importance of diverse community representation during the preparation phase can be found in Nebraska. Our team facilitated an evaluation of the state's standards revision process. The Nebraska Department of Education (NDE) and the Nebraska State Board of Education (NSBE) requested an evaluation of their content standards revision process as part of an ongoing effort to ensure Nebraska standards are rigorous and reflect the diversity of perspectives and expertise in the state. As part of that evaluation, a landscape scan was generated to compare the selection process for review committees across states in order to recommend (among other items) how Nebraska could include diverse perspectives throughout the revision stages. We found that educators serving diverse populations—across geographic locations, district sizes, district settings, socioeconomic and ethnic diversity, grade bands, content area expertise, and roles—were an integral component of the selection process in many states.

Step 2: Revise

The second part of the process focuses on the actual revision and development of state social studies standards content. Development refers to the processes involved in creating new standards or revising a set of existing standards and includes planning as well as writing and/or revising. The work of development entails a specific set of steps that research and experiences suggest SEAs should follow to maximize the likelihood that the standards will be adopted. Those steps include planning and organizing, writing or revising, gathering feedback, revising based on feedback, and approving/adopting the standards.

Writing standards is a unique process that most members of a writing team will not be familiar with. Our team often asks members of the writing team first to reflect on what they value, and what they see as the ultimate purpose of the civics standards. Next, we ask members of the writing team to review existing standards (in their state and others) and national standards/frameworks using a rubric criteria review of academic standards. This tool outlines and defines major criteria present in existing high-quality standards. Criteria in the tool include examples such as rigor, focus, specificity, and clarity/accessibility. By reviewing civics standards with these criteria in mind, writing teams have a greater probability of developing their own standards that are of similar quality.

Gathering feedback is critical, perhaps more critical than the writing process itself. To effectively gather feedback, it is important to determine who is most critical to gather feedback from and how the feedback will be collected and shared with those responsible for making revisions and the wider public (Education Commission of the States, 2021). Methods of feedback vary from state to state but often include examples such as online surveys, focus groups, public forums/hearings, national feedback, state-specific community partner organizations, and/or a separate standards review team.

After gathering multiple forms of feedback, the team reviews the feedback and revises as needed. This focus is intrinsically civic-minded: input and an iterative process from all members of a community are both major tenants of the standards revision process and a major principle of civic ideals. As is often true, the specific stages of revision based on feedback vary from state to state. But nearly all feedback revision includes prioritizing the types of revisions recommended, cataloging and combining similar types of revisions together, and drafting justification statements that correlate to each recommendation.

In the final stage of this step, the revised civics standards undergo an approval/adoption process. Each state has their own process for approval/adoption of the standards. In some states, a simple sign off is required by the SEA director. In others, the State Board of Education or legislature must approve the standards. Each of these processes is unique and often has their own unique timeline. In many SEAs, formal presentations are required of the State Board of Education or legislature.

As noted, each step of this process is heavily impacted by core civic principles. This fact is exemplified in the New Mexico social studies standards revision in 2022. The state followed our steps for revision, ultimately outlining strong anchor, content, and inquiry standards aligned to civic principles. New Mexico Civics anchor standards include civic and political institutions; processes, rules, and laws; civic dispositions and democratic principles; and roles and responsibilities of civic life. Further, the state's guiding principles include "empowering students to develop pride in their identity, history, culture, and region by incorporating a community-based approach while preparing students to be part of a global environment." And finally, one of New Mexico's inquiry standards includes "taking informed action" which states that students should "participate in deliberative and democratic procedures to make decisions about and act on civic problems or issues in their classrooms." Indeed, the cumulative impact of these components of the standards reinforces the state's commitment to civic ideals, a commitment that was mirrored in their civics standards revision process and duplicated in the standards content themselves.

Step 3: Implement

The third phase of the civics standards process involves implementation mapping. An implementation map provides practitioners with a useful way to analyze the extent to which new standards are being integrated with fidelity. Further, implementation mapping helps to set and assess goals by identifying drivers of standards implementation and can be used to both analyze and determine the current status of implementation at each stage to develop detailed plans and access sufficient resources for implementation.

Such implementation can enhance SEAs' ability to develop solutions that meet the needs of districts and schools as they implement their civics standards. In addition, SEAs can use such a tool at various intervals of the standards process to build and sustain continuous systemic supports for implementation. It also allows SEAs and regional service agencies to assist communities with developing and assessing clear standards implementation goals at each stage.

Implementation support is essential for states to meet their goals regarding standards revision. The team compiled multiple state and territory implementation plans, ultimately selecting 11 plans for the report. Plans were selected based on several factors and topics such as geographic diversity, date of implementation, subject area(s) addressed, division of roles/responsibilities, and AIR team member familiarity with plan development.

The report outlines numerous considerations for states building implementation plans, including items that specifically address the goals of effectively implementing civics standards. The first recommendation is to develop a communication plan to establish administration support early. It is important to create communication plans early and continually reevaluate them throughout the process. This means having a two-way channel between State and Local Education Agencies and educators to share and receive information. States such as Minnesota have a district leader network where they share struggles and needs, while the USVI utilizes a survey (Minnesota Department of Education, n.d.). When communicating, utilizing clear, plain language diminishes the possibility that technical terms become lost in the translation. If there is crucial terminology for everyone to understand, it is important to revisit it on an ongoing basis. Such an interactive and communicative process is intrinsic to the ideals inherent in civics standards.

The second relevant recommendation from the implementation report was to include a structured approach to PD supports (Desimone, 2009). The state department of education plays an essential role in the development of PD modules, and districts and administrators are afforded options to individualize PD strategies to best support their diverse teacher populations. The addition of explicit opportunities for feedback and reflection on PD strategies is an important component of many state strategies. Providing space for feedback and revision can be a powerful tool to ensure PD remains effective and relevant to educators in the state.

Finally, the report recommends providing methods to assess high-quality instructional materials (HQIMs). Multiple state implementation plans note structured criteria to review and assess HQIMs. For instance, Nebraska explicitly refers to "high-quality instructional materials" (or HQIMs) and asks districts to "utilize resources developed by the NDE to select high-quality instructional materials...aligned to content area standards" (Nebraska Department of Education, 2019). Indeed, the need to assess the quality of instructional materials aligned to new standards is integral to the development of an implementation strategy, as it provides educators with practical materials and methods to plan curricula that align to the new civics standards.

To address this need for HQIM assessment in civics and other social studies disciplines, AIR partnered with EdReports to develop a draft rubric for identifying HQIMs in social studies that includes evidence guides (American Institutes for Research, 2023). The evidence guide provides elaborate details for indicators in an evaluation rubric, along with the indicator's purpose, relevant research or standards, and resources to support the review.

Before the evidence guides could be created, AIR investigated the state of social studies, standards, and current work on HQIMs across the U.S. in individual states. From this investigation, AIR developed gateways and criteria to organize and focus the evaluation rubrics. These gateways included Standards Alignment, Social Studies Practices, Equity and Inclusion, Usability, Instructional Supports, and Assessment. Criteria were built based on commonalities between state social studies standards and were reviewed by the social studies collaborative at the Council of Chief State School Officers and the Council of State Social Studies

(Council of State Social Studies Specialists, n.d.). Once the gateways and criterion were solidified, AIR turned their attention to creating evidence guides.

The team reviewed select curriculum review tools and research on the state of social studies curricula. Relevant review criteria were identified and used to frame or guide the development of the requirements for indicators in each gateway. Once the evidence guides were drafted, six social studies state representatives from Arkansas, Kansas, Kentucky, Maryland, Ohio, and Oklahoma, along with representatives from Washington, D.C., and the Department of Defense Education Activity (DoDEA), reviewed the evidence guides. Each representative provided unique and critical perspectives in refining and expanding the evidence guides to inform key requirements and "look fors" when evaluating social studies instructional materials. Our team is currently piloting versions of the evidence guides in Hawaii and the USVI, and workshopping with social studies publishers. These pilots will inform future iterations of the guides. The evidence guides support a vision for continuous improvement and advancement in civics education.

From preparation to draft, revision, and implementation, the procedures to develop civics standards are foundationally rooted in an iterative and transparent process that is inclusive of all interested members of the affected community. This highlights the civic ideals inherent in the work and is reflected in the civics standards and assessment content generated in each state. Such experiences and practices have revealed certain civic principles that our team has compiled; principles that inform our work and the products developed.

Civic Principles for Standards Revision

In civics standards revision, responsibility lies with a diverse group of partners, including educators, administrators, subject matter experts, community members, and sometimes students, all working together to analyze current standards, identify areas for improvement, gather feedback, and develop revised standards that accurately reflect the necessary knowledge and skills for students to achieve success; this often involves a collaborative process with clear roles for each participant to ensure comprehensive review and implementation.

Through our work we have identified five key civic principles for standards revision: *transparency*, *representation*, *accountability*, *plurality*, and *civility*. These principles are essential to the civics standards revision process because they foster an environment that ensures fairness, inclusivity, and effectiveness, while maintaining trust and integrity.

Transparency

Transparency in the civics standards revision process is critical because it builds trust and credibility among all partners in education, including educators, students, higher education, administrators, legislators, and the broader community. When the process is transparent, partners are clear about how decisions are made, what factors are being considered, and what the intended outcomes are. This openness reduces suspicions of bias or unfair influence and helps participants feel more invested in the process. Additionally, transparency ensures that the rationale behind revisions is communicated clearly, making the changes easier to understand and support (Manna, 2015).

Transparent revision of civics standards is essential for improving the quality of education and ensuring broad support for new policies. Key aspects of a transparent revision process include public notice, where the intent to revise is announced with a clear timeline and opportunities for public input. The process needs to have extensive community involvement, where educators, administrators, higher education faculty, students, legislators, and community partners collaborate to provide a wide-ranging perspective on the revisions. Draft standards should be readily accessible online, allowing the community to review and provide feedback. Engaging a diverse range of partners—such as teachers, administrators, parents, and community members—is critical for gathering varied perspectives, while providing multiple feedback mechanisms, including online surveys, public hearings, and written comments, ensures that everyone has an opportunity to contribute. In order to be transparent, the process must include documentation and record-keeping of every step, including feedback and decision-making processes, which ensures accountability and creates a trail of evidence for future reference. Feedback mechanisms, such as surveys and public comment periods, empower partners to contribute their insights and concerns, promoting a sense of shared ownership. Additionally, explaining the rationale behind proposed changes and revising standards based on constructive feedback helps create a more inclusive, comprehensive set of guidelines. The process also needs clear communication about the reasons for changes, the process, and the expected outcomes to help demystify the revisions for all involved, whether through public meetings, documents, or other accessible channels.

The benefits of transparency are numerous: it builds public trust, improves the quality of the standards through diverse input, and ensures greater buy-in from the community. By clearly communicating goals, processes, and timelines, providing regular updates, and documenting all processes, a transparent approach helps ensure that the final standards reflect the needs and expectations of the community, while also maintaining accountability throughout the revision process.

Example: Kentucky

While states each have their own standards revision processes, certain fundamental principles guide the way. Every step of the process, from the initial planning conversations with constituents, to facilitating and supporting standards development and assessing their efficacy, will require a rigorous approach with clear communication on procedural steps and goals. Consistency and transparency ensure trust among partners.

AIR partnered with staff at the Kentucky Department of Education (KDE) to coordinate, plan, and facilitate every component of the social studies standards review work. Kentucky law KRS 158.6453 (2)(g)(1) (g) requires transparency throughout the standards revision process. *1. The review process implemented under this subsection shall be an open, transparent process that allows all Kentuckians an opportunity to participate. The department shall ensure the public's assistance in reviewing and suggesting changes to the standards and alignment adjustments to corresponding state assessments by establishing a website dedicated to collecting comments by the public and educators. An independent third party, which has no prior or current affiliation with a curriculum or assessment resources vendor, shall be selected by the department to collect and transmit the comments to the department for dissemination to the appropriate advisory panel for review and consideration* (Kentucky General Assembly, 2024).

Throughout this project, AIR worked closely with KDE to develop processes, tools, and resources to ensure that the decisions and processes for the standards review and revision process were public. The work included creating protocols to comply with the Open Meetings Act, including press releases prior to and after each meeting, agendas released to the public prior to each meeting, and detailed minutes, capturing roll call, motions, discussions, and official actions that are posted to the KDE standards review news webpage. This organized process ensures clear communication and proper documentation throughout the standards revision process.

Representation

Representation in civics standards revision requires ensuring that a diverse group of partners, including teachers, administrators, parents, community members, subject matter experts, and potentially students, are involved in the process of reviewing and updating civics standards, so that the revised standards reflect the needs and perspectives of the wider educational community. Representation in civics standards revision is a critical process that ensures the revised standards reflect the diverse needs and perspectives of the broader educational community (Gay, 2018). This process involves a wide range of partners, including teachers, administrators, parents, community members, subject matter experts, and potentially students, to ensure that the standards are relevant, inclusive, and equitable. By incorporating diverse perspectives—such as those from different demographic backgrounds, educational experiences, and geographic regions—the standards are more likely to be accessible and effective for all students. Key to this process is engaging a variety of community partners, from classroom teachers to community leaders, and ensuring subject matter experts contribute to the accuracy and rigor of the standards. Representation also plays a crucial role in improving the quality of civics standards, as a broader array of input leads to more comprehensive and well-rounded guidelines. Additionally, involving diverse groups fosters increased buy-in and support for the revised standards, as partners who feel involved are more committed to their successful implementation. Finally, a focus on representation ensures that the revised standards promote equity and access, addressing the needs of students from all backgrounds, including those from marginalized communities, and helping to create a more inclusive and effective educational system.

Representation in civics standards revision is vital for creating a fair, supportive, and equitable educational environment. To promote inclusivity, several strategies can be employed. Diverse representation in the revision process ensures that a wide array of voices—spanning various disciplines, student backgrounds, and underrepresented communities—are included. This can be achieved by forming committees that reflect the diversity of the student body and faculty. Broad consultation further strengthens representation by reaching out to students, alumni, community members, and industry professionals, ensuring that the standards address the needs and perspectives of all partners. Additionally, developing culturally responsive standards acknowledges the value of different knowledge systems, learning styles, and cultural practices, creating a more inclusive educational experience for students from diverse backgrounds. Accessibility considerations are also critical, ensuring that the language used in civics standards is clear, and that materials are available in multiple formats and languages, particularly for students with disabilities. Structured feedback mechanisms, such as focus groups or surveys, provide all partners with opportunities to voice concerns and contribute to the revision process. Clear, transparent rationale for changes helps build trust, ensuring that the revisions align with inclusive goals.

Example: Alaska

AIR partnered with the Alaska Department of Education and Early Development (DEED) to facilitate the revision of their social studies standards. DEED wanted to ensure that the revised standards/indicators would be designed so that ALL students felt represented and reflected in the standards. This meant that the process needed to also include representation reflective of the diversity of Alaskans. DEED identified the need for three workgroups of diverse education professionals and/or leaders to support the work: the Guiding Principles Workgroup (GPWG), Alaska History Workgroup (AHWG), and Educator Workgroup (EWG).

The GPWG was composed of approximately nine individuals, including representatives from organizations such as the Alaska Municipal League, the Institute of the North, and the Alaska Association of School Boards, along with a superintendent and social studies curriculum coordinator. The function of the GPWG was to develop guiding principles for the standards revision process.

The AHWG was composed of eight individuals, including educators, education leaders, and representatives of Alaska tribes. This included representation from the Sitka Tribe of Alaska, the Goldbelt Heritage Foundation, and the Alaska Native Heritage Center. The function of the AHWG was to develop guidance for the inclusion of state history, tribal government, and Indigenous histories.

The EWG was composed of 18 educators in Alaska with a wide variety of experience in K-12 social studies education. The function of the EWG was to refine, revise, and develop appropriate standards to meet Alaska's current needs that align with current national standards and reflect the cultural perspectives of Alaska. When choosing writers, the selection committee considered statewide representation for public elementary, middle, and high school educators across Alaska, particularly from different locales and district sizes.

Accountability

Accountability ensures that the revision process remains focused, responsible, and aligned with the state's educational goals. It means that those involved in the revision process are answerable for their decisions, and there are systems in place to track progress, evaluate outcomes, and address concerns. When accountability is embedded in the revision process, it prevents decisions from being made in isolation or without adequate justification. It also promotes continuous improvement by allowing for feedback and regular assessment of how the revisions impact student outcomes and educational quality. Without accountability, the process risks becoming opaque or disconnected from its intended purpose (Gill et al., 2017).

Accountability requires that the revision of standards be done thoughtfully and with a clear focus on measurable outcomes. When those involved in the revision process are accountable to each other and to the broader community, they are more likely to design evidence-based indicators that can be objectively measured and linked to student performance. Accountability also ensures that there are mechanisms in place to track progress and assess the effectiveness of civics-related teaching and learning.

Example: New Mexico

The process of drafting the civics standards and rule-making for instructional materials in New Mexico was a collaborative and structured approach, inclusive of a wide range of partners throughout the process. AIR worked with the New Mexico Public Education Department (NMPED) to ensure accountability throughout the process. NMPED brought together an Advisory Council of content experts, including representatives from higher education, cultural institutions, and sovereign tribal entities, to set the guiding principles and vision for the standards. The educator writing teams were held to these guiding principles throughout the process.

Once a draft set of standards was developed, NMPED and AIR conducted focus groups to ensure accountability to the community. These focus groups engaged parents, superintendents, board members, teachers, principals, tribal education leaders, and students, to gather valuable feedback. The educator writing teams utilized this feedback to revise and refine the draft standards.

The standards were then posted online for a 45-day public comment and a public hearing was held, where community members could provide input. After the public comment period, the educator writing teams reconvened to revise the standards based on the feedback received. This thorough, inclusive process ensured the educators were accountable to the guiding principles and all community members throughout the process ensuring the standards were shaped by diverse perspectives and aligned with the needs of New Mexico's educational community.

Plurality

Plurality emphasizes the inclusion of diverse perspectives and knowledge systems, recognizing that no single viewpoint can fully represent the complexity of modern education. Civics standards should reflect a variety of cultural, intellectual, and methodological approaches, and should be responsive to global trends, interdisciplinary insights, and different learning styles. By ensuring plurality, states can create standards that better address the needs of a diverse student population, preparing them for success in a globalized and multifaceted world. Additionally, embracing plurality enriches the academic environment by encouraging innovative thinking and preventing the dominance of any single perspective or tradition.

Plurality in civics standards revision is essential for ensuring that educational criteria reflect the diverse needs, backgrounds, and experiences of students. This approach involves incorporating multiple perspectives through community engagement, where students, educators, parents, and community members collaborate to ensure the standards address a variety of viewpoints. Interdisciplinary approaches further enrich the process by integrating knowledge from different fields, creating standards that are both comprehensive and relevant across disciplines. Additionally, cultural competence plays a crucial role in making sure that the standards are inclusive, acknowledging the diversity of student populations and promoting equity in education. To ensure the standards remain adaptable to societal and educational changes, feedback mechanisms are put in place, allowing for continuous input and adjustments. Finally, the revision process is grounded in research-based practices, ensuring that revisions are informed by the latest educational research and best practices. By embracing plurality in the revision process, civics standards become more relevant, equitable, and effective, supporting all students in reaching their full potential.

Example: U.S. Virgin Islands

AIR worked with the Virgin Islands Department of Education (VIDE) to support the revision of their social studies standards. VIDE wanted to ensure the revised standards reflected the diverse needs and experiences of the entire VI community. One critical element to ensure plurality in the process was ensuring the civics standards revision process was grounded in research-based practices, drawing from a wide range of studies and educational theories to ensure that the standards are informed by the best available evidence, ultimately leading to higher quality and more effective educational outcomes.

Prior to drafting the standards, the educator writing team convened virtually to craft guiding principles that would serve as a guide for the standards revision work. For this process, each group built their background knowledge on national and state trends, and state policies impacting the social studies standards in USVI in order to review and identify strengths and gaps in the current VIDE social studies standards. They engaged in a visioning activity in which they brainstormed criteria for determining high-quality social studies standards and identified key knowledge, skills, and dispositions (KSDs) that all students need to master in USVI.

Next, the groups reviewed current research/best practices, the national landscape of social studies, and various state standards in order to identify key components or "must haves" that could inform the social studies revision work in USVI. The "must haves" were organized into themes and then written as draft action statements to guide the revision of the social studies standards.

Civility

Civility is fundamental to maintaining a respectful, productive, and collaborative environment during the revision process. Civics standards revision often involves discussions on sensitive topics, and differing opinions are inevitable. Civility ensures that disagreements are handled with respect and that all voices are heard without fear of personal attack or disrespect. A civil process fosters a constructive atmosphere where ideas can be debated and refined, leading to better, more thoughtful outcomes. By modeling and encouraging civil behavior, states can create an environment where dialogue is not only respectful but also focused on achieving shared goals rather than personal agendas.

Civility in the revision process ensures that civics standards are developed in a way that encourages respectful and constructive dialogue about civic responsibilities, ethical behavior, and social issues. Civility promotes a climate where all viewpoints are considered and valued, especially when determining what constitutes important aspects of civic knowledge and engagement. When civility is central to the process, the resulting civics standards are more likely to reflect respect for diverse opinions and inclusive perspectives. Moreover, civility encourages the creation of standards that focus not just on students' knowledge of civics but also on their ability to engage in productive discourse and navigate conflicts respectfully, important skills in both local and global civic participation.

Example: South Dakota

AIR worked with the South Dakota Department of Education (SD DOE) to conduct the initial revision of their social studies standards. AIR worked closed SD DOE to build a research-based consensus process to ensure all participants on the standards writing team were able to share ideas to reach a consensus throughout the process. We built a research-based consensus process that prioritized evidence, collaboration, and systematic decision-making to ensure that revisions were grounded in best practices and reflected broad agreement among all involved participants. The process began with defining the purpose and scope of the revisions, and establishing a guiding framework rooted in current educational research. It then included the identification of diverse partners to write the standards ensuring the revised standards meet the needs of all communities involved. AIR then built a thorough literature review to inform the revisions, partnering with SD DOE to determine the diverse set of research and evidence-based practices that correlated to meet the needs of the South Dakota context. During the writing process, we had specific protocol to help the writers engage in structured dialogue, to reach consensus on the revisions, promoting active listening, empathy, and civility throughout the process. This process not only enhances the quality of civics standards but also ensures that the revised standards are academically rigorous, inclusive, and responsive to both educational trends and real-world needs.

A research-based consensus process for civics standards revision ensures that revisions are both evidence-driven and widely supported by partners. By involving diverse groups such as faculty, students, administrators, and industry experts early in the process, this approach fosters inclusivity and ensures that the revised standards meet the needs of all parties. The process begins with a clear definition of the purpose and scope of revisions, grounded in current research and data on student performance, followed by the collection of input through surveys, focus groups, and collaborative discussions. Through a structured, consensus-building approach, partners work together to refine standards based on best practices and data, fostering transparency and trust. Feedback loops are incorporated to ensure that revisions are practical, and the final standards are tested and reviewed before implementation. This iterative process, focused on continuous improvement, ensures that civics standards are not only rigorous and effective but also adaptable to evolving educational needs, while promoting a culture of collaboration and accountability within the academic community.

How Principles Lead to Measurable Civics Assessment Indicators

These principles—*transparency*, *representation*, *accountability*, *plurality*, and *civility*—serve as the foundation for a revision process that is fair, effective, and inclusive. They help ensure that civics standards evolve in a way that is aligned with the needs of the state and its diverse community, and that revisions are made in a responsible, inclusive, and respectful manner. By aligning with these principles, the development of standards becomes a collaborative, transparent, and inclusive process. The resulting standards are more likely to be the following:

- Clear and objective: Transparent processes allow partners to understand what is being measured and why, ensuring that indicators are straightforward and measurable.
- Inclusive and holistic: Representation and plurality ensure that the indicators reflect the diversity of civic experiences, including different cultures, backgrounds, and social perspectives, leading to more comprehensive assessments.
- Relevant to contemporary issues: The feedback mechanisms and regular reviews embedded in the principles of accountability and civility ensure that the indicators stay aligned with evolving civic expectations and educational goals.
- Fair and equitable: Representation and accountability ensure that the indicators measure the civic engagement of all students, recognizing their different paths to civic involvement and ensuring that no group is disadvantaged.
- Focused on meaningful outcomes: Civility and transparency help to keep the revision process centered on constructive and actionable goals, resulting in civics assessments that encourage real-world civic participation, respect, and democratic engagement.

Inclusion of these principles in the civics standards revision process plays a crucial role in shaping the effectiveness and fairness of civics assessment indicators. When the process of revising civics standards is transparent, representative, accountable, plural, and civil, it allows for clear communication about how the standards are developed, what values they prioritize, and how they are aligned with the broader goals of democratic education. This helps ensure that all partners—such as educators, policymakers, students, parents, and the public—understand the rationale behind the criteria used to evaluate civic knowledge and skills.

Grounding the civics standards revision process in these principles helps ensure that the assessment indicators reflect a diverse set of civic competencies. For example, if the civics standards revision process is open, educators and other partners can advocate for the inclusion of critical thinking, media literacy, and active participation as key components of civics education. As a result, the assessment indicators will be more comprehensive, capturing not just factual knowledge about government and history but also the ability to engage meaningfully in civic life.

When the revision process is grounded in these principles, partners can track how the standards and the corresponding assessments evolve, ensuring that any changes are based on clear objectives rather than political or ideological motivations. This can help build public trust in the fairness and objectivity of civics assessments, which is particularly important in a subject that shapes students' understanding of democracy, rights, and responsibilities.

A civics standards revision process built on these principles invites input from a broad range of perspectives, including those of marginalized or underrepresented groups. By considering diverse viewpoints, the civics standards and their corresponding assessment indicators are more likely to be inclusive and relevant to all students, reflecting the values of equity and social justice.

Finally, a civics standards revision process grounded in these principles encourages the use of evidence-based practices. When the public and educators can see the data, research, and feedback driving the revision process, it ensures that the assessment indicators are based on sound educational practices and are likely to improve civic education outcomes.

Aligning the civics standards revision process to the principles of *transparency, representation, accountability, plurality,* and *civility* ensures that when civics assessment indicators are developed, based on the standards, they are inclusive, measurable, and relevant to all students. This alignment contributes to the creation of civics assessment tools that effectively evaluate students' readiness to participate in civic life, promote democratic values, and engage with diverse communities both locally and globally.

Lessons Learned from Creating Civics Standards and Assessment Indicators: Key Considerations for Standards Development

Our experiences working with SEAs, in combination with insights from national frameworks such as the NAEP Civics, U.S. History, Geography, and Economics assessments, point to several essential takeaways for those engaged in revising civics standards and developing corresponding assessment indicators. The following five lessons reflect not only the technical dimensions of this work but also the civic values that must guide it to ensure equity, transparency, and meaningful impact.

1. Civics Standards Revision Requires Shared Responsibility and Collaborative Design

One of the most important lessons learned is that the responsibility for civics standards revision must be shared across a diverse group of partners—including educators, administrators, subject matter experts, community members, and, in some cases, students. These collaborators work together to analyze existing standards, identify areas for improvement, gather public feedback, and draft revised frameworks that reflect the KSDs students need for civic success. Clearly defined roles and an inclusive, structured process are essential to ensure that revisions are comprehensive, equitable, and responsive to a wide range of perspectives.

2. A Rigorous and Transparent Process Builds Public Trust

Beyond inclusivity, transparency is a foundational principle in maintaining stakeholder trust throughout the standards revision process. From early planning conversations to public review and implementation, each step must be communicated clearly and consistently. Transparent processes not only mitigate concerns about partisanship or bias but also signal a commitment to democratic practice within the educational system itself. A rigorous and open approach builds broad-based support and promotes accountability throughout the development and adoption phases.

3. Discipline-Specific Civic Skills Deepen Student Learning and Engagement

A growing body of research and practitioner experience supports the integration of discipline-specific civic skills into standards and assessments. Skills such as source analysis, argument construction, civic dialogue, and policy evaluation do not replace content knowledge—they reinforce it. These competencies help students apply their learning in real-world contexts, preparing them for active and informed participation in civic life. Frameworks that prioritize inquiry, deliberation, and critical thinking not only enhance knowledge retention but also reflect the dynamic nature of democracy itself.

4. Representation Must Be Central to Civics Standards Development

The revision of civics standards and indicators presents an opportunity to broaden whose stories, experiences, and contributions are reflected in civic education. Many states have made intentional efforts to ensure that their standards and indicators are more representative of the diverse populations they serve. Including historically marginalized voices—such as Indigenous communities, immigrants, and communities of color—strengthens both the educational validity and cultural relevance of civics content. States like New Mexico and Alaska have demonstrated how early and sustained engagement with community partners results in standards that are more inclusive, accurate, and meaningful to all students.

5. Thoughtful Civic Indicators Help Measure What Matters

Developing effective assessment indicators for civics requires attention to both content and values. Civic learning cannot be fully captured through rote recall or narrow testing mechanisms; instead, assessment indicators should reflect a broad set of competencies—such as critical reasoning, collaborative problem-solving, ethical thinking, and engagement with diverse viewpoints. Civic indicators must also be flexible enough to respect local contexts while still supporting statewide comparability and instructional coherence. When designed thoughtfully, these indicators reinforce instructional goals and provide educators with actionable insights, without constraining the richness of civic learning.

This framework of shared responsibility, principled engagement, and evidence-based design can guide SEAs and their partners toward civics standards and assessment indicators that are inclusive, effective, and democratically grounded.

References

Alabama State Department of Education. (2024). *Alabama course of study: Social studies.* https://www.alabamaachieves.org/wp-content/uploads/2025/01/AS_20250110_2024-Alabama-Course-of-Study-Social-Studies_V1.0.pdf

American Institutes for Research. (2023). *Evaluating high-quality instructional materials: A framework for K–12 educators.* Retrieved from https://www.air.org/resources/example-hqim-framework-url

American Institutes for Research. (2024). *The state of K–12 social studies education.* https://www.air.org/sites/default/files/2024-03/State-of-K-12-Social-Studies-Education-Report-March-2024.pdf

American Institutes for Research. (2025). *Standards and assessments in social studies.* https://www.air.org/resource/spotlight/standards-and-assessments-social-studies

Council of State Social Studies Specialists. (n.d.). *Council of State Social Studies Specialists.* Retrieved from https://www.socialstudies.org/cs4

Desimone, L. M. (2009). Improving impact studies of teachers' professional development: toward better conceptualizations and measures. *Educational Researcher, 38*(3), 180–198. https://doi.org/10.3102/0013189X08331140

Education Commission of the States. (2021). *Processes for creating and evaluating state education standards.* https://www.ecs.org/wp-content/uploads/State-Information-Request_Processes-for-Creating-and-Evaluating-State-Education-Standards-1.pdf

Gay, G. (2018). *Culturally responsive teaching: Theory, research, and practice* (3rd ed.). Teachers College Press.

Gill, B., Gill, M. J., & Miller, R. (2017). Reimagining accountability in K–12 education. *Behavioral Science & Policy, 1*(1), 63–75. https://behavioralpolicy.org/wp-content/uploads/2017/05/BSP_vol1is1_Gill.pdf

Kentucky General Assembly. (2024). *Kentucky revised states: KRS chapter 158.* https://apps.legislature.ky.gov/law/statutes/chapter.aspx?id=37853

Learning Policy Institute. (2022, August 9). *Technical assistance for community schools: Enabling strong implementation.* https://learningpolicyinstitute.org/product/technical-assistance-community-schools-brief

Levy, J. S. (2021). Measuring the impact of a supplemental civic education program on students' civic attitude and efficacy beliefs. *Journal of Social Studies Education Research, 2*(1), 1–18.

Manna, P. (2015). "Transparency in education policy." In J. D. Saultz (Ed.), *The Palgrave handbook of education policy analysis* (pp. 525–540). Palgrave Macmillan.

Minnesota Department of Education. (n.d.). *Minnesota multi-tiered system of supports (MnMTSS) roadmap.* Retrieved from https://education.mn.gov/mde/dse/mtss/roadmap/

Morrow, E., Kabala, B. Z., & Hartness, C. (2024). In pursuit of civic engagement in Texas: Leveraging trust in a changed legal landscape. *Arts, 14*(1), 9.

National Council for the Social Studies. (1994). *National curriculum standards for social studies: Executive summary.* https://www.socialstudies.org/standards/national-curriculum-standards-social-studies-executive-summary

Nebraska Department of Education. (2019). *Nebraska social studies standards implementation.* https://www.education.ne.gov/wp-content/uploads/2019/11/Nebraska-Social-Studies-Standards-Final-11-2019.pdf

Ohio Department of Education and Workforce. (2018). *Ohio's learning standards for social studies.* https://education.ohio.gov/Topics/Learning-in-Ohio/Social-Studies/Ohio-s-Learning-Standards-for-Social-Studies]

South Carolina Code Ann. § 59-29-240 (2024). Retrieved from https://law.justia.com/codes/south-carolina/title-59/chapter-29/section-59-29-240/

The National Assessment of Educational Progress. (2023). *NAEP report card in civics: Student group scores and score gaps.* https://www.nationsreportcard.gov/civics/results/groups/

8
Assessing Student Engagement in a U.S. History and Civics Curriculum

Leah Bueso, Marsha Ing, Abigail Dym, and Joseph Kahne

Increasing student engagement is a common goal for educators and for good reason. Student engagement is positively associated with academic achievement, attendance, retention, and social-emotional learning (Greene, 2015; Klem & Connell, 2004; Reschly & Christenson, 2012). While the promise of such benefits has drawn increased attention to the study of engagement over the past three decades, researchers disagree about how to define and measure the construct (Azevedo, 2015). Moreover, student engagement research efforts in education have centered around specific content areas like reading, science, and math (see Guthrie & Klauda, 2014; Ing et al., 2015; Wang et al., 2016) with social studies largely neglected (Taboada Barber et al., 2017).

There is consensus among social studies educators that student engagement matters for improving learning outcomes (Anderson & Cook, 2014; Gehlbach, 2011; Schmitt et al., 2022). However, there is a lack of consensus about how to assess student engagement in social studies classrooms generally (Marks, 2000; Stevenson, 1990; Taboada Barber et al., 2017) and minimal evidence about how to do so in civics specifically (Beck, 2000; Cohen et al., 2021; Stolte et al., 2013). To better understand student engagement in social studies classrooms implementing civics curricula, this study describes a mixed-methods approach to measuring student engagement as a multidimensional construct. We administered surveys of student engagement to more than 800 middle school students across six school districts implementing the same U.S. history and civics curriculum to assess their behavioral, emotional, and cognitive engagement and observed classrooms across these six school districts.

Conceptualizing Student Engagement

Student engagement can be conceptualized at different "grain sizes" ranging from the microlevel to the macrolevel depending on the context and purpose of the research (Sinatra et al., 2015, p. 2). While research at the microlevel tends to focus on individual students and uses physiological or psychological indicators like eye movements and response time (Miller, 2015), research at the macrolevel looks at groups of students and employs analytical perspectives like summaries of student survey responses and classroom observations (Ryu & Lombardi, 2015).

DOI: 10.4324/9781003476825-10
This chapter has been made available under a CC BY-NC-ND license.

There is no consensus on how to conceptualize different types of student engagement. Some researchers focus on particular types of engagement, while others (e.g., Fredricks et al., 2004, 2016) describe engagement as a multidimensional construct that includes behavioral, emotional, and cognitive perspectives. Within this framework, behavioral engagement considers the extent to which students attend school, follow the rules, and pay attention; cognitive engagement focuses on students' investment in their learning (Chi, 2009; Chi & Wylie, 2014; Dinsmore & Alexander, 2012); and emotional engagement considers students' attitudes, interests, and values (Heddy & Sinatra, 2013). Notably, there are different ways to operationalize the construct even within similar perspectives of engagement. For example, cognitive engagement can be measured using self-report surveys to gauge metacognitive effort (e.g., coping with failure, monitoring study plans) and observations of the frequency of different cognitive strategies used (Fredricks et al., 2011; Gobert & Sao Pedro, 2017; Greene, 2015).

A multidimensional construct of engagement aligns with the goals of social studies and civics classrooms. Indeed, across all content areas, teachers aim to foster classroom environments where students pay attention and follow the rules (behavioral engagement), take interest in and enjoy the content (emotional engagement), and engage in deep processing of the material and ideas covered (cognitive engagement). Compared with other content areas, however, social studies and civics classrooms are more heavily influenced by cultural and political dynamics in and out of schools that hold a uniquely powerful impact on curriculum and instruction. For example, talking about current events and controversial issues is understood to be a part of the core content to a greater degree than in other subjects. As a result, students are more likely to have opportunities to connect classroom content to their own lived experiences and those of their communities. These opportunities may prompt sizable differences in student engagement, particularly emotional engagement, and require distinct or supplementary assessment methods compared to other content areas (Helme & Clarke, 2001; Nystrand et al., 2001; Stevenson, 1990). In addition, the extent to which student engagement in social studies and civics instruction is reflective of and responsive to students' diverse backgrounds and experiences (Cohen et al., 2018; Ladson-Billings, 2001) may vary across communities. Thus, measuring student engagement, especially in a politically polarized school or classroom climate, poses challenges that are unique to social studies and civics (Fredricks & McColskey, 2012; Lawson & Lawson, 2013).

Although methods used to measure student engagement are linked to perspectives or theories on student engagement, there is always concern about whether the measure can be used to make inferences about student engagement. Consistent with current research, we consider validation as an ongoing process and that a measure in and of itself is not valid or invalid. Instead, validation concerns the quality of evidence and theory that supports the actual interpretations made on the basis of a measure (American Educational Research Association, National Council for Measurement in Education, & American Psychological Association [APA], 2014; Kane, 2013; Shepard, 1997). Our investigation is not complete after running a factor analysis or conducting cognitive interviews with respondents from a single sample (Ericsson & Simon, 1980; Flake, 2021; Flake & Fried, 2020). Instead, the investigation continues until consistency in findings across multiple samples is achieved (Haertel, 2018; Moss, 2016). Thus, this study describes an initial step in investigating the extent to which student survey responses could be used to make inferences about student engagement in middle school social studies classrooms implementing a U.S. history and civics curriculum. We intend for student survey responses to eventually be used to make inferences about student engagement such that higher levels of student engagement are related to more positive learning outcomes and lower levels of student engagement are related to less positive learning outcomes. We also anticipate that these student survey responses could eventually be used to identify learning opportunities that support more positive student engagement. While we do not yet have the data to investigate these possible intended uses of the measure or how the measure is actually taken up in practice, in this study we take a first step to determine whether it is useful to pursue additional data collection.

Methods

This study used a mixed-methods approach to explore the quality of inferences about student engagement in middle school social studies classrooms based on student self-reports. We investigate a multidimensional construct of student engagement that includes items designed to measure students' behavioral engagement, emotional engagement, and cognitive engagement.

Sample Population and Context

The sample population for this study included more than 800 seventh and eighth grade students from six school districts across five states: California, Colorado, Louisiana, New Mexico, and Oklahoma. Although we did not collect demographic information about individual students, the demographics of each school district are presented in Table 8.1. School district #1 is plurality White and #2 is majority White, school district #3 is majority Black, and school districts #4, #5, and #6 are majority Latinx. All six school districts have 31% or fewer of their student population living below the poverty line. The demographics of the schools in our sample population roughly align with the demographics of their respective school districts. For example, White students make up 45% of the overall population in district #1 and 39% of the sample of schools in district #1. Similarly, Latinx students make up 76% of the overall population in district #4 and 81% of the sample of schools in district #4.

All six districts were implementing the same U.S. history and civics curriculum created by iCivics called *U.S. History Through Inquiry: Beginning to 1877*. To participate in the pilot implementation of this curriculum, school districts submitted applications to and were chosen by the national nonprofit that created the curriculum. School districts were given the option to take part in an independent evaluation of the curriculum managed by our research team. We were approved to conduct this study through the institutional review board at the University of California, Riverside as well as the research offices of each of the participating school districts.

The U.S. history and civics curriculum was designed to cover an entire school year's scope and sequence (roughly 8 units made up of 120 lessons). Each unit follows an arc of inquiry driven by a compelling question and the analysis of authentic primary and secondary sources. Students are asked to demonstrate their learning through daily, informal writing tasks and a culminating project-based assessment at the end of the unit. Although the assessments differ with each unit, students are always asked to answer the compelling question in a product or performance that can be shared with a broader audience beyond their teacher (e.g., museum exhibit, documentary, collage). The curriculum aligns to both national and state standards for social studies and civics (see, e.g., National Council for the Social Studies, 2013; New Mexico Public Education Department, 2022; Oklahoma State Department of Education, 2019).

Table 8.1 Demographics of School Districts

District	Size	Locale	Race/Ethnicity	Below Poverty
1	>25,000	Midsize suburb	45% White, 36% Latinx, 10% Asian	7%
2	>75,000	Large city	51% White, 19% Latinx, 12% Black	6%
3	>50,000	Midsize city	74% Black, 12% White, 7% Latinx	29%
4	>25,000	Midsize city	76% Latinx, 19% White, 2% Black	25%
5	>25,000	Small city	75% Latinx, 18% White, 3% Two or more races	16%
6	>50,000	Large city	54% Latinx, 20% Black, 17% White	31%

Note. The three largest percentages are reported for each district under race/ethnicity.

Data Collection

In February 2024, at least one member of the research team visited each of the six school districts for a period of two or three days. During those visits, we conducted classroom observations of teachers implementing the new curriculum and administered surveys to students in the observed classes.

Classroom Observations. We conducted 50 classroom observations of 20 teachers across 18 schools. Each teacher was observed for multiple class periods over the course of one school day, but the total number of class periods observed varied among teachers due to differences in their scheduling (e.g., some teachers taught U.S. history for two periods a day, while others taught it for five periods). Similarly, classroom observations ranged in length from 45 to 90 minutes depending on the schedule for each school. Teachers implemented the same lesson across all class periods during which they were observed but did not necessarily implement the same lesson as other teachers across the sample.

During the observations, a member of the research team took narrative and descriptive notes on teacher-student and student-student interactions that related to behavioral, emotional, and cognitive engagement. We were not able to identify individual students in the observations so to maintain confidentiality, students were assigned a number and that number was used to match students' in-class interactions with their survey responses.

Survey. The *Social Studies Student Engagement* survey was administered at the end of each class period by a member of the research team. The research team members passed out paper copies of the survey to students and provided instructions on how to complete it. We notified students that their participation in the survey was voluntary and that their responses would not impact their grades or standing in the class. We also encouraged students to provide honest answers and reminded them that their responses would not impact their teacher in any way. The survey included a total of nine items with three items for each perspective of engagement – behavioral, emotional, and cognitive. All nine items were yes/no questions. It took students an average of 5 minutes to complete the survey.

The survey items used to assess behavioral engagement were drawn from the *School Engagement Measure* (Fredricks et al., 2005) and modified to fit the context of this study. For example, since the survey asked students to reflect on their behavioral engagement at the end of a specific class period, verbs were shifted to past tense (e.g., "I pay attention in class" became "I paid attention in class today"). We also replaced general references to "school" with specific references to "class" and we substituted certain phrases to better reflect our focus on day-of, in-class behavior (e.g., "I follow the rules at school" became "I stayed on task during class today"). The modified survey items for behavioral engagement were presented as follows:

- "I turned in my assignments for today."
- "I stayed on task during class today."
- "I paid attention during class today."

To measure emotional engagement, we started with items from the *5Essentials* survey that were designed to provide diagnostic information about evidence-based indicators that lead to improved student outcomes (University of Chicago, 2023). These survey items were developed by members of the research team several years ago in consultation with civic education leaders from Chicago Public Schools. While the *5Essentials* survey includes over 120 items in its entirety, we focused on two items used in the social studies subset related to student engagement (University of Chicago, 2024). We modified these items by adding the specific class title and updating the timing qualifiers in line with the parameters of this study (e.g., "I usually look forward to my social science class" became "I look forward to what we are learning in my U.S. history class tomorrow"). We also divided one of the existing survey items into two new items to gauge students' sensitivity to the adjectives "meaningful" and "important." Thus, the survey items for emotional engagement were expanded as follows:

- "What we learned about in class today was meaningful to me."
- "What we learned about in class today was important to me."
- "I look forward to what we are learning in my U.S. history class tomorrow."

The survey items used to assess cognitive engagement were based on research that suggests that explaining one's own thinking and comparing one's ideas with others' ideas can help students identify misunderstandings or deficiencies, reveal differences in perspectives, and develop more complex reasoning skills (Chi, 2000; Chi et al., 2018; Roscoe & Chi, 2008). Research in mathematics education examined students' participation in different settings (Webb et al., 2014, 2021, 2023) and found that students who construct arguments and critique the reasoning of others were related to productive student outcomes (Ing et al., 2015). Drawing from this previous research, we developed the following survey items for cognitive engagement:

- "I defended or argued my ideas with another student today."
- "I asked other students questions about their ideas today."
- "I debated ideas with other students today."

Data Analysis

We used multiple methods to investigate whether we feel confident making inferences about student engagement based on self-report surveys. To better understand the psychometric properties of the items, exploratory and confirmatory factor analyses were conducted (Rodriguez et al., 2016a, 2016b). These analyses provide guidance as to whether we can consider the nine survey items as a total score (Reise et al., 2010) and the extent to which there are three subscales representing theoretically distinct constructs (behavioral engagement, cognitive engagement, emotional engagement) that can provide scores after accounting for the general factor of student engagement (Reise et al., 2013).

Factor analysis was conducted using the Mplus software version 8.2 (Muthén & Muthén, 1998–2011). The weighted least square mean and variance-adjusted estimation method were used due to the categorical response options of the nine items. The sample of 807 cases were randomly split into two samples. The first sample ($n = 404$) was used to conduct the exploratory factor analysis and the second sample ($n = 403$) was used to conduct the confirmatory factor analysis. After the two samples were created, data from each sample was checked to ensure that students from different school districts and teachers were represented. In addition, chi-square tests were conducted to determine whether there were any differences in the responses to the nine items across the two samples. There were no differences across any of the items, so the analysis proceeded on each sample.

In addition to the quantitative analyses, we analyzed classroom observations of student engagement in conjunction with the self-report survey responses. All class periods were observed on the same day in which the student surveys were administered. Based on the observation notes, we assigned codes to each class period to reflect the level of students' behavioral, cognitive, and emotional engagement. Class periods with higher levels of engagement were given a "1," and class periods with lower levels of engagement were given a "0." Table 8.2 provides examples of the codes for each perspective of engagement.

Table 8.2 Examples of Classroom Observation Coding

	Behavioral	Emotional	Cognitive
Lower engagement	Students spend most of their time off task during small group work (e.g., talking about movies, listening to music on their phones)	Relatively few students are following along with the group task during small group work	Students are not talking with each other during small group work (i.e., no discussion)
Higher engagement	Students spend most of their time completing assigned tasks (e.g., annotating primary sources)	A majority of students ask substantive follow-up questions about the lesson material (e.g., Why would people leave their peaceful farm to work in a dirty factory?)	Students take turns reading primary sources out loud and debating answers to the guiding questions

The observations and coding were carried out by the research team. To investigate the consistency of the coding, all four authors coded the same seven observations. These seven class periods were selected to reflect differences across the entire sample; however, the amount of variation due to differences between class periods was low (16%; Shavelson & Webb, 1991). The amount of variation due to differences between these four raters was also low (4%) with most of the variation due to differences between the type of engagement (39%). Due to the low variation among raters, a single rater coded the remainder of the observations (generalizability coefficient = 0.74).

Results

The initial sample included 894 student survey responses across six school districts, 18 middle schools, 20 middle school teachers, and 50 class periods. There were 87 surveys with at least one item response missing. To handle missing data, we checked the original paper copies of the survey to see whether there were any data entry issues or systematic ways in which the responses were missing. We did not find any patterns and missing responses were not concentrated in a particular school district, school, teacher, or item. We then considered different options to handle the missing data such as imputing values. After running initial descriptive analyses and finding a similar outcome between the imputed values and non-imputed data, we decided to exclude responses that were missing data on at least one item. Thus, the final sample size used in the analyses was 807. Table 8.3 lists the response rates for each of the nine survey items.

Table 8.3 Survey Responses ($n=807$)

Survey item	Response	
	No	Yes
I turned in my assignments for today	157 (19%)	650 (81%)
I stayed on task during class today	116 (14%)	691 (86%)
I paid attention during class today	62 (8%)	745 (92%)
I asked other students questions about their ideas today	368 (46%)	439 (54%)
I debated ideas with other students today	453 (56%)	354 (44%)
I defended or argued my ideas with other students today	556 (69%)	251 (31%)
What we learned about in class today was meaningful to me	313 (39%)	494 (61%)
What we learned about in class today was important to me	311 (39%)	496 (61%)
I look forward to what we are learning in my U.S. history class tomorrow	286 (35%)	521 (65%)

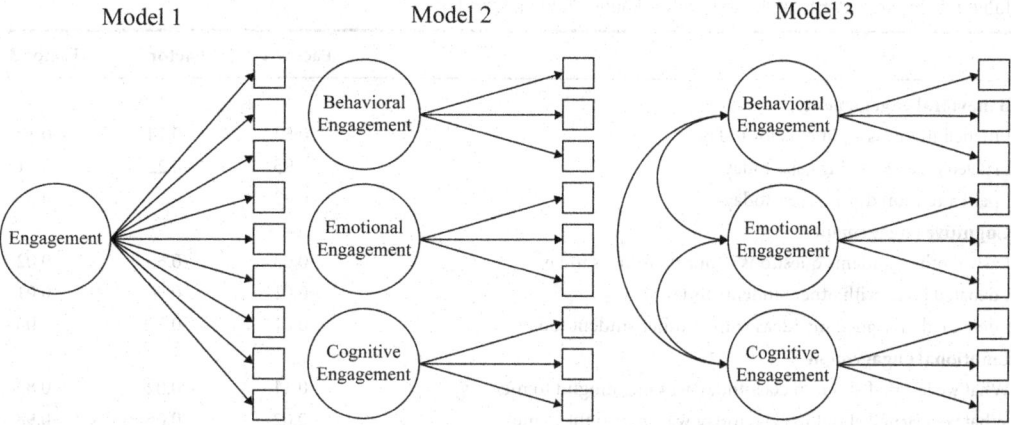

Figure 8.1 Models Tested.

Initial tests did not indicate concerns with singularity or multicollinearity. In addition, Bartlett's test of sphericity testing the null hypothesis that the correlation matrix is an identity matrix suggests that factor analysis is appropriate for this data ($\chi^2(N = 36) = 1309.77$, $p < 0.001$). Exploratory factor analysis was conducted on the first sample for a one-factor model of engagement where all nine items were included as a single factor (engagement). The fit of the one-factor model was compared with a two-factor and three-factor model. Confirmatory factor analysis was conducted with the second sample on the model with the best fit based on the exploratory factor analysis results. Figure 8.1 illustrates how we used confirmatory factor analysis to test a model where the factors were correlated with a model where the factors were not correlated.

Several fit statistics were used to identify the number of factors to retain based on the exploratory factor analysis (Finch, 2020). Compared to one and two factors, the comparative fit index (1.00) and Tucker-Lewis index (1.00) were highest and the root mean square error of approximation estimate was the lowest (0.02) for three factors. The chi-square test of model fit for the three-factor model was not significant, $\chi^2(N = 12) = 6.55$, $p = 0.89$. The estimated eigenvalue of the first factor was 2.76, compared to 2.27 for the second factor, 1.81 for the third factor, and 0.65 for the fourth factor. In addition, when comparing the models, the three-factor compared to the four-factor model was not significant, $\chi^2(N = 6) = 4.71$, $p = 0.58$, but the two-factor compared to the three-factor model was significant, $\chi^2(N = 7) = 113.01$, $p < 0.01$. Table 8.4 shows the results of the exploratory factor analysis for the three-factor model. The three factors were consistent with the behavioral, emotional, and cognitive engagement framework grounding this study (Fredricks et al., 2004, 2016).

Using the second sample, a confirmatory factor analysis was conducted for the three-factor model. The chi-square difference test indicated that the three-factor model with correlated factors fit the data, $\chi^2(N = 27) = 62.50$, $p < 0.01$, and was a statistically better fit compared to the three-factor model where the factors were not correlated, $\chi^2(N = 3) = 16.63$, $p < 0.01$. The three-factor model with correlated factors using confirmatory factor analysis, $\chi^2(N = 24) = 37.35$, $p = 0.04$, was structurally consistent with the three-factor model with correlated factors using exploratory factor analysis.

Using the total sum score of survey responses, we also compared class periods where there were relatively different levels of reported student engagement. The use of survey responses in this way can be problematic when compared to latent variable methods. In particular, the sum scores may be less accurate and do not consider measurement error (McNeish, 2023;

Table 8.4 Exploratory Factor Analysis with Oblique Rotation (*n*=404)

	Factor 1	Factor 2	Factor 3
Behavioral engagement			
I turned in my assignments for today	0.53	0.14	−0.17
I stayed on task during class today	0.95	−0.22	0.01
I paid attention during class today	0.83	0.01	0.05
Cognitive engagement			
I asked other students questions about their ideas today	0.03	0.65	0.02
I debated ideas with other students today	−0.01	0.98	0.01
I defended or argued my ideas with another student today	0.01	0.72	−0.05
Emotional engagement			
What we learned about in class today was meaningful to me	0.11	−0.02	0.83
What we learned about in class today was important to me	−0.02	0.06	0.98
I look forward to what we are learning in my U.S. history class tomorrow	0.01	0.10	0.66

McNeish & Wolf, 2020). However, we made the decision to use sum scores in service of better understanding whether these survey responses would allow for inferences about student engagement. Across the entire sample included in this study, students varied in their reported engagement (78% of the reported behavioral engagement, 82% in reported emotional engagement, and 71% in reported cognitive engagement). The variation between teachers is consistent with the expectation that opportunities to engage in class on any day depend on the content covered, the learning activities chosen, and the ways in which teachers facilitate opportunities for engagement (Gould et al., 2011; Stevenson, 1990; Taboada Barber et al., 2017).

While these results suggest three subscales (behavioral engagement, cognitive engagement, emotional engagement) can be used to make inferences about student engagement, additional information is needed to better understand whether student responses were consistent with other sources of information such as teacher reports of their students' engagement. The use of factor analysis to support inferences is important, but insufficient in theoretical and applied settings (e.g., Bostic et al., 2019; Chang & Cochran-Smith, 2022; Delis et al., 2003; Flake et al., 2017, 2022; Maul, 2017). Since this investigation of the factorial composition does not provide information about the extent to which student responses could be used to make inferences about behavioral, emotional, and cognitive engagement (e.g., Flake, 2021; Goodwin, 1999; Moss, 2016), qualitative data from classroom observations were analyzed.

To compare the data from the self-report surveys, we compared classroom averages of student responses to the classroom observations ($n = 50$). There were no surveys administered to students in one of the observed class periods, so it was excluded from the analyses ($n = 49$). Although measures collecting student-level data are ideal for making comparisons to survey responses (Ericsson, 2017; Ericsson & Simon, 1993, 1998; Leighton, 2017, 2021), students could not be individually identified through classroom observations or administrative data (e.g., demographics, standardized test scores) in this study. Despite this limitation, we collected classroom-level data about student engagement that provided context to better understand students' responses to the survey. The classroom observations and survey responses were positively correlated in terms of behavioral ($r = 0.45$), cognitive ($r = 0.33$), and emotional ($r = 0.36$) engagement. Students in classrooms coded as having higher engagement by the research team also self-reported higher levels of engagement. In addition, there were significant differences in survey responses between classrooms that were coded as having lower

Table 8.5 Classroom Observations and Average Classroom Survey Responses ($n=50$)

	Classroom Observations				t-test
	Lower Engagement		Higher Engagement		
	Mean	SD	Mean	SD	
Behavioral	2.28	0.48	2.67	0.27	−3.49
Cognitive	1.22	0.44	1.65	0.67	−2.41
Emotional	1.83	0.57	2.29	0.52	−2.62

levels of engagement and classrooms that were coded as having higher levels of engagement (Table 8.5). These results suggest moderate consistency between the survey responses and classroom observations and provide initial tentative evidence that observations of engagement were consistent with student perceptions about their engagement in that class period. Furthermore, such additional information helped contextualize survey responses and further support our findings that multidimensional survey items could be used to make inferences about student engagement.

Discussion

Drawing from a sample of more than 800 middle school students from 18 schools across six school districts, this study explores a mixed-methods approach to measuring student engagement in social studies classrooms. We examined whether self-report surveys supported a multidimensional construct of student engagement and the extent to which classroom observations aligned with inferences from students' self-reports of their engagement.

Multidimensional Construct of Student Engagement

The results of this study demonstrate that student engagement in the social studies classroom can be measured as a multidimensional construct (Fredricks et al., 2004, 2016). Although all three perspectives included in the survey – behavioral, emotional, and cognitive engagement – are distinct, our analysis revealed an interdependence among the perspectives. This finding is consistent with the observations of the research team during development of the coding manual for the classroom observations, as it was difficult to determine where one type of engagement started and another ended. For example, the extent to which a student is staying on task can be an indicator of both behavioral and emotional engagement or just behavioral. While one could argue that a student is showing emotional engagement by staying on task, another could argue that staying on task alone is not sufficient to indicate emotional engagement, but rather a reflection of a student's desire to "do school" (i.e., follow directions and complete their work to get good grades). As another example, the frequency with which a student asks substantive questions about the lesson material can be an indicator of both emotional and cognitive engagement or just cognitive. Is the student asking questions because the material is meaningful to them or because they want to develop their own new ideas about the material? As we grappled with the overlapping qualities of the three types of engagement, it helped to remind us that all nine survey items are related and cannot be neatly placed into separate buckets. Instead, we must think about student engagement as a cluster of indicators that reflect three different, but interdependent facets of the overarching construct of engagement.

One potential next step in our research is to consider ways to conceptualize engagement through other perspectives and analytical frameworks such as rational/technical, interpretive/student-centered, or critical/transformative (Vibert & Shields, 2003). A rational/technical lens views the primary purpose of education as successful competition in the labor market (e.g., job market, university), and thus, engagement is not an end but an instrument to enhance human capital (e.g., grades, standardized test scores). An interpretive/student-centered lens centers on self-discovery and individual fulfillment through curricular opportunities for student choice and autonomy (e.g., students working productively on a project that interests them and over which they have control). A critical/transformative lens views education as potentially transformative of the lives of individuals and communities and asks teachers to commit to the democratic purposes of schooling, political dimensions of education, and explicitly call attention to issues of social difference (e.g., race, class, gender). These frameworks might help us further situate the unique characteristics of student engagement in social studies and civics classrooms as differences in how and why students choose to engage behaviorally, cognitively, and emotionally.

Furthermore, it is important for future research to consider the utility and value of a multidimensional construct of student engagement to examine whether particular social studies or civic pedagogies, curricula, or professional development can promote any or all three perspectives. Access to this information can guide educators implementing continuous improvement cycles and bring awareness to new concerns that may require additional modifications or considerations.

Comparing Self-Report Surveys with Classroom Observations

Our mixed-methods approach allowed us to investigate students' self-reports of their engagement. Even though middle school students are familiar with taking surveys, it doesn't necessarily mean that their responses are indicators of their engagement. By comparing the survey responses to the classroom observations, we challenge our confidence in self-reports as a valid measure of student engagement. In other words, triangulating different sources of information about students' engagement helped us to further investigate whether students were as engaged (or not engaged) as they reported themselves to be. For example, students in classrooms coded as having higher engagement by the research team also self-reported higher levels of engagement across all three perspectives. Likewise, students in classrooms coded as having lower engagement self-reported lower levels of engagement across all three perspectives. Given the consistency in the ratings of student engagement from the classroom observations and student surveys, there is initial support for the use of the nine survey items to make inferences about student engagement in middle school social studies classrooms.

Implications

While there is great potential in self-reports of student engagement, we recognize the need for ongoing validation efforts to better understand the extent to which inferences about student engagement are supported. For example, students who are particularly disengaged might not willingly report their lack of engagement. These students might overestimate or inflate their engagement, which calls into question the extent to which responses to these items fully capture their engagement. This limitation might be more prevalent for certain types of engagement (behavioral) compared to other types of engagement (emotional) and might not reflect actual variation in student engagement. Given this limitation of self-reports as objective indicators, we recommend continuing to investigate inferences about student engagement. In addition, we expect but do not have evidence that student responses of their engagement are related to student outcomes (e.g., academic, civic). Investigating potential relations among the factors (such as greater emotional engagement associated with greater behavioral engagement) has implications for targeting interventions on types of engagement. This type of evidence would allow education researchers to examine productive student engagement and then support teachers to use this information in their classrooms. For example, if students' self-reported cognitive engagement was related to learning, but only if students also reported emotional engagement, lessons could be designed and implemented in ways that support both cognitive and emotional engagement. Future research in these directions could help address questions of whether emotional or cognitive engagement are both desirable outcomes and necessary factors for student learning. It is also the case that additional types of engagement (e.g., social) might be more central to the democratic purposes of civic education. If such were the case, teachers could use data from student survey responses to identify strategies to support students' engagement and gather feedback about the extent to which their students were engaged. While we were not able to investigate the relationship in this study, this is a necessary future direction in the conceptualization and measurement of engagement in civics.

We also acknowledge that self-reports from a single time point might not generalize to other parts of the class period or other lessons, so additional work is needed to investigate potential variation in reported engagement and the factors that influence such variation. This type of research would require more in-depth data collection that follows students and teachers working on the same lessons for longer periods of time. In doing so, researchers could investigate variation across lessons, classrooms, and students in the hopes of providing recommendations for implementation in ways that will increase student engagement. As part of ongoing validity efforts, future studies should test alternative models of engagement and conduct additional tests of the relationship between the focal construct (engagement) and other conceptually related latent variables (motivation). In addition, testing for differences between groups is important when considering if a multidimensional construct is similar across different populations (Flake et al., 2022; Hussey & Hughes, 2020). For example, testing this construct with students who were included in this study who had opportunities to engage in civic learning opportunities and students who were not included in this study who did not have opportunities to engage in civic learning opportunities. Furthermore, it would be worthwhile to consider student engagement from the perspective of both students and teachers (Herman et al., 2000). These research strategies are necessary to highlight the diverse ways in which students can be supported to engage in social studies classrooms.

Acknowledgments

This study was supported through a subcontract for an independent evaluation from iCivics and funded as part of a larger grant from the Schusterman Foundation. The chapter's authors are solely responsible for all content and any views expressed do not necessarily reflect those of iCivics or the Schusterman Foundation.

References

American Educational Research Association, American Psychological Association, & National Council on Measurement in Education. (2014). *Standards for educational and psychological testing*. American Educational Research Association.

Anderson, D., & Cook, T. (2014). Committed to differentiation and engagement: A case study of two American secondary social studies teachers. *Journal of Social Studies Education Research, 5*(1), 1–19.

Azevedo, R. (2015). Defining and measuring engagement and learning in science: Conceptual, theoretical, methodological and analytical issues. *Educational Psychologist, 50*(1), 84–94.

Beck, T. A. (2000, November 16–19). *Using problem-solving steps and audience roles to increase student engagement in elementary civics instruction* [Paper presentation]. Annual Meeting of the National Council for the Social Studies.

Bostic, J., Krupa, E. E., & Shih, J. C. (Eds.). (2019). *Quantitative measures of mathematical knowledge: Researching instruments and perspectives.* Routledge.

Chang, W.-C., & Cochran-Smith, M.(2022). Learning to teach for equity, social justice, and/or diversity: Do the measures measure up? *Journal of Teacher Education.* https://doi.org/10.1177/00224871221075284

Chi, M. T. H. (2000). Self-explaining expository texts: The dual processes of generating inferences and repairing mental models. In R. Glaser (Ed.), *Advances in instructional psychology: Educational design and cognitive science* (pp. 161–238). Erlbaum.

Chi, M. T. H. (2009). Active-constructive-interactive: A conceptual framework for differentiating learning activities. *Topics in Cognitive Science, 1,* 73–105.

Chi, M. T. H., Adams, J., Bogusch, E. B., Bruchok, C., Kang, S., Lancaster, M., Levy, R., Li, N., McEldoon, K. L., Stump, G. S., Wylie, R., Xu, D., & Yaghmourian, D. L. (2018). Translating the ICAP theory of cognitive engagement into practice. *Cognitive Science, 42*(6), 1777–1832.

Chi, M. T. H., & Wylie, R. (2014). The ICAP framework: Linking cognitive engagement to active learning outcomes. *Educational Psychologist, 49*(4), 219–243.

Cohen, A. K., Fitzgerald, J. C., Ridley-Kerr, A., Maker Castro, E., & Ballard, P. J. (2021). Investigating the impact of generation citizen's action civics education program on student academic engagement. *The Clearing House: A Journal of Educational Strategies, Issues and Ideas, 94*(4), 168–180.

Cohen, C., Kahne, J., & Marshall, J. with Anderson, V., Brower, M., & Knight, D. (2018). *Let's go there: Race, ethnicity, and a lived civics approach to civic education.* GenForward at the University of Chicago.

Delis, D. C., Jacobson, M., Bondi, M. W., Hamilton, J. M., & Salmon, D. P. (2003). The myth of testing construct validity using factor analysis or correlations with normal or mixed clinical populations: Lessons from memory assessment. *Journal of the International Neuropsychological Society, 9,* 936–946.

Dinsmore, D. L., & Alexander, P. A. (2012). A critical discussion of deep and surface processing: What it means, how it is measured, the role of context, and model specification. *Educational Psychology Review, 24,* 499–567.

Ericsson, K. A. (2017). Protocol analysis. In W. Bechtel & G. Graham (Eds.), *A companion to cognitive science* (pp. 425–432). Wiley.

Ericsson, K. A., & Simon, H. A. (1980). Verbal reports as data. *Psychological Review, 87*(3), 215–251.

Ericsson, K. A., & Simon, H. A. (1993). *Protocol analysis: Verbal reports as data.* MIT Press.

Ericsson, K. A., & Simon, H. A. (1998). How to study thinking in everyday life: Contrasting think-aloud protocols with descriptions and explanations of thinking. *Mind, Culture, and Activity, 5*(3), 178–186.

Finch, W. H. (2020). Using fit statistic differences to determine the optimal number of factors to retain in an exploratory factor analysis. *Educational and Psychological Measurement, 80*(2), 217–241.

Flake, J. K. (2021). Strengthening the foundation of educational psychology by integrating construct validation into open science reform. *Educational Psychologist, 56*(2), 132–141.

Flake, J. K., Davidson, I. J., Wong, O., & Pek, J. (2022). Construct validity and the validity of replication studies: A systematic review. *American Psychologist, 77*(4), 576–588.

Flake, J. K., & Fried, E. I. (2020). Measurement schmeasurement: Questionable measurement practices and how to avoid them. *Advances in Methods and Practices in Psychological Science, 3*(4), 456–465.

Flake, J. K., Pek, J., & Hehman, E. (2017). Construct validation in social and personality research: Current practice and recommendations. *Social Psychological and Personality Science, 8*(4), 1–24.

Fredricks, J., McColskey, W., Meli, J., Mordica, J., Montrosse, B., & Mooney, K. (2011). *Measuring student engagement in upper elementary through high school: A description of 21 instruments* (Issues & Answers Report, REL 2011–No. 098). Department of Education, Institute of Education Sciences, National Center for Education Evaluation and Regional Assistance, Regional Educational Laboratory Southeast.

Fredricks, J. A., Blumenfeld, P. C., & Paris, A. H. (2004). School engagement: Potential of the concept, state of the evidence. *Review of Educational Research, 74,* 59–109.

Fredricks, J. A., Blumfeld, P. C., Friedel, J., & Paris, A. (2005). School engagement. In K. A. Moore & L. H. Lippman (Eds.), *What do children need to flourish? Conceptualizing and measuring indicators of progress* (pp. 305–321). Springer.

Fredricks, J. A., Filsecker, M., & Lawson, M. A. (2016). Student engagement, context, and adjustment: Addressing definitional, measurement, and methodological issues. *Learning and Instruction, 43,* 1–4.

Fredricks, J. A., & McColskey, W. (2012). The measurement of student engagement: A comparative analysis of various methods and student self-report instruments. In S. Christenson, A. Reschly, & C. Wylie (Eds.), *Handbook of research on student engagement* (pp. 763–782). Springer.

Gehlbach, H. (2011). Making social studies social: Engaging students through different forms of social perspective taking. *Theory Into Practice, 50*(4), 311–318.

Gobert, J. D., & Sao Pedro, M. A. (2017). Digital assessment environments for scientific inquiry practices. In A. A. Rupp & J. P. Leighton (Eds.), *The Wiley handbook of cognition and assessment frameworks, methodologies, and applications* (pp. 508–534). John Wiley & Sons.

Goodwin, L. D. (1999). The role of factor analysis in the estimation of construct validity. *Measurement in Physical Education and Exercise Science*, 3(2), 85–100.

Gould, J., Jamieson, K. H., Levine, P., McConnell, T., Smith, D. B., McKinney-Browning, M., & Cambell, K. (Eds.). (2011). *Guardian of democracy: The civic mission of schools*. The Lenore Annenberg Institute for Civics of the Annenberg Public Policy Center at the University of Pennsylvania and the Civic Mission of Schools.

Greene, B. A. (2015). Measuring cognitive engagement with self-report scales: Reflections from over 20 years of research. *Educational Psychologist*, 50(1), 14–30.

Guthrie, J. T., & Klauda, S. L. (2014). Effects of classroom practices on reading comprehension, engagement, and motivations for adolescents. *Reading Research Quarterly*, 49(4), 387–416.

Haertel, E. H. (2018). Tests, test scores, and constructs. *Educational Psychologist*, 53(3), 203–216.

Heddy, B. C., & Sinatra, G. M. (2013). Transforming misconceptions: Using transformative experience to promote positive affect and conceptual change in students learning about biological evolution. *Science Education*, 97, 723–744.

Helme, S., & Clarke, D. (2001). Identifying cognitive engagement in the mathematics classrooms. *Mathematics Educational Journal*, 13, 133–153.

Herman, J. L., Klein, D. C. D., & Abedi, J. (2000). Assessing students' opportunity to learn: Teacher and student perspectives. *Educational Measurement: Issues and Practice*, 19(4), 16–24.

Hussey, I., & Hughes, S. (2020). Hidden invalidity among 15 commonly used measures in social and personality psychology. *Advances in Methods and Practices in Psychological Science*, 3, 166–184.

Ing, M., Webb, N. M., Franke, M. L., Turrou, A. C., Wong, N. S., & Fernandez, C. H. (2015). Student participation in elementary mathematics classrooms: The missing link between teacher practices and student achievement? *Educational Studies in Mathematics*, 90(3), 341–356.

Kane, M. T. (2013). Validating the interpretations and uses of test scores. *Journal of Educational Measurement*, 50(1), 1–73.

Klem, A. M., & Connell, J. P. (2004). Relationships matter: Linking teacher support to student engagement and achievement. *Journal of School Health*, 74(7), 262–273.

Ladson-Billings, G. (2001). Crafting a culturally responsive social studies approach. In E. W. Ross (Ed.), *Social studies curriculum: Purposes, problems, and possibilities* (pp. 201–215). State University of New York Press.

Lawson, M. A., & Lawson, H. A. (2013). New conceptual frameworks for student engagement research, policy, and practice. *Review of Educational Research*, 83(3), 432–479.

Leighton, J. P. (2017). *Using think-aloud interviews and cognitive labs in educational research*. Oxford University Press.

Leighton, J. P. (2021). Rethinking think-alouds: The often-problematic collection of response process data. *Applied Measurement in Education*, 34(1), 61–74.

Marks, H. M. (2000). Student engagement in instructional activity: Patterns in the elementary, middle, and high school years. *American Educational Research Journal*, 37(1), 153–184.

Maul, A. (2017). Rethinking traditional methods of survey validation. *Measurement: Interdisciplinary Research and Perspectives*, 15(2), 51–69.

McNeish, D. (2023). Psychometric properties of sum scores and factor scores differ even when their correlation is 0.98: A response to Widaman and Revelle. *Behavior Research Methods*, 55(8), 4269–4290.

McNeish, D., & Wolf, M. G. (2020). Thinking twice about sum scores. *Behavioral Research*, 52, 2287–2305.

Miller, B. (2015). Using reading times and eye-movements to measure cognitive engagement. *Educational Psychologist*, 50(1), 31–42.

Moss, P. A. (2016). Shifting the focus of validity for test use. *Assessment in Education: Principles, Policy & Practice*, 23(2), 236–251.

Muthén, L. K., & Muthén, B. O. (1998–2011). *Mplus user's guide* (6th ed.). Muthén & Muthén.

National Council for the Social Studies. (2013). *College, career, and civic life (C3) framework for social studies state standards: Guidance for enhancing the rigor of K-12 civics, economics, geography, and history*. https://www.socialstudies.org/system/files/2022/c3-framework-for-social-studies-rev0617.2.pdf

New Mexico Public Education Department. (2022). *New Mexico social studies standards*. https://webnew.ped.state.nm.us/wp-content/uploads/2022/02/NM-Standards-508.pdf

Nystrand, M., Wu, L. L., Gamaron, A., Zeiser, S., & Long, D. (2001). *Questions in time: Investigating the structure and dynamics of unfolding classroom discourse*. National Research Center on English Learning & Achievement.

Oklahoma State Department of Education. (2019). *Oklahoma academic standards: Social studies*. https://oklahoma.gov/content/dam/ok/en/osde/documents/services/standards-learning/social-studies/Oklahoma-Academic-Standards-for-Social-Studies.pdf

Reise, S. P., Moore, T. M., & Haviland, M. G. (2010). Bifactor models and rotations: Exploring the extent to which multidimensional data yield univocal scale scores. *Journal of Personality Assessment*, 92(6), 544–559.

Reise, S. P., Moore, T. M., & Haviland, M. G. (2013). Applying unidimensional item response theory models to psychological data. In K. F. Geisinger, B. A. Bracken, J. F. Carlson, J.-I. C. Hansen, N. R. Kuncel, S. P. Reise, & M. C. Rodriguez (Eds.), *APA handbook of testing and assessment in psychology*, Vol. 1. Test theory and testing and assessment in industrial and organizational psychology (pp. 101–119). American Psychological Association.

Reschly, A. L., & Christenson, S. L. (2012). Jingle, jangle, and conceptual haziness: Evolution and future directions of the engagement construct. In S. J. Christenson, A. L. Reschly, & C. Wylie (Eds.), *Handbook of research on student engagement* (pp. 3–19). Springer.

Rodriguez, A., Reise, S. P., & Haviland, M. G. (2016a). Applying bifactor statistical indices in the evaluation of psychological measures. *Journal of Personality Assessment, 98*(3), 223–237.

Rodriguez, A., Reise, S. P., & Haviland, M. G. (2016b). Evaluating bifactor models: Calculating and interpreting statistical indices. *Psychological Methods, 21*(2), 137–150.

Roscoe, R. D., & Chi, M. (2008). Tutor learning: The role of instructional explaining and responding to questions. *Instructional Science, 36*(4), 321–350.

Ryu, S., & Lombardi, D. (2015). Coding classroom interactions for collective and individual engagement. *Educational Psychologist, 50*(1), 70–83.

Schmitt, H. A., Witmer, S. E., & Rowe, S. S. (2022). Text readability, comprehension instruction, and student engagement: Examining associated relationships during text-based social studies instruction. *Literacy Research and Instruction, 61*(1), 62–83.

Shavelson, R. J., & Webb, N. M. (1991). *Generalizability theory: A primer*. Sage Publications.

Shepard, L. A. (1997). The centrality of test use and consequences for test validity. *Educational Measurement: Issues and Practice, 16*(2), 5–24.

Sinatra, G. M., Heddy, B. C., & Lombardi, D. (2015). The challenges of defining and measuring student engagement in science. *Educational Psychologist, 50*(1), 1–13.

Stevenson, R. B. (1990). Engagement and cognitive challenge in thoughtful social studies classes: A study of student perspectives. *Journal of Curriculum Studies, 22*(4), 329–341.

Stolte, L. C., Isenbarger, M., & Cohen, A. K. (2013). Measuring civic engagement processes and youth civic empowerment in the classroom: The CIVVICS observation tool. *The Clearing House: A Journal of Educational Strategies, Issues and Ideas, 87*(1), 44–51.

Taboada Barber, A. M., Buehl, M. M., & Beck, J. S. (2017). Dynamics of engagement and disaffection in a social studies classroom context. *Psychology in the Schools, 54*(7), 736–755.

University of Chicago. (2023). *5Essentials: Survey administration manual*. University of Chicago Urban Education Institute. https://impactsurveys.my.site.com/s/article/Illinois-5Essentials-Survey-Administration-Manual

University of Chicago. (2024). *5Essentials survey*. University of Chicago Consortium on School Research. https://uchicagoimpact.org/sites/default/files/2024%20CPS%205Essentials%20Student%20Survey.pdf

Vibert, A., & Shields, C. (2003). Approaches to student engagement: Does ideology matter? *McGill Journal of Education, 38*(2), 221–240.

Wang, M. T., Fredricks, J. A., Ye, F., Hofkens, T. L., & Linn, J. S. (2016). The math and science engagement scales: Scale development, validation, and psychometric properties. *Learning and Instruction, 43*, 16–26.

Webb, N. M., Franke, M. L., Ing, M., Wong, J., Fernandez, C. H., & Shin, N. (2014). Engaging with others' mathematical ideas: Interrelationships among student participation, teachers' instructional practices and learning. *International Journal of Educational Research, 63*, 79–93.

Webb, N. M., Franke, M. L., Johnson, N. C., Ing, M., & Zimmerman, J. (2023). Learning through explaining and engaging with others' mathematical ideas. *Mathematical Thinking and Learning, 25*(4), 438–464.

Webb, N. M., Ing, M., Burnheimer, E., Johnson, N. C., Franke, M. L., & Zimmerman, J. (2021). Is there a right way? Productive patterns of interaction during collaborative problem solving. *Education Sciences, 11*(5), 1–18.

9
Measuring Civic Values to Assess Civic Identity Development in Adolescents

David C. Kidd and Nicolás Riveros Medelius

The most crucial task of civic education is to prepare young people to "take on the demanding responsibilities of engaged, responsible citizenship over a lifetime" (Levinson & Levine, 2013, p. 341). This mission, though long neglected (Rebell, 2018), has been revived in the face of increasing political polarization (Kingzette et al., 2021; Tyler & Iyengar, 2023) and waning democratic commitments (Diamond, 2020). Notably, several states have launched initiatives to improve civic education (Journell, 2015; Stern et al., 2021; Wilson et al., 2019). Among them, Massachusetts, the setting for this project, recently introduced new K-12 history and social science standards accompanied by a mandate to implement student-led civics projects in grade 8 and high school.

These new requirements called for new curricula, and, among other providers stepping forward to meet the need for civics resources, the Democratic Knowledge Project (DKP), founded at the Edmond & Lily Safra Center for Ethics at Harvard University, developed a grade 8 curriculum, *Civic Engagement in Our Democracy*, aligned with the new standards and with a commitment to deeper civic learning (Mehta & Fine, 2019). Rooted in project-based learning, which research shows improves traditional knowledge-based academic outcomes (Chen & Yang, 2019), the curriculum is intended support learners to develop authentic civic identities (Allen & Kidd, 2022; Haduong et al., 2024), which the DKP understands in terms of a sociocultural theory of learning (Lave & Wenger, 1991; Wenger, 2010).

This chapter first briefly describes the DKP's account of civic identity development and shows how it helps to clarify constructs for assessment. Then, drawing on the framework for evaluating sources of evidence for the valid use and interpretation of tests (American Educational Research Association et al., 2014), it will focus on the development of the civic values questionnaire (CVQ) to measure a core component of civic identity, commitment to shared civic values. Finally, it will present guidelines for the valid use of the CVQ along with suggestions for using similar methods to develop tools for assessing civic learning.

Civic Identity Development

To participate in civic life is to engage with fellow members of a shared political community to shape the present and future. Civic identity development lays the groundwork for participation

DOI: 10.4324/9781003476825-11
This chapter has been made available under a CC BY-NC-ND license.

in civic life (Allen & Kidd, 2022), and specific kinds of educational experiences can be powerful supports for such identity development (Haduong et al., 2024). Although models of identity formation vary, empirical findings converge in highlighting the roles of mentors and peers in supporting learning and the production of personally meaningful work recognized as competent by community members (Brickhouse et al., 2000; Godwin et al., 2016; Pfund et al., 2016).

To develop a civic identity, young people need to be inducted into the community of practice of civic life. Communities of practice consist of behavioral repertoires, norms, and ways of thinking that guide activity in specific domains (Lave & Wenger, 1991; Wenger, 2010), and learning can be understood as a social process of identifying as a member of a particular community of practice while gaining the robust knowledge, skills, and capacities to actively participate in it (Hand & Gresalfi, 2015).

Understanding learning as identity formation within communities of practice helps clarify the task of civic education in a democracy: it must help young people form a civic identity of their own and prepare them to authentically fill a range of roles in the complex community of practice that is our democracy. Civic participants must master the values and norms, specific knowledge, and skills that make up a shared "thin" civic identity that is "thickened" by the diverse experiences, needs, goals, and values that characterize different individuals and groups (Allen & Kidd, 2022; Haduong et al., 2024).

Assessing Civic Identity Development

While the goal of civic education may be to cultivate learners' development of "thick" civic identities (Haduong et al., 2024), the focus of assessment in civic education should remain on the development of the core "thin" identity elements of civic knowledge, civic values, and civic skills. Even the "thin" conception of civic identity, though, is complex, and it seems implausible that a single assessment method can address its elements. Accordingly, the DKP has worked to develop an assessment toolkit designed to provide a holistic account of civic identity development.

In doing so, it was necessary to work from broad definitions of civic knowledge, values, and skills toward more narrow and concrete operational definitions aligned with the DKP's grade 8 curriculum. In the case of civic knowledge, it was possible to draw on conventional methods of item development to create a brief multiple-choice style test aligned with the curriculum. However, the assessment of civic values and civic skills required more complex methods. While a full account of the design of the civic skills assessment is the subject of another manuscript, the development of an assessment tool for civic values, the CVQ, is the subject of this chapter.

Civic Values Questionnaire (CVQ)

A 2021 report by the Institute of Education Sciences catalogued over 110 published measures of civic attitudes, political attitudes, and civic-related skills or character traits. Given the sheer volume of existing scales, indices, and related instruments, there is little that is novel about the act of measuring civic values. However, consistent with recent observations of educational research (Flake, 2021), many of these measures lack conventional evidence supporting their use, and consideration of other forms of validity evidence, with the exception of evidence based on content, is even more rare. Choosing among the many available measures or developing new ones to include in the CVQ, therefore, required evaluating evidence that they could be used to make valid inferences about the civic values relevant to the DKP's curriculum.

Following the most recent standards for testing published by the American Educational Research Association, American Psychological Association, and National Council on Measurement in Education (2014), this process included: evaluating evidence based on content (strong theoretical underpinnings); investigating response processes (activation and reflection of intended constructs); examining internal structure (psychometric qualities); testing relations to other variables (convergence with related constructs, independence from unrelated constructs, predictive value); and determining the appropriate uses and intended consequences of testing (valid interpretation and use of results). Each of these forms of evidence is described below, drawing on both theoretical work and a series of empirical studies.

Evidence Based on Content

Perhaps the most obvious place to look for evidence that an assessment can be used to make valid inferences about a construct is to look at the items. They should have strong theoretical ties to the construct, and they should be appropriate for the context of assessment and the population who will be assessed. In the present case, the first step is to define the shared civic values in ways that are consistent with how they are addressed in the grade 8 curriculum. Then, it is possible to identify existing measurement tools or develop new ones to represent the values.

A difficult challenge in defining a set of shared civic values is that there is much disagreement, often rooted in different political philosophies, regarding the role of schools in promoting values through civic education (Westheimer & Kahne, 2004). In some cases, they seem consistent with personally responsible or participatory citizenship (e.g., civic duty, Zaff et al., 2010; nationalism, Hart et al., 2011; patriotism, Petrilli & Finn, 2020), to use Westheimer and Kahne's (2004) typology, while in others they seem better aligned with more creative forms of justice-oriented citizenship (e.g., civic purpose, Malin et al., 2015; critical consciousness, Diemer et al., 2017). The selection of civic attitudes and dispositions as targets of assessment for civic education necessarily elevates them as shared civic values. This introduces a risk of ideological bias, making it essential to transparently define the civic values and explain how they support democracy as a form of shared governance (e.g., political equality, informed engagement), rather than a particular ideological account of what the democracy should do (e.g., protect the environment, reduce taxes).

By limiting the focus of civic education to the values important to a "thin" conception of civic identity, it is possible to leave it to learners to "thicken" their civic identities by connecting them with the experiences, views, values, and goals associated with their other personal or social identities (Allen & Kidd, 2022). Our shared civic values should promote the responsible pursuit of authentic goals while respecting the political equality of others and the integrity of our democracy. With this in mind, the DKP proposes that the shared civic values of civic self-confidence, civic reciprocity, and civic self-care provide a set of guardrails and guidelines for civic participation in our modern, diverse, and complicated democracy (Allen & Kidd, 2022).

Civic Self-Confidence

Civic self-confidence is not just a self-report of skills and knowledge. Of course, it does, or should, reflect actual participatory readiness, and there is substantial evidence of a reciprocal relationship of civic efficacy and civic participation (Bandura, 1993; Cohen & Chaffee, 2012; Gastil & Xenos, 2010; Kahne & Westheimer, 2006). But, from a sociocultural learning theory perspective, it can also be understood as a sense of being a legitimate participant in the civic domain, of feeling recognized by others as a political equal (Allen & Kidd, 2022).

Given its long history as a subject of study across multiple disciplines, civic efficacy can be assessed reliably using measures backed by substantial evidence that they can be used with validity, primarily for purposes of studying large groups. Among the most rigorously developed and widely used measures are the measures of Citizenship Self-Efficacy and Internal Political Efficacy administered in the 2009 International Civic and Citizenship Education Study (ICCS;

Schulz et al., 2010). The former asks respondents how well they can do certain things (e.g., organize a group of students in order to achieve changes at school), framing efficacy in terms of skills. The Internal Political Efficacy scale, in contrast, asks respondents the extent to which they see themselves as competent and legitimate participants in the civic domain (e.g., I have a good understanding of the political issues facing this country; I have political opinions worth listening to.). This conception of efficacy aligns closely with the concept of civic self-confidence, leading to the inclusion of the Internal Political Efficacy measure in the initial CVQ to represent civic self-confidence.

Civic Reciprocity

The value of civic reciprocity calls for good-faith power-sharing among political equals who, despite pursuing different interests, do so with awareness of and care for the fact that all of their fates are bound up in a single democratic community (Allen, 2004, 2023; Allen & Kidd, 2022). This requires learning about and acknowledging the sacrifices of others, and ensuring that those on the losing side of political contests have good reasons to come back to the table.

For example, advocates of an environmental policy that would threaten jobs in a community might practice civic reciprocity by working with members of that community to develop new employment opportunities. This would show good-faith participation by demonstrating that the needs of the potentially affected workers and their community are being taken seriously, even in the face of disagreement. Setting aside rivalrous self-interest and seeking reciprocity among political equals provides a necessary foundation of trust in a diverse democracy.

To measure the value of civic reciprocity, as described above, a brief self-report scale was developed to elicit respondents' endorsement of democracy-sustaining principles. Specifically, participants are asked to "rate how important it is for members of your community to do the following things." Then, participants rate the importance of five behaviors indicative of civic reciprocity on a five-point scale ranging from *not at all important* to *necessary*. The items were designed to address respect for the political equality of others (i.e., *respect the equal rights of all Americans; listen to the opinions of others and acknowledge that everyone has a right to have a say in how the country is run*), good-faith participation (i.e., *be trustworthy and fair when discussing and participating in politics, even if others are not*), and explicit endorsements of reciprocity (i.e., *think about how achieving one's political goals, such as helping a candidate win an election or getting a law passed, will affect everyone, including those with different viewpoints; be willing to compromise in politics [or be willing to give up some of what one wants] to make sure that everyone feels their needs and values are being taken seriously*).

Civic Self-Care

Civic participation is not without costs or risks. Beyond exhaustion or the neglect of other domains of life, civic actors must confront the threats of misinformation and the prospect of harassment or even violence. In the interest of personal flourishing and sustainable civic engagement, individuals need to place value on their own civic self-care in the face of the epistemic, emotional, and physical hazards of the political domain (Allen, 2023; Allen & Kidd, 2022).

Civic engagement is increasingly pursued online (Cho et al., 2020), and young civic participants need to be prepared for the heightened risks of misinformation and harassment in digital spaces (Allen & Light, 2015; Kahne & Bowyer, 2017; Weinstein & James, 2022). Discourse surrounding civic issues online often includes misinformation, which can lead to diminished trust and increase the likelihood of radicalization (Hodgin & Kahne, 2018; Wilf et al., 2023). Becoming a participant in discourse exposes one to new risks, including becoming the victim of online harassment or establishing a regretful digital footprint (Jones & Mitchell, 2016; Weinstein & James, 2022). In this context, civic self-care for 8th graders can be understood as including both being a responsible consumer of information and a careful participant in civic spaces, especially online.

Media literacy has received increasing attention from researchers and civic educators (McGrew & Kohnen, 2024; von Gillern et al., 2024). Most concretely, media literacy is a skill, the ability to ascertain the credibility and purposes of sources, and it can be assessed using realistic tasks (e.g., McGrew & Breakstone, 2023). It can also be understood as knowledge of how the media works (e.g., Maksl et al., 2015), but, as a civic value, it reflects a commitment to an epistemically healthy democracy in which people make good-faith efforts to ascertain the truth. In this case, a measure developed by Vraga et al. (2015), Value for Media Literacy, is closely aligned with this definition, addressing the extent to which individuals see the media and their own media consumption as important to democracy.

Despite a growing research literature on the risks of online civic participation, there were no apparent measures of the extent to which young people are aware of and respond to these risks. Most empirical research on digital citizenship focuses primarily on media literacy and online civic engagement (e.g., von Gillern et al., 2022), with relatively little attention given to ethics and misuse (Richardson et al., 2021), despite the importance of these to broader frameworks (e.g., Ribble, 2015; Richardson et al., 2021). Noting a lacuna of empirical measures appropriate for the multiple dimensions of digital citizenship, Jones and Mitchell (2016) developed simple self-report measures for adolescents of two components of digital citizenship, including civic participation and, most relevant to the measurement of civic self-care, a 7-item subscale for Online Respect that was negatively correlated with the measures of online harassment victimization and perpetration.

Given these qualities, this scale was used as the foundation for a new 5-item scale. Two items address responsibilities toward others (i.e., *I try to avoid posting or sharing things online that would hurt other peoples' feelings, even if they are just meant to be funny*; *when I post or share something online, I do research to make sure that the information is accurate*), and three items are about minimizing risks to oneself (i.e., *Before I post or share something online, I make sure to think about how people might take it out of context or use it to try to harm or embarrass me*; *when I post or share something online, I think about how it might look to others in a few years*; *before putting something online, I make sure it would not embarrass me if other people found out I did it.*).

As illustrated above, assembling measures in the CVQ to represent the three core civic values of civic self-confidence, civic reciprocity, and civic self-care involved both identifying existing measures aligned with the values or developing or modifying items for new scales to achieve alignment. That said, these are complex constructs, and they could surely be defined in different ways for the middle school context. For example, others could reasonably argue for the inclusion of items directly mapping onto perceptions, experiences, and commitments toward the political recognition of oneself and others when measuring civic self-confidence. Similarly, items measuring attitudes toward other forms of risk could be highly relevant in specific contexts. Therefore, we stress that scores derived from the measures included in the CVQ should be understood as indicators of important aspects of the three civic values, not as full accounts.

Evidence Based on Response Processes

A second form of validity evidence comes from the analysis of participants' response processes, often using qualitative interview methods (Leighton, 2017; Willis, 2015). The purpose of understanding response processes is to help ensure that respondents draw on the intended knowledge, skills, or attitudes when responding to items. For example, a self-report measure of civic efficacy may include an item addressing one's perceived ability to discuss current events with peers. While the item is meant to assess respondents' own sense of confidence that they understand current events and can articulate their views, some respondents may instead consider whether their peers would be interested in such a discussion or reflect on social norms regarding the desirability of engaging in political discourse. In such cases, the intended interpretation of the score should be revised to include these additional dimensions of civic efficacy, or the item should be updated, modified, or replaced to better capture the construct. Understanding how respondents interpret items and what factors influence their responses provides a basis for evaluating whether scores can be reliably interpreted and informs item revisions to promote consistency in response processes.

The measures in the assessment toolkit were refined through cognitive interviews with a small sample of Massachusetts 8th and 9th graders ($N = 10$) recruited through social media networks and after school programs. Despite the small sample, the interviews provided information key to improving the measures in the CVQ. For example, interviews on the civic self-confidence items revealed a need to clearly define terms like "politics" and "civic life" or adjust vocabulary to help reliably elicit evidence of participants' attitudes. Based on our findings, instructions for the CVQ were updated, as were 10 (45%) of the items. Overall, the cognitive interviews helped us identify how to maximize the likelihood of ensuring that responses could be interpreted as intended by making sure that adolescents understood the items and response options.

Evidence Based on Internal Structure

Evidence of validity from internal structure is perhaps the most widely available form of validity, and it refers to evidence that responses to items in a measure reflect the intended number of underlying constructs. Statistical techniques such as confirmatory factor analysis can help determine whether a measure addresses one or more underlying constructs by revealing patterns of responses across items. The basic logic behind factor analysis is that responses to items measuring the same construct should be correlated with the same latent variable. For example, a measure of civic efficacy may include items related to internal efficacy (feelings of one's own capacity for civic engagement) and external efficacy (confidence that the government and institutions are responsive to community members). A factor analysis would be expected to reveal that these items are associated with distinct latent factors corresponding to internal and external efficacy. Demonstrating evidence of validity from internal structure is key to establishing that a measure addresses the expected number of constructs, and evaluating the internal structure of measures can also help improve measures by removing or modifying items with low or ambiguous relations with factors.

Empirical Studies

Online Youth Study

To evaluate the internal structures and test–retest reliability of the CVQ and other measures in the assessment toolkit, we conducted a study of volunteer adolescent participants in Massachusetts who were currently enrolled in 8th or 9th grade. Despite offering substantial compensation and conducting extensive recruitment efforts through a social media marketing campaign (which yielded many spam responses) and schools, we were able to recruit and retain only 69 participants who completed the CVQ and a knowledge test at two time points separated by at least a week.

This small sample size precluded conducting a confirmatory factor analysis, including all items on the CVQ representing the four measures associated with the three civic values as expressed in the DKP's curriculum: civic self-confidence, civic reciprocity, and civic self-care (i.e., valuing media literacy, and risk awareness). However, an exploratory factor analysis, albeit underpowered, was conducted for each of the four measures to evaluate unidimensionality.

Two methods were used to evaluate dimensionality based on exploratory factor analysis. One, parallel analysis, identifies factors using bootstrapping methods (O'Connor, 2000). The other draws on the criteria used by Tedeschi et al. (2021), with good support for the factor structure indicated by loadings of at least 0.50 on a single factor and no loadings of greater than 0.50 on other factors, and moderate support indicated if at least half of the items have a loading of at least 0.50 on a single factor. Parallel analysis suggested a single factor for all four measures, and only the measure of civic reciprocity failed to meet the threshold for good support, with one item having a loading of less than 0.50. These findings suggest that each measure is unidimensional, but the analyses cannot address the question of whether or not the overall structure of the CVQ corresponds with the expected four factors.

Implementation Study

Although the sample size of the study evaluating test–retest reliability was too small to support meaningful tests of internal structure, data from a pilot administration of the assessment from a separate study of the curriculum's implementation yielded a sample of 375 8th grade civics students in MA (due to the de-identification of data, no demographic information is available). Only responses to the civic knowledge test and CVQ were available, each administered at the end of the 2023 school year.

For the CVQ ($n = 333$), a structural equations model with each of the four civic values measures modeled as distinct but correlated factors was tested. Using conventional guidelines (Nye, 2023), indices suggested moderate fit (i.e., RMSEA = .054, 90% CI [.047, .062]; CFI = .906; TLI = .893; and SRMR = .058). While these findings support the anticipated internal structure of the CVQ, they are preliminary, with larger samples needed to test more sophisticated models, including tests of measurement invariance across demographic groups.

Online Adult Study

As part of an otherwise unrelated study on political attitudes, a sample of 150 MA young adults, 91% with at least some college education (see Table 9.1 for other characteristics) was recruited via Prolific for a compensated online survey. Relevant to this project, these participants completed the full CVQ, as well as the test of civic knowledge from the assessment toolkit. Given the small sample size, an exploratory factor analysis on the full CVQ was conducted.

Parallel analysis suggested four factors, and a subsequent factor analysis using an oblimin rotation yielded results consistent with a moderately good model fit (Tedeschi et al., 2021). Specifically, only two of the 22 items had loadings of less than 0.50 on their expected factors, and no items had loadings greater than 0.50 on more than one factor. Given the relatively small sample size and, most importantly, the fact that this is an adult sample, this analysis provides limited evidence for the intended factor structure of the CVQ that can only be tentatively generalized to the context of its intended use. Nonetheless, in combination with the results of the other studies, each with their own notable limitations, these findings suggest that the four measures included in the CVQ are distinct from each other and unidimensional.

Overall, there is modest evidence that the internal structures of the measures in the CVQ are consistent with their intended uses. The measures of civic self-confidence, civic reciprocity, media literacy, and risk awareness appear to be capturing distinct elements of civic identity aligned with the DKP's conception of civic values. Yet, these findings are preliminary, and

Table 9.1 Characteristics of Participants

	Online Youth Sample			Online Adult Sample		
Characteristic	M	SD	95%CI	M	SD	95%CI
Age	14.57	0.49	14.46, 14.69	27.18	4.28	26.48, 27.87
Political liberalism	3.47	1.03	3.22, 3.72	3.94	1.05	3.77, 4.11
Civic knowledge[a]	14.14	5.95	12.71, 15.57	8.17	2.26	7.80, 8.53
Civic self-confidence	3.68	0.69	3.52, 3.85	3.27	0.92	3.12, 3.42
Civic reciprocity	4.19	0.49	4.07, 4.30	4.21	0.61	4.11, 4.31
Media literacy	4.21	0.65	4.06, 4.37	4.47	0.51	4.39, 4.55
Risk awareness	3.91	0.70	3.74, 4.08	4.08	0.75	3.96, 4.21
		n	%		n	%
Female		31	44.93		76	50.67
Male		33	47.83		65	43.33
Other gender		5	7.25		9	6.00
Arab		1	1.47		0	3.13
Asian		21	30.88		26	17.33
Black or African American		6	8.82		13	8.67
Native Hawaiian or Pacific Islander		2	2.94		2	1.33
West Asian		1	1.47		0	0
White		35	51.47		105	70.00
Race not provided		2	2.94		2	1.33
Hispanic or Latino/a/e		14	20.29		8	5.33
Not Hispanic or Latino/a/e		55	79.71		142	94.67

Notes: All items were responded to on a 5-point scale.
[a]Civic knowledge scores for the Online Youth Study are based on 24 items completed over two sessions. Those for the Online Adult Study are based on 12 items completed during a single session.

the internal structure of the CVQ should be further investigated. Critically, future analyses should utilize data gathered as part of regular classroom assessment practices. Such data would contribute to a much larger sample, but, most important, they would also likely be more representative of ordinary students than volunteers in online studies.

Reliability

Alongside testing the internal structure of the CVQ, we also sought to investigate its reliability, a property distinct from internal structure and necessary but insufficient for valid use and interpretation. A measure that yields consistent estimates of an underlying construct is considered reliable. While a reliable assessment can be used in ways that are either valid or not valid, an unreliable assessment cannot be used with validity, making reliability a condition for valid use.

Most commonly, reliability is estimated as a dimension of internal consistency, conventionally represented by Cronbach's alpha. Although a common metric, Cronbach's alpha is upwardly biased by the inclusion of additional items to a measure, so the average inter-item correlation (AIC) was also calculated to serve as a more direct indicator of internal consistency (see Table 9.2). Based on the criteria used by Tedeschi et al. (2021) for evaluating Cronbach's alpha, all of the measures demonstrated at least medium reliability (i.e., .70–.79), with

Table 9.2 Internal Consistency of CVQ Measures by Study

	Cronbach's Alpha (Average Inter-Item Correlation)			
	Online Youth		Implementation	Online Adult
Measure	Time 1	Time 2		
Self-confidence	.87 (.56)	.83 (.46)	.81 (.42)	.89 (.58)
Reciprocity	.66 (.28)	.64 (.26)	.75 (.38)	.78 (.41)
Media literacy (self-care)	.84 (.40)	.79 (.41)	.77 (.36)	.77 (.35)
Risk awareness (self-care)	.77 (.40)	.77 (.41)	.78 (.41)	.78 (.42)

the exception of civic reciprocity, which had low reliability in the Online Youth Study, but medium reliability in the larger two studies. Notably, all measures had AIC values that fell within recommended ranges (Clark & Watson, 2019). While acceptable for aggregate analyses, however, the internal consistencies of the measures in the CVQ do not yield the sort of precision needed for high-stakes decisions about individuals, a point returned to in the final section of this chapter about intended uses.

Statistical indices measuring internal consistency, including those discussed above, account only for random error and error associated with items. Supplementing analysis of internal consistency with an analysis of test–retest reliability makes it possible to ascertain the degree to which scores are likely to vary randomly within individuals across time. This form of reliability is estimated by testing the relations of scores obtained at one time with scores obtained at a later time, assuming that no meaningful change in the underlying construct could have occurred in the interval. When this form of reliability is high, it is possible to be more confident that a student's score today will not be substantially different from their score a week from now simply due to random variation.

To evaluate test–retest reliability, participants in the Online Youth Study completed the CVQ twice, with sessions separated by at least a week. Scores at the two time points were significantly correlated for civic self-confidence ($r(65) = .71, p < .001$), civic reciprocity ($r(65) = .60, p < .001$), media literacy ($r(64) = .67, p < .001$), and risk assessment ($r(64) = .67, p < .001$).

In addition, intraclass correlation coefficients were calculated using the ICC(2,1) model (i.e., two-way mixed effects, absolute agreement) to estimate test–retest reliability (Koo & Mae, 2016). All analyses were conducted using the Intracc Macro (Hamer, 1991) for SAS, modified to calculate confidence intervals. Using guidelines for interpretation proposed by Koo and Mae, ICC values with lower-bound confidence intervals above 0.5 are considered moderate, and those with lower bounds above 0.75 are considered excellent. All four measures in the CVQ met the threshold for moderate reliability based on confidence intervals: civic self-confidence (ICC = .79, 95% CI [.72, .85]); civic reciprocity (ICC = .69, 95% CI [.59, .78]), media literacy (ICC = .80, 95% CI [.59, .78]; risk awareness (ICC = .77, 95% CI [.69, .84]).

Using more conventional, though less conservative, interpretive guidelines set forth by Cicchetti (1994), the civic reciprocity measure met the threshold for good clinical significance, and the other three measures met the threshold for excellent clinical significance. It is important to note that the small sample size leads to relatively large confidence intervals, so it is most reasonable to characterize the measures as having moderate test–retest reliability until larger studies are able to more precisely estimate ICC values.

Overall the measures included in the CVQ demonstrate moderately good internal consistency and, though based on limited data, moderate test–retest reliability. Accordingly, the precision of the scores makes aggregate analysis more valid than using scores to make decisions about individuals. The reason for this is that random measurement errors associated with individual observations are likely to balance out in an aggregate analysis but could lead to miscategorization at the individual level.

Evidence Based on Relations with Other Variables

In considering the first forms of evidence (i.e., content, response processes, internal structure) for valid use, the measures in the CVQ were analyzed independently of other constructs or measures. Yet, confidence that the scores on the CVQ measures can be interpreted as intended can also be bolstered by examining how those scores relate to theoretically related and unrelated scores. This form of evidence may include findings that scores on a measure are strongly positively related to other measures of the same construct, that scores are not substantially related to measures of theoretically unrelated constructs, and that scores predict an important outcome. For example, scores on a new measure of internal civic efficacy should be positively correlated with scores from extant measures of the same construct but not correlated with a theoretically unrelated measure of liberal political ideology. Additional evidence from relations with other variables may come from the finding that internal civic efficacy scores predict future civic engagement, since there are theoretical and empirical reasons to expect that efficacy motivates behavior.

For the measures on the CVQ, evidence based on correlations varies depending on how widely researchers have used the measures. For example, the measure of civic self-confidence, very lightly adapted from the original measure of civic self-efficacy, is known to correlate with various forms of civic engagement in adolescents, ranging from attending to civic information (e.g., Arens & Watermann, 2017) to expected participation (e.g., Diemer & Li, 2011; Manganelli et al., 2014). Similarly, the measure of media literacy, at least in adults, has been shown to predict knowledge about the new media, knowledge of current events, and healthy skepticism toward the media (Vraga et al., 2015).

In the present Online Youth Study and Online Adult Study, both the measure of civic self-confidence ($r(66) = .48, p < .001$) and the measure of media literacy ($r(66) = .25, p = .03$) were positively related with scores on a civic knowledge test. In the Online Adult Study, where additional measures were collected, civic self-confidence was negatively related ($r(148) = -.40, p < .001$) to intellectual humility (IH) in the political domain (Hoyle et al., 2016) but positively related ($r(148) = .23, p < .01$) to a single-item measure of importance of democracy (Foa & Mounk, 2016). In contrast, media literacy was positively correlated with both IH ($r(148) = .21, p < .01$) and importance of democracy ($r(148) = .31, p < .001$). These patterns seem consistent with the theoretical definitions of the two constructs. Media literacy entails both a commitment to truthfulness in democracy and an awareness of the difficulty of overcoming biases and gaining good information, explaining the positive relations with pro-democracy attitudes and IH. In contrast, the positive relation of civic self-confidence with support for democracy and negative relation with IH is consistent with the higher levels of political conviction that often accompany civic efficacy (Stapleton & Wolak, 2024).

Overall, the evidence from prior research and the studies conducted as part of this project bolsters confidence that scores derived from these measures will support valid inferences about learners' civic self-confidence and media literacy, a component of civic self-care. Put through their own development processes and already situated in the research literature, the extant evidence from correlations with other variables for the measures of civic self-confidence (i.e., Internal Political Efficacy; Schulz et al., 2010) and media literacy (i.e., Value for Media Literacy; Vraga et al., 2015) will continue to accrue as the measures are used in future research.

The measures of civic self-care and of risk awareness, a component of self-care, however were developed specifically for the CVQ. Although some items in the measure of risk awareness have roots in Jones and Mitchell's (2016) well-developed Online Respect scale, the measure is new and, like the measure of civic reciprocity, has not been used elsewhere. Currently, there is little evidence from correlations to support these measures, with the exception of findings from the Online Youth Study and Online Adult Study.

The measure of civic reciprocity was positively related to civic knowledge in the Online Youth Study ($r(66) = .31, p = .01$) but not the Online Adult Study ($r(148) = .12, p = .13$). However, it was positively related with IH ($r(148) = .35, p < .001$) and importance of democracy ($r(148) = .25, p < .01$). In contrast, the measure of risk awareness was not related to civic knowledge ($rs < .18, ps > .12$), IH ($r(148) = .13, p = .12$), or importance of democracy ($r(148) = .07, p = .35$). Notably, while it is clear that both IH and commitment to democracy are theoretically related to civic reciprocity, their non-significant relations with risk awareness are not surprising. Unlike the other values, risk awareness, though important for sustained civic participation, is not conceptualized as a necessarily pro-democracy value.

Overall, evidence from correlations in support of the measures in the CVQ is mixed, with relatively strong support associated with the measures of civic self-confidence and media literacy, weaker support for the measure of civic reciprocity, and no substantive evidence for the measure of risk awareness. Larger studies are needed to better understand how the measures in the CVQ relate with theoretically similar constructs, and studies with more easily recruited young adults might also provide valuable insight into how these measures relate to more advanced forms of civic participation.

Evidence Based on Uses and Consequences of Testing

Ultimately, for an assessment tool to be used with validity, it must serve its intended purposes. In this case, it must support credible inferences about learners' civic values that enable educators and other stakeholders to make informed judgments about the quality of civic education. In the sections above, evidence from the content of the measures, the response processes elicited by the items, the internal structures and reliabilities of the measures, and the relations of the measures with other variables has been mustered to support the claim that the measures in the CVQ yield scores that are meaningful indicators of civic self-confidence, civic reciprocity, and civic self-care. Yet, this evidence also points to important constraints on the use of the CVQ.

Notably, the reliability of the measures, both internally and across time, is moderately good, at best. As discussed in the section on reliability above, the measures are suitable for aggregate analyses, but they should not be used to make judgments about individuals. They are simply too imprecise to give scores to individuals that reliably differentiate among those with different degrees of civic readiness. This limitation, though, is also a guardrail. With the history of Jim Crow literacy tests at the ballot box still clearly visible in the rearview mirror, more recent proposals to make passing the United States Citizenship and Immigration Services naturalization exam a condition for voting only highlight the real risk that students' civics transcripts might be used to challenge their political equality.

The intended use of the CVQ is to assess the quality of civic education for groups of students at the classroom level and higher. For example, the CVQ could be used to measure changes over the course of a year, with scores obtained at the end of the year compared to those recorded at the start. Or, district leaders could compare scores across schools to monitor the consistency of civic development. Over longer periods of time, CVQ data could be linked with data on learning opportunities and student characteristics to identify the drivers of civic identity development across diverse groups of students or learning contexts. As the CVQ is implemented fully, it will be important to understand the extent to which and how it is used to monitor and improve civic education.

Educators or researchers who use the CVQ must consider the important limitations to the evidence supporting its use presented here. The limited reliability of the measures has already been discussed, but it is also important to note that all of the statistical evidence comes from small studies. To a significant extent, this reflects the difficulty of obtaining assessment data from adolescents in voluntary research studies, but all of the statistical findings reported here should be interpreted with some caution until they can be corroborated in larger samples that would produce more reliable results. Also, it is unclear if the CVQ can be used with validity to assess civic values among learners with limited literacy or other construct-irrelevant differences that set them apart from the bulk of their peers. Accordingly, future work is critical to evaluate the performance of these measures in specific subgroups of students, including those defined by demographic characteristics.

Measurement development is an ongoing process that should be continuously informed by new data and new thinking. The CVQ will almost certainly be modified over time to more accurately align with the constructs it is designed to assess, as well as to improve its internal structure and reliability. The evidence presented in this chapter, therefore, must be expanded and re-evaluated as the CVQ is more widely implemented.

Conclusion

Accepting the limitations discussed above, the CVQ can be used to assess civic self-confidence, civic reciprocity, and civic self-care as defined by the DKP in the context of its grade 8 civics curriculum. There is, however, no single ideal set of outcomes to pursue in civic education, much less a universally applicable set of assessment tools. Rather, civic educators and the resource developers who support them should identify or create assessment tools aligned with their own theoretical understanding of civic development.

Providing transparent definitions of outcomes, especially civic values, will not only help others use and interpret measures, it will also help the field guard against unintended ideological bias and build trust with stakeholders. Despite these complications, there is simply no way to ensure that all students experience high quality civic education unless we design rigorous assessments we can use to hold ourselves accountable to meeting that mission.

References

Allen, D. (2004). *Talking to strangers: Anxieties of citizenship since Brown v. Board of Education.* University of Chicago Press.
Allen, D. (2023). *Justice by means of democracy.* University of Chicago Press.
Allen, D., & Kidd, D. (2022). Civic learning for the 21st century: Disentangling the "thin" and "thick" elements of civic identity to support civic education. In R. Curren (Ed.), *Routledge handbook of philosophy of education* (pp. 27–41). Routledge.
Allen, D., & Light, J. S. (2015). *From voice to influence: Understanding citizenship in a digital age.* University of Chicago Press.
American Educational Research Association, American Psychological Association, & National Council on Measurement in Education. (2014). *Standards for educational and psychological testing.* American Educational Research Association.
Arens, A. K., & Watermann, R. (2017). Political efficacy in adolescence: Development, gender differences, and outcome relations. *Developmental Psychology, 53*(5), 933.
Bandura, A. (1993). Perceived self-efficacy in cognitive development and functioning. *Educational Psychologist, 28*(2), 117–148. https://doi.org/10.1207/s15326985ep2802_3
Brickhouse, N. W., Lowery, P., & Schultz, K. (2000). What kind of a girl does science? The construction of school science identities. *Journal of Research in Science Teaching, 37*(5), 441–458.
Chen, C. H., & Yang, Y. C. (2019). Revisiting the effects of project-based learning on students' academic achievement: A meta-analysis investigating moderators. *Educational Research Review, 26,* 71–81.
Cho, A., Byrne, J., & Pelter, Z. (2020). *Digital civic engagement by young people.* UNICEF Office of Global Insight and Policy.
Cicchetti, D. V. (1994). Guidelines, criteria, and rules of thumb for evaluating normed and standardized assessment instruments in psychology. *Psychological Assessment, 6*(4), 284. https://doi.org/10.1037/1040-3590.6.4.284

Clark, L. A., & Watson, D. (2019). Constructing validity: New developments in creating objective measuring instruments. *Psychological Assessment*, 31(12), 1412–1427. https://doi.org/10.1037/pas0000626

Cohen, A. K., & Chaffee, B. W. (2012). The relationship between adolescents' civic knowledge, civic attitude, and civic behavior and their self-reported future likelihood of voting. *Education, Citizenship and Social Justice*, 8(1), 43–57. https://doi.org/10.1177/1746197912456339

Diamond, L. (2020). Breaking out of the democratic slump. *Journal of Democracy*, 31(1), 36–50.

Diemer, M. A., & Li, C. H. (2011). Critical consciousness development and political participation among marginalized youth. *Child Development*, 82(6), 1815–1833.

Diemer, M. A., Rapa, L. J., Voight, A. M., & McWhirter, E. H. (2017). Critical consciousness: A developmental approach to addressing marginalization and oppression. *Child Development Perspectives*, 11(4), 240–245. https://doi.org/10.1111/cdep.12230

Flake, J. K. (2021). Measurement schmeasurement: Questionable measurement practices and how to avoid them. *Advances in Methods and Practices in Psychological Science*, 4(2). https://doi.org/10.1177/2515245920952393

Foa, R. S., & Mounk, Y. (2016). The danger of deconsolidation: The democratic disconnect. *Journal of Democracy*, 27(3), 5–17. https://doi.org/10.1353/jod.2016.0049

Gastil, J., & Xenos, M. (2010). Of attitudes and engagement: Clarifying the reciprocal relationship between civic attitudes and political participation. *Journal of Communication*, 60(2), 318–343. https://doi.org/10.1111/j.1460-2466.2010.01484.x

Godwin, A., Potvin, G., Hazari, Z., & Lock, R. (2016). Identity, critical agency, and engineering: An affective model for predicting engineering as a career choice. *Journal of Engineering Education*, 105(2), 312–340. https://doi.org/10.1002/jee.20118

Haduong, P., Jeffries, J., Pao, A., Webb, W., Allen, D., & Kidd, D. (2024). Who am I and what do I care about? Supporting civic identity development in civic education. *Education, Citizenship and Social Justice*, 19(2), 185–201.

Hamer, R. M. (1991, February 7). *intracc.sas: Intraclass correlations macro* [Computer software]. SAS Sample Library. https://support.sas.com/documentation/onlinedoc/stat/ex_code/141/intracc.html

Hand, V., & Gresalfi, M. (2015). The joint accomplishment of identity. *Educational Psychologist*, 50(3), 190–203. https://doi.org/10.1080/00461520.2015.1075401

Hart, D., Richardson, C., & Wilkenfeld, B. (2011). Civic identity. In S. J. Schwartz, K. Luyckx, & V. L. Vignoles (Eds.), *Handbook of identity theory and research* (pp. 771–787). Springer.

Hodgin, E., & Kahne, J. (2018). Misinformation in the information age: What teachers can do to support students. *Social Education*, 82(4), 208–212.

Hoyle, R. H., Davisson, E. K., Diebels, K. J., & Leary, M. R. (2016). Holding specific views with humility: Conceptualization and measurement of specific intellectual humility. *Personality and Individual Differences*, 97, 165-172.

Jones, L. M., & Mitchell, K. J. (2016). Defining and measuring youth digital citizenship. *New Media & Society*, 18(9), 2063–2079. https://doi.org/10.1177/1461444815577797

Journell, W. (2015). We still need you! An update on the status of K-12 civic education in the United States. *PS: Political Science & Politics*, 48(4), 630–634. https://doi.org/10.1017/S104909651500089X

Kahne, J., & Bowyer, B. (2017). Educating for democracy in a partisan age: Confronting the challenges of motivated reasoning and misinformation. *American Educational Research Journal*, 54(1), 3–34. https://doi.org/10.3102/0002831216679817

Kahne, J., & Westheimer, J. (2006). The limits of political efficacy: Educating citizens for a democratic society. *PS: Political Science & Politics*, 39(2), 289–296. https://doi.org/10.1017/S1049096506060471

Kingzette, J., Druckman, J. N., Klar, S., Krupnikov, Y., Levendusky, M., & Ryan, J. B. (2021). How affective polarization undermines support for democratic norms. *Public Opinion Quarterly*, 85(2), 663–677.

Koo, T., & Mae, L. (2016). A guideline of selecting and reporting intraclass correlation coefficients for reliability research. *Journal of Chiropractic Medicine*, 15, 155–163.

Lave, J., & Wenger, E. (1991). *Situated learning: Legitimate peripheral participation*. Cambridge University Press.

Leighton, J. P. (2017). *Using think-aloud interviews and cognitive labs in educational research*. Oxford University Press.

Levinson, M., & Levine, P. (2013). Taking informed action to engage students in civic life. *Social Education*, 77(6), 339–341.

Maksl, A., Ashley, S., & Craft, S. (2015). Measuring news media literacy. *Journal of Media Literacy Education*, 6(3), 29–45.

Malin, H., Ballard, P. J., & Damon, W. (2015). Civic purpose: An integrated construct for understanding civic development in adolescence. *Human Development*, 58(2), 103–130. https://doi.org/10.1159/000381655

Manganelli, S., Lucidi, F., & Alivernini, F. (2014). Adolescents' expected civic participation: The role of civic knowledge and efficacy beliefs. *Journal of Adolescence*, 37(5), 632–641.

McGrew, S., & Breakstone, J. (2023). Civic online reasoning across the curriculum: Developing and testing the efficacy of digital literacy lessons. *AERA Open*, 9, 23328584231176451.

McGrew, S., & Kohnen, A. M. (2024). Tackling misinformation through online information literacy: Structural and contextual considerations. *Journal of Research on Technology in Education*, 56(1), 1–6.

Mehta, J., & Fine, S. (2019). *In search of deeper learning: The quest to remake the American high school*. Harvard University Press.

Nye, C. D. (2023). A review of global fit statistics in psychology from the perspective of predictive validity. *Psychological Methods*. Advance online publication. https://doi.org/10.1037/met0000527

O'Connor, B. P. (2000). SPSS and SAS programs for determining the number of components using parallel analysis and Velicer's MAP test. *Behavior Research Methods, Instruments, & Computers, 32*(3), 396–402. https://doi.org/10.3758/BF03200807

Petrilli, M. J., & Finn, C. E. (2020). Conclusion: How to educate an American. In M. J. Petrilli & C. E. Finn (Eds.), *How to educate an American: The conservative vision for tomorrow's schools* (pp. 251–260). Templeton Foundation Press.

Pfund, C., Byars-Winston, A., Branchaw, J., Hurtado, S., & Eagan, K. (2016). Defining attributes and metrics of effective research mentoring relationships. *AIDS and Behavior, 20*(2), 238–248. https://doi.org/10.1007/s10461-016-1384-z

Rebell, M. A. (2018). *Flunking democracy: Schools, courts, and civic participation*. University of Chicago Press.

Ribble, M. (2015). *Digital citizenship in schools: Nine elements all students should know*. International Society for Technology in Education.

Richardson, J. W., Martin, F., & Sauers, N. (2021). Systematic review of 15 years of research on digital citizenship: 2004–2019. *Learning, Media and Technology, 46*(4), 498–514.

Schulz, W., Ainley, J., Fraillon, J., Kerr, D., & Losito, B. (2010). *ICCS 2009 international report: Civic knowledge, attitudes, and engagement among lower-secondary school students in 38 countries*. International Association for the Evaluation of Educational Achievement.

Stapleton, C. E., & Wolak, J. (2024). Political self-confidence and affective polarization. *Public Opinion Quarterly, 88*(1), 79–96.

Stern, J. A., Brody, A. E., Gregory, J. A., Griffith, S., & Pulvers, J. (2021). *The state of state standards for civics and US history in 2021*. Thomas B. Fordham Institute.

Tedeschi, S. E. J., Brodersen, R. M., Schramm, K., Haines, M., Liu, J., McCullough, D., Eide, M., & Cherasaro, T. (2021). *Measuring civic readiness: A review of survey scales*. Institute of Education Sciences.

Tyler, M., & Iyengar, S. (2023). Learning to dislike your opponents: Political socialization in the era of polarization. *American Political Science Review, 117*(1), 347–354.

von Gillern, S., Gleason, B., & Hutchison, A. (2022). Digital citizenship, media literacy, and the ACTS Framework. *The Reading Teacher, 76*(2), 145–158.

von Gillern, S., Korona, M., Wright, W., Gould, H., & Haskey-Valerius, B. (2024). Media literacy, digital citizenship and their relationship: Perspectives of preservice teachers. *Teaching and Teacher Education, 138*, 104404.

Vraga, E. K., Tully, M., Kotcher, J. E., Smithson, A. B., & Broeckelman-Post, M. (2015). A multi-dimensional approach to measuring news media literacy. *Journal of Media Literacy Education, 7*(3), 41–53.

Weinstein, E., & James, C. (2022). *Behind their screens: What teens are facing (and adults are missing)*. MIT press.

Wenger, E. (2010). Communities of practice and social learning systems: The career of a concept. In C. Blackmore (Ed.), *Social learning systems and communities of practice* (pp. 179–198). Springer.

Westheimer, J., & Kahne, J. (2004). What kind of citizen? The politics of educating for democracy. *American Educational Research Journal, 41*(2), 237–269. https://doi.org/10.3102/00028312041002237

Willis, G. B. (2015). *Analysis of the cognitive interview in questionnaire design*. Oxford University Press.

Wilf, S., Wray-Lake, L., & Saavedra, J. A. (2023). Youth civic development amid the pandemic. *Current Opinion in Psychology, 52*, 101627.

Wilson, J. J., Sadler, J., Cohen-Vogel, N., & Willis, C. (2019). An examination of changes to state civic education requirements, 2004–2016. *Peabody Journal of Education, 94*(1), 48–62.

Zaff, J. F., Boyd, M. J., Li, Y., Lerner, J. V., & Lerner, R. M. (2010). Active and engaged citizenship: Multi-group and longitudinal factorial analysis of an integrated construct of civic engagement. *Journal of Youth and Adolescence, 39*(7), 736–750. https://doi.org/10.1007/s10964-010-9541-6

10
Defining and Monitoring K-12 Civic Learning Opportunities in the United States

Margarita Olivera-Aguilar, Laura S. Hamilton,
Corey Savage, and Samuel H. Rikoon

Throughout this volume, authors have presented data suggesting that the state of civic competencies[1] among America's young people is concerning, if not dire. The generally poor performance on tests of relevant outcomes, including knowledge and skills in democratic citizenship, government, and American constitutional democracy; historical knowledge and thinking; and digital information literacy points to an urgent need for institutions to cultivate the competencies young people will need to engage effectively in community and civic life (Breakstone et al., 2024; The Nation's Report Card, 2022). High-quality civic learning in schools can yield benefits for individuals' success and well-being while also benefiting society at large, including through the potential for an informed citizenry to resist the allure of non-democratic forms of governance (Barton & Ho, 2021; Sant, 2019). Although education systems that serve students in grades kindergarten through twelve (K-12) do not bear sole responsibility for civic learning, they are arguably the set of institutions that is best positioned to contribute due to the large number of young people they serve and the significant impact they have on child and adolescent development (Winthrop, 2020).

Evidence regarding the current state of students' civic competencies highlights the nature and magnitude of the challenge schools face. It does not, however, point to clear solutions. Should states or school districts mandate additional coursework in social studies? Should all students be required to engage in a service-learning project before they graduate? Or does the answer lie in revamping preservice teacher preparation to ensure that educators develop the necessary expertise and commitment to foster civic learning in their classrooms? Existing research on civic learning practices and interventions suggests some promising approaches, including project-based learning and integration of civics instruction into other subjects such as science (Fitzgerald et al., 2021; Rimm-Kaufman et al., 2021; Teegelbeckers et al., 2023). Still, policymakers and education leaders at all levels often lack not only the evidence but also the systematic data they need to make sound decisions about how to improve civic learning in schools and to determine whether those decisions lead to the desired outcomes.

DOI: 10.4324/9781003476825-12
This chapter has been made available under a CC BY-NC-ND license.

In this chapter, we discuss the need for improved systems and tools to measure students' *civic learning opportunities (CLO)*. We discuss the rationale for investing in a CLO indicator system and present a framework that could guide the development of a CLO indicator system at the classroom and school levels. We finalize the chapter by summarizing the conditions that would need to be in place to support its use and effectiveness.

What Are Civic Learning Opportunities, and Why Should We Monitor Them?

Numerous educators, scholars, and advocates have described the wide variety of approaches schools and other youth-serving institutions can adopt to foster the development of civic competencies. We refer to these approaches as *CLO*. In recent decades, the civic purposes of public schools have been increasingly overshadowed by their economic purposes, with policy and accountability reforms emphasizing the need for schools to prepare students for college and careers through an emphasis on literacy and numeracy (Hamilton & Martinez, 2024). But several factors, including growing awareness of threats to civil democracy and the test-score data mentioned earlier, have subsequently led to a widespread call for a return to schools' civic mission (Lee et al., 2021; Vinnakota, 2019). Moreover, advances in the science of learning and in research on employability skills have made it clear that competencies such as the ability to understand and engage with perspectives different from one's own are not only relevant to civic learning but are related to the most in-demand competencies among employers (Kyllonen et al., 2024; Yoder et al., 2020). The education research and policy community has increasingly acknowledged that preparation for civic life is likely to enhance, rather than detract from, schools' responsibilities to prepare students for economic and personal success.

Of course, recognizing the importance of civic learning does not translate directly into the ability to foster it. The past several decades have seen several efforts to identify strategies for advancing civic learning in K-12 schools. The Campaign for the Civic Mission of Schools identified six "proven practices" (Gould et al., 2011), and subsequent reports included four additional practices (Hansen et al., 2018; Levine & Kawashima-Ginsberg, 2017), that research suggests are likely to lead to improved civic learning outcomes when implemented effectively. These 10 practices, which we refer to as "promising" rather than "proven," are shown in Table 10.1.

More recently, a National Academy of Education report emphasized additional features of high-quality civic learning instruction, including the importance of addressing moral, ethical, and identity development, the value of project-based and inquiry-based learning, the need to attend to new forms of media, and the value of integrating this instruction into all academic subjects (Lee et al., 2021). Today, any discussion of how to increase access to CLO in schools must recognize the breadth of approaches and the variety of educational contexts in which they are offered.

The Policy Relevance of Opportunity to Learn

CLO can be considered a specific instantiation of the concept of *opportunity to learn*, or OTL. The concept of OTL has evolved significantly over the past decades, reflecting changes in educational policy and research. When this concept first emerged in the 1960s, most OTL definitions were fairly narrow, emphasizing the overlap between what students were taught and what they were tested on (Banicky, 2000). Importantly, however, these early conceptions of OTL correctly recognized the difference between the intended curricula (e.g., state standards) and the implemented curricula (i.e., what is actually taught in the classroom) and the importance of documenting and measuring both (Schmidt & Maier, 2009). By the 1990s, the definition

Table 10.1 Practices That Research Suggests Can Foster Civic Learning in Schools

Practices	Description
1. Classroom instruction	Instruction covering government, history, economics, law, and democracy.
2. Discussion of current events and controversial issues	Discussion of current local, national, and international issues and events into the classroom, particularly those that young people view as important to their lives.
3. Service learning	Opportunities provided by schools for students to apply what they learn through community service linked to the formal curriculum and classroom instruction.
4. Extracurricular activities	Opportunities facilitated by schools for young people to get involved in their schools or communities outside of the classroom.
5. School governance	Opportunities for students to participate in school governance.
6. Simulations of democratic processes	School opportunities for students to participate in simulations of democratic processes and procedures.
7. News media literacy	Instruction to help students access, analyze, create, and share news appropriately.
8. Action civics	Opportunities for students to participate in their communities and act as citizens (with rights and responsibilities) and where they are encouraged to consider influencing institutional policies.
9. Social and emotional learning	Learning opportunities for students to understand and manage emotions, set and achieve positive goals, feel and show empathy for others, establish and maintain positive relationships, and make responsible decisions.
10. School climate reform	School climate that promotes a healthy, safe school environment that fosters learning and respectful engagement with peers, considering the harmful effects that disciplinary actions (e.g., suspensions) may have.

Note: Practices 1–6 are described by Gould et al. (2011), while practices 7–10 are described by Hansen et al. (2018) and Levine and Kawashima-Ginsberg (2017).

extended to include the resources that state and district policymakers should provide to ensure that students and teachers could meet the high expectations set by state standards, and calls for monitoring OTL to inform policy and incentivize school and district actions emerged (McDonnell, 1995). The idea of incorporating OTL measures into policy was incorporated into the *Goals 2000: Educate America Act*, which included language regarding measurement of learning conditions, practices, and resources that students need to learn the material included in academic content standards (Goals 2000: Educate America Act, 1994).

Over time, the definition of OTL has broadened to encompass the quality of resources, school conditions, curricula, the teaching that students experience, and how the education system helps students meet standards (Banicky, 2000; Marion, 2020; Pritchard, 1996). A recent Aspen Institute report described OTL as "the resources, experiences, and expectations students get access to," which "enable students to pursue their purpose, develop their agency, and contribute as community members and informed citizens" (Aspen Institute Education & Society Program, 2022, p. 2). Some contemporary understandings of OTL also emphasize the relationship between learners and their learning environments, which not only include their schools and classrooms but also their communities at large.

In alignment with the conceptualization of OTL that extends beyond the classroom, definitions of CLO emphasize the conditions and resources in both school and community settings that promote civic learning outcomes. For instance, the Institute for Citizens & Scholars (2023) defines CLO as "the systems, platforms, programs, laws, and processes for individuals and groups to practice and build the civic dimensions of understanding, participation, connection, and belief" (p. 13). Similarly, in their proposal for a large-scale system of indicators for civic learning outcomes and opportunities, Hamilton and Kaufman

(2022) emphasize that civic learning occurs not only in classrooms and schools but also within an ecosystem that includes students' communities (e.g., community groups that partner with schools).

The Importance of Monitoring CLO

The policy argument for adopting OTL standards (also called school delivery standards) in the early 1990s did not ultimately result in those standards being enacted in federal or state legislation. However, the rationale for including them remains relevant today, perhaps best exemplified in the 2019 National Academies of Sciences, Engineering, and Medicine (NASEM) *Monitoring Educational Equity* report (National Academies of Sciences, Engineering, and Medicine, 2019). The report called for a wide-ranging set of indicators of both outcomes and opportunities, noting that efforts to address low levels of student achievement and attainment will benefit from data on students' access to and participation in high-quality educational opportunities. A systematic approach to gathering data on OTL over time could contribute to a data infrastructure that could allow researchers and policymakers to examine how changes in OTL factors influence student outcomes.

The NASEM (2019) report focused specifically on indicators of *equity* in both outcomes and opportunities, stating that "Educational equity requires that educational opportunity be calibrated to need, which may include additional and tailored resources and supports to create conditions of true educational opportunity" (NASEM, 2019, p. 24). The NASEM report's authors noted the importance of civic learning outcomes and opportunities but did not recommend specific indicators in this domain due to the lack of appropriate measures available at the time of its publication. However, evidence of disparities (e.g., Bueso, 2022; Hamilton et al., 2024a; Kahne & Middaugh, 2008; Kahne & Sporte, 2008; Kiesa et al., 2022; Savage & Ikoma, 2023) in access to CLO points to a clear need for a more robust approach to monitoring these opportunities and identifying those students who could benefit from an infusion of resources (Hamilton & Kaufman, 2022).

Current State of CLO Monitoring

Recent assessment and accountability policy has reflected a modest shift toward recognizing the potential benefits of monitoring OTL. For instance, the Every Student Succeeds Act (2015) allows states to incorporate OTL indicators into their statewide accountability systems as part of the school quality and student success (SQSS) indicator. Some states have adopted indicators related to OTL factors such as access to advanced coursework, but only a small number of states included such indicators, and when they are included, the weight allocated to them in the accountability system is small (Hall, 2017).

Because the United States has not participated in cross-national studies of civic education since 1999, the only current nationwide effort to monitor civic learning outcomes as well as opportunities on a regular basis is the National Assessment of Educational Progress (NAEP). In addition to the student achievement assessments, NAEP gathers data on several CLO domains through its school questionnaires that are administered to school leaders, teachers, and students. Some of the CLO-related topics included in the civics student questionnaire, for example, have been the extent to which students studied civics content in their social studies class (e.g., the three branches of government, current political and social issues), instructional approaches (e.g., field trips to learn about civics topics, writing assignments, political debates and discussions at school), and the extent to which students have opportunities outside of school settings (e.g., discussing political events with family and friends).

The NAEP CLO data from the civics and U.S. history questionnaires are valuable, but at the time of writing this chapter, NAEP gathered data on civic learning only from 8th graders and only at the national level (in contrast with the mathematics and reading assessments, for which state-level data are available). Other data on CLO is hard to come by. One reason is the lack of resources (including but not limited to funding) and infrastructure for large-scale data collection on civic-related topics. Aside from NAEP there have been a few sporadic efforts to gather data on a national scale (Diliberti et al., 2023; Kahne et al., 2025). This work has generated valuable evidence but has not covered the full scope of CLO, nor has it resulted in systematic, ongoing data collection.

A second factor contributing to the lack of CLO data is the relative dearth of high-quality measures that can be used to systematically monitor CLO. In a recent report, the Institute for Citizens & Scholars (2023) documented their review of tools for measuring both civic readiness, defined as "an individual's preparation to be an effective citizen" (p. 13), and CLO (see also Gallos et al., this volume). The review identified questionnaires and other measurement tools designed to provide evidence of learning opportunities in school settings ranging from kindergarten to college, as well as in non-school settings, such as the civic infrastructure in communities. The analysis shows that available tools measure a limited number of opportunities, such as classroom instruction that helps students build critical thinking skills and opportunities for agency through student government. The authors noted that there are numerous learning opportunities for which measurement tools are largely unavailable, such as opportunities to learn how to address differences and conflicts through activities like discussions of contested issues. Other constructs related to CLO that are not systematically measured in the United States include antecedents that facilitate the provision of CLO, such as teachers' perspectives regarding the importance of teaching or supporting students in developing civic knowledge, skills, and dispositions, as well as their confidence in teaching and the barriers they face.

Toward a System of CLO Indicators

The discussion above highlighted the potential benefits of a systematic approach to monitoring CLO and identified some of the gaps in measures, infrastructure, and policy that hinder efforts to understand the opportunities young people have to develop civic competencies. In this section, we describe a vision for a system of CLO indicators that policymakers and other groups could use to monitor the state of CLO in U.S. schools and inform decision-making at all levels of the education system.

One critical consideration related to any proposed monitoring system is identifying the parties who are responsible for designing, implementing, and updating the system. In this chapter, we do not prescribe a specific approach to assigning this responsibility or to developing a governance plan for the system. Given the decentralized nature of public education in the United States, along with the recent dismantling of many federal supports for data collection and reporting, we anticipate that any robust CLO monitoring system will require participation by state and local education agencies in partnership with policy, research, and community-serving organizations. States might be the best-positioned entities to lead on this effort, and at the time of this writing, numerous state agencies and legislatures were exploring and implementing new systems and structures related to data and indicators (Camborda, 2025).

To contribute to the design of a comprehensive set of CLO indicators, we drew on the work by Hamilton and Kaufman (2022) and reviewed several civic learning frameworks and papers to identify specific practices and opportunities that can be documented at the classroom and school levels. We classified these practices and opportunities into categories to provide a blueprint of the content of CLO indicators. Importantly, we propose the inclusion of antecedents to CLO as they can potentially facilitate (or hinder if they are absent) the provision of CLO. This discussion is not intended to provide an exhaustive overview of potential CLO-related practices, their antecedents, and measures but instead aims to lay out a broad outline of what a comprehensive CLO indicator system might look like. In addition, our proposed framework consists of CLO and antecedents that can be documented at the school, teacher, or classroom level. We do not propose an approach to gathering data at the district, state, or community levels, though such data collection would be important for providing a more comprehensive view of policies and practices that promote civic learning.

It is also important to recognize that the level at which an aspect of CLO is measured might be different from the level at which it is offered and that whether we measure availability of, or participation in, an opportunity will produce different information. For example, below we discuss the importance of gathering data on student coursetaking. An indicator that documents the number and characteristics of civic-related courses that school districts offer will lead to different inferences, and perhaps subsequent policy decisions, than one that provides that information at the school level or that focuses on the percentages of students who enroll in or complete those courses. We return to these issues later in this chapter. Table 10.2 provides a list of the proposed categories of indicators and antecedents; we describe each category in detail below.

Classroom- and Teacher-Level Indicators

Instructional Activities and Content

Indicators of instructional activities and content are necessary to examine the enacted curricula, which refers to how teachers implement the intended curricula (Pak et al., 2020). Indicators for instructional activities may include the extent to which teachers incorporate deliberations and discussions, simulations and role-play, action civics and service learning, and inquiry-based approaches in their classroom practices (Conklin et al., 2021; Educating for American Democracy (EAD), 2021). These practices have been linked to various civic learning outcomes, including increased political knowledge, self-efficacy, civic engagement, political interest, tolerance of diverse perspectives, tolerance of disagreements, trust, participation, understanding of the complex nature of political issues, intentions of civic participation, and actual electoral participation (Barton & Avery, 2016; Celio et al., 2011; Hess, 2002, 2009; Hess & McAvoy, 2014; Kahne et al., 2013) but still require further research into whether the relationships with student outcomes are causal.

Table 10.2 Proposed Categories of CLO Indicators and Antecedents

Level	Category of CLO Indicators	Antecedent Indicators
Classroom/teacher	Instructional activities and content Instructional quality Instructional materials and assessments	Teacher capacity Teachers' attitudes and beliefs
School	Courses and curricula Student voice opportunities Service learning Positive school climate	Staffing supports

Indicators of instructional activities related to civic learning may also include practices focused on developing social and emotional competencies (i.e., self-awareness, self-management, social awareness, relationship skills, and responsible decision-making), given the considerable practical and theoretical overlap in the skills, behaviors, and attitudes between civic and social/emotional competencies (for a more detailed discussion of this overlap, see Hamilton et al., 2024b). Additional indicators may include the adoption of practices that emphasize positive relationships with the teacher and classmates, drawing on students' assets and backgrounds, in a rigorous environment that challenges them (Stembridge, 2020). Creating small learning communities and fostering student voice and agency are two examples of practices that can facilitate positive school relationships and increase student engagement (Hernández & Darling-Hammond, 2024).

Content indicators may consist of survey items regarding the extent to which students are exposed to various curricular topics. However, the specific topics to examine may vary depending on the framework adopted or the state standards (described in the section of school-level indicators). When considering indicators for both instructional activities and content, we should keep in mind that responses from teachers and students might show discrepancies, and that students' reports about their teachers or their classrooms will vary across students even for the same teachers or classrooms. We discuss this issue later in the chapter.

Instructional Quality

In addition to the content delivered and the instructional approaches used, it is important to measure and monitor the quality of instruction (Gitomer, 2018; Pianta & Hamre, 2009), which to date has not been a major focus of the field of civic learning. Instructional (or teaching) quality research and policy have tended to focus on mathematics and language arts, but literature is emerging on instructional quality in the context of civic learning (e.g., Alscher et al., 2022).

One promising framework is an adapted version of the German framework of Three Basic Dimensions (see Praetorius et al., 2018 for a description of the original framework). The Three Basic Dimensions include classroom management, cognitive activation (i.e., teachers' ability to promote higher-order thinking in the classroom), and student support (i.e., classroom climate). Applications of the Three Basic Dimensions tend to utilize student survey measures, which can be integrated into large-scale indicator systems more easily than classroom observations. Researchers have recently started to adapt this framework for the context of civic learning (Alscher et al., 2022) by integrating the rich, international evidence base on open classroom climate – a classroom climate where political topics are discussed openly with respect for differences in viewpoints (see e.g., Campbell, 2008; Persson, 2015; Schulz et al., 2018). While research is ongoing, Alscher et al. (2022) provided some early validity evidence for measures of two of the three dimensions.

Instructional Materials and Assessments

The materials and assessment tools teachers use influence the instructional practices they implement (Kaufman et al., 2020). As such, their quality and the topics they cover are relevant to documenting CLO. Using nationally representative data from K-12 teachers, Hamilton et al. (2020) found that most elementary teachers and secondary teachers reported that half or more of the instructional materials they use in social studies classes are those they found themselves. Furthermore, a smaller but substantial proportion of teachers (31% of elementary teachers, and 44% of secondary teachers) reported creating from scratch half or more of their materials. Continued systematic data collection is needed to examine these results in more detail to understand why the materials provided by the school or district, which theoretically have been approved given their high quality, may not be sufficient. The materials, for example, may not cover all the content teachers include in their lessons or may not be relevant or engaging to their students and cultural backgrounds.

Classroom assessments are an important tool that teachers can use to examine how well students have mastered civic learning topics and to identify the areas that need more emphasis (will add references to relevant chapters in this volume). Assessments should also be used to give students the opportunity to reflect on their own learning. A system of CLO indicators should measure the extent to which teachers use assessments as a tool to guide their instructional approaches to give students opportunities for self-reflection.

Teacher Capacity

Teachers have substantial influence on what is taught in classrooms and how, particularly in non-tested subjects, and their decisions are determined in part by their knowledge about a particular subject (Winfield & Woodard, 1994). Hence, a comprehensive approach to understanding students' learning opportunities requires attending to teachers' professional knowledge, experiences, and certifications (Banicky, 2000; Valencia et al., 2024). Broadly, this set of indicators might include measures of teacher knowledge, information about teacher education and certification, and years of experience. These indicators should be specific to civic learning and could include, for example, the number of years teaching social studies, history, or other civic-related disciplines and teachers' educational coursework in those fields. In addition, this category could include teachers' participation in professional learning opportunities related to their civic learning. As we note in the section below in staffing supports, even when professional learning opportunities are offered schoolwide, individual teachers within a school might vary in their participation.

Teachers' Attitudes and Beliefs

Another set of influences on teachers' instructional approaches is their attitudes and beliefs about the importance of civic learning topics and their beliefs about students' capacities (Conklin et al., 2021; Winfield & Woodard, 1994). Teachers' beliefs, including views on the challenges and supports they face in their daily work, can play a crucial role in creating CLO (Domitrovich et al., 2022; Hamilton & Kaufman, 2022) and have been shown to be significant predictors of student learning outcomes (Organisation for Economic Co-Operation and Development, 2009; Schonert-Reichl, 2017).

Hamilton et al. (2020) found that teachers' beliefs on the importance of students' civic development were positively related to their reported emphasis on civics topics (e.g., voting, the Constitution), civics instructional approaches (e.g., discussion of current and controversial events, media literacy), and civic-related skills (e.g., conflict resolution). Indicators for teachers' attitudes and beliefs may also include measures of teachers' beliefs regarding whether all students have the capacity to learn complex and rigorous content, teachers' appreciation of student diversity, and teachers' attitudes regarding self-reflection and cultivating self-knowledge (EAD, 2021).

School-Level Indicators

Courses and Curricula

Decisions about what courses to offer are typically made at the district or school level, as are many decisions about formal curricula adoption. It is important to distinguish between (a) the formal set of curricula materials and guidance that reflect the goals of education leaders at the school, district, or even state level, and (b) decisions that teachers make regarding the adoption of classroom-specific instructional materials and practices (discussed above). These teacher-level decisions are described by Choppin et al. (2022), who write that "The operational curriculum includes the teacher-intended curriculum (the lessons teachers design from the designated curriculum) and the enacted curriculum…[which] involves what happens in classrooms when students and teachers interact around content and tasks" (p. 124).

In addition to monitoring the specific courses and curricula focused on civic-related content that tends to be taught in social studies classrooms (e.g., voting, the Constitution, history, geography), indicators of CLO should also capture information about schools' adoption of courses and curricula that emphasize practices linked to a broad range of civic learning outcomes, such as those that provide opportunities for inquiry and critical thinking (EAD, 2021), the use of tools and strategies to engage in respectful debates and discussions of controversial topics (Conklin et al., 2021; Kraatz et al., 2022), and opportunities to civically engaging with communities (Darling-Hammond & McGuire, 2023), among others. Furthermore, considering the prominent space that digital media takes in youth's civic engagement, courses and curricula are needed to teach students to judge the accuracy of information and interact safely and responsibly with others through digital media (Garcia et al., 2021).

Student Voice Opportunities

Schools function as a microcosm of democratic society, reflecting its structures, norms, and dynamics. As such, schools represent a space in which students can engage in their school communities and decisions, similar to the opportunities they may face as adults (Darling-Hammond & McGuire, 2023). School opportunities for students to express their views include participation in school-wide debates and panel discussions about school issues (Barber et al., 2021; Littenberg-Tobias, 2021), use of student government, participation in school budgeting, and decision-making in school issues relevant to students (Jagers et al., 2019; Littenberg-Tobias, 2021; Yoder et al., 2021).

Service Learning

When implemented well, service learning offers students opportunities to develop civic dispositions and become active citizens (Flanagan, 2014). Indicators of service learning may include participation in daily experiences with civic institutions, community volunteer projects or services, writing letters to state an opinion or solve a community problem. Furthermore, service learning offers the opportunity to engage in project-based learning requiring students to engage in authentic problems of interest to them and their communities; use inquiry and critical thinking to analyze the problem, evaluate alternative solutions, design and/or implement a solution; practice metacognition skills by reflecting on what they have learned about their schools and communities; and practice communication skills by working on public products of their experiences and solutions to the problem (Darling-Hammond & McGuire, 2023; Jagers et al., 2019). As such, indicators may include survey items of participation in project-based learning to solve problems in their communities.

Positive School Climate

A positive school climate is essential for fostering an environment where students can learn and thrive. It is characterized by active engagement, ensuring both emotional and physical safety, and maintaining a supportive environment that addresses students' physical and mental health needs (National Center on Safe Supportive Learning Environments, n.d.). Engagement involves students, staff, and families actively participating in school activities and decision-making processes. Safety encompasses emotional and physical security, protecting students from bullying and violence. The environment includes well-maintained facilities and resources that support student health and well-being.

A positive school climate plays a crucial role in promoting civic learning by creating an environment where students feel valued and empowered to participate in civic activities and safe to share their viewpoints. This includes opportunities for students to engage in open discussions about social and political issues, interact with others who may hold conflicting opinions, participate in community service projects, and develop a sense of responsibility toward their community (Barber et al., 2021; Conklin et al., 2021; Darling-Hammond & McGuire, 2023).

Staffing Supports

As classroom instruction is inherently intertwined with the instruction-related supports teachers receive, professional development is one OTL indicator typically included in surveys to teachers (e.g., Organisation for Economic Co-operation and Development, 2023; Valencia et al., 2024). Potential indicators include access to and participation in professional learning that focuses on civic-related topics or pedagogical approaches and that incorporates strategies associated with effective professional development, such as tailoring to teachers' classroom contexts and ongoing, personalized support through coaching (Darling-Hammond et al., 2017). Additionally, we propose the inclusion of teachers' self-perception of the need for professional development and their self-reported confidence in teaching civic learning topics (Hamilton, Kaufman & Hu, 2020; Hamilton et al., 2024a), as teachers are a critical source of information about their own learning needs. We recognize that professional development can be teacher-specific, and variation between teachers should also be monitored.

Conditions Needed to Support a CLO Indicator System

As schools, districts, and states strive to promote civic learning among young people, it is imperative that they also organize and make informed use of robust indicator systems to track both their own and students' development. These systems should make use of the types of classroom- and school-level indicators described above, going beyond just capturing data to summarize it in formats easily interpreted by educational leaders and policymakers. Collected on a regular basis (every one to four years, with the frequency being determined based on considerations of cost, feasibility, and magnitude of anticipated changes), the resulting information on civic learning environments would facilitate the understanding of where additional resources may be needed to ensure all students are afforded educational opportunities to develop civic competencies and dispositions sufficient to sustain engaged and productive participation in society. Below we suggest conditions that would be ideal to support the collection of high-quality data supporting CLO indicator systems.

Incorporate Data from Multiple Sources

Using multiple sources of data is essential for capturing accurate information on CLOs. As we discussed earlier, survey questionnaires are widely used to gather data on a large scale. Despite challenges associated with obtaining good response rates and creating items that are resistant to response biases, we expect surveys to remain valuable in this context due to their cost-effectiveness, the relative ease with which they can be developed versus other types of measures, and their applicability across a wide range of potential topics and constructs. Surveys also have a history of strong evidence supporting their reliability and validity for group-level monitoring

(Hart et al., 2020; Valencia et al., 2024). Collecting data from a variety of sources (e.g., students, teachers, other school staff) and being careful about how we interpret such data sources, weighing them based on their relative strengths and limitations, can facilitate building a more comprehensive understanding of the educational environment with respect to CLOs. Taking a multiple-source approach may also help mitigate misperceptions that could arise from relying only on information from a single group, improving our understanding of and insights into how CLOs are made available or delivered in a given context.

There are multiple additional benefits education systems might expect to accrue from integrating multiple sources of CLO data. Systems using this approach might expect to improve the effectiveness of decision-making around targeting interventions or resources, for example, as a direct result of knowing how different respondent groups align versus diverge in their perspectives on or experience with CLOs. A system incorporating multiple data sources (perhaps collected at multiple time points) can also expect to be able to adapt to shifting educational contexts that may impact how different individuals experience CLOs. Such a system would allow for continuous monitoring and timely adjustments based on multi-source feedback, helping ensure that civic-related educational strategies remain relevant and responsive to current needs. Additionally, it is important to have flexibility in the system to incorporate indicators specific to each state, district, or other relevant entity, while maintaining a core set of indicators that would allow comparability. This balance ensures that local contexts are respected and addressed, while also enabling broader comparisons and assessments of CLO across different regions. Finally, school community engagement could be expected to benefit from direct participation in a state or district's CLO indicator system. Seeking data from multiple groups can help build a sense of ownership in the sense that helping students, teachers, and staff see that their input is valued and utilized can enhance their commitment to the state or district's civic learning goals and initiatives.

Of course, incorporating multiple data sources introduces challenges related to interpretation and synthesis. For instance, teachers' reports about classroom climate might lead to different inferences than students' reports, and student survey results typically show extensive variability even when students are reporting about the same teacher or classroom (see Schweig et al., 2019, for additional discussion of considerations when interpreting school and classroom climate survey data).

Explore Alternate Approaches to Measurement

For any large-scale indicator system to be both feasible and useful, we must rely on methods for gathering data quickly and efficiently across a broad range of topics. This likely means continued reliance on survey questionnaires but, given their limitations (e.g., Primi et al., 2022), developers of CLO indicator systems should explore ways to leverage advances in technology and measurement methodology to improve on these traditional approaches. Potentially promising alternatives to traditional surveys are the uses of forced-choice and situational judgment test (SJT) items and scales which can provide nuanced, contextualized insights into respondents' preferences, behavioral tendencies, and knowledge of effective or helpful ways to respond to challenging situations. Applications of generative AI offer promising possibilities for automated item generation and customization, as well as for enhancing the assessment reporting and feedback process (though they also introduce risks; see Tucker & Baker, this volume). Beyond its application to assessment techniques, the collection of classroom artifacts such as written documents or student-produced multimedia content could be analyzed efficiently using AI (aided by human review), providing rich data on CLOs to complement information provided by quantitative measures. More broadly and with appropriate instructions and fairness guardrails in place, large language models or other forms of AI could be deployed to help users of CLO indicators (or indicator systems) interpret variation objectively within and across those indicators. This would support evidence-based inference and decision-making, ideally by improving the efficiency of (and thus encouraging) holistic reviews of CLO indicator results. By integrating multiple components across innovative approaches, the field can develop more robust indicator systems equipped to capture complex CLO phenomena and support student success.

Prioritize Measurement Quality

As with any assessment or evaluation endeavor, the cornerstone of an effective indicator system lies in the quality of its component measures and resulting data. "Quality" in this case is defined by the extent to which the system's results can be used to generate valid and reliable inference aligned with their intended use cases. Note the key nuance that – following the *Standards for Educational and Psychological Testing* (American Educational Research Association et al., 2014) – like their component indicators or measures, indicator systems themselves should not be characterized as "valid" or "reliable." They are instead a mechanism for supporting the valid and reliable interpretation of data on CLO in a specific context. Gathering validity and reliability evidence for the use of CLO indicators should be conducted on an ongoing basis to reflect changes in the contexts and populations in which they are used. Lacking evidence for measurement quality, any inferences made based on data from an indicator system are called into question (Flake & Fried, 2020). In addition to the measurement quality of the indicators, it is essential to provide clear guidance on how the data should be interpreted and used to support the validity interpretation of CLO indicators. Without such guidance, we risk scores being misused or misinterpreted, undermining their intended purpose. Additionally, ongoing monitoring of potential negative consequences is crucial to ensure the use of these indicators does not inadvertently reinforce inequities or distort educational practices.

Evidence of the validity and reliability of CLO indicators for large-scale monitoring should be collected through the various phases of their development, collection, and interpretation, for example, through providing clear operational definitions, consistent training of any required data collectors (e.g., classroom observers), and standardized data collection procedures. Importantly, the adoption of CLO indicators should be backed by initial feasibility and larger-scale pilot studies, bearing in mind that the types of measures and evidence we rely upon to support valid interpretations may vary by various characteristics such as school level (e.g., different instructional strategies or learning activities appropriate for elementary vs. secondary students) or geographic region (e.g., community-based learning opportunities may vary in rural vs. urban contexts). The validity of adopted CLO indicators can also be supported by evidence of their meaningfulness (i.e., reflective of clearly defined constructs) and usefulness for informing future decisions.

Connect CLO Indicators to Data on Civic Readiness

A system measuring CLO without capturing elements of civic learning outcomes would result in an incomplete picture of their relationships. Measuring the two domains in combination is essential to understand how opportunities may combine with other contextual factors or policy levers to support development of outcomes (Valencia et al., 2024). Informed by the growing literature on CLO and civic readiness (e.g., Alscher et al., 2022; Bowyer & Kahne, 2020; Bringle & Clayton, 2021), such a holistic approach would enable schools, districts, and states to identify those CLO with potential to drive meaningful improvements in civic learning outcomes. Indicator data could be used to form part of the justification for targeting supportive resources toward schools whose students appeared to lack access, with continued monitoring to determine whether any CLO disparities observed previously among student populations have been reduced by the provision of additional supports. Moving beyond descriptive analyses, having access to both types of indicators would also pave the way for more rigorous studies exploring longitudinal trends and using research designs appropriate to explore the causal mechanisms linking CLO-related policy shifts to student outcomes (Savage et al., 2023).

Design a System to Support Longitudinal Monitoring

Tracking CLO over time and understanding whether school-, district-, or state-level interventions have been effective requires collecting the same indicator data repeatedly using the same or similar mechanisms. Longitudinal measurement of both CLO and civic learning outcomes is needed to support studies to reveal how trends in both phenomena develop over time and interact with each other, and, in combination with rigorous experimental or quasi-experimental research designs, to answer causal research questions (e.g., did implementing policy A cause a change in Y student outcome?). Cross-sectional data on CLO and civic learning outcomes are useful for describing patterns or illuminating disparities at a single point in time, but they are insufficient for answering pressing questions in the field around, for example, the extent to which changing social and cultural contexts might affect how CLO are provided in different types of classroom instructional environments, which in turn are related to student outcomes (Wang et al., 2020). While NAEP collects large-scale data and provides valuable information about 8th-graders' civics and U.S. history outcomes and learning opportunities, the program currently lacks both detailed OTL indicators and scales summarizing those indicators (Valencia et al., 2024). Civic learning is a dynamic process that unfolds over the course of students' educational experiences. As such, CLO should be viewed not as one-time snapshots but rather as evolving phenomena that interact with and potentially influence students' developmental trajectories when it comes to civic learning outcomes (e.g., media literacy, community involvement, future voting behavior). Building indicator systems incorporating longitudinal data at multiple levels enhances their capacity to both reveal those trajectories and inform policies and practice.

Conclusion

High-quality civic learning in K-12 schools is crucial for individual success and societal well-being. Schools are well-positioned to cultivate civic competencies due to their significant impact on child and adolescent development. As such, it is important for policy and decision-makers to have access to information regarding the CLO students receive in schools. While various studies have gathered information on the state of CLOs, there has been no effort to construct a comprehensive system of CLO indicators and systematically track those opportunities over time.

We propose a framework for developing a CLO indicator system to monitor learning opportunities and support effective decision-making by policymakers and education leaders. Establishing an effective indicator system to track and address equity in CLO necessitates careful attention to measurement quality, the integration of measures of both CLO and civic readiness, and longitudinal implementation. Through a careful design process involving stakeholders with different interests and lived experiences, educational agencies of all sizes and areas of focus can develop robust indicator systems that not only track equity in CLO but also contribute to the advancement of research and the promotion of effective civic education practices. Providing access to such systems to policymakers, researchers, and the public alike, can be instrumental to educational and community efforts intended to help prepare students to become informed, engaged citizens eager to make productive contributions toward civil society.

Note

1 Throughout this chapter, we use the phrase "civic competencies" to refer to the broad set of skills, knowledge, and dispositions that help people engage effectively in civic and community life (see Chapter 1).

References

Alscher, P., Ludewig, U., & McElvany, N. (2022). Civic education, teaching quality and students' willingness to participate in political and civic life: Political interest and knowledge as mediators. *Journal of Youth and Adolescence*, 51(10), 1886–1900. https://doi.org/10.1007/s10964-022-01639-9

American Educational Research Association, American Psychological Association, & National Council on Measurement in Education. (2014). *Standards for educational and psychological testing*. American Educational Research Association. https://www.testingstandards.net/uploads/7/6/6/4/76643089/standards_2014edition.pdf

Aspen Institute Education & Society Program. (2022). *Opportunity to learn, responsibility to lead*. https://www.aspeninstitute.org/publications/opportunity-to-learn-responsibility-to-lead/

Banicky, L. (2000). Opportunity to learn. *Education Policy Brief*, 7.

Barber, C., Clark, C. H., & Torney-Purta, J. (2021). Learning environments and school/classroom climate as supports for civic reasoning, discourse, and engagement. In C. D. Lee, G. White, & D. Dong (Eds.), *Educating for civic reasoning and discourse* (pp. 273–318). National Academy of Education. https://naeducation.org/wp-content/uploads/2021/03/Chapter-6.pdf

Barton, K. C., & Avery, P. G. (2016). Research on social studies education: Diverse students, settings, and methods. In D. H. Gitomer & C. A. Bell (Eds.), *Handbook of research on teaching* (5th ed., pp. 985–1038). American Educational Research Association.

Barton, K. C., & Ho, L. C. (2021). *Curriculum for justice and harmony: Deliberation, knowledge, and action in social and civic education*. Routledge.

Bowyer, B., & Kahne, J. (2020). The digital dimensions of civic education: Assessing the effects of learning opportunities. *Journal of Applied Developmental Psychology*, 69, 101162.

Breakstone, J., McGrew, S., & Smith, M. (2024). Measuring what matters: Investigating what new types of assessments reveal about students' online source evaluations. *Harvard Kennedy School (HKS) Misinformation Review*. https://doi.org/10.37016/mr-2020-133

Bringle, R. G., & Clayton, P. H. (2021). Civic learning: A sine qua non of service learning. *Frontiers in Education*, 6, 606443. https://doi.org/10.3389/feduc.2021.606443

Bueso, L. (2022). Civic equity for students with disabilities. *Teachers College Record*, 124(1), 62–86.

Camborda, C. (2025). *Three state legislative actions we're watching for in 2025 and resources to guide the way*. Data Quality Campaign. https://dataqualitycampaign.org/legislative-actions-were-watching-for-in-2025/

Campbell, D. (2008). Voice in the classroom: How an open classroom climate fosters political engagement among adolescents. *Political Behavior*, 30, 437–454.

Celio, C. I., Durlak, J., & Dymnicki, A. (2011). A meta-analysis of the impact of service-learning on students. *Journal of Experiential Education*, 34(2), 164–181.

Choppin, J., McDuffie, A. R., Drake, C., & Davis, J. (2022). The role of instructional materials in the relationship between the official curriculum and the enacted curriculum, *Mathematical Thinking and Learning*, 24(2), 123–148. https://doi.org/10.1080/10986065.2020.1855376

Conklin, H. G., Lo, J. C., McAvoy, P., Monte-Sano, C. B., Howard, T., & Hess, D. E. (2021). Pedagogical practices and how teachers learn. In C. D. Lee, G. White, & D. Dong (Eds.), *Educating for civic reasoning and discourse* (pp. 353–398). National Academy of Education. https://naeducation.org/wp-content/uploads/2021/03/Chapter-8.pdf

Darling-Hammond, L., Hyler, M. E., & Gardner, M. (2017). *Effective teacher professional development* (research brief). Learning Policy Institute.

Darling-Hammond, L., & McGuire, K. (2023). Policy for civic reasoning. *The ANNALS of the American Academy of Political and Social Science*, 705, 232–248.

Diliberti, M. K., Woo, A., & Kaufman, J. H. (2023). *The missing infrastructure for elementary (K–5) social studies instruction: Findings from the 2022 American Instructional Resources Survey* (RR-A134-17). RAND. https://www.rand.org/pubs/research_reports/RRA134-17.html

Domitrovich, C. E., Harris, A. R., Syvertsen, A. K., Morgan, N., Jacobson, L., Cleveland, M., Moore, J. E., & Greenberg, M. T. (2022). Promoting social and emotional learning in middle school: Intervention effects of Facing History and Ourselves. *Journal of Youth and Adolescence*, 51, 1426–1441.

Educating for American Democracy (EAD). (2021). *Educating for American democracy: Excellence in history and civics for all learners*. iCivics.

Every Student Succeeds Act. 20 U.S.C. 6301 (2015). https://www.congress.gov/114/plaws/publ95/PLAW-114publ95.pdf

Fitzgerald, J. C., Cohen, A. K., Maker Castro, E., & Pope, A. (2021). A systematic review of the last decade of civic education research in the United States. *Peabody Journal of Education*, *96*(3), 235–246. https://doi.org/10.1080/0161956X.2021.1942703

Flake, J. K., & Fried, E. I. (2020). Measurement schmeasurement: Questionable measurement practices and how to avoid them. *Advances in Methods and Practices in Psychological Science*, *3*(4), 456–465.

Flanagan, C. (2014). Teaching a larger "sense of community." *Analysis of Social Issues and Public Policy*, *14*(1), 423–425.

Garcia, A. G., McGrew, S., Mirra, N., Tynes, B., & Kahne, J. (2021). Rethinking digital citizenship: Learning about media, literacy, and race in turbulent times. In C. D. Lee, G. White, & D. Dong (Eds.), *Educating for civic reasoning and discourse* (pp. 319–352). National Academy of Education. https://naeducation.org/wp-content/uploads/2021/03/Chapter-7.pdf

Gitomer, D. H. (2018). Evaluating instructional quality. *School Effectiveness and School Improvement*, *30*(1), 68–78. https://doi.org/10.1080/09243453.2018.1539016

Goals 2000: Educate America Act. 20 U.S.C. 5801 (1994). https://www.govtrack.us/congress/bills/103/hr1804/text/enr.

Gould, J., Jamieson, K. H., Levine, P., McConnell, T., & Smith, D. B. (2011). *Guardian of democracy: The civic mission of schools*. The Leonore Annenberg Institute for Civics of the Annenberg Public Policy Center at the University of Pennsylvania. https://www.carnegie.org/publications/guardian-of-democracy-the-civic-mission-of-schools/

Hall, E. (2017). *Identifying a school Quality/Student success indicator for ESSA: Requirements and considerations*. The National Center for the Improvement of Educational Assessment, Inc. https://www.nciea.org/wp-content/uploads/2023/04/CCSSO_SQSS_Brief.pdf

Hamilton, L. S., & Kaufman, J. H. (2022). Indicators of equitable civic learning in U.S. public schools. *Educational Assessment*, *27*, 187–196. https://doi.org/10.1080/10627197.2022.2087623

Hamilton, L. S., Kaufman, J. H., & Hu, L. (2020). *Preparing children and youth for civic life in the era of truth decay* (RR-A112-6). RAND. https://www.rand.org/pubs/research_reports/RRA112-6.html

Hamilton, L. S., & Martinez, J. F. (2024). Policy influences on ambitious classroom instruction, assessment, and learning. In Marion, S.F., Pellegrino, J.W., & Berman, A.I. (Eds.), *Implementation and use of balanced assessment systems* (pp. 274–308). National Academy of Education. https://naeducation.org/wp-content/uploads/2024/04/Chapter-9_Reimagining-Balanced-Assessment-Systems.pdf

Hamilton, L. S., Olivera-Aguilar, M., & Rikoon, S. (2024a). *Cultivating civic learning and engagement in U.S. schools*. American Institutes for Research. https://www.air.org/sites/default/files/2024-04/cultivating-civic-learning-engagement-US-schools.pdf

Hamilton, L. S., Rikoon, H. S., & Olivera-Aguilar, M. (2024b). How SEL can support civic learning in K-12 schools. In J. A. Durlak, C. E. Domitrovich, & J. L. Mahoney (Eds.), *Handbook of social and emotional learning* (2nd ed., pp. 260–272). Guilford Press.

Hansen, M., Levesque, E., Valant, J., & Quintero, D. (2018). *The 2018 Brown Center report on American education: How well are American students learning*. Brown Center on Education Policy at the Brookings Institution. https://www.brookings.edu/wp-content/uploads/2018/06/2018-Brown-Center-Report-on-American-Education_Final.pdf

Hart, H., Young, C., Chen, A., Zou, A., & Allensworth, E. M. (2020). *Supporting school improvement: Early findings from reexamination of the 5Essentials survey*. University of Chicago Consortium on School Research. https://files.eric.ed.gov/fulltext/ED608120.pdf

Hernández, L., & Darling-Hammond, L. (with Nielsen, N.). (2024). *Cultivating relationships in secondary schools: Structures that matter*. Learning Policy Institute.

Hess, D. (2009). *Controversy in the classroom: The democratic power of discussion*. Routledge.

Hess, D., & McAvoy, P. (2014). *The political classroom: Ethics and evidence in democratic education*. Routledge.

Hess, D. E. (2002). Discussing controversial public issues in secondary social studies classrooms: Learning from skilled teachers. *Theory & Research in Social Education*, *30*(1), 10–41.

Institute for Citizens & Scholars. (2023). *Mapping civic measurement: How are we assessing readiness and opportunities for an engaged citizenry?* citizensandscholars.org.

Jagers, R. J., Rivas-Drake, D., & Williams, B. (2019). Transformative social and emotional learning (SEL): Toward SEL in service of educational equity and excellence. *Educational Psychologist*, *54*, 162–184. https://doi.org/10.1080/00461520.2019.1623032

Kahne, J., Crow, D., & Lee, N. J. (2013). Different pedagogy, different politics: High school learning opportunities and youth political engagement. *Political Psychology*, *34*(3), 419–441.

Kahne, J., & Middaugh, E. (2008). *Democracy for some: The civic opportunity gap in high school* [Circle Working Paper 59]. Center for Information and Research on Civic Learning and Engagement (CIRCLE).

Kahne, J., Rogers, J., & Kwako, A. (2025). The new politics of education and the pursuit of a diverse democracy. *AERA Open*, *11*. https://doi.org/10.1177/23328584241311819

Kahne, J. E., & Sporte, S. E. (2008). Developing citizens: The impact of civic learning opportunities on students' commitment to civic participation. *American Educational Research Journal*, *45*(3), 738–766.

Kaufman, J. H., Hamilton, L. S., & Hu, L. (2020). *Teachers' civics instructional materials: Civic development in the era of Truth Decay* [RR-A112-3]. RAND Corporation. https://www.rand.org/pubs/research_reports/RRA112-3.html

Kiesa, A., Booth, R., Hayat, N., Kawashima-Ginsberg, K., & Medina, A. (2022). *Growing voters: Building institutions and community ecosystems for equitable election participation*. Center for Information and Research on Civic Learning and Engagement.

Kraatz, E., von Spiegel, J., Sayers, R., & Brady, A. C. (2022). Should we "just stick to the facts"? The benefit of controversial conversations in classrooms. *Theory Into Practice*, 61(3), 312–324.

Kyllonen, P. C., Martin-Raugh, M., & Kell, H. J. (2024). SEL competencies in the workplace. In J. A. Durlak, C. E. Domitrovich, & J. L. Mahoney (Eds.), *Handbook of social and emotional learning* (2nd ed., pp. 324–336). Guilford Press.

Lee, C. D., White, G., & Dong, D. (Eds.). (2021). *Educating for civic reasoning and discourse*. National Academy of Education.

Levine, P., & Kawashima-Ginsberg, K. (2017). *The republic is (still) at risk—and civics is part of the solution*. Jonathan M. Tisch College of Civic Life, Tufts University.

Littenberg-Tobias, J. (2021). Teaching citizens: What can NAEP civics tell us about active learning in civics? *Peabody Journal of Education*, 96:3, 247–260. https://doi.org/10.1080/0161956X.2021.1942704

Marion, S. (2020). *Using opportunity-to-learn data to support educational equity*. National Center for the Improvement of Educational Assessment. https://files.eric.ed.gov/fulltext/ED611325.pdf

McDonnell, L. M. (1995). Opportunity to learn as a research concept and a policy instrument. *Educational Evaluation and Policy Analysis*, 17(3), 305–322. https://doi.org/10.3102/01623737017003305

National Academies of Sciences, Engineering, and Medicine (NASEM). (2019). *Monitoring educational equity*. The National Academies Press.

National Center on Safe Supportive Learning Environments. (n.d.). *School climate improvement*. https://safesupportivelearning.ed.gov/school-climate-improvement

Organisation for Economic Co-operation and Development. (2009). *Creating effective teaching and learning environments: First results from TALIS*. https://www.oecd.org/education/school/43023606.pdf

Organisation for Economic Co-operation and Development. (2023). *PISA 2022 assessment and analytical framework*. OECD Publishing. https://doi.org/10.1787/dfe0bf9c-en

Pak, K., Polikoff, M. S., Desimone, L. M., & Saldívar García, E. (2020). The adaptive challenges of curriculum implementation: Insights for educational leaders driving standards-based reform. *AERA Open*, 6, 1–15. https://doi.org/10.1177/2332858420932828

Persson, M. (2015). Classroom climate and political learning: Findings from a Swedish panel study and comparative data. *Political Psychology*, 36(5), 587–601. https://doi.org/10.1111/pops.12179

Pianta, R. C., & Hamre, B. K. (2009). Conceptualization, measurement, and improvement of classroom processes: Standardized observation can leverage capacity. *Educational Researcher*, 38(2), 109–119.

Praetorius, A. K., Klieme, E., Herbert, B., & Pinger, P. (2018). Generic dimensions of teaching quality: The German framework of three basic dimensions. *ZDM – Mathematics Education*, 50, 407–426. https://doi.org/10.1007/s11858-018-0918-4

Primi, R., Hauck-Filho, N., & Valentini, F. (2022). Self-report and observer ratings: Item types, measurement challenges, and techniques of scoring. In J. Burrus, S. Rikoon, & M. Brenneman (Eds.), *Assessing competencies for social and emotional learning* (1st ed., pp. 99–116). Routledge.

Pritchard, I. (1996). Judging standards in standards-based reform. *Perspective*, 8, 1–20.

Rimm-Kaufman, S. E., Merritt, E. G., Lapan, C., DeCoster, J., Hunt, A., & Bowers, N. (2021). Can service-learning boost science achievement, civic engagement, and social skills?: A randomized controlled trial of connect science. *Journal of Applied Developmental Psychology*, 74. https://doi.org/10.1016/j.appdev.2020.101236.

Sant, E. (2019). Democratic education: A theoretical review (2006–2017). *Review of Educational Research*, 89(5), 655–696. https://doi.org/10.3102/0034654319862493

Savage, C., Hamilton, L. S., Scholz, C., & Murray, O. (2023). *Pressing needs in research on K–12 civic learning: A call to the field*. https://www.air.org/sites/default/files/2023-09/Pressing-Needs-in-Research-on-K-12-Civic-Learning-September-2023.pdf

Savage, C., & Ikoma, S. (2023). *Access to civics content and evidence-based instructional approaches in U.S. schools* [AIR-NAEP Working Paper #2023-07]. American Institutes for Research.

Schmidt, W. H., & Maier, A. (2009). Opportunity to learn. In G. Sykes, B. Schneider, & D. N. Plank (Eds.), *Handbook of education policy research* (pp. 541–559). Routledge.

Schonert-Reichl, K. A. (2017). Social and emotional learning and teachers. *The Future of Children*, 27(1), 137–155.

Schulz, W., Ainley, J., Fraillon, J., Losito, B., Agrusti, G., & Friedman, T. (2018). Becoming citizens in a changing world. IEA International Civic and Citizenship Education Study 2016 International Report. *Springer Open*. https://doi.org/10.1007/978-3-319-73963-2

Schweig, J., Hamilton, L. S., & Baker, G. (2019). *School and classroom climate measures: Considerations for use by state and local education leaders* (RR-4259-FCIM). RAND. https://www.rand.org/pubs/research_reports/RR4259.html

Stembridge, A. (2020). *Culturally responsive education in the classroom: An equity framework for pedagogy*. Routledge. https://doi.org/10.4324/9780429441080

Teegelbeckers, J. Y., Nieuwelink, H., & Oostdam, R. J. (2023). School-based teaching for democracy: A systematic review of teaching methods in quantitative intervention studies. *Educational Research Review, 39*, 100511. https://doi.org/10.1016/j.edurev.2023.100511

The Nation's Report Card. (2022). *The Nation's Report Card: Civics*. Students group scores and score gaps. https://www.nationsreportcard.gov/civics/results/groups/

Valencia, S. W., Pellegrino, J. W., & Durán, R. P. (2024). *An exploration of opportunity to learn and implications for NAEP*. NAEP Validity Studies (NVS) Panel American Institutes for Research.

Vinnakota, R. (2019). *From civic education to a civic learning ecosystem: A landscape analysis and case for collaboration*. Red & Blue Works. https://citizensandscholars.org/wp-content/uploads/2022/12/Civic-Learning-White-Paper.pdf

Wang, M. T., Degol, J. L., Amemiya, J., Parr, A., & Guo, J. (2020). Classroom climate and children's academic and psychological wellbeing: A systematic review and meta-analysis. *Developmental Review, 57*, 100912.

Winfield, L. F., & Woodard, M. D. (1994). Assessment, equity, and diversity in reforming America's schools. *Educational Policy, 8*(1), 3–27. https://doi.org/10.1177/0895904894008001001

Winthrop, R. (2020, June 4). *The need for civic education in 21st-century schools*. The Brookings Institution. https://www.brookings.edu/policy2020/bigideas/the-need-for-civic-education-in-21st-century-schools/

Yoder, N., Atwell, M. N., Godek, D., Dusenbury, L., Bridgeland, J. M., & Weissberg, R. (2020). *Preparing youth for the workforce of tomorrow: Cultivating the social and emotional skills employers demand*. Collaborative for Academic, Social, and Emotional Learning.

Yoder, N., Ward, A. M., & Wolforth, S. (2021). Instructional practices that integrate equity-centered social, emotional, and academic learning. *American Institutes for Research*. https://www.air.org/sites/default/files/2021-12/Social-Emotional-Learning-Equity-Centered-Instructional-Practices-December-2021.pdf

11
Can Discrete-Choice Measures and Situational-Judgment Tests Address Ongoing Questions about How to Quantify Global Citizenship?

Michael Thier

Global citizenship education (GCE), like many educational concepts that are characterized as useful extensions to mainstay instructional targets such as literacy and numeracy, faces ongoing problems of how to define and measure it. After providing an overview of those problems, I offer discrete-choice measures (DCMs) and situational-judgment tests (SJTs) as potential solutions. Also known as forced-choice measures, DCMs are more commonly found in economic and market research than in education. They prompt respondents to select from a choice set, allowing researchers to quantify the relative value of different attributes that the choices represent. SJTs offer respondents scenarios with lists of possible responses, so their responses enable researchers to analyze attributes underlying their choices. Both approaches offer alternatives to the Likert-type items that predominate the measurement of GCE. Overall, I intend for readers to think of DCMs and SJTs as encouraging possibilities, not silver bullets.

Each section of this chapter features a question I attempt to address. First, I consider "What is global citizenship?", exploring its ever-increasing and contested definitional space. Second, I ask "Why measure GCE?", highlighting reasons such as providing schools with evidence to justify GCE over traditional education models and ensuring equitable access. Third, I quickly review a historical path, which has produced a measurement base that seems wider than deep, as I wonder: "How did we get here?" Fourth, I ask, "If there are so many measures, why not use them?", examining conceptual, methodological, and political challenges to extant measures that, at least nominally, inhabit this space. Fifth, I offer possible solutions, wondering: "How can DCMs and SJTs improve the situation?" Sixth, I conclude with a provocation: "How do we move forward?"

What Is Global Citizenship?

Global citizenship lacks a consensus definition (Deardorff, 2009; Reysen & Katzarska-Miller, 2018), raising considerable challenges for how to measure it (Osterlind, 2009). One cannot read beyond the second paragraph of influential papers on global citizenship before seeing

DOI: 10.4324/9781003476825-13
This chapter has been made available under a CC BY-NC-ND license.

the construct described as hotly contested (e.g., Davies, 2006; Goren & Yemini, 2017; Oxley & Morris, 2013; Schattle, 2009). To select one of many possible starting points for our purposes, we could use a definition from UNESCO (2021), which regards global citizenship as a sense of belonging to a broader community beyond national boundaries, emphasizing a common humanity and shared responsibility for the planet. Organizationally, UNESCO characterizes global citizenship as an ethos rather than a legal status, though Banks (2008), among others, takes an expansionist view of global citizenship involving individual rights, opportunity for political participation, and availability of social goods such as education. UNESCO's global citizenship ethos features dimensions that are *cognitive* (knowledge, understanding, and critical thinking about global issues), *socio-emotional* (sense of belonging to a common humanity, sharing values, and fostering empathy, solidarity, and respect for diversity), and *behavioral* (acting responsibly at local, national, and global levels to promote peace and sustainability).

Thier (2020) sampled nearly two dozen global citizenship definitions published in peer-reviewed journals between 2006 and 2016, illustrating those definitions' considerable variation in their simultaneous incorporation of dispositions, knowledge, skills, and behaviors. In many instances, Thier's review found scholarly definitions to conflate those aspects within the definition itself, further muddying the operational space around global citizenship. Unsurprisingly, some of global citizenships' most ardent advocates refer to the construct as:

- "too abstract" for meaningful inclusion in education (Davies, 2006, p. 5)
- too convoluted a definitional space for practitioners and researchers (Shultz, 2007)
- a loose association of varying agendas (Marshall, 2011)
- a "floating signifier" (Mannion et al., 2011, p. 134)
- "universally understood, but [...] rarely conceptually or operationally defined" (Morais & Ogden, 2011, p. 445)
- "elusive subject matter" and "quite difficult to isolate" (Goren & Yemini, 2017, p. 173)
- having "capacity to cause significant confusion for policy makers and educators" (Clark & Savage, 2017, p. 406)
- considerably diverse (Pashby et al., 2020)
- "ever-increasing" and "romanticized" (Estellés & Fischman, 2021, pp. 1–2)

Many scholars (e.g., Gándara et al., 2021; Reysen & Katzarska-Miller, 2018; Singh & Qi, 2013) raise further doubts about global citizenship, specifically frequent interchanges of it with terms that Bailey and colleagues (2023) have called "construct cousins"[1] such as:

- cosmopolitanism
- global awareness
- global identity
- identification with the world (or with humanity ... or with the world community)
- intergroup empathy
- International Baccalaureate (IB)'s term: "international-mindedness"
- internationalism
- social justice
- valuing diversity
- world citizenship

Amid such confusion, GCE has arisen broadly as an attempt to empower learners who might actively seek to resolve local, global, and glocal challenges.[2] Fittingly, developing global citizens has become common parlance in many schools and across the internet in an age of increasing globalization. As an example of the concept's growing popularity, 2012 saw the first Global Citizen Festival, now an annual musical event that draws about 60,000 people to New York City (Reysen & Katzarska-Miller, 2018). True to the brand of a fuzzy construct, the festival's goals run the gamut from defending the planet to defeating poverty.

As artificial intelligence (AI) is quickly becoming a trusted aid for sense-making in a complex world, I asked Microsoft Copilot for a "consensus definition" of global citizenship, finding the concept to be:

generally understood as ... transcend[ing] national boundaries and identities, emphasizing a sense of belonging to a global community. It involves recognizing the interconnectedness of life, respecting cultural diversity and human rights, advocating for global social justice, and feeling a moral responsibility for the planet.

Furthermore, Copilot noted key aspects such as:

interconnectedness (understanding how global issues and events affect individuals and communities worldwide), cultural respect (valuing and respecting cultural diversity and promoting inclusivity), human rights (upholding and advocating for universal human rights), global justice (working towards social justice on a global scale), and environmental responsibility (taking action to protect the environment and promote sustainability)

(search conducted on 27 October 2024)

Three days later, I asked Copilot the same question, this time finding a new "consensus definition":

individuals recogniz[ing] themselves as part of a broader, interconnected world community. It emphasizes shared values, responsibilities, and the understanding that local events are influenced by global dynamics and vice versa. Global citizens champion fundamental human rights, promote diversity, empathy, and perspective, and work towards fostering international understanding. In essence, global citizenship is about acknowledging our interdependence and working towards a more just, sustainable, and interconnected world.

(search conducted on 30 October 2024)

These identical searches of a construct's "consensus definition" yielded one set of 20 concepts and another set of 12 concepts with minimal direct overlap (see Figure 11.1). Seemingly, global citizenship is bearing out Humes' (2008) warning about many citizenship concepts: "vague, feel-good rhetoric, a term that can mean everything and nothing" (p. 45).

Furthermore, the Covid-19 pandemic—an accelerant to many global challenges—seems to have exacerbated the challenge of how to operationalize global citizenship. Saperstein (2023) suggested a new term: post-pandemic citizenship education, emphasizing public health, empathy, compassion, self-sacrifice, and a cooperative spirit. In the face of such definitional diffusion, measurement of global citizenship remains problematic.

Why Measure GCE?

More than a decade ago, scholars, policymakers, and other observers began characterizing GCE among education's fastest-growing reforms (e.g., Dill, 2012). In part, the choice to focus explicitly on global citizenship prompted the United Nations' shift from its previous eight

27 October 2024	30 October 2024
1. transcending national boundaries 2. transcending national identities 3. sense of belonging to a global community 4. recognizing interconnectedness of life 5. respecting cultural diversity 6. [respecting] human rights 7. advocating for global social justice 8. feeling moral responsibility for the planet 9. interconnectedness 10. understanding how global issues and events affect individuals and communities worldwide 11. cultural respect 12. valuing cultural diversity 13. respecting cultural diversity 14. promoting inclusivity 15. upholding universal human rights 16. advocating for universal human rights 17. working towards social justice on a global scale 18. environmental responsibility 19. taking action to protect the environment 20. taking action to promote sustainability	1. individuals recognizing themselves as part of a broader, interconnected world community 2. emphasizing shared values, responsibilities 3. understanding that local events are influenced by global dynamics and vice versa 4. championing fundamental human rights 5. promoting diversity 6. promoting empathy 7. promoting perspective 8. fostering international understanding 9. acknowledging our interdependence 10. working toward a more just world 11. working toward a sustainable world 12. working toward an interconnected world

Figure 11.1 Two Microsoft Copilot Searches for a "Consensus Definition" of Global Citizenship Conducted Three Days apart that Reveal Minimal Conceptual Overlap.

Millennium Development Goals to 17 Sustainable Development Goals in 2015. In response, Wilkinson et al. (2015) cast global citizenship as "basic" education's most important outcome, a 21st-century necessity to participate in "all facets of the public sphere and private enterprise" (p. 23). However, a school community's desire to implement GCE[3] and that community having the permissions and/or funding needed to do so are separate issues. In many jurisdictions, schools cannot unilaterally endorse an education model without demonstrating its promise to decision-makers, often those who govern the school externally through structures such as districts. Decision-makers might only greenlight GCE if data suggest a need (i.e., a deficit among students' global citizenship dispositions), pathways to desirable outcomes, or both. Therefore, measurement would be, in many contexts, a prerequisite to generate sufficient evidence to lobby for procuring resources to facilitate GCE implementation. Even among GCE programs that are already in flight, measurement is necessary to inform valid inference-making about how global citizenship-relevant pedagogical practices work, which promising practices might be ready for scale-up, what additional resources might be needed, and/or how to respond to pressures from governments or other agencies (Reysen & Katzarska-Miller, 2018; Rigling et al., 2021; Thier, 2020). Without measurement, well-intentioned educators' anecdotes might provide the only GCE information available. A reliable measurement approach would be a necessary supplement to what is currently a paucity of information.

Under the assumption that GCE represents promising pedagogy, those who prioritize educational equity would also need adequate measures to determine whether gaps exist between those who can and cannot access it. Availability of IB programs—perhaps the world's most recognizable GCE model—provides a useful proxy to detect GCE's school-level availability. As of this writing, nearly 6000 schools worldwide offer at least one of the four programs that IB authorizes for students aged 3–19 and expect their schools' missions to emphasize concepts that are central to many GCE definitions. About one-third of those schools are in the U.S., making IB more frequently available in U.S. communities than anywhere else in the world. Moreover, about 90% of U.S. IB schools receive public funding, a stark difference from the other 160 countries with at least one IB school. Outside the U.S., public funding accounts for 25% of IB schools (International Baccalaureate, 2024), typically privileging access to students from fee-paying families. However, the large number of schools in the U.S. overall masks the fact that less than 2% of publicly funded schools offer IB (Thier & Beach, 2021).

All told, these statistics suggest limited GCE access, especially when the nation with the most IB programs and the highest likelihood of public availability occurs in only 2% of schools. Therefore, one's zip code or enrollment in a magnet school within a central location determines GCE access. This challenge is especially relevant outside major metropolitan areas or geographically well-positioned suburbs, where mass transit options can facilitate school choice for students and their families (Provasnik et al, 2007; Thier & Beach, 2021).

Moreover, within-school access might further diminish one's GCE opportunities, particularly for students from historically marginalized ethno-racial groups (Donaldson, 2017; Perna et al., 2015). And just because a school intends to offer GCE to some or all students, its teachers are not necessarily ready to deliver GCE. UNESCO (2021) and Education International published results of a global survey of 58,000 teachers, revealing pronounced gaps regarding teachers' beliefs about their own GCE readiness. Despite nearly 95% of surveyed teachers believing it would be at least "important" to teach about issues such as climate change, only about 40% felt confident in doing so. Many teachers expressed reluctance to teach about other GCE-relevant topics. Among surveyed teachers, about:

- 25% felt they could not teach human rights, gender equality, or themes related to sustainable development, global citizenship, or peace; and
- 15% felt they could not explain histories of racism and discrimination.

Any given student's chances of receiving a robust GCE experience seem minimal when considering the combined effects of schools' limited likelihoods of offering GCE, teachers' self-reported impediments to delivering it, and then the compounding effects for students whose demographics do not associate with historical advantage (Donaldson, 2017; Gardner-McTaggart, 2016; Thier & Beach, 2021). If GCE is an essential outcome of schooling, as many scholars and policymakers have asserted (Estellés & Fischman, 2021), examining the extent to which its opportunities are equally distributed becomes a necessity. Measurement can aid that pursuit, perhaps contributing to GCE becoming part of education's basic menu. Especially until a substantial proportion of students can access GCE, we should know and understand where it can be found, who can access it, and to what extent it works. But despite many measures being available, questions remain regarding their fitness for the purpose of measuring GCE in K-12 settings.

How Did We Get Here?

The concept of global citizenship dates to the 5th and 6th centuries BCE, when Diogenes of Sinope (Ancient Greece) and Kaniyan Pungundranar of Tamil Nadu (in modern-day India) separately eschewed dominant notions of their times by self-identifying as global citizens rather than members of a city-state or other geographic jurisdiction. More recently, global citizenship played a central role in measurement's overall history. Likert's (1932) dissertation resulted in his now ubiquitous approach to scaling individuals' attitudes. The seminal study that produced the Likert-type item was an attempt to scale internationalism, a precursor to global citizenship, as developed nations grappled with international interdependence between the two world wars. Offering ease of use, Likert-type items have become a standard approach to measuring dispositional aspects of many constructs, especially global citizenship. However, Likert-type items' potential to introduce social desirability bias and other forms of bias (e.g., reference bias) reduces their utility, especially if a measure is intended to inform consequential decisions such as whether to continue offering a program such as GCE.

After several decades of Likert-type items predominating scholarly thought about how to measure international attitudes, the 1950s–1980s yielded individuals and small groups of scholars developing hundreds of self-report instruments. Beneficially, interest in global citizenship soared. The unintentional drawback: a construct with no shared understanding of its most important ingredients. More recently, large organizations such as the World Values Survey and the Programme for International Student Assessment (PISA) have attempted population-level (or for large samples) measurement of global citizenship's construct cousins, again elevating its profile but inviting a host of critiques (see Bailey et al., 2023; Gándara et al., 2021; Reysen & Katzarska-Miller, 2018), several of which I echo in this chapter. For fuller examinations of large-scale assessments of civic learning and engagement, see Goodman and Kirsch and Shulz and Domniani (Chapters 5 and 6, respectively).

As noted by Brown and Maydeu-Olivares (2011), Thurstone pioneered models for modeling pairwise preference data nearly a century ago (Thurstone, 1927, 1931). Those models have since been adapted to accommodate multidimensional constructs (Anguiano-Carrasco et al., 2015; Brown & Maydeu-Olivares, 2013), of which global citizenship is one. Furthermore, investment in SJTs began as early as World War II (Brenneman et al., 2016). More recently, SJTs have employed virtual-reality or live-action situations to enable tests of someone's response to cross-cultural encounters (e.g., Johnson et al., 2011).

If There Are So Many Measures, Why Not Use Them?

The existence of global citizenship measures is not a problem; many exist (Reysen & Katzarska-Miller, 2018; Zhao, 2016). However, the availability of measures that suit someone interested in gathering information on pre-university students regarding global citizenship, especially their dispositions, is rare (Thier, 2020). Barriers to using the myriad measures that are characterized as ways to assess global citizenship—except perhaps the few recent examples of DCMs and SJTs—might be conceptual, methodological, or political.

Conceptual Barriers

Three conceptual barriers to fit-for-purpose measures of global citizenship in secondary schools include: (a) definitional variety, including susceptibility to the jingle-jangle fallacies (Brandt, 2024); (b) multidimensionality; and (c) potential for cultural universality. Having devoted a previous section to global citizenship's definitional challenges, I focus here on the latter two conceptual barriers.

Multidimensionality

As Osterlind (2009) notes, assessments can incorporate items that reflect unidimensionality *and* multidimensionality across the entirety of a measure, but each individual item should tap directly into only one dimension. Several scholars recognize global citizenship's

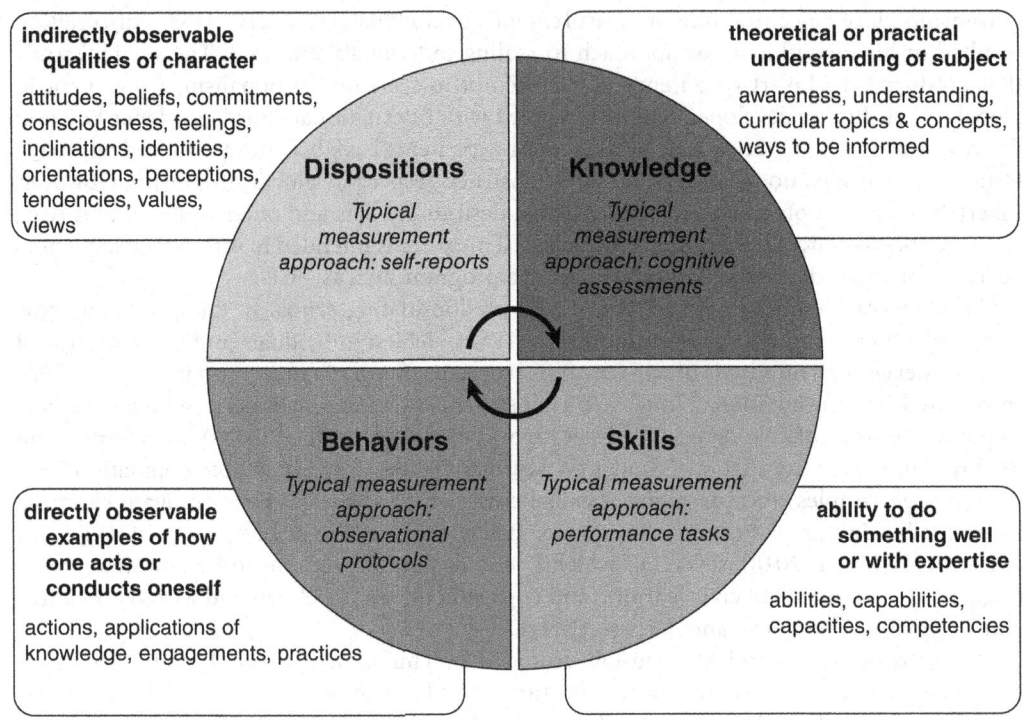

Figure 11.2 A Four-Dimensional Framing for Constructs Such as Global Citizenship with Each's Typical Measurement Approach (Thier, 2020).

multidimensionality, despite considerable variation in how they conceptualize those dimensions (Deardorff, 2009; 2015; Gándara et al., 2021; Morais & Ogden, 2011; Reysen & Katzarska-Miller, 2013). In Thier's (2020) framing (see Figure 11.2), global citizenship can be thought of as containing dispositions, knowledge, skills, and behaviors, with each dimension requiring its own approach to measurement. When I led a team of coders (Thier et al., 2025) to examine Likert-type items from three prominent GCE-relevant measures—Global Citizenship Scale (Morais & Ogden, 2011), Global Citizen Scale (Reysen & Katzarska-Miller, 2013), and Global Perspective Inventory (Braskamp et al., 2014)—we found 80% of the items combined dispositions, knowledge, skills, and/or behaviors. Such overlap might prompt different respondents (or perhaps one respondent on different measurement occasions) to interpret items in fundamentally different ways, making them wonder if an item was meant to elicit how they are disposed, and/or what they know, and/or what they can do, and/or how they act.

Potential for Cultural Universality

Many psychological constructs—those with global implications and not—might manifest differently across cultural, historical, and other contextual divides within single, diverse jurisdictions or cross-jurisdictionally (Chen & Gabrenya, 2021). However, there has been limited empirical work to examine the cross-cultural applicability of global citizenship and related constructs (Gándara et al., 2021). Therefore, whether global citizenship and its "construct cousins" can be shown to possess cultural universality will remain theoretical until someone defines such constructs across contexts (Choi et al., 2012; Gándara et al., 2021; Vogt, 2006).

In the meantime, several challenges exist to cross-cultural applications of measures that were, in most cases, developed within a single cultural context (often a Western one), such as

- a bias toward the measure's (or developer's) culture of origin;
- translation issues, particularly if words/phrases do not have semantic equivalence; or
- interpreting results across cultures that might frame concepts differently (e.g., Western-Eastern differences in individualistic v. collectivistic approaches).

As noted previously, the Organisation for Economic Co-operation and Development (OECD) added a measure of what it called "global competence", referring to a multidimensional construct (knowledge, skills, attitudes, and values), one applies to global issues or intercultural situations, to its PISA battery in 2018. The addition drew swift critiques, in large part due to concerns of cultural applicability across dozens of PISA-participating jurisdictions (Auld & Morris, 2019; Bailey et al., 2023; Engel et al., 2019; Grotlüschen, 2018; Ledger et al., 2019; Robertson, 2021; Sälzer & Roczen, 2018). Several smaller-scale studies have flagged intercultural differences with well-known measures such as:

- Gándara et al. (2021) using World Values Survey items in six nations
- Lawthong (2003) using Hett's (1993) U.S.-developed Global-mindedness scale in Thailand
- Hagel et al. (2022) and Boffi et al. (2022) using the Identification with All Humanity scale in nearly a dozen European countries
- new factor structures that Seo (2016) and Cheon (2017) found when using Morais and Ogden's (2011) U.S.-developed Global Citizenship Scale in Korea.

Consequently, the global citizenship literature sorely needs research on measurement invariance or differential item functioning based on respondents' culture.

Methodological Barriers

Reviews from Reysen and Katzarska-Miller (2018), Gándara et al. (2021), and Thier (2020) reveal methodological challenges among currently available global citizenship measures. One such barrier is the construct's complexity (Deardorff, 2006; Goren & Yemini, 2017; Ledger et al., 2019; Reysen & Katzarska-Miller, 2018), which I discussed previously in terms of its multidimensionality. And while other important methodological challenges remain, I will briefly note a few here before delving more deeply into perhaps the field's most widespread issue: the ubiquity of self-reports and response-style biases they can present (see Anderson et al., 2017). Other issues include limited resources available to develop GCE measures, forcing reliance on non-representative, convenience samples, often university students in psychology classrooms or employees in multinational corporations (Anguiano-Carrasco et al., 2017; Conley, 2013; Deardorff, 2014, 2015; Morais & Ogden, 2011).

Even if resources suddenly became available to develop stronger measures, and if educators and researchers agreed on which approach(es) would provide the greatest utility (Thier, 2020), the field leans heavily on self-reports, which are fraught with biases stemming from participants responding in ways perceived to be socially desirable. Such self-presentation bias is possible because self-report instruments measure dispositions indirectly *and* without either comparing them to standardized responses or relatively against an alternative response, creating space for conscious or subconscious inaccuracies (Brown & Maydeu-Olivares, 2013; Cao, 2016; Deardorff, 2006; 2015; Duckworth & Yeager, 2015; Huws et al., 2009; Krumpal, 2013; Kuokkanen & Sun, 2016; Miller, 2012; Tourangeau & Yan, 2007).

One type of self-presentation bias, social desirability bias, involves participants feeling real or perceived social pressure to alter their responses to make their attitudes or dispositions more palatable. Deardorff (2015) noted how social desirability bias limits self-reported measures of dispositions for constructs with intercultural loadings, such as global citizenship. These biases are considered more likely to occur under high-stakes situations (Duckworth & Yeager, 2015; Huws et al., 2009; Lagattuta et al., 2012; Miller, 2012; Tourangeau & Yan, 2007). Social desirability bias can explain some weak correlations that researchers have found between scores from self-report measures of a given construct and scores from behavioral measures of the same construct (see Dang et al., 2020). Furthermore, scores on the frequently used Global Identity Scale and the Identification with All Humanity Scale correlate at least moderately with indicators of social desirability and impression management (McFarland et al., 2012; Phelps et al., 2011; Türken & Rudmin, 2013). Supporting these conclusions are qualitative findings such as those from Palasinski et al. (2012), who observed Polish Catholic men living in the United Kingdom adopting a common humanity approach to manage self-impression, not to benefit others. Taken together, there seems to be weakness in typical GCE measures, raising questions about whether they can be useful in practice (Brown & Maydeu-Olivares, 2011, 2012, 2013; Gándara et al., 2021; Kopcha & Sullivan, 2007; Lagattuta et al., 2012; Reysen & Katzarska-Miller, 2018).

Setting aside the possibility that a respondent might not respond with full accuracy, the imprecision of Likert-type items could raise doubts among researchers who might legitimately question whether Participant A's 5 = strongly agree is as strong as Participant B's 5 = strongly agree. Or even whether Participant A's 5 = strongly agree remains consistently strong across measurement occasions, as in a pre-test/post-test design or across items within a single occasion. Extending that skepticism to classrooms, where measurement most likely would occur, imagine you are a Year 9 student attending a school with GCE embedded in its mission. Perhaps your parents urged you to attend this school, though you do not value global citizenship and don't really want to participate in that pedagogy. To avoid embarrassment or negative consequences from classmates, teachers, or your parents, who you perceive to have a GCE-friendly agenda, you might be able to detect the GCE-relevant response to an item you are presented with when given a self-report instrument. Understandably, you might feel compelled to respond in ways that mask your true disposition. Very likely conformity and avoiding perceived punishment are more salient for you than accuracy in measurement. It seems clear that the combination of measuring dispositions indirectly, human need for social approval, and preference for embarrassment avoidance might all lead some respondents to overreport traits deemed desirable or underreport traits that are not desirable (Krumpal, 2013; Kuokkanen & Sun, 2016; Tourangeau & Yan, 2007).

Thus, the ambiguity that self-reports can yield might create space for feeling indoctrinated among students whose values do not necessarily align with what their school, family, or community labels "correct". If researchers continued to opt for the self-report approach, they could also employ scales to detect social desirability bias, which van de Mortel (2008) recommends after finding <1% of 14,000-plus healthcare studies did so, and nearly half of the studies that did had social desirability influencing results. Other scholars call for social desirability to be vetted when using self-report instruments (Miller, 2012; Tourangeau & Yan, 2007), especially if social desirability scales might *under*estimate such bias (Holden, 2008).

Political Barriers

In the past decade, several political barriers have stymied efforts to strengthen global citizenship research. On the political right of most well-resourced nations, nationalist movements, perhaps hardened by COVID-19 pandemic responses, have demonstrated backlashes to globalism (Reysen & Katzarska-Miller, 2018). Many national elections have empowered authoritarian leaders in countries with previous traditions of liberal democracy, alongside the 2016

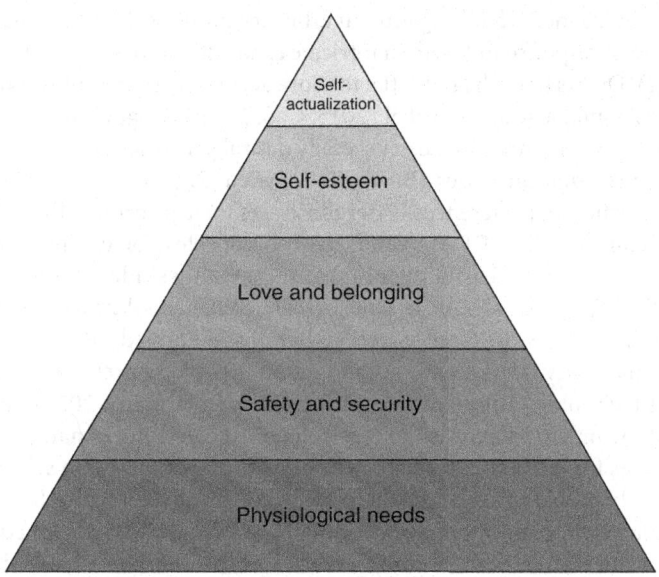

Figure 11.3 An Overview of Maslow's (1954) Hierarchy of Needs.

Brexit vote. And there is reason to think such sentiments have only grown during and since the pandemic (Bieber, 2020; Elias et al., 2021).

Meanwhile, many on the political left view global citizenship not as a need, per the United Nations' Sustainable Development Goals, but rather a privilege for affluent individuals in highly developed societies (Gardner-McTaggart, 2016). A GCE critic could justifiably wonder: if someone cannot sustain their basic physiological needs, do higher-order levels of Maslow's hierarchy (1954) even matter at all (see Figure 11.3)? Furthermore, regardless of one's location on the political spectrum, it seems easy to agree that attempts to measure global citizenship have not enjoyed the political will—and corresponding funding to support—the kinds of efforts that have led to optimizing measurement as with literacy and numeracy (Conley, 2013).

How Can DCMs and SJTs Improve the Situation?

Two alternatives to Likert-type, self-report instruments—DCMs and SJTs—offer promise to address some of these challenges. Next, I will define each of these two measurement approaches and provide some of the limited examples to date, before summarizing their potential benefits and limitations in comparison to self-reports.

Discrete-Choice Measures (DCMs)

DCMs involve two or more hypothetical choices of descriptive dimensions enabling rank-ordered preferences, ultimately yielding weighted statistical estimates that prioritize dimensions (Kennelly et al., 2014). As a construct's number of dimensions can vary, so can a DCM's complexity and corresponding cognitive load (Aubusson et al., 2014; Roberts et al., 2015). Helpfully, DCMs can reduce susceptibility to faked responses and social desirability bias, providing more accurate representations of a respondent than self-reports might (Cao, 2016; Drasgow et al., 2012).

DCMs feature blocks of Likert-type statements, compelling respondents to wrestle in a time-efficient manner with the complexity of what is relatively "most like" or "least like" them rather than responding to items individually against an arbitrary numerical rating scale. By design, self-reports exist for ease of response rather than intricate examination of a construct (Brown & Maydeu-Olivares, 2011). DCMs have the potential to more accurately represent respondents' levels of certain constructs (Anguiano-Carrasco et al., 2015; Cao, 2016; Drasgow et al., 2012). If designing a DCM with blocks of statements that cluster socially desirable responses equally, a researcher can mitigate some self-presentation biases (Brown & Maydeu-Olivares, 2013). Then, respondents' rank-ordering or selection of preferences better illustrates their priorities (Kennelly et al., 2014).

Despite initial concerns that DCMs would be too complex for use in secondary schools, recent studies have shown their feasibility for measuring young students' attitudes (e.g., Anguiano-Carrasco et al., 2015; Li et al., 2024; Thier, 2020). Still, school-based applications remain limited, especially in the U.S. In Greece, researchers have applied DCMs to assess teachers' practices in physical activity (Grammatikopoulos et al., 2019) and preferences regarding methods of integrating technology into pedagogy (Kostaki & Linardakis, 2024), just as Aubusson et al. (2014) had done in Australia. Also in Australia, Burke and Buchanan (2022) used DCMs to examine incentives for attracting teachers to work in rural and remote schools.

However, the only global citizenship-focused DCM—and one of the few attempted with students in secondary schools—appears to be one that Thier (2020) developed with participation of high school students in the U.S. and Sweden. For this initiative, I culled 437 items from 32 extant self-reports that are used to measure GCE-related constructs. I scrutinized those measures' Likert-type items before showing 120 of them to an 18-member panel of global citizenship scholars from 12 nations. Retaining 89 items from that phase, I tested their correlations with a well-known social desirability measure (Crowne & Marlowe, 1960), finding 65 (73%) to correlate significantly with social desirability scores. Then, ranking items by the magnitudes of those correlations with social desirability bias, I arrayed the items into DCM blocks to minimize social desirability's influence on respondent selections, following a process from Anguiano-Carrasco et al. (2015).

In contrast to traditional Likert-type items, my DCM avoided the problem of about 3-in-every-4 items indicating social desirability, which would have undermined understanding of what the measure could indicate about global citizenship. The DCM I developed demonstrated:

- strong internal consistency ($\alpha > .91$) and structural associations (loadings > .50)
- stable factors based on inter-item correlations ($r = .40–.50$; see Clark & Watson, 1995) and that covaried significantly without raising multicollinearity concerns
- adequate model fit for a relatively small study (The COVID-19 pandemic reduced the number of available schools and respondents per participating school).

Ultimately, this DCM made it possible to assess secondary students from GCE-missioned schools in two nations for their students' dispositions toward global citizenship, isolating dispositions from the associated knowledge, skills, or behaviors. With so few DCMs in use in schools, this measure provided proof of concept for other developers to generate DCMs that might help educators re-organize pedagogical activities to target GCE dispositions. Of additional importance, my DCM was nearly 22% quicker to administer (18.44 minutes) than a corresponding Likert-type approach (22.40 minutes), a key finding given schools' hectic schedules.

Situational-Judgment Tests (SJTs)

SJTs involve hypothetical scenarios in authentic contexts to approximate decision-making or problem-solving (Anderson et al., 2017; Lievens & Sackett, 2012). SJTs can leverage multimedia to engage participants and collect data in forms ranging from multiple choice to constructed response to rankings to Likert-style ratings (Roberts et al., 2015). As with DCMs, school-based applications of SJTs remain limited. In fact, many SJTs developed to date have involved military use (e.g., McCloskey et al., 2012), a facet of this approach that might prompt some GCE stakeholders to bristle given GCE's typical incorporation of peace education. One such example, the Virtual Cultural Awareness Trainer (VCAT), is a computer simulation Johnson et al. (2011) developed to train military members to negotiate foreign linguistic and cultural settings. Following digitized role-playing scenarios, VCAT participants demonstrate capacities in intercultural communication, problem-solving, and cultural knowledge. In addition to providing scores that can be used in statistical analyses, the VCAT also provides real-time feedback, allowing formative and summative uses. As Anderson et al. (2017) note:

> When [VCAT] respondents err, simulated coaches, who are culturally and linguistically native to designed settings, target mistakes through body language and/or verbal feedback. These nuances may enhance relevance and both cognitive and emotional engagement of realistic scenarios.
>
> Blending curriculum with assessment, they may create more overt feedback than would be typical in K-12 classrooms.
>
> (p. 54)

Two systematic literature reviews on SJT use in educational contexts indicate the approach's considerable uptick in use overall in the last decade but still wider use in European countries (Nadmilail & Matore, 2021) and its prevalence to date for evaluating applicants' "non-academic abilities", typically in higher education settings (Chao et al., 2019; Webster et al., 2020). Some school-based SJTs include:

- confronting teachers with socio-emotionally challenging student situations and having teachers self-rate their response choices for effectiveness in self-regulating their own emotions or creating positive teacher-student engagement (Aldrup et al., 2020);
- selecting applicants for initial teacher education (Klassen et al., 2020) and student teaching in middle schools (Chao et al., 2019);
- examining socio-emotional competency development among youth in Spain (Rodríguez-Pérez et al., 2021) or empathy, assertiveness, communication, and ethics among university-level pharmacy students (Smith et al., 2022).

Consequently, SJTs remain ripe for exploration. In comparison to self-reports, DCMs and SJTs offer many benefits and, of course, some drawbacks. DCMs and SJTs seem more resistant to several self-presentation biases and more efficient for gathering data. For DCMs, the efficiency exists in real time as they distribute their items' cumulative cognitive load into blocks, prompting respondents to review an equivalent number of items relatively rather than individually (i.e., gathering more data with fewer prompts). For SJTs, the efficiency stems from offering the flexibility of being useful for formative and summative assessment simultaneously.

Challenges remain regarding the complexity and cost of developing DCMs and SJTs. Minimally, DCM development requires researchers to create choice sets, elicit preferences (often via surveys), and identify or follow an approach to quantify respondent preferences. Likewise, SJT development requires researchers to conduct job analysis, design scenarios, seek input from experts, and create or follow a scoring schema. Fakability might be more easily avoided with DCM design, but the issue remains salient for SJTs due to the construct under consideration, response options, and scoring schema (Oostrom et al., 2015). Meanwhile, respondents' experience with DCMs might suffer because of possible additional time, effort, or frustration needed to make relative decisions when compared to Likert-type alternatives (Sass et al., 2020).

And that assumes a designer can resolve issues that might stem from multidimensionality concerns or DCM's potential for poor model fit (Anguiano-Carrasco et al., 2015; 2017; Sass et al., 2020). Meanwhile, SJTs also involve the tradeoff of measurement efficiency with respondent burden when compared to Likert-type items (Anderson et al., 2017).

How Do We Move Forward?

If we accept that (a) education stakeholders have compelling reasons to measure GCE among K-12 students in schools and (b) the mere existence of many measures does not guarantee that any are fit for use outside of universities or multinational corporations, then we recognize that we have work to do. According to Deardorff (2009), "[I]nterculturally competent global citizens generally do not occur naturally. If this phenomenon were naturally occurring, programs would not need to address this" (p. 351). Consequently, adequate measures are crucial for understanding how programs are faring toward that goal. Without such measures, there is justifiable worry regarding groupthink in support of GCE without evidence to justify endorsement of it.

DCMs and SJTs show promise, so encouraging their development is crucial to overcoming the self-report default. Initially, in non-educational settings, and more recently in some schools, DCMs and SJTs' studies have offered proof of concept for reliably capturing information about students' attitudes without self-presentation biases that are common to self-reports. DCMs and SJTs also demonstrate precision and efficiency. Considerable momentum toward this aim existed before the COVID-19 pandemic disrupted the already challenging enterprise of conducting research in schools. With school schedules having returned to some degree of normalcy, the time is right to engage further with these measurement types. Problematically, funding for projects with international dimensions is quite challenging to find for domestic projects, especially in jurisdictions where popular and/or political opinions reject global notions. Therefore, foundations, non-government agencies, or private citizens will need to identify resources to improve understanding of global citizenship as a construct and DCMs and SJTs as approaches for measuring such constructs with dispositional dimensions and cross-cultural implications.

Notes

1 Scholars tend to flag this issue as the jingle-jangle fallacies. The jingle fallacy occurs when one term is defined differently across disciplines. The jangle fallacy occurs when different terms are used to refer to the same construct.
2 Robertson (1994) popularized the term "glocal" to emphasize concurrent focus on local matters and globalization.
3 In one well-known example of GCE implementation, IB expects its authorized schools to emphasize the Learner Profile, IB's framework that invites students to develop as inquirers, knowledgeable, thinkers, communicators, principled, open-minded, caring, risk-takers, balanced, and reflective. As Rizvi et al. (2020) note, Learner Profile implementation can invite contextual variation based on national, local, and other jurisdictional factors.

References

Aldrup, K., Carstensen, B., Köller, M. M., & Klusmann, U. (2020). Measuring teachers' social-emotional competence: Development and validation of a situational judgment test. *Frontiers in Psychology, 11*. https://doi.org/10.3389/fpsyg.2020.00892

Anderson, R., Thier, M., & Pitts, C. (2017). Interpersonal and intrapersonal skill assessment alternatives: Self-reports, situational-judgment tests, and discrete-choice experiments. *Learning and Individual Differences, 53*, 47–60. https://doi.org/10.1016/j.lindif.2016.10.017

Anguiano-Carrasco, C., MacCann, C., Geiger, M., Seybert, J. M., & Roberts, R. D. (2015). Development of a forced-choice measure of typical-performance emotional intelligence. *Journal of Psychoeducational Assessment, 33*(1), 83–97. https://doi.org/10.1177%2F0734282914550387

Anguiano-Carrasco, C., Petway, K. T., Brenneman, M. W., & Kurzum, C. (2017). *Feasibility of forced-choice assessments in middle and high school students*. Paper presented at the annual meeting of the American Educational Research Association.

Aubusson, P., Burke, P., Schuck, S., Kearney, M., & Frischknecht, B. (2014). Teachers choosing rich tasks: The moderating impact of technology on student learning, enjoyment, and preparation. *Educational Researcher*, *43*(5), 219–229. https://doi.org/10.3102/0013189X14537115

Auld, E., & Morris, P. (2019). Science by streetlight and the OECD's measure of global competence: A new yardstick for internationalisation? *Policy Futures in Education*, *17*(6), 677–698. https://doi.org/10.1177/1478210318819246

Bailey, L., Ledger, S., Thier, M., & Pitts, C. M. (2023). Global competence in PISA 2018: deconstruction of the measure. *Globalisation, Societies and Education*, *21*(3), 367–376. https://doi.org/10.1080/14767724.2022.2029693

Banks, J. A. (2008). Diversity, group identity, and citizenship education in a global age. *Educational Researcher*, *37*(3), 129–139. https://journals.sagepub.com/doi/10.3102/0013189x08317501

Bieber, F. (2020). Global nationalism in times of the COVID-19 pandemic. *Nationalities Papers*, *50*(1), 13–25. https://doi.org/10.1017/nps.2020.35

Boffi, M., Rainisio, N., & Inghilleri, P. (2022). The psychological impact of global education approach to SDGs. A study on emotions and sustainability attitudes of European teachers. *Frontiers in Psychology*, *13*. https://doi.org/10.3389/fpsyg.2022.926284

Brandt, W. C. (2024). *Competencies of the future: A review of the literature on intercultural understanding*. Center for Assessment. https://www.nciea.org/wp-content/uploads/2024/10/InterculturalUnderstandingReport-Final.pdf

Braskamp, L. A., Braskamp, D. C., Merrill, K. C., & Engberg, M. (2014). *Global Perspective Inventory (GPI): Its purpose, construction, potential uses, and psychometric characteristics*. http://gpi.central.edu/

Brenneman, M. W., Klafehn, J., Burrus, J., Roberts, R. D., & Kochert, J. (2016). Assessing cross-cultural competence: A working framework and prototype measures for use in military contexts. In J. L. Wildman et al. (Eds.), *Critical issues in cross-cultural management* (pp. 103–131). Springer International. doi: https://link.springer.com/chapter/10.1007/978-3-319-42166-7_8

Brown, A., & Maydeu-Olivares, A. (2011). Item response modeling of forced-choice questionnaires. *Educational and Psychological Measurement*, *71*(3), 460–502. https://doi.org/10.1177/0013164410375112

Brown, A., & Maydeu-Olivares, A. (2012). Fitting a Thurstonian IRT model to forcedchoice data using Mplus. *Behavior Research Methods*, *44*(4), 1135–1147. https://doi.org/10.3758/s13428-012-0217-x

Brown, A., & Maydeu-Olivares, A. (2013). How IRT can solve problems of ipsative data in forced-choice questionnaires. *Psychological Methods*, *18*(1), 36–52. https://doi.org/10.1037/a0030641

Burke, P. F., & Buchanan, J. (2022). What attracts teachers to rural and remote schools? Incentivising teachers' employment choices in New South Wales. *Australian Journal of Education*, *66*(2), 115–139. https://doi.org/10.1177/00049441211066357

Cao, M. (2016). Examining the fakability of forced-choice individual differences measures (Doctoral dissertation, University of Illinois at Urbana-Champaign).

Chao, T. Y., Sung, Y. T., & Huang, J. L. (2019). Construction of the situational judgment tests for teachers. *Asia-Pacific Journal of Teacher Education*, *48*(4), 355–374. https://doi.org/10.1080/1359866X.2019.1633621

Chen, X., & Gabrenya, W. K. Jr (2021). In search of cross-cultural competence: A comprehensive review of five measurement instruments. *International Journal of Intercultural Relations*, *82*, 37–55. https://doi.org/10.1016/j.ijintrel.2021.02.003

Cheon, S.-H. (2017). *Primary school teachers' global citizenship types and perceptions of global citizenship education: Focusing on Seoul, South Korea*. (Master's thesis, Seoul National University).

Choi, J., Kushner, K. E., Mill, J., & Lai, D. W. L. (2012). Understanding the language, the culture, and the experience: Translation in cross-cultural research. *International Journal of Qualitative Methods*, *11*(5), 652–665. https://doi.org/10.1177/160940691201100508

Clark, E. B., & Savage, G. C. (2017). Problematizing 'global citizenship' in an international school. In S. Choo, D. Sawch, A. Villanueva, & R. Vinz (Eds.), *Educating for the 21st century* (pp. 405–424). Springer. https://doi.org/10.1007/978-981-10-1673-8

Clark, L. A., & Watson, D. (1995). Constructing validity: Basic issues in objective scale development. *Psychological Assessment*, *7*(3), 309–319. https://doi.org/10.1037/1040-3590.7.3.309

Conley, D. T. (2013). Rethinking the notion of "noncognitive". *Education Week*, *32*(18), 20–21.

Crowne, D. P., & Marlowe, D. (1960). A new scale of social desirability independent of psychopathology. *Journal of Consulting Psychology*, *24*(4), 349–354. https://doi.org/10.1037/h0047358

Dang, J., King, K. M., & Inzlicht, M. (2020). Why are self-report and behavioral measures weakly correlated? *Trends in Cognitive Sciences*, *24*(4), 267–269. https://doi.org/10.1016/j.tics.2020.01.007

Davies, L. (2006). Global citizenship: abstraction or framework for action? *Educational Review*, *58*(1), 5–25. https://doi.org/10.1080/00131910500352523

Deardorff, D. K. (2006). Identification and assessment of intercultural competence as a student outcome of internationalization. *Journal of Studies in International Education*, *10*(3), 241–266. https://doi.org/10.1177/1028315306287002

Deardorff, D. K. (2009). Understanding the challenges of assessing global citizenship. In R. Lewin (Ed.), *The handbook of practice and research in study abroad: Higher education and the quest for global citizenship* (pp. 346–364). Routledge. https://doi.org/10.1111/j.1467-9647.2010.00680.x

Deardorff, D. K. (2014). *Some thoughts on assessing intercultural competence*. Viewpoints. *National Institute of Learning Outcomes Assessment*. https://www.learningoutcomesassessment.org/wp-content/uploads/2019/08/Viewpoint-Deardorff.pdf

Deardorff, D. K. (2015). Intercultural competence: Mapping the future research agenda. *International Journal of Intercultural Relations, 48*, 3–5. https://doi.org/10.1016/j.ijintrel.2015.03.002

Dill, J. S. (2012). Protestant evangelical schools and global citizenship education. In W. Jeynes & D. Robinson D. (Eds.), *International handbook of Protestant education, Vol 6* (pp. 615–632). Springer. https://doi.org/10.1007/978-94-007-2387-0_34

Donaldson, K. (2017). *The implementation of the International Baccalaureate Diploma Program: Equity, access, and effectively maintained inequality* (Doctoral dissertation, University of Notre Dame).

Drasgow, F., Stark, S., Chernyshenko, O. S., Nye, C. D., Hulin, C., & White, L. A. (2012). Development of the Tailored Adaptive Personality Assessment System (TAPAS) to support Army selection and classification decisions. *U.S. Army Research Institute for the Behavioral and Social Sciences*. https://apps.dtic.mil/dtic/tr/fulltext/u2/a564422.pdf

Duckworth, A. L., & Yeager, D. S. (2015). Measurement matters: Assessing personal qualities other than cognitive ability for educational purposes. *Educational Researcher, 44*(4), 237–251. https://doi.org/10.3102/0013189X15584327

Elias, A., Ben, J., Mansouri, F., & Paradies, Y. (2021). *Race and ethnicity in pandemic times*. Routledge.

Engel, L. C., Rutkowski, D., & Thompson, G. (2019). Toward an international measure of global competence? A critical look at the PISA 2018 framework. *Globalisation, Societies and Education, 17*(2), 117–131. https://doi.org/10.1080/14767724.2019.1642183

Estellés, M., & Fischman, G. E. (2021). Who needs global citizenship education? A review of the literature on teacher education. *Journal of Teacher Education, 72*(2), 223–236. https://doi.org/10.1177/0022487120920254

Gándara, F., Reeves, A., & Schmenner, D. (2021). Global-mindedness in International Baccalaureate schools. *International Baccalaureate*. https://sts-international.org/wp-content/uploads/2024/03/wherewework_IBO_report.pdf

Gardner-McTaggart, A. (2016). International elite, or global citizens? Equity, distinction and power: The International Baccalaureate and the rise of the South. *Globalisation, Societies and Education, 14*(1), 1–29. https://doi.org/10.1080/14767724.2014.959475

Goren, H., & Yemini, M. (2017). Global citizenship education redefined: A systematic review of empirical studies on global citizenship education. *International Journal of Educational Research, 82*, 170–183. https://doi.org/10.1016/j.ijer.2017.02.004

Grammatikopoulos, V., Gregoriadis, A., & Linardakis, M. (2019). Discrete choice modeling in education: An innovative method to assess teaching practices. *Educational Measurement: Issues and Practice, 38*(3), 46–54. https://doi.org/10.1111/emip.12255

Grotlüschen, A. (2018). Global competence—Does the new OECD competence domain ignore the global South? *Studies in the Education of Adults, 50*(2), 185–202. https://doi.org/10.1080/02660830.2018.1523100

Hagel, M. L., Trutzenberg, F., & Eid, M. (2022). Perceived parenting and identification with all humanity: Insights from England and Germany. *Frontiers in Psychology, 13*. https://doi.org/10.3389/fpsyg.2022.924562

Hett, E. J. (1993). *The development of an instrument to measure global-mindedness* (Doctoral dissertation, University of San Diego).

Holden, R. R. (2008). Underestimating the effects of faking on the validity of self-report personality scales. *Personality and Individual Differences, 44*(1), 311–321. https://doi.org/10.1016/j.paid.2007.08.012

Humes, W. (2008). The discourse of global citizenship. In *Global citizenship education* (pp. 41–52). Brill. https://doi.org/10.1163/9789087903756_004

Huws, N., Reddy, P. A., & Talcott, J. B. (2009). The effects of faking on non-cognitive predictors of academic performance in university students. *Learning and Individual Differences, 19*(4), 476–480. https://doi.org/10.1016/j.lindif.2009.04.003

International Baccalaureate. (2024). *Find an IB World School*. https://www.ibo.org/programmes/find-an-ib-school/

Johnson, W. L., Friedland, L., Schrider, P., Valente, A., & Sheridan, S. (2011). The Virtual Cultural Awareness Trainer (VCAT): Joint Knowledge Online's (JKO's) solution to the individual operational culture and language training gap. Proceedings of ITEC. Clarion Events.

Kennelly, B., Flannery, D., Considine, J., Doherty, E., & Hynes, S. (2014). Modeling the preferences of students for alternative assignment designs using discrete choice experiment methodology. *Practical Assessment, Research & Evaluation, 19*(16), 1–14. https://doi.org/10.7275/y9r2-nc06

Klassen, R. M., Kim, L. E., Rushby, J. V., & Bardach, L. (2020). Can we improve how we screen applicants for initial teacher education? *Teaching and Teacher Education, 87*, 1–11. https://doi.org/10.1016/j.tate.2019.102949

Kopcha, T. J., & Sullivan, H. (2007). Self-presentation bias in surveys of teachers' educational technology practices. *Educational Technology Research and Development, 55*(6), 627–646. https://www.jstor.org/stable/30221255

Kostaki, S. M., & Linardakis, M. (2024). Revealing primary teachers' preferences for general characteristics of ICT-based teaching through discrete choice models. *Education and Information Technologies*, 1–22. https://doi.org/10.1007/s10639-024-13182-0

Krumpal, I. (2013). Determinants of social desirability bias in sensitive surveys: A literature review. *Quality & Quantity, 47*(4), 2025–2047. https://doi.org/10.1007/s11135-011-9640-9

Kuokkanen, H., & Sun, W. (2016). Social desirability and cynicism: Bridging the attitude- behavior gap in CSR surveys. *Emotions and Organizational Governance*, *12*, 217–247. https://doi.org/10.1108/S1746-979120160000012008

Lagattuta, K. H., Sayfan, L., & Bamford, C. (2012). Do you know how I feel? Parents underestimate worry and overestimate optimism compared to child self-report. *Journal of Experimental Child Psychology*, *113*(2), 211–232. https://doi.org/10.1016/j.jecp.2012.04.001

Lawthong, N. (2003). A development of the global-mindedness scale in Thai socio-cultural context. *SOUTH EAST ASIA (JIRSEA)*.

Ledger, S., Thier, M., Bailey, L., & Pitts, C. (2019). OECD's approach to measuring global competency: Powerful voices shaping education. *Teachers College Record*, *121*(8), n8.

Li, M., Zhang, B., & Mou, Y. (2024). Though forced, still valid: Examining the psychometric performance of forced-choice measurement of personality in children and adolescents. *Assessment*. https://doi.org/10.1177/10731911241255841

Lievens, F., & Sackett, P. R. (2012). The validity of interpersonal skills assessment via situational judgment tests for predicting academic success and job performance. *The Journal of Applied Psychology*, *97*(2), 460–468. https://doi.org/10.1037/a0025741

Likert, R. (1932). A technique for the measurement of attitudes. *Archives of Psychology*, *22*, 140–194.

Mannion, G., Biesta, G., Priestley, M., & Ross, H. (2011). The global dimension in education and education for global citizenship: Genealogy and critique. *Globalisation, Societies and Education*, *9*(3–4), 443–456. https://doi.org/10.1080/14767724.2011.605327

Marshall, H. (2011). Instrumentalism, ideals and imaginaries: Theorising the contested space of global citizenship education in schools. *Globalisation, Societies and Education*, *9*(3–4), 411–426. https://doi.org/10.1080/14767724.2011.605325

Maslow, A. H. (1954). The instinctoid nature of basic needs. *Journal of Personality*, *22*, 326–347.

McCloskey, M. J., Behymer, K. J., Papautsky, E. L., & Grandjean, A. (2012). *Measuring learning and development in cross-cultural competence*. US Army Research Institute for the Behavioral and Social Sciences. https://apps.dtic.mil/sti/tr/pdf/ADA568555.pdf

McFarland, S., Webb, M., & Brown, D. (2012). All humanity is my ingroup: A measure and studies of identification with all humanity. *Journal of Personality and Social Psychology*, *103*(5), 830–853. https://doi.org/10.1037/a0028724

Miller, A. (2012). Investigating social desirability bias in student self-report surveys. *Educational Research Quarterly*, *36*(1), 30–47.

Morais, D. B., & Ogden, A. C. (2011). Initial development and validation of the global citizenship scale. *Journal of Studies in International Education*, *15*(5), 445–466. https://doi.org/10.1177/1028315310375308

Nadmilail, A. I., & Matore, M. E. E. M. (2021). Trend of using situational judgement test on school teachers: A systematic literature review. *The Journal of Contemporary Issues in Business and Government*, *27*(2), 6117–6141. https://cibgp.com/au/index.php/1323-6903/article/view/1501

Oostrom, J. K., De Soete, B., & Lievens, F. (2015). Situational judgment testing: A review and some new developments. *Employee Recruitment, Selection, and Assessment*, 172–189. https://ink.library.smu.edu.sg/lkcsb_research/5808

Osterlind, S. J. (2009). *Theory, principles, and applications of mental appraisal* (2nd ed.). Allyn & Bacon/Pearson.

Oxley, L., & Morris, P. (2013). Global citizenship: A typology for distinguishing its multiple conceptions. *British Journal of Educational Studies*, *61*(3), 301–325. https://doi.org/10.1080/00071005.2013.798393

Palasinski, M., Abell, J., & Levine, M. (2012). Intersectionality of ethno-cultural identities and construal of distant suffering outgroups. *The Qualitative Report*, *17*(17), 1–17.

Pashby, K., Da Costa, M., Stein, S., & Andreotti, V. (2020). A meta-review of typologies of global citizenship education. *Comparative Education*, *56*(2), 144–164. https://doi.org/10.1080/03050068.2020.1723352

Perna, L. W., May, H., Yee, A., Ransom, T., Rodriguez, A., & Fester, R. (2015). Unequal access to rigorous high school curricula: An exploration of the opportunity to benefit from the International Baccalaureate Diploma Programme (IBDP). *Educational Policy*, *29*(2), 402–425. https://doi.org/10.1177/0895904813492383

Phelps, J. M., Eilertsen, D. E., Türken, S., & Ommundsen, R. (2011). Integrating immigrant minorities: Developing a scale to measure majority members' attitudes toward their own proactive efforts. *Scandinavian Journal of Psychology*, *52*(4), 404–410. https://doi.org/10.1111/j.1467-9450.2011.00876.x

Provasnik, S., Kewal Ramani, A., Coleman, M. M., Gilbertson, L., Herring, W., & Xie, Q. (2007). *Status of education in rural America* (NCES 2007-040). National Center for Education Statistics, Institute of Education Sciences, U.S. Department of Education.

Reysen, S., & Katzarska-Miller, I. (2013). A model of global citizenship: Antecedents and outcomes. *International Journal of Psychology*, *48*(5), 858–870. https://doi.org/10.1080/00207594.2012.701749

Reysen, S., & Katzarska-Miller, I. (2018). *The psychology of global citizenship: A review of theory and research*. Rowman & Littlefield.

Rigling, C., Wood, T., & Thier, M. (2021). Field studies: inspiring critical-thinking global citizens. *Multicultural Education Review*, *13*(3), 260–272. https://doi.org/10.1080/2005615X.2021.1996943

Rizvi, F., Savage, G. C., Quay, J., Acquaro, D., Sallis, R. J., & Sobhani, N. (2020). Transnationalism and the International Baccalaureate learner profile. *Prospects*, *48*(3), 157–174. https://link.springer.com/article/10.1007/s11125-019-09447-z

Roberts, R. D., Martin, J. E., & Olaru, G. (2015). *A Rosetta Stone for noncognitive skills: Understanding, assessing, and enhancing noncognitive skills in primary and secondary education*. Asia Society and ProExam.

Robertson, R. (1994). Globalisation or glocalisation? *Journal of International Communication*, *1*(1), 33–52. https://doi.org/10.1080/13216597.1994.9751780

Robertson, S. L. (2021). Provincializing the OECD-PISA global competences project. *Globalisation, Societies and Education*, *19*(2), 167–182. https://doi.org/10.1080/14767724.2021.1887725

Rodríguez-Pérez, S., Sala-Roca, J., Doval, E., & Urrea-Monclús, A. (2021). Design and validation of a situational judgment test of socioemotional competences development in young people (SCD-Y). *Relieve*, *27*(2). http://doi.org/10.30827/relieve.v27i2.22431

Sälzer, C., & Roczen, N. (2018). Assessing global competence in PISA 2018: Challenges and approaches to capturing a complex construct. *International Journal of Development Education and Global Learning*, *10*(1). https://doi.org/10.18546/IJDEGL.10.1.02

Saperstein, E. (2023). Post-pandemic citizenship: The next phase of global citizenship education. *Prospects*, *53*(3), 203–217. https://doi.org/10.1007/s11125-021-09594-2

Sass, R., Frick, S., Reips, U. D., & Wetzel, E. (2020). Taking the test taker's perspective: Response process and test motivation in multidimensional forced-choice versus rating scale instruments. *Assessment*, *27*(3), 572–584. https://kops.uni-konstanz.de/server/api/core/bitstreams/c1b1be78-cbe0-4652-a8e3-c18c4c0b1137/content

Schattle, H. (2009). Global citizenship in theory and practice. In R. Lewin (Ed.), *The handbook of practice and research in study abroad: Higher education and the quest for global citizenship* (pp. 3–20). Routledge. https://doi.org/10.1111/j.1467-9647.2010.00680.x

Seo, H. (2016). *A study on secondary school teachers' global citizenship type and perceptions of global citizenship education*. (Master's thesis, Seoul National University).

Shultz, L. (2007). Educating for global citizenship: Conflicting agendas and understandings. *Alberta Journal of Educational Research*, *53*(3), 248–258. https://doi.org/10.11575/ajer.v53i3.55291

Singh, M., & Qi, J. (2013). *21st century international mindedness: An exploratory study of its conceptualisation and assessment*. International Baccalaureate Organization. https://www.ibo.org/globalassets/publications/ib-research/singhqiibreport27julyfinalversion.pdf

Smith, K. J., Neely, S., Dennis, V. C., Miller, M. M., & Medina, M. S. (2022). Use of situational judgment tests to teach empathy, assertiveness, communication, and ethics. *American Journal of Pharmaceutical Education*, *86*(6). https://doi.org/10.5688/ajpe8761

Thier, M. (2020). *A Global Set of Dispositions? Applying Discrete-choice Method to Measure Global Citizenship Dispositions of Secondary-school Students in Two Nations* (Doctoral dissertation, University of Oregon).

Thier, M., & Beach, P. T. (2021). Still where, not if, you're poor: International Baccalaureate opportunities to learn international-mindedness and proximity to US cities. *Journal of Advanced Academics*, *32*(2), 178–206. https://doi.org/10.1177/1932202X20974024

Thier, M., Kim, M. H., & Graham, M. C. (2025). *Towards a multidimensional framework for measuring global citizenship: Disentangling dispositions, knowledge, skills and behaviors*.

Thurstone, L. L. (1927). A law of comparative judgment. *Psychological Review*, *79*, 281–299.

Thurstone, L. L. (1931). Rank order as a psychological method. *Journal of Experimental Psychology*, *14*, 187–201.

Tourangeau, R., & Yan, T. (2007). Sensitive questions in surveys. *Psychological Bulletin*, *133*(5), 859–883. *https://doi.org/10.1037/0033-2909.133.5.859*

Türken, S., & Rudmin, F. W. (2013). On psychological effects of globalization: Development of a scale of global identity. *Psychology & Society*, *5*(2), 63–89.

UNESCO. (2021). *Teachers have their say: Motivation, skills and opportunities to teach education for sustainable development and global citizenship*. https://doi.org/10.54675/YXRW9784

van de Mortel, T. F. (2008). Faking it: social desirability response bias in self-report research. *Australian Journal of Advanced Nursing*, *25*(4), 40–48.

Vogt, K. (2006). Can you measure attitudinal factors in intercultural communication? Tracing the development of attitudes in e-mail projects. *ReCALL*, *18*(2), 153–173. https://doi.org/10.1017/S095834400600022X

Webster, E. S., Paton, L. W., Crampton, P. E., & Tiffin, P. A. (2020). Situational judgement test validity for selection: A systematic review and meta-analysis. *Medical Education*, *54*(10), 888–902. https://doi.org/10.1111/medu.14201

Wilkinson, M. N., Thomas, M. A. M., Heyman, C., Bartlett, L., Godbole, P., Hodge, S., Naidu, S., Switzer, T., & Vavrus, F. (2015). Capturing quality, equity & sustainability: An actionable vision with powerful indicators for a broad and bold education agenda post- 2015. *Open Society Foundations*. https://www.opensocietyfoundations.org/sites/default/files/wilkinson-qualityequity-sustainability-20150520.pdf

Zhao, Y. (2016). *Counting what counts: Reframing education outcomes*. Solution Tree.

Section 3
Assessment to Foster Civic Learning Opportunities in the Classroom and Beyond

12
Assessing Digital Literacy as a Civic Skill in K-12 Classrooms

Mark Smith, Joel Breakstone, and Sam Wineburg

Introduction

In a digital age, the ability to discern the credibility of information on the internet is vital for informed civic engagement. The internet has become indispensable for accessing current information on nearly every issue of civic importance, and informed civic engagement requires the ability to identify trustworthy information online. However, depending on the internet for information can be perilous without the ability to sort fact from fiction. Bad actors peddle scams and lies with impunity, and social media feeds are misinformation minefields. If schools are to prepare students for civic life, they must help them develop the skills needed to gauge the credibility of information in this chaotic online environment. Unfortunately, educators have few proven options for assessing student proficiency in this realm. In this chapter, we examine assessment tools developed by researchers in education and psychology for measuring digital literacy skills and discuss how they might be adapted for use in K-12 settings.

Young people in the United States are deeply immersed in online environments. A 2022 Pew Research Center survey found that 97% of teenagers in the United States use the internet daily, and a majority of teens 15–17-years-old report being online "almost constantly" (Vogels et al., 2022). A 2023 Gallup poll revealed that American teenagers spend an average of 4.8 hours per day on social media platforms, more time than they spend on homework (Rothwell, 2023).

Young Americans also rely heavily on the internet to get news and information, particularly social media platforms (Deloitte, 2021; Pew Research Center, 2024). Roughly three-quarters of American teens say they get news from social media (Wronski, 2025). TikTok has seen especially rapid growth as a source of information for American teenagers, with nearly two-thirds of teens aged 13–17 on the platform (Anderson et al., 2023). Polling data suggests the majority of TikTok users in the United States *regularly* use the platform to consume news (Leppert & Matsa, 2024).

A widespread misconception has persisted for decades that young people are more equipped than older generations to handle the information they find on the internet because they are "digital natives" (Prensky, 2001). On the contrary, research suggests that young people struggle to evaluate the credibility of the information that floods their screens (e.g., Barzilai & Zohar,

DOI: 10.4324/9781003476825-15
This chapter has been made available under a CC BY-NC-ND license.

2012; Breakstone et al., 2022; Coiro et al., 2015; McGrew et al., 2018). Breakstone, Smith, Wineburg et al. (2021), for example, surveyed 3446 students who reflected the racial, ethnic, and gender demographic profile of high school students in the United States and found that they struggled to evaluate the credibility of internet sources. Over half of the students in the sample believed that a bogus social media video showing ballot stuffing in Russia was strong evidence of election fraud in the United States, and two-thirds were unable to distinguish news stories from ads on a popular website's home page. A recent survey by YouGov (2023) indicated that Gen Z may actually be less able to spot incorrect information than older generations, leading some scholars to conclude that younger Americans could be especially vulnerable to misinformation (cf., Kelly, 2024; University of Cambridge, 2023).

Evidence also suggests that preparedness to navigate digital information landscapes may be an emerging equity issue. Black and Hispanic teens report spending more time online than white teens, possibly exposing them to more of the perils of toxic online content. A Pew Research Center poll revealed that 54% of African American teens and 55% of Hispanic teens report being online "almost constantly," compared to 38% of their white peers (Anderson et al., 2023). Racial and ethnic minorities may also be especially vulnerable to bad actors who are propagating disinformation. A report on election interference from the U.S. Senate Select Committee on Intelligence (2019) concluded that Russia's infamous troll farm, the Internet Research Agency, "targeted African Americans more than any other group or demographic." Polling research also suggests that Spanish-language social media pages may convey misinformation at especially high rates (cf. Equis Institute, 2022). Lawmakers and Latino advocacy groups have called out social media companies for failing to address the proliferation of misinformation in Spanish and other non-English languages (Paul, 2022).

There is a growing consensus that schools have an important role to play in preparing young people from all backgrounds for participation in civic life by teaching them to navigate the information that flows across their screens. A study by the American Institutes for Research, for example, found that 93% of teachers in the United States thought it was "essential" or "very important" for K-12 public schools to develop students' "ability to assess the credibility of information (e.g., information shared online)" (Hamilton et al., 2024, p. 6). A recent survey also found strong bipartisan support for students learning to evaluate online information, with 88% of Republicans and 94% of Democrats agreeing that schools should include activities for students to "learn to detect false information online" (Saavedra et al., 2025). The U.S. Surgeon General (2023) and the National Academies of Sciences, Engineering, and Medicine (2024) have recently recommended that schools provide students with training in how to navigate digital environments. State governments and departments of education have also increasingly acknowledged the need. Thirty-five states have incorporated aspects of information literacy or media literacy in their learning standards; only 17 had similar guidelines in 2021 (CivxNow, 2023).

Research suggests that school-based digital literacy instruction can be effective. Interventions with middle school, high school, and college students have shown that students can learn to evaluate the credibility of online information more effectively with explicit instruction (Addy, 2020; Breakstone, Smith, Connors, et al., 2021; Brodsky, Brooks, Scimeca, Galati, et al., 2021; Brodsky, Brooks, Scimeca, Todorova, et al., 2021; McGrew & Breakstone, 2023; McGrew et al., 2019). Wineburg et al. (2022), for example, conducted a cluster-randomized, treatment-and-control intervention in an urban school district. Students in the treatment group were taught strategies that professional fact checkers use to evaluate online information in six 1-hour lessons across three months in a district-mandated government course. Compared to students receiving the standard government curriculum, students in the treatment group improved significantly in their ability to judge the credibility of digital content.

Currently, educators have a dearth of assessment options for assessing students' abilities to evaluate the credibility of online information, and to our knowledge, there are no large-scale efforts underway to systematically develop them for use in K-12 settings. If K-12 schools are to implement digital literacy instruction effectively, they will need assessments to efficiently and inexpensively evaluate student learning and track the progress of their efforts over time. Classroom teachers will need assessments aligned to digital literacy instruction, now mandated in 19 states (Media Literacy Now, 2024), that provide evidence of student thinking to monitor progress and adjust instruction to meet students' needs. States and districts will need assessment instruments that allow them to reliably monitor achievement and learning among large groups of students over time. If our educational system is to prepare students for civic life, it will need support from states, education agencies, and the research community to develop assessment tools to measure students' digital literacy skills.

Overview

Researchers in the fields of psychology and education have developed a variety of digital literacy outcome measures in recent years that might serve as useful models for generating new kinds of K-12 assessments that measure students' abilities to evaluate the credibility of online content. In this chapter, we will discuss several approaches that researchers have developed over the past decade for measuring aspects of digital literacy, which we define as the ability to evaluate the credibility of information online.[1] We will outline three broad types of assessments that have featured prominently in peer-reviewed research and provide examples of how each of these approaches has been used to gauge participants' digital literacy abilities. We will then discuss the strengths and limitations of each approach for use in K-12 settings.

Digital Literacy Assessments

Approach 1: Evaluating Headlines

Misinformation researchers in the cognitive and psychological sciences have widely employed digital literacy assessments that ask research participants to evaluate whether news headlines or brief social media posts are true, real, or accurate (e.g., Guess et al., 2020; Lee et al., 2024; Maertens et al., 2021; Moore & Hancock, 2022; Pennycook & Rand, 2019; Pennycook et al., 2020; Roozenbeek & van der Linden, 2019; Swire et al., 2017). In this approach, participants are typically asked to evaluate headlines or posts by judging them as true or false or rating their credibility on a Likert scale. Participants are not typically asked to explain or elaborate on the reasoning behind their decision, leaving only a scale rating as evidence of the strategies or processes they used to evaluate the headline or post. Researchers frequently create an index score by taking an average of all ratings or calculating the difference in true and false ratings (Maertens et al., 2024). Researchers have often used these numerical index scores as indicators of participants' abilities to discern the accuracy of information or their susceptibility to misinformation.

Researchers using this approach often expect participants to take headlines and social media posts at face value; that is, participants in these studies are not encouraged or expected to seek information on the internet to help them assess the information in the headline or to evaluate the trustworthiness of the source of information (e.g., Pennycook & Rand, 2019; Pennycook et al., 2020; Roozenbeek & van der Linden, 2019). However, researchers from the Stanford Social Media Lab have allowed participants access to the internet when evaluating headlines and then asked them if they had done any research before deciding whether the headline was true (e.g., Lee et al., 2024; Moore & Hancock, 2022).

The application of the evaluating headlines approach has varied across studies. The number of headlines or posts researchers have presented to participants has ranged from 6 (e.g., Roozenbeek & van der Linden, 2019) to 30 (e.g., Pennycook & Rand, 2019). The ratio of true to false headlines or posts has also varied. In some studies, participants are shown mostly false headlines (e.g., Roozenbeek et al., 2020), and in others, they are shown a balanced blend of both true and false (e.g., Pennycook & Rand, 2019).

The nature of the stimulus materials presented to participants has also varied, and researchers have disagreed on the best approach for generating stimulus materials for participants to evaluate. Specifically, researchers have debated the relative merits of three approaches: (1) evaluating real headlines, (2) evaluating simulated headlines or posts, and (3) evaluating both real and simulated headlines. Below, we discuss each approach to generating stimulus materials and provide examples of how researchers have employed these approaches.

Evaluating Real Headlines

In the Evaluating Real Headlines approach, participants evaluate a series of news headlines or social media posts about real events that have been published online, some of which report true information and others false. True headlines are typically taken from reputable news outlets, and untrue headlines are generated from stories that have been deemed false by fact-checking sites. Pennycook and Rand (2019), for example, ran a pair of studies with 3446 adult Mechanical Turk respondents that examined how individual propensity to engage in analytical reasoning (as measured by the Cognitive Reflection Test) was related to individual ability to discern the accuracy of news stories with different political alignments (Republican-consistent, Democrat-consistent, or politically neutral). To measure news discernment, researchers presented adult participants with a series of stories they had classified as either "entirely true" or "entirely false." The true headlines were taken from the websites of reputable news outlets (e.g., *The Wall Street Journal*, *The Washington Post*), and the false headlines were selected from stories that had been fact-checked as "false" by the fact-checking outlet Snopes. Stories were formatted as social media posts that included a headline, an image, and a lead sentence. Although the headlines were from real stories, the social media posts were created by researchers and were not live internet sources embedded in a connected social media platform. Participants did not have access to the full news story or the website on which it had originally appeared, and they were not afforded the opportunity to search for information on the internet when evaluating the stories. Participants were asked to judge whether each post was "accurate" on a four-category Likert-type scale ranging from "very accurate" to "not at all accurate." Researchers found a significant relationship between adult participants' ratings of news stories and their Cognitive Reflection Test scores, regardless of whether the stories aligned with participants' political allegiances, which led the researchers to conclude that individual susceptibility to believing misinformation was better explained by "lazy thinking"—an unwillingness to think analytically—than by political allegiance.

Advocates of the Real Headlines approach hold that having participants evaluate real headlines formatted as static social media posts provides a better approximation of online behavior than having them evaluate headlines wholly generated by researchers, thus providing a more accurate picture of participants' abilities to evaluate online information in real-world environments (Maertens et al., 2024; Pennycook et al., 2021).

Evaluating Simulated Headlines

Researchers employing the Evaluating Simulated Headlines approach ask participants to evaluate the veracity of news headlines or social media posts that researchers have generated rather than scraping them from news websites (e.g., Maertens et al., 2021; Roozenbeek & van der Linden, 2019, 2020). Some of the headlines include information that is true. Others include false information or feature common misinformation techniques. Researchers from the Cambridge Social Decision-Making Lab, for example, used the simulated headlines approach in an influential study that tested the effectiveness of Bad News, an online game designed to "confer cognitive resistance against fake news strategies" by asking players to assume the role of an internet content producer who uses six misinformation techniques to create social media posts (Roozenbeek & van der Linden, 2019). To gauge the effectiveness of the game for combating misinformation, researchers asked participants to answer six questions that required them to evaluate six simulated headlines formatted as social media posts at both pretest and posttest. Two were "control" headlines and four were "treatment." Treatment headlines were crafted to simulate real headlines that employed one of the six misinformation techniques in the game. For example, the misinformation technique of *impersonation* was simulated by a post with a handle of "HBÖ" (instead of HBO) that announced the postponement of a season of Game of Thrones. Control headlines were created to mimic real news from reputable outlets and did not feature misinformation techniques. One treatment headline, for example, had "New York Times" as the handle and read, "President Trump wants to build a wall between the United States and Mexico." Participants rated each headline on a seven-point scale (1 = reliable; 7 = unreliable). Researchers found that participants, on average, rated the treatment posts as less reliable at posttest than they did at pretest, but they found no statistically significant differences from pre to post for the control items, which researchers interpreted as evidence that participants' abilities to "spot and resist misinformation" had improved after playing the game (Roozenbeek & van der Linden, 2019, p. 1).

Advocates of this approach believe that researcher-generated stimulus materials can offer advantages over sources generated from real news stories for assessing participants' abilities. Proponents maintain that researcher-generated headlines may be less susceptible to memory effects and identity effects (Maertens et al., 2024).

Blended Approach

In the blended approach, participants are presented with both real and simulated headlines. This approach was developed by Maertens et al. (2024), who maintained that many of the digital literacy outcome measures employed in misinformation research have lacked rigorous evaluation. As they explained, "Scholars have been inventive in the way that they employ individually constructed misinformation tests, often with the best intentions to create a good scale, but typically without formal validation" (Maertens et al., 2024, p. 1864). To address the need for an assessment supported by reliability and validity evidence that could be used as a common measure of "misinformation susceptibility" across studies, Maertens et al. (2024) developed the Misinformation Susceptibility Test (MIST). MIST presents participants with decontextualized news headlines (i.e., with no source attribution or other clues about where the headlines are from) and asks them to make a binary determination about whether each is "real" or "fake." The "real" headlines were selected from news stories that had been published online and that researchers had deemed true and nonpartisan through expert review. To generate "fake" headlines, researchers asked ChatGPT2 to create headlines inspired by extant misinformation belief scales (e.g., the Belief in Conspiracy Theories Inventory, the Generic Conspiracist Beliefs scale). Using piloting data from 8504 adults recruited on survey sites (CloudResearch, Prolific, Respondi), Maertens and colleagues gathered evidence about the factor structure and reliability of three versions of the MIST [8-item, 16-item, and 20-item; cf. Maertens et al. (2024) for details]. An open-source version of the 20-item version of the assessment is available online (Maertens et al., 2024).

The creators of MIST believe it is "a novel approach that combines the best of both worlds" (Maertens et al., 2024, p. 1870). They argue that MIST benefits from the "ecological validity" that comes from presenting students with real items for "true" headlines, while minimizing potential confounds from identity effects and memory effects that could arise from prior exposure to the content by using simulated sources for the untrue headlines.

Discussion: Evaluating Headlines

The evaluating headlines approach may be an attractive option for state and district administrators looking to develop large-scale digital literacy measures. Assessments that ask students to rate headlines or posts can be administered quickly. The 20-item version of the MIST, for example, can be administered in about 2 minutes (Maertens et al., 2024). Assessments that use such items would also be quick and inexpensive to score, requiring only the computation of students' binary or scale ratings. Districts and or states could easily incorporate headline-type items into extant standardized assessments.

However, this approach has potential limitations. One is that the task prompts students to engage in an ineffective evaluation strategy. Although the ability to judge the veracity of a headline or post on its face is preferable to being duped, relying wholly on intuition to judge the accuracy of information can be problematic. On the internet, truthful claims are often indistinguishable from sham without a deeper investigation into the credibility of the sources conveying the information (Caulfield & Wineburg, 2023). Consider a headline featured in a study by Basol et al. (2021) that evaluated the effectiveness of the previously discussed Bad News game: "Worldwide rise of left-wing extremist groups damaging world economy: UN report." Savvy students were expected to label the headline as misinformation because it employed the misinformation technique of "polarization." However, a similar headline actually appeared in the prominent journal *Foreign Policy*: "Far-right extremism is a global problem" (Ashby, 2021). Headlines that seem far-fetched, such as, "Seals with high-tech hats are collecting climate data in the Antarctic," turn out to be true (Wu, 2019). In short, this approach may encourage students to think that they can evaluate online information by a headline alone—which is not always the case.

The evaluating headlines approach is also limited with respect to classroom-based assessment, particularly formative assessment. The assessments that rely on true/false or Likert scales provide little information about the thinking behind students' responses. If classroom teachers are to monitor student growth and tailor instruction to their needs, they will require assessments that yield more information about how and why students came to the conclusions they did.

This approach to digital literacy assessment has proven effective in detecting changes in adult research participants' judgments of news headlines after experimental treatments, but additional research is needed to test its effectiveness for use in K-12 settings. For example, how do these kinds of items function with younger populations who have less background knowledge? It is possible that the kinds of items that have been tested with adult participants would be much more difficult for younger populations that have less exposure to news and less experience judging whether headlines are true.

In studies with adult participants, little work has been done to systematically gather evidence about the psychometric properties of instruments employing the headlines approach. Few researchers employing this approach have reported reliability estimates for these scales or presented evidence that supports a validity argument for the use of these scales to measure participants' digital literacy abilities. A notable exception is a study by Maertens et al. (2024) that gathered extensive evidence about how the MIST functioned as a measure of "news veracity" among adults in the United States and the United Kingdom. The researchers gathered evidence of score reliability, factor structure, and concurrent relationships with other research outcome measures employing the headlines approach. The study is a welcome step in building a corpus of research on the psychometric properties of measures that employ the headlines approach. However, if these forms are to be used as standardized measures in K-12 settings, work is needed to understand how they function as measures of digital literacy.

Approach 2: Evaluating Live Internet Sources

Originally developed by the Stanford History Education Group[2]—which became the Digital Inquiry Group in 2024—the evaluating live sources approach involves asking students to complete short performance tasks that require them to evaluate the credibility of real internet sources while connected to the internet (Breakstone, Smith, Connors, et al., 2021; Breakstone, Smith, Wineburg, et al., 2021; McGrew, 2020; McGrew & Breakstone, 2023; McGrew et al., 2018, 2019; Wineburg et al., 2022). Each task includes one or two live internet sources (websites, social media posts, news articles, advertisements) that address topics of civic importance (e.g., climate change, minimum wage policy). Rather than merely rating a source's credibility using a binary or Likert scale, participants respond to questions that elicit their underlying reasoning about the source. Consider an item developed by the Stanford History Education Group (SHEG) that presented students with an article on minimum wage policy from minimumwage.com, a project of the Employment Policies Institute, an organization that describes itself as a "non-profit research organization." In reality, the site is run by a Washington, DC, public relations firm working on behalf of the restaurant lobby, a fact readily discovered with a quick browser search of the organization. The assessment asked students: "Is this a reliable source of information about the minimum wage? (yes/no) Explain your answer, citing evidence from any webpages you used to decide" (Digital Inquiry Group, n.d.a). The assessment instructed students that they could search online and asked them to explain their reasoning (Breakstone et al., 2022; McGrew et al., 2018).

The Evaluating Live Sources approach is grounded in research on how professional fact checkers at news organizations evaluate information on the internet. Wineburg and McGrew (2019) asked professional fact checkers from prominent news organizations, Stanford University undergraduates, and professional historians to think aloud as they evaluated live internet sources and searched for information on topics of civic importance. Interview protocol analysis revealed that professional fact checkers employed search strategies that efficiently yielded accurate judgments about the credibility of online sources, while the students and academics did not. Principal among these strategies was *lateral reading*, the practice of leaving an online source to seek information about who is behind it.

SHEG developed live-source assessments to gauge students' mastery of the strategies fact checkers use to evaluate online sources. In developing the assessments, SHEG first defined *civic online reasoning* (COR), a measurement construct comprising the fact-checking skills students need to evaluate the credibility of information online. SHEG then engaged in iterative item development in which they piloted and revised assessments with secondary and college students across the United States (cf. McGrew et al., 2018). They also conducted think-aloud interviews with students to examine whether the assessments tapped the intended thinking processes and examined whether students' written responses were good indicators of the thinking processes they used to evaluate sources (McGrew et al., 2018). SHEG eliminated items that did not pass muster in the development process and published items that did on their website (Digital Inquiry Group, n.d.b).

The Digital Inquiry Group has developed both constructed-response and multiple-choice versions of their live-source assessments. Below is a discussion of these two formats and how they have been used by researchers to gauge students' thinking about online sources.

Constructed-Response

Constructed-response COR items ask students to decide if one or more internet sources are credible and briefly explain their reasoning. Student responses are typically evaluated with a three-level rubric, which allows scorers to quickly identify gradations in student thinking (Beginning – 0; Emerging – 1; Mastery – 2). In Mastery responses, students demonstrate clear proficiency in the targeted reasoning processes. Emerging responses are partially correct but incomplete or include both proficient and problematic reasoning. Beginning responses reveal completely incorrect or irrelevant reasoning about the sources in question (Breakstone, Smith, Wineburg et al., 2021; McGrew et al., 2018).

Constructed-response COR items were designed with formative classroom assessment in mind (cf. Stanford History Education Group, 2016). Teachers can give students a task in class and then quickly scan their short responses to get a sense of their thinking, gauge whether they have mastered civic online reasoning skills, and adjust instruction accordingly to meet student needs (Breakstone et al., 2024).

These items have also been used effectively in research studies to measure students' abilities to evaluate information on the internet (e.g., Breakstone, Smith, Connors, et al., 2021; Brodsky, Brooks, Scimeca, Todorova, et al., 2021; Brodsky et al., 2023; McGrew & Byrne, 2020; McGrew et al., 2019). Wineburg et al. (2022), for example, used two parallel assessments comprising seven constructed-response items as pre- and post-measures in a large-scale quasi-experiment that tested the effectiveness of new curricular materials in government classes at all high schools in an urban Midwestern school district. Two independent raters used a three-level rubric to score each task blind to treatment condition for both the pretest and posttest. Interrater reliability was high for both pretest and posttest, with weighted kappa estimates above .90 for each task, and alpha estimates of internal consistency were .58 at pretest and .69 at posttest. Researchers found that students who had received six digital literacy lessons were more likely to show improvement from pretest to posttest than students in the control condition who received their standard curriculum, which suggests that the assessment instrument was sensitive to changes in students' thinking about online sources.

Constructed-response items have also been used effectively to survey student thinking about online sources. Breakstone, Smith, Wineburg, et al. (2021) administered an assessment comprising six constructed-response COR tasks to a sample of 3446 high school students. The survey revealed that students struggled to evaluate the credibility of all the online sources they were asked to evaluate. For example, 96% of students failed to identify that a climate change website claiming to "disseminate factual reports" was actually funded by fossil fuel companies. Estimates of interrater reliability were high, with kappa coefficients between .93 and .97 for each task, and a Cronbach's alpha estimate of internal consistency was .58.

Multiple-Choice

The Digital Inquiry Group has developed multiple-choice versions of COR assessments to have options for assessing student thinking that are more efficient to administer and less labor-intensive to score (Breakstone et al., 2024). The multiple-choice items were developed from extant constructed-response items that had been used extensively in prior research (cf. Breakstone, Smith, Wineburg, et al., 2021; McGrew et al., 2018). The multiple-choice versions of the items include the same question stem and internet sources as the constructed-response item, but rather than generate a written response, participants are asked to identify one correct line of reasoning about the source from a list of four or five choices. The answer choices presented to students in the multiple-choice items reflect the kinds of reasoning—both correct and incorrect—observed most frequently in students' written responses to constructed response versions of the items. Correct answers provide evidence that they can evaluate the credibility of a source. Incorrect responses provide educators with information about the fallacious lines of reasoning that tripped students up (Breakstone et al., 2024).

The multiple-choice items have been effectively incorporated into the outcome measures of research studies. McGrew and Breakstone (2023), for example, tested the effectiveness of a digital literacy curriculum intervention in ninth-grade biology and geography courses at a large suburban high school. Researchers developed two six-item outcome measures with three constructed response COR items and three multiple-choice. Each student was randomly assigned one form at pretest and then took the other form at posttest. ANOVA analysis revealed that students' scores improved significantly from pretest to posttest regardless of the order in which they answered the two forms, which suggests that the measure comprising multiple-choice items was sensitive to changes in students' evaluation of digital sources.

Discussion: Evaluating Live Sources

The live sources approach provides options for educators and policy makers looking for short performance tasks that can be used to gauge whether students can employ fact-checking strategies. The two assessment formats DIG has used in their research—constructed-response and multiple-choice—likely have different applications in K-12 settings. Constructed-response items may be best suited for applications where educators are interested in gathering evidence about how students evaluate sources and have the time to score responses. School districts could use the constructed response items to get a snapshot of how their students—or cross sections of their students—reason about online sources. Classroom teachers could use constructed-response items strategically across a school year to formatively assess student thinking about online content and use the information to tailor instruction to student needs.

Multiple-choice versions of live source assessments may offer schools and states a more efficient and affordable option than constructed-response items for tracking digital literacy among large groups of students. Multiple-choice assessments can be scored accurately and reliably in an instant, and the relative speed of administration per item may support the development of tests that tap a broader array of skills in the same amount of time as a constructed-response test with fewer items (Haladyna, 2004).

Although there are some theoretical advantages to using multiple-choice items instead of constructed response items for large-scale assessments, additional research is needed to gather evidence about the strengths and limitations of these two item formats for drawing conclusions about students' higher-order digital literacy skills. Multiple-choice questions can be used to measure higher-order thinking and complex cognition in some domains (Downing, 2006; Haladyna & Rodriguez, 2013), but constructed-response items may have a broader range for assessing complex skills in others (Martinez, 1999; Rodriguez, 2015). It is possible that constructed-response items are better suited for measuring some aspects of digital literacy.

There are challenges to implementing the live sources approach, particularly for educational institutions looking for assessments that can be used to track student abilities over time. These assessments feature live internet sources, which can change frequently and without notice, presenting challenges for longitudinal tracking of student performance. Even if the stimulus materials are stable, the information that students encounter when reading laterally about a source or topic can change as well, rendering comparisons across time difficult. Unlike math problems that remain evergreen for decades, assessments that feature live internet stimuli on important civic issues can become dated.

More research is needed to explore the psychometric properties of assessments featuring the live sources approach. Some evidence has emerged that suggests live source items tap the intended digital literacy constructs (McGrew et al., 2018), that live source assessments can be sensitive to student learning (McGrew & Breakstone, 2023; Wineburg et al., 2022), and that live source assessments used in school-based research exhibit high estimates of reliability and moderate internal consistency (Breakstone, Smith, Wineburg, et al., 2021; Wineburg et al., 2022). However, the corpus of psychometric research is modest, and any instrument employing this approach to assessing digital literacy would need to undergo examination before being deployed in schools as a standardized measure.

Approach 3: Self-Report Surveys

Researchers investigating aspects of digital literacy have used self-report scales to measure knowledge, feelings, or behaviors related to digital literacy, often as part of a broader suite of outcome variables in intervention studies. Participants have been asked to report the frequency of their own fact-checking behaviors (Brodsky, Brooks, Scimeca, Todorova, et al., 2021), confidence in their own ability to engage in digital literacy strategies (Brodsky, Brooks, Scimeca, Galati, et al., 2021; News Literacy Project, 2024; Reeves et al., 2024), and understanding of digital literacy strategies (Lee et al., 2024) using Likert-type scales. Below are two approaches to self-report surveys that have been utilized in peer-reviewed research in recent years: reporting behaviors and reporting understanding.

Reporting Behaviors

One self-report assessment strategy that researchers have employed is asking participants to report how frequently they engage in digital literacy practices (Brodsky, Brooks, Scimeca, Todorova, et al. 2021) or how likely they are to engage in behaviors related to digital literacy evaluations, like sharing a social media post with others (Roozenbeek & van der Linden, 2020). Brodsky, Brooks, Scimeca, Todorova, et al. (2021) used a four-item self-report assessment of lateral reading as one of their pre- and post-outcome measures in a curriculum intervention ($N = 230$) in a college civics course in Canada. The intervention taught students lateral reading across three class sessions. The self-report measure asked students to report on a Likert scale how frequently (1 = never; 5 = constantly) they used four practices related to lateral reading (e.g., Check the information with another source; Look for the original source of information). An ANOVA analysis revealed no significant interaction between time (pretest to posttest) and condition (treatment vs. control), which suggested that the magnitude of change in self-reported lateral reading behaviors from pretest to posttest for treatment group students was not significantly different from that of control group students. It is unclear the extent to which this null result was attributable to the effectiveness of the intervention (i.e., the intervention did not affect the frequency of student lateral reading) or the instrument's lack of sensitivity to changes in student behavior (i.e., student answers to the questions did not accurately reflect their behaviors).

Reporting Understanding

In this approach, researchers estimate participants' digital literacy skills by asking them to rate how well they understand key digital literacy concepts or strategies. Lee et al. (2024), for example, developed a six-item self-report assessment that asked participants to rate their own comprehension of six digital literacy skills (lateral reading, click restraint, monitoring emotional reactions to headlines, reverse image search, using fact-checking resources, and using search engines) on a five-point scale (1 = no understanding; 5 = full understanding). They administered the assessment at pretest and posttest in two studies that examined the effectiveness of an intervention designed to improve resilience to misinformation in communities of color.

The intervention included 30-minute webinars on five of the six digital literacy skills included in the self-report scales (all but "using search engines" from the list above). In the first study, which was a treatment-only design, researchers found that participants were significantly more likely to report that they understood three of the six skills (lateral reading, reverse image search, and click restraint) at posttest. In the second study, a randomized control trial, researchers found that treatment group participants were significantly more likely than control participants to increase the rate at which they reported understanding all five of the skills covered in intervention materials.

Lee et al. (2024) adapted this approach from the work of Hargittai (2002, 2005), who had developed similar types of self-report questions to participants about their proficiency in technological skills (e.g., "Do you know how to download a file from the World Wide Web to your computer?") and then conducted observational studies to establish that a positive relationship between participants' self-reports and their actual proficiencies in using digital technologies. However, a later study by Hargittai et al. (2010) found a gaping disconnect between what participants reported they would do when evaluating websites and what they actually did during observations of their behavior. Among the college students in this study who said they would investigate the source or the author when judging a website, "none actually followed through" (p. 480).

Discussion: Self-Report Surveys

Self-report scales may have some utility for educators or policymakers interested in gathering quick information about students' confidence in—or beliefs about—their own digital literacy knowledge or skills. Self-report scales can be quick to administer and inexpensive to score, potentially making self-evaluation approaches attractive to districts and states looking for digital literacy assessments to use with large groups of students. Unlike assessments that feature live sources or headlines, self-report scales do not require stimulus materials that might function differently with test takers as civic issues evolve and internet sources change, likely making self-report scales more stable than live source or headline assessments for monitoring student progress over time.

Although self-report scales may have some useful applications, more research is needed to gauge the validity of their use for measuring digital literacy skills. Self-report evaluations have faced legitimate questions about validity since their inception (Allport, 1927; LaPiere, 1934; Paulhus & Vazire, 2007). A great deal of research shows that individuals frequently misreport their behaviors or abilities on self-evaluation assessments, often by overestimating their abilities or desirable behaviors (Brenner & DeLamater, 2016; Donaldson & Grant-Vallone, 2002; Kruger & Dunning, 1999; Maxwell & Lopus, 1994; Paulhus & Vazire, 2007), and little work has been done to examine whether student responses to the kinds of digital literacy self-report scales developed thus far accurately reflect their knowledge or behaviors. Self-report scales can also be vulnerable to reference bias, which arises when participants in different populations have different implicit standards for evaluating behaviors (Lira et al., 2022). Students in an academically competitive school, for example, may rate their own academic abilities as lower, on average, than students in a less competitive school, even though their true abilities are similar.

Future Directions

The three approaches to assessing digital literacy outlined in this chapter provide a starting point for more concerted efforts to develop new assessments that K-12 schools can use to gauge students' digital literacy, but significant work remains to develop the kinds of assessments needed to monitor student abilities and learning. School districts and state agencies will likely require standardized measures that they can readily administer with large numbers of students. The "headline evaluation" and "self-report" approaches discussed in this chapter may provide avenues for developing broader measures that can be administered quickly and scored inexpensively, but such assessments would depend on first collecting evidence indicating that student responses accurately reflect proficiency in digital literacy. To date, very little work has been done to systematically gather evidence about the psychometric properties of the instruments that have been used as outcome measures in research, and there is little extant evidence about whether sound conclusions can be drawn about students' digital literacy from their responses to these kinds of items.

Evidence suggests that items employing the "evaluating live sources" approach can be used to gauge the digital literacy processes students use to evaluate internet sources among secondary students (McGrew et al., 2018), but their use in standardized measures would require further work. Live internet sources change frequently over time, which makes live-internet assessments impractical for standardized tests. One potential avenue going forward is the development of assessments that ask students to reason about sources on a closed intranet with curated sources that approximate the experience of searching for information on the live internet. Although the development of intranet-based assessments would likely be more expensive than other modes of assessment, they could potentially address the limitations of live-internet assessments while retaining their strengths in approximating the kinds of source evaluation behaviors schools hope students will learn through instruction.

Teachers will also likely need ready-to-use classroom assessments that can be used formatively. Evidence suggests that the evaluating live sources approach can be an effective tool for assessing whether students can employ fact-checking strategies when prompted to reason about one or two internet sources (McGrew et al., 2018; Wineburg et al., 2022), but research is needed into how best to embed these kinds of assessments into extant K-12 curriculum.

Research is also needed to explore options for broader performance tasks. Performance assessments that present students with a problem space that is broader than a targeted question about a source or two could give educators more options for determining whether students can coordinate an array of digital literacy skills when reasoning about civic issues. One option would be to develop digital literacy tasks for K-12 students that are similar in structure to the Collegiate Learning Assessment (CLA+), which asks students to consider a variety of sources of information to complete a complex and realistic task (e.g., prepare a memo with recommendations to a company about whether to purchase an aircraft; Arum & Roksa, 2011).

Conclusion

Digital literacy is crucial for informed civic engagement, and evidence suggests that young people do not acquire effective digital literacy skills just by being immersed in digital environments. Instead, they need targeted instruction in how to make sense of the information that floods their screens. A growing body of research, including studies in the United States, Canada, Sweden, Germany, and Italy, indicates that we can move the needle in people's ability to evaluate the credibility of online information with targeted curricular strategies (Caulfield & Wineburg, 2023; McGrew, 2024). If teachers and districts are to implement digital literacy instruction effectively, they will need assessments to track student abilities and growth over time. Unfortunately, no established off-the-shelf options exist for educators to readily deploy. Significant research and development must take place to create assessments appropriate for measuring digital literacy in K-12 settings and to test the validity of the inferences drawn from them. Assessments created by researchers provide models that can serve as a starting point for this work, but creativity is also needed in the generation of new approaches. It is up to myriad stakeholders—including researchers, policy makers, and education testing agencies—to pick up the mantle of developing innovative tools that K-12 educators can use effectively to measure digital literacy.

Notes

1 Note, digital literacy is sometimes defined more broadly (cf. Greene & Crompton, 2025). This chapter does not address assessments that target some of the abilities or constructs sometimes included under the digital literacy umbrella, including proficiency in using digital technology (e.g., smartphone applications, email), technological preparedness for work or school, or using technology safely or responsibly (e.g., avoiding scams, preventing bullying). Digital literacy is also distinct from news or media literacy. Although definitions of news and/or media literacy may incorporate aspects of digital literacy, they also address aspects of traditional journalism, digital citizenship, or media production that are not within the purview of our definition of digital literacy in this chapter.
2 In this chapter, we will use Stanford History Education Group (SHEG) when discussing research that was completed by SHEG. We will use Digital Inquiry Group (DIG) when discussing ongoing work that DIG has continued or work that has been completed by DIG.

References

Addy, J. M. (2020). The art of the real: Fact checking as information literacy instruction. *Reference Services Review*, 48(1), 19–31. https://doi.org/10.1108/RSR-09-2019-0067

Allport, F. H. (1927). Self-evaluation: A problem in personal development. *Mental Hygiene*, 11, 570–583.

Anderson, M. A., Faverio, M., & Gottfried, J. (2023, December 11). *Teens, social media and technology 2023*. Pew Research Center. https://www.pewresearch.org/internet/2023/12/11/teens-social-media-and-technology-2023/

Arum, R., & Roksa, J. (2011). *Academically adrift: Limited learning on college campuses*. University of Chicago Press.

Ashby, H. (2021, January 15). Far-right extremism is a global problem. *Foreign Policy*. https://foreignpolicy.com/2021/01/15/far-right-extremism-global-problem-worldwide-solutions/

Barzilai, S., & Zohar, A. (2012). Epistemic thinking in action: Evaluating and integrating online sources. *Cognition and Instruction*, 30(1), 39–85. https://doi.org/10.1080/07370008.2011.636495

Basol, M., Roozenbeek, J., Berriche, M., Uenal, F., McClanahan, W. P., & van der Linden, S. (2021). Towards psychological herd immunity: Cross-cultural evidence for two prebunking interventions against COVID-19 misinformation. *Big Data & Society*, 8(1), 1–18. https://doi.org/10.1177/20539517211013868

Breakstone, J., McGrew, S., & Smith, M. (2024). Measuring what matters: Investigating what new types of assessments reveal about students' online source evaluations. *Harvard Kennedy School Misinformation Review*. https://doi.org/10.37016/mr-2020-133

Breakstone, J., Smith, M., Connors, P., Ortega, T., Kerr, D., & Wineburg, S. (2021). Lateral reading: College students learn to critically evaluate Internet sources in an online course. *Harvard Kennedy School Misinformation Review*, 2(1), 1–17. https://doi.org/10.37016/mr-2020-56

Breakstone, J., Smith, M., Wineburg, S., Rapaport, A., Carle, J., Garland, M., & Saavedra, A. (2021). Students' civic online reasoning: A national portrait. *Educational Researcher*, 50(8), 505–515. https://doi.org/10.3102/0013189X211017495

Breakstone, J., Smith, M., Ziv, N., & Wineburg, S. (2022). Civic preparation for the digital age: How college students evaluate online sources about social and political issues. *Journal of Higher Education*, 93(7), 963–988. https://doi.org/10.1080/00221546.2022.2082783

Brenner, P. S., & DeLamater, J. (2016). Lies, damned lies, and survey self-reports? Identity as a cause of measurement bias. *Social Psychology Quarterly*, 79(4), 333–354. https://doi.org/10.1177/0190272516628298

Brodsky, J. E., Brooks, P. J., Pavlounis, D., & Johnston, J. L. (2023). Instruction increases Canadian students' preference for and use of lateral reading strategies to fact-check online information. *AERA Open*, 9, 23328584231192106. https://doi.org/10.1177/23328584231192106

Brodsky, J. E., Brooks, P. J., Scimeca, D., Galati, P., Todorova, R., & Caulfield, M. (2021). Associations between online instruction in lateral reading strategies and fact checking COVID-19 news among college students. *AERA Open*, 7(1), 1–17. https://doi.org/10.1177/23328584211038937

Brodsky, J. E., Brooks, P. J., Scimeca, D., Todorova, R., Galati, P., Batson, M., Grosso, R., Matthews, M., Miller, V., & Caulfield, M. (2021). Improving college students' fact-checking strategies through lateral reading instruction in a general education civics course. *Cognitive Research: Principles and Implications*, 6(23), 1–18. https://doi.org/10.1186/s41235-021-00291-4

Caulfield, M., & Wineburg, S. (2023). *Verified: How to think straight, get duped less, and make better decisions about what to believe online*. University of Chicago Press.

CivxNow. (2023, September 28). *2023 civic education state policy scan results*. https://civxnow.org/now-live-2023-civic-education-state-policy-scan-results/

Coiro, J., Coscarelli, C., Maykel, C., & Forzani, E. (2015). Investigating criteria that seventh graders use to evaluate the quality of online information. *Journal of Adolescent and Adult Literacy*, 59(3), 287–297. https://doi.org/10.1002/jaal.448

Deloitte. (2021). *Digital consumer trends 2021: Are younger generations moving away from traditional news sources?* https://www2.deloitte.com/dk/da/pages/technology-media-and-telecommunications/topics/digital-consumer-trends/are-younger-generations-moving-away-from-traditional-news-sources.html

Digital Inquiry Group. (n.d.a). *Civic online reasoning: Article evaluation*. https://cor.inquirygroup.org/curriculum/assessments/article-evaluation

Digital Inquiry Group. (n.d.b). *Civic online reasoning: Curriculum*. https://cor.inquirygroup.org/curriculum/?tab=assessments

Donaldson, S. I., & Grant-Vallone, E. J. (2002). Understanding self-report bias in organizational behavior research. *Journal of Business and Psychology*, 17, 245–260. https://doi.org/10.1023/A:1019637632584

Downing, S. M. (2006). Selected-response item formats in test development. In S. M. Downing & T. M. Haladyna (Eds.), *Handbook of test development* (pp. 287–301). Routledge.

Equis Institute. (2022). *Latinos and a growing crisis of trust*. https://www.weareequis.us/research/disinfo-landscape-latinos

Greene, J. A., & Crompton, H. (2025). Synthesizing definitions of digital literacy for the web 3.0. *TechTrends*, 69(1), 21–37. https://doi.org/10.1007/s11528-024-01015-3

Guess, A. M., Lerner, M., Lyons, B., Montgomery, J. M., Nyhan, B., Reifler, J., & Sircar, N. (2020). A digital media literacy intervention increases discernment between mainstream and false news in the United States and India. *Proceedings of the National Academy of Sciences*, 117(27), 15536–15545. https://doi.org/10.1073/pnas.1920498117

Haladyna, T. M. (2004). *Developing and validating multiple-choice test items*. Routledge.

Haladyna, T. M., & Rodriguez, M. C. (2013). *Developing and validating test items*. Routledge. https://doi.org/10.4324/9780203850381

Hamilton, L. S., Olivera-Aguilar, M., & Rikoon, S. H. (2024). *Cultivating civic learning and engagement in US schools*. American Institutes for Research. https://www.air.org/sites/default/files/2024-04/cultivating-civic-learning-engagement-US-schools.pdf

Hargittai, E. (2002). Beyond logs and surveys: In-depth measures of people's web use skills. *Journal of the American Society for Information Science and Technology*, 53(14), 1239–1244. https://doi-org.stanford.idm.oclc.org/10.1002/asi.10166

Hargittai, E. (2005). Survey measures of web-oriented digital literacy. *Social Science Computer Review*, 23(3), 371–379. https://doi.org/10.1177/0894439305275911

Hargittai, E., Fullerton, L., Menchen-Trevino, E., & Thomas, K. Y. (2010). Trust online: Young adults' evaluation of web content. *International Journal of Communication*, 4, 27.

Kelly, J. (2024, September 6). *Research finds Gen Z, Millennials more vulnerable to fake news*. UVAToday. https://news.virginia.edu/content/research-finds-gen-z-millennials-more-vulnerable-fake-news

Kruger, J., & Dunning, D. (1999). Unskilled and unaware of it: How difficulties in recognizing one's own incompetence lead to inflated self-assessments. *Journal of Personality and Social Psychology*, 77(6), 1121–1134. https://doi.org/10.1037/0022-3514.77.6.1121

LaPiere, R. T. (1934). Attitudes vs. actions. *Social Forces*, 13(2), 230–237. https://doi.org/10.2307/2570339

Lee, A. Y., Moore, R. C., & Hancock, J. T. (2024). Building resilience to misinformation in communities of color: Results from two studies of tailored digital media literacy interventions. *New Media & Society*, 14614448241227841. https://doi-org.stanford.idm.oclc.org/10.1177/14614448241227841

Leppert, R., & Matsa, K. E. (2024, September 17). *More Americans—Especially young adults—Are regularly getting news on TikTok*. Pew Research Center. https://www.pewresearch.org/short-reads/2024/09/17/more-americans-regularly-get-news-on-tiktok-especially-young-adults/

Lira, B., O'Brien, J. M., Peña, P. A., Galla, B. M., D'Mello, S., Yeager, D. S., Defnet, A., Kautz, T., Munkacsy, K., & Duckworth, A. (2022). Large studies reveal how reference bias limits policy applications of self-report measures. *Scientific Reports*, 12, 19189. https://doi.org/10.1038/s41598-022-23373-9

Maertens, R., Götz, F. M., Golino, H. F., Roozenbeek, J., Schneider, C. R., Kyrychenko, Y., Kerr, J., Stieger, S., McClanahan, W. P., Drabot, K., He, J., & van der Linden, S. (2024). The Misinformation Susceptibility Test (MIST): A psychometrically validated measure of news veracity discernment. *Behavior Research Methods*, 56(3), 1863–1899. https://doi.org/10.3758/s13428-023-02124-2

Maertens, R., Roozenbeek, J., Basol, M., & van der Linden, S. (2021). Long-term effectiveness of inoculation against misinformation: Three longitudinal experiments. *Journal of Experimental Psychology: Applied*, 27(1), 1. https://doi.org/10.1037/xap0000315

Martinez, M. E. (1999). Cognition and the question of test item format. *Educational Psychologist, 34*(4), 207–218. https://doi.org/10.4324/9780203850381

Maxwell, N. L., & Lopus, J. S. (1994). The Lake Wobegon effect in student self-reported data. *The American Economic Review, 84*(2), 201–205. http://www.jstor.org/stable/2117829

McGrew, S. (2020). Learning to evaluate: An intervention in civic online reasoning. *Computers & Education, 145*, 1–13. https://doi.org/10.1016/j.compedu.2019.103711

McGrew, S. (2024). Teaching lateral reading: Interventions to help people read like fact checkers. *Current Opinion in Psychology, 55*, 101737. https://doi.org/10.1016/j.copsyc.2023.101737

McGrew, S., & Breakstone, J. (2023). Civic online reasoning across the curriculum: Developing and testing the efficacy of digital literacy lessons. *AERA Open, 9*. https://doi.org/10.1177/23328584231176451

McGrew, S., Breakstone, J., Ortega, T., Smith, M., & Wineburg, S. (2018). Can students evaluate online sources? Learning from assessments of civic online reasoning. *Theory and Research in Social Education, 46*(2), 165–193. https://doi.org/10.1080/00933104.2017.1416320

McGrew, S., & Byrne, V. L. (2020). Who is behind this? Preparing high school students to evaluate online content. *Journal of Research on Technology in Education, 53*(4), 457–475. https://doi.org/10.1080/15391523.2020.1795956

McGrew, S., Smith, M., Breakstone, J., Ortega, T., & Wineburg, S. (2019). Improving students' web savvy: An intervention study. *British Journal of Educational Psychology, 89*(3), 485–500. https://doi.org/10.1111/bjep.12279

Media Literacy Now. (2024). *U.S. media literacy policy report 2023: A state-by-state status of media literacy education laws for K-12 schools*. https://medialiteracynow.org/policyreport/

Moore, R. C., & Hancock, J. T. (2022). A digital media literacy intervention for older adults improves resilience to fake news. *Scientific Reports, 12*(1), 6008. https://doi.org/10.1038/s41598-022-08437-0

National Academies of Sciences, Engineering, and Medicine. (2024). *Social media and adolescent health*. The National Academies Press. https://doi.org/10.17226/27396

News Literacy Project. (2024, October). *News literacy in America: A survey of teen information attitudes, habits and skills (2024)*. https://newslit.org/wp-content/uploads/2024/10/NLP-Teen-Survey-Report-2024.pdf

Paul, K. (2022, October 6). Disinformation in Spanish is prolific on Facebook, Twitter and YouTube despite vows to act. *The Guardian*. https://www.theguardian.com/media/2022/oct/06/disinformation-in-spanish-facebook-twitter-youtube

Paulhus, D. L., & Vazire, S. (2007). The self-report method. In R. C. Fraley, R. W. Robins, & R. F. Krueger (Eds.), *Handbook of research methods in personality psychology* (pp. 224–239). Guilford.

Pennycook, G., Binnendyk, J., Newton, C., & Rand, D. G. (2021). A practical guide to doing behavioral research on fake news and misinformation. *Collabra: Psychology, 7*(1), 25293. https://doi.org/10.1525/collabra.25293

Pennycook, G., McPhetres, J., Zhang, Y., Lu, J. G., & Rand, D. G. (2020). Fighting COVID-19 misinformation on social media: Experimental evidence for a scalable accuracy-nudge intervention. *Psychological Science, 31*(7), 770–780. https://doi.org/10.1177/0956797620939054

Pennycook, G., & Rand, D. G. (2019). Lazy, not biased: Susceptibility to partisan fake news is better explained by lack of reasoning than by motivated reasoning. *Cognition, 188*, 39–50. https://doi.org/10.1016/j.cognition.2018.06.011

Pew Research Center. (2024, September 17). *Social media and news fact sheet*. https://www.pewresearch.org/journalism/fact-sheet/social-media-and-news-fact-sheet/

Prensky, M. (2001). Digital natives, digital immigrants part 2: Do they really think differently? *On the Horizon, 9*(6), 1–6. https://doi.org/10.1108/10748120110424843

Reeves, R. H., Duffin, D. L., & Ziebarth-Bovill, J. (2024). Gauging growth in undergraduate information literacy: A case study in library-faculty collaboration. *The Journal of Academic Librarianship, 50*(6), 102968. https://doi.org/10.1016/j.acalib.2024.102968

Rodriguez, M. C. (2015). Selected-response item development. In S. Lane, M. R. Raymond, & T. M. Haladyna (Eds.), *Handbook of test development* (2nd ed., pp. 259–273). Routledge. https://doi.org/10.4324/9780203102961

Roozenbeek, J., Schneider, C. R., Dryhurst, S., Kerr, J., Freeman, A. L. J., Recchia, G., van der Bles, A. M., & van der Linden, S. (2020). Susceptibility to misinformation about COVID-19 around the world. *Royal Society Open Science, 7*(10), 201199. https://doi.org/10.1098/rsos.201199

Roozenbeek, J., & van der Linden, S. (2019). Fake news game confers psychological resistance against online misinformation. *Palgrave Communications, 5*(1), 1–10. https://doi.org/10.1057/s41599-019-0279-9

Roozenbeek, J., & van der Linden, S. (2020). Breaking Harmony Square: A game that "inoculates" against political misinformation. *Harvard Kennedy School Misinformation Review, 1*(8), 1–26. https://doi.org/10.37016/mr-2020-47

Rothwell, J. (2023, October 13). *Teens spend an average of 4.8 hours on social media per day*. Gallup. https://news.gallup.com/poll/512576/teens-spend-average-hours-social-media-per-day.aspx

Saavedra, A. R., Polikoff, M., Rapaport, A., Silver, D., Scollan-Rowley, J., & Garland, M. W. (2025, February). *Agreement across the aisle: Schools should prepare students for the rights and responsibilities of citizenship*. Center for Economic and Social Research, University of Southern California. https://dornsife.usc.edu/cesr/wp-content/uploads/sites/54/2025/03/UAS_CARE_Agreement_Across_The_Aisle.pdf

Stanford History Education Group. (2016). *Evaluating information: The cornerstone of civic online reasoning.* https://stacks.stanford.edu/file/druid:fv751yt5934/SHEG%20Evaluating%20Information%20Online.pdf

Swire, B., Berinsky, A. J., Lewandowsky, S., & Ecker, U. K. (2017). Processing political misinformation: Comprehending the Trump phenomenon. *Royal Society Open Science, 4*(3), 160802. https://doi.org/10.1098/rsos.160802

U.S. Senate Select Committee on Intelligence. (2019, October 8). *Senate intel committee releases bipartisan report on Russia's use of social media* [Press release]. https://www.intelligence.senate.gov/press/senate-intel-committee-releases-bipartisan-report-russia's-use-social-media

U.S. Surgeon General. (2023). *Social media and youth mental health: The U.S. Surgeon General's advisory.* https://www.hhs.gov/sites/default/files/sg-youth-mental-health-social-media-advisory.pdf

University of Cambridge. (2023). *First misinformation susceptibility test finds 'very online' Gen Z and Millennials are most vulnerable to fake news.* Phys.org. https://phys.org/news/2023-06-misinformation-susceptibility-online-gen-millennials.html#google_vignette

Vogels, E. A., Gelles-Watnick, R., & Massarat, N. (2022, August 10). *Teens, social media, and technology 2022.* Pew Research Center. https://www.pewresearch.org/internet/2022/08/10/teens-social-media-and-technology-2022/

Wineburg, S., Breakstone, J., McGrew, S., Smith, M., & Ortega, T. (2022). Lateral reading on the open internet: A district-wide field study in high school government classes. *Journal of Educational Psychology, 114*(5), 893–909. https://doi.org/10.1037/edu0000740

Wineburg, S., & McGrew, S. (2019). Lateral reading and the nature of expertise: Reading less and learning more when evaluating digital information. *Teachers College Record, 121*(11), 1–40. https://doi.org/10.1177/016146811912101102

Wronski, L. (2025). *Common Sense Media | Survey Monkey poll: Teen media literacy.* Common Sense Media & Survey Monkey. https://www.surveymonkey.com/curiosity/common-sense-media-teen-media-literacy/#

Wu, K. (2019, December 6). Seals with high-tech hats are collecting climate data in the Antarctic. *Smithsonian Magazine.* https://www.smithsonianmag.com/smart-news/seals-high-tech-hats-are-collecting-climate-data-antarctic-180973709/

YouGov. (2023, April 3–9). *Misinformation susceptibility.* https://d3nkl3psvxxpe9.cloudfront.net/documents/Misinformation_Susceptibility_poll_results.pdf

13
Reasoning with Content
Complex Scenarios as Performance Assessments

Jane C. Lo, Sheila W. Valencia, and Walter C. Parker

Introduction

As authoritarian rule gains footing, scholars, politicians, and pundits have been sounding alarms about democracy in peril (e.g., Levitsky & Ziblatt, 2018). At the same time, work on democracy-building around the world suggests that people need both to identify with democracy (Onuch, 2022) and have healthy skepticism rather than blind faith (Norris, 2022). In other words, democracy can only survive if people both believe in the process and are willing to think deeply with the evidence they are given. The dual-sided nature of trust (faith in democracy and skepticism of demagogues) means that to educate *for* democracy, teachers need to not only present their students with content about democracy but also help them to reason better with the information they have before them. In this chapter, we present a low-stakes, summative, performance assessment of deeper learning as a tool to determine how well students do this kind of reasoning with content (RWC). We argue that the Complex Scenario Test (CST) is an assessment of deeper social studies learning that can help teachers better understand how well their students think with evidence about problems of democracy.[1]

The CST was developed as a part of a larger design-based study of project-based learning (PBL) in the high school Advanced Placement (AP) U.S. Government and Politics course (Parker et al., 2013, 2017). At the time of the project, AP curriculum was experiencing a surge in popularity through its "democratization" (Lacey, 2010, p. 34): more and more schools were encouraging *all* students to take at least one AP course, with AP U.S. Government and Politics being one of the most popular. As a result, enrollment in our PBL version of the course included students with a wider range of academic, linguistic, and cultural backgrounds than typically was represented in AP classes. We wanted the newcomers not only to enroll in the course but to succeed in it. We were attentive, therefore, to issues of equitable access, engagement, and learning for all students in the course and on our assessment of deeper learning.

Deeper learning, usually contrasted with superficial or rote learning, is promoted across numerous initiatives. It was a somewhat novel idea with Resnick and Klopfer's publication of *Toward the Thinking Curriculum* in 1989 but then took hold and has become an expectation in educational scholarship, curriculum standards, and assessment of student learning (e.g., Hewlett Foundation's *Deeper Learning Initiative* [2013]; National Research Council's *Education for Life and Work: Developing Transferable Knowledge and Skills in 21st Century Skills* [2012]; OECD [2018]). Although time-on-topic has been the unit of analysis in some research on deeper learning (Schwartz et al., 2008), we concentrate our work on the *kind of understanding* (in this case, RWC) that students achieve and how to assess that understanding.

Following Bransford and Schwartz (2000), we characterize deeper learning as complex and adaptive. To say that an understanding is complex means that it is nuanced and differentiated or shaded and varied. To say that it is adaptive means that it can be applied flexibly, bending as needed to novel problems. In this way, deep understanding facilitates learning now and action in the future when conditions have changed. Hatano and Inagaki (1986) call this "adaptive expertise" (p. 266). We narrow our focus to deeper *civic* learning, the curricular aim of our redesigned *government* course, and the target of our assessment. By deeper civic learning, we mean complex and adaptive knowledge of, and reasoning with, the concepts, structures, and functions of national and local government and politics, as well as the rights and responsibilities of citizens (see Figure 13.1). We believe this kind of deeper civic learning can help students develop the kind of reasoning necessary to support a healthy democracy.

Many high school teachers, like those in our project, depend on classroom-based summative assessments as an indicator of student learning at the end of a course. Our work on the CST, a low-stakes, summative assessment of deeper learning, fell at the intersection of existing research on large-scale performance assessment, typically summative and high stakes (e.g., Niemi et al., 2007), and classroom-based performance assessment, typically formative and low stakes (e.g., Black & Wiliam, 1998; Heritage et al., 2009). Accordingly, we looked to both literatures for insights. Following Miller and Linn (2000) and the *Standards for Educational and Psychological Testing* (American Educational Research Association et al., 2014), we focused on issues of validity (using evidence based on the test content, its internal structure, response processes, and consequences of testing) and scoring (both reliability and practical efficiency). This resulted in a summative CST that sought (1) to assess individual students' learning as contrasted to collaborative projects in which group learning might be assessed; (2) to assess students' long-term learning across quasi-repetitive activity cycles; and (3) to provide evidence of student learning that would inform revisions to the course as it was implemented across seven years and additional sites. Working alongside the teachers, we designed and tested a model for a classroom-based, summative assessment of deeper learning that was tried out, scored, analyzed, and revised over time.

More recently, there have been calls to better embed equity into assessment praxis (e.g., Montenegro & Jankowski, 2020; Shepard et al., 2020). Although equity-minded assessment was not an initial design principle of the CST, we aimed to design both a PBL version of the course and a summative assessment of deeper learning that were meaningful, relevant, and fair to students from diverse academic, cultural, and linguistic backgrounds. We believe the CST, in its existing form, attends to several aspects of equity and fairness but could be redesigned to be more focused on issues of equity. In this chapter, we discuss the existing features and elaborate on adaptations that may enhance its reach. Specifically, toward the end of the chapter, we draw on Evans's (2023) culturally responsive classroom assessment framework to describe how the CST, as a low-stakes classroom assessment, might be adapted to attend to the tenets of culturally responsive education.

Note that the CST was not developed in a style or discourse typical of work on large-scale assessment. To the contrary, it was developed as part of an ongoing collaboration with teachers to improve curriculum and instruction in a particular course with an eye toward deepening student learning. There were successive trials and revisions in various classrooms, schools, and districts across seven years. In all, approximately 1,200 students from 13 primarily high-poverty schools in 4 states participated in the development of the CST.[2] There was not, consequently, a stable sample of students or classrooms over the years. In the sections below, we describe the context of the study that produced the CST, present the assessment, provide validity and reliability evidence, and identify ways that the assessment can be adapted to be a still fairer and equitable tool for deeper civic learning.

Context[3]

The test-development research reported here focuses on assessing student learning in a durable site of civic education in the United States: the high school government course. Nearly all students in the U.S. take it in one form or another (Hansen et al., 2018). We situated our work in the AP version of this course (hereafter APGOV). AP is a platform where rapid test-prep instruction predominates—an approach we call "breadth-speed-test" (Parker et al., 2013). Teachers are understandably committed to curriculum coverage so their students have a fair chance of earning a high score on the AP test and, potentially, earning college credit.[4] Over seven years, we worked with 13 APGOV teachers from 18 schools, both affluent and poverty-impacted, to redesign the APGOV course for deeper learning and develop the CST, a summative assessment of deeper learning. Design-Based Intervention Research (DBIR) afforded us opportunities to study and revise the CST over time while teachers were implementing an engaging, experiential, PBL version of the course.

Design Principles

In an effort to drive deeper learning into this course, in 2008, the research team at the University of Washington built on the work of Bransford and Schwartz (2000) and the National Research Council (2000) to develop a PBL model for APGOV. It had four main design principles, and each sought to engage students in deeper, flexible learning of important concepts:

1) Rigorous projects as the spine of the course, where each project is the unit itself, rather than a culminating activity at the end of a unit. In essence, students do all of their learning through political simulations. The curriculum and pedagogical approaches demand that students "perform" many tasks as part of their projects as they problem-solve, construct responses, and display their understandings of course material.
2) Engagement first, where the projects place students in roles at the beginning of each project, engaging them before they learn about the content or skills they will acquire through the project tasks. The assigned roles in the projects provide students with a "need to know" (Schwartz & Bransford, 1998) how political processes and governmental institutions work together.
3) In order for the projects to be aligned with content standards and practical for teachers in the classroom, the research team included teachers as collaborators. Rather than seeing teachers as adopters or adapters of a ready-made curriculum, we needed teachers to be co-designers of the curriculum to ensure the applicability of the design principles.
4) Quasi-repetitive project cycles drive deeper learning through the course. These learning cycles (Bransford et al., 2006; National Research Council, 2000), or what our collaborating teachers call "looping," give students multiple opportunities to re-engage with questions, skills, and concepts throughout the course. In a course known for having so much information to cover, it seems incredulous to advise teachers to revisit any content. We accomplished this by focusing on essential concepts and then placing multiple examples across units in the course to expand students' understanding of each of them.[5]

Together, the four principles constitute the theoretical framework for this study. Since the depth of learning was a goal, we needed a way to measure it. The APGOV exam administered by the College Board served as a good measure of breadth, but an alternative assessment was needed to measure depth. To that end, the CST was born.

The PBL-APGOV Course

Before presenting the CST, we provide a brief overview of the curriculum and instructional framework of the course for which the CST was designed. We do so because aligning assessment with the concepts and strategies taught in a course is an essential step to examining the validity of any assessment results. Working with teachers of the course, we developed a pedagogical model based on the design principles. Students participate in five-week-long simulations, each highlighting the workings of the U.S. government and politics (e.g., arguing a Supreme Court case, participating in elections) while re-engaging with core concepts and strategies. They try out their fledgling understandings in iterative cycles, building prior knowledge for later encounters, remodeling misconceptions, and addressing new material, resulting in deeper understandings.

While looping through multiple learning cycles addresses the *how* of deeper learning, "deliberative content selection" (Parker & Lo, 2016, p. 206) drives curricular decisions about *which* content and strategies are worth looping. Working from the College Board's APGOV official course description along with released prior exam questions, we deliberated with our collaborating teachers across multiple meetings, striving to distinguish peripheral content from what might be fundamental, generative concepts and reasoning strategies. The Board's content list was itself the result of a deliberative process in a committee of disciplinary scholars convened by the Board who teach the corresponding college course. But that list does not lend itself to in-depth instruction, but rather, as one of our teachers quipped, to test-prep, "duck and cover" instruction. Sorting and sifting this content list, our group identified five disciplinary concepts and five disciplinary reasoning strategies (Figure 13.1). This process stems from Schwab's (1970) seminal work on content selection and involves iterative face-to-face dialogue and decision-making among the stakeholders.

Core Disciplinary Concepts

1. Limited government
2. Separation of powers (federalism, three branches, checks and balances)
3. Constitutionalism (rule of law, precedent)
4. Civil rights and liberties
5. Institutions linking citizens to government (elections, interest groups, political parties, media)

Core Disciplinary Reasoning Strategies

1. Constitutional reasoning (reasoning about policy on the basis of the Constitution)
2. Deliberation (discussion to decide among alternatives; evidentiary warrant)
3. Perspective taking (e.g., trying on diverse political ideologies and social positions)
4. Political autonomy (making uncoerced decisions, consenting to be governed, voting for candidate X)
5. Close, interpretive reading of subject-specific texts

Figure 13.1 PBL-APGOV Core Disciplinary Concepts and Reasoning Strategies.

Next, we looped these concepts and skills throughout the revised course in order to build deeper understanding, facilitate transfer, and encourage coherent instruction. These core concepts and reasoning strategies became the deeper-learning targets of the revised PBL version of the course, hereafter PBL-APGOV, and consequently, of the assessment we aimed to develop. Hence, they are the key to the whole enterprise of teaching, learning, and assessment.

The Assessment

CST Development

We drew on features of principled or construct-driven assessment design as well as evidence-centered design to develop and test our summative measure of deeper learning (Messick, 1994; Mislevy & Haertel, 2006; Pellegrino et al., 2001). This approach begins by (1) identifying the essential subject-matter concepts or content standards to be assessed, as well as the cognitive demands of the learning process. It also (2) specifies the assessment tasks that will elicit the targeted knowledge and thinking, as well as (3) the scoring approaches that will be used to evaluate student performance. This three-pronged approach to assessment design mitigates some of the challenges that have plagued performance assessments, among which are the labor-intensiveness of designing the assessments and the variability across assessment tasks and scoring rubrics. Principled assessment design addresses these concerns by creating a conceptual blueprint that supports the design of prototypes or "shells" (Solano-Flores & Shavelson, 1997, p. 18) that can be applied across course content.

Our assessment shell was specific to deeper civic learning. We reviewed the core disciplinary concepts and reasoning strategies (Figure 13.1) and then constructed assessment tasks that required students to apply them. As with other summative assessments, the CST was designed to capture a representative sample from the universe of course objectives (Shavelson et al., 1993) through the above-mentioned deliberative process. We chose not to include two disciplinary reasoning strategies—deliberation and political autonomy—because they were discussion-based and better assessed during classroom activities rather than in a summative classroom assessment. And to make the CST meaningful and authentic (Messick, 1994; Newmann & Associates, 1996, 1996), we designed the tasks around contemporary issues that are relevant to high school students, both in school and out.

CST Design and Scoring Rubric

In keeping with our definition of deeper learning, the CST requires students to apply content knowledge and disciplinary reasoning strategies learned in the course to novel problems (scenarios) drawn from real-life situations that are similar to, but not the same as, subject matter students have studied in the course. A chief goal is to integrate assessment of core course content and reasoning strategies into each scenario. Here we describe the shell and the scoring rubric.

Test Shell

In the introduction to the CST, students are presented with a contemporary political problem relevant to their lives, such as a GPS tracking device hidden on vehicles that is used to find drug dealers, or a high school locker search (targeting the core concepts of *constitutionalism, civil rights and liberties, limited government*). Then, they are put in the role of an advisor to a client: an interest group with a particular policy agenda on this problem (*perspective taking*). Information about the problem is presented in the form of an actual newspaper or magazine article, abridged (*close interpretive reading*). After reading, students are asked to give knowledgeable and well-reasoned advice (*constitutional reasoning*) to the interest group on how to advance its policy agenda, and the advice they give is to be based on information they are given in the test itself and concepts and reasoning strategies learned across the course. Students mobilize concepts, facts, and disciplinary reasoning relevant to the scenario and to the perspective and aims of their particular client (*interest group, political party, media, branches of government*).

After the teacher reads the overview and directions aloud, students begin the assessment on their own. They begin by reading a short framing paragraph that orients them to the problem and their role as advisor, and then introduces them to the first article containing new information. Then, students answer three short constructed-response questions prompting them to apply content taught in the course (e.g., What is the Constitutional issue involved in this case? Why is it controversial?) and then they write an extended response providing advice to the interest group and reasoning for that advice (i.e. Describe the three most important steps that this group should take to advance its cause, and then explain why each step is important).

Next, students are introduced to a "critical incident," a second abridged article, in which they are given additional, often conflicting, information on the same scenario. In two additional extended response questions, students are asked to consider the new information and to revise their original advice as needed. In this way, the CST elicits two samples of students' adaptive transfer of disciplinary concepts and reasoning. The first is their initial advice to the interest group based on the first source document; the second is their response to additional information provided in the second document.

Rubric Design

A challenge for classroom assessments of deeper learning is designing scoring rubrics and procedures that have evidence of validity and reliability while also offering efficiency. In the case of a classroom assessment administered and scored by teachers (e.g., CST), this can make the difference between assessments that are used and valued by teachers and those that are not.

Over several years of DBIR, we developed and tried out various rubrics with the aim of achieving acceptable levels of scoring reliability and validity. We experimented with five-point scales for each question and rubrics organized by the two dimensions of the course outcomes—deep content knowledge and disciplinary reasoning. However, the scales proved unreliable across raters, and a factor analysis did not support the two factors (i.e., content knowledge and disciplinary reasoning were highly correlated [Pearson's $r = .68$]). Because of this, the final scoring rubrics were designed to measure students' disciplinary RWC.[6] They require scorers to consider content and reasoning simultaneously as they rate each response. Each item had its own dichotomous tree rubric. Adapted from a model developed at Tennessee Technological University for the Critical-Thinking Assessment Test,[7] a dichotomous tree rubric takes scorers through a series of yes/no questions that flow through the rubric via various pathways (Valencia et al., 2023).

Each rubric begins by prompting the grader to choose yes or no on a question about the response they are grading (e.g., Does the response explicitly provide an appropriate Constitutional amendment or clause?), the yes/no choice then branches into other questions (e.g., Does the response refer to a violation of the Constitutional amendment or clause?), until the grader comes to an end of the dichotomous tree. The simplicity of a series of yes/no choices for each response increased the consistency of scoring. Additionally, it provided a way to see multiple pathways of student thinking (the branching), rather than just a cumulative score of student performance. In the case of the PBL-APGOV course, some forms of disciplinary reasoning are better than others (i.e., there are more or less informed ways of arriving at the same conclusion); these are rated as high, mid, and low in disciplinary reasoning. Similarly, content is assigned points based on accuracy, quality, and completeness. This type of rubric allows students to receive credit for different depths of understanding and ways of thinking about a problem.

These different pathways were then translated into categories of disciplinary reasoning (high, mid, low). And to incorporate the contribution of reasoning into students' final scores, the categories were converted to numeric weights using Solver (Microsoft Excel 2016). The weight was multiplied by the content score to get a total RWC score for each item.[8] A strong reasoning path (high) enhances the content score, and a weak path (low) diminishes the content score. Furthermore, a somewhat weaker content score combined with stronger disciplinary reasoning earns more points than the reverse. Figure 13.2 provides example responses that showcase this difference. The highest-scoring response includes the most complete correct content, while providing disciplinary reasoning about the appeals process. The second-highest-scoring response did not name the level of government (incomplete content) but gave strong reasoning about the appeals process. The lowest-scoring response identified the correct level and branch of government (the most basic correct content) but did not include any content or reasoning on the judicial appeals process or why this particular case would merit action at these levels of government.

Validity and Reliability Evidence

In the next section, we describe the challenges and efforts to address validity and reliability issues of implementing the CST in the context of the PBL-APGOV course. Over seven years, using DBIR methodology, we engaged in iterative cycles of collaborative design and implementation to achieve sustainable innovation. As mentioned before, this is atypical of large-scale summative assessment design work; however, the DBIR context is important for two reasons: First, teachers were partners in the ongoing design and implementation of both the curriculum

---

Question: Which level and branch of government would be the best place for the interest group to begin their work? Explain your thinking.

Total Score 7.2 = Content Score: 6; Reasoning Score: H
"The federal judicial branch, because there are already lower court decisions on this issue of the right to privacy. If the interest group believes the lower court decision misinterpreted the constitution, they can appeal to the supreme court for judicial action."

Total Score 3.6 = Content Score: 3; Reasoning Score: H
"The lower courts have made their decision and if the interest group feels like the decision misinterpreted the law, higher courts can overturn the decision."

Total Score 3.2 = Content Score: 4; Reasoning Score: M
"Federal because the right to privacy is stated in the Constitution, and judicial because the issue is a court case."

Figure 13.2 Potential Responses and Scoring.

and assessment. This ensured there was alignment between the PBL-APGOV course and the end-of-course assessment as each morphed and matured. Second, the participating teachers and schools changed over time, which resulted in iterative versions of the CST that were investigated with different cohorts of teachers and students. We organize our validity and reliability work in four sections: (1) reading and writing difficulty, (2) tasks and questions, (3) content and constructs, and (4) scoring rubrics.

Working with Reading and Writing Difficulty

Many assessments of deeper learning include documents that students must read in order to respond to the assessment tasks. This is one way to assess the application or transfer of the content and reasoning strategies learned in a course. Students must use existing knowledge strategies to analyze the new information. The challenge for assessment development, however, is that reading and writing ability can confound assessment of the targeted outcomes and become a source of construct-irrelevant variance (Haladyna & Downing, 2004; Miller & Linn, 2000).

In the context of "AP for all," we gathered information about the reading ability of students enrolled in the PBL-APGOV classes during the second and third years of our work. Existing standardized reading scores revealed a wide range of reading abilities on the PSAT (Pre Scholastic Aptitude Test) reading section (5th–98th percentile), with approximately 40% of students scoring in the lowest quartile. These data suggested that reading difficulty, and perhaps writing difficulty, on the CST would need to be carefully considered to not threaten the validity of students' performance or lead them to feel frustrated or disengaged.

We addressed the reading challenges of the CST in two ways. First, we examined all the text contained in the CST (written directions, framing language, documents, and constructed-response questions) and applied findings from research on text difficulty and complexity (Valencia et al., 2014) to identify potential challenges. These included text length, density of concepts, uncommon figures of speech (e.g., "short end of the stick"), challenging vocabulary unrelated to course content (e.g., "pervasive"), academic language (e.g., write a "memo"), and other factors that might impact readability and, consequently, contribute to construct-irrelevant variability. It is important to note that many of these factors that influence difficulty are not included in automated reading difficulty estimators such as Lexiles® (Stenner et al., 2006) or Text Evaluator (Sheehan et al., 2014) that are often applied to texts included on disciplinary content tests. Qualitative analysis revealed that all of these text-based elements of the CST needed some minor or major revision.

Second, we conducted cognitive think-alouds (Pressley & Afflerbach, 1995) with a stratified sample of students (i.e., students scoring across all quartiles on the PSAT reading section). This was done to assess students' abilities to both read and comprehend the revised CST. We found that students were proficient at decoding; they were able to correctly read texts and test questions with a high degree of accuracy (>95%). However, most of them exhibited difficulty comprehending some aspects of the texts at both the literal and interpretive levels. Taken together, these findings led to further revisions of the CST to reduce the reading load of the test documents and to require teachers to read directions aloud, which likely decreased students' frustration and enhanced their sense of self-efficacy. Over the next two years, the reading demands of the CST were reviewed and adjusted to reduce construct-irrelevant variance and address fairness in the assessment of the targeted learning outcomes.

Working with Tasks and Questions

Moving from the targets of assessment (deeper understanding of and reasoning about the core curricular objectives in Figure 13.1) to specific assessment tasks and questions (the CST format) is particularly difficult when designing assessments of deeper learning. The goal here is to create a test that best elicits students' learning rather than obscuring it.

Qualitative analyses of a subset of student responses over the first four years of CST trials revealed that students' understandings of many course concepts were reasonably complex. However, they did not elaborate on their reasoning and provided only vague explanations and a few details in their written responses. This suggested that the structure and language of the questions and tasks on early versions of the CST might be obscuring more valid information about students' understandings. Heeding Messick's (1994) caution about the need for balance between complex performance tasks and structured exercises, the CST was revised to add more structure, facilitating student performance. For example, the task was divided into two parts (described above under Test Shell) so that students considered each case/document sequentially rather than at once. In addition, several explicit short-answer questions were added that targeted factual information judged essential to the course objectives but often omitted in students' explanations. Additional scaffolding was added as well to support students' written responses. Overall, these revisions were intended to reduce the construct-irrelevant cognitive load associated with responding to the complex scenario tasks. At the same time, they provided more structure so that students could demonstrate the knowledge they had learned.

Two other features of the assessment tasks were designed to make them more accessible to students and responsive to their cultural identities and experiences. First, students were told that their written responses would not be scored for spelling or grammar—they were scored for the content and reasoning of their ideas. A second feature was the flexibility of the shell to adapt the scenarios and supporting articles to students' experiences and interests while staying aligned with the disciplinary concepts and reasoning strategies of the course. In fact, we experimented with these adaptations by piloting two forms of the CST and found no significant difference in students' scores using different scenarios (Valencia et al., 2023).

Working with Content and Constructs

Evidence related to test content is often examined using expert review. Following Miller and Linn (2000), we convened two different panels of expert teachers to judge how well the CST's tasks represented the course content and constructs—its core concepts and disciplinary reasoning strategies—and how well it measured the goal of deeper understanding. Prior to convening these panels, we conducted classroom observations to document implementation of the PBL-APGOV curriculum. Our goal was to ensure that there was alignment between the course (content, pedagogical approach, participation structures) and the summative assessment. One review panel, composed of three teachers who had implemented the PBL-APGOV course and participated in prior CST scoring, provided an "insider" check that the assessment aligned with the curriculum being taught. A second panel was composed of four APGOV teachers who were not familiar with the revised course or the CST but who had been recognized by the College Board as accomplished APGOV teachers. This "outsider" panel provided a check on how the CST measured up to the core content and reasoning strategies defined for the course. Neither group of teachers had participated in the development of the CST.

The panels evaluated the CST on three criteria: disciplinary content, deeper learning, and authenticity. Panelists independently assigned a rating of 1 (strongly disagree) to 5 (strongly agree) on each of the three criteria. The panels concluded, with a high degree of agreement (>4.4, SD = .53–.70), that the CST, overall, (1) covered the core disciplinary concepts and reasoning skills from the course, (2) measured deeper learning, and (3) assessed meaningful content and reasoning applied to authentic, meaningful contexts. This was one indication that we had met our goals for this summative test of deeper learning.

Concurrent evidence for validity based on relationships with other measures was difficult to establish because there were no existing assessments that aligned with the goal of assessing deeper learning of the specific disciplinary concepts and strategies of the PBL-APGOV course. Therefore, following Shavelson et al. (1992), we examined correlations of students' CST scores with their performance on the APGOV test. This made sense because the course content is drawn from and aligned with the College Board's APGOV curriculum and its APGOV test. As with other studies of correlations between performance assessments and non-performance-based standardized measures (National Research Council, 2001), we anticipated a moderate—neither high nor low—correlation between the CST and the APGOV test. This was to be expected because the AP test emphasizes breadth over depth, while the CST is focused on students' deep disciplinary reasoning as well as their content knowledge.

We also examined the correlation between the CST and the ACT (American College Testing) Composite score, an overall measure of achievement in English, science, mathematics, and reading. Here we posited a lower correlation than with the APGOV test, as the CST is a measure of deeper learning in a specific subject area rather than general academic ability. This lower correlation was of special interest to our work and to the validity of the CST because the PBL-APGOV course had been designed to support all students, including those in urban, culturally diverse, poverty-impacted schools who until recently had rarely been admitted to or succeeded in AP courses. We reasoned that students should be able to perform well on the CST because they had learned the content and disciplinary reasoning in the course, not simply because they had general school ability (Miller & Linn, 2000). These hypotheses were borne out: the correlation of the final version of the CST with the College Board APGOV test was moderate (n=241, Pearson's r = .60), and the correlation with ACT was substantially lower (n=225, Pearson's r = .33). These comparisons with other tests provided a helpful check on the validity and fairness of the CST—that it was measuring the course content rather than general school ability.

Working with Scoring the CST

Using the dichotomous tree rubric and weighting the quality of both content and disciplinary reasoning, scores were generated for each question, and reliability was examined. As described and exemplified above, disciplinary reasoning was prioritized. All item scores were summed to create a total RWC CST score for each student.

Teachers scored the CST. After 2–3 hours of training and calibrating scores, they were able to score each test in approximately 10 minutes. Six raters each scored a random sample of the total papers (n=385), with approximately 10% (n=38) of the papers double-scored. Interrater reliability was calculated for scores on individual items to learn more about the efficacy of the rubrics for scoring complex, open-ended items. Results for Cohen's Kappa were generally in the "good—very good range" (70%–93%).[9] Results for exact agreement for individual item scores across the same set of papers were in an acceptable range (82%–97%; Niemi et al., 2007) especially when considering the CST as a low-stakes assessment.

The Potential of the CST to Address Cultural Responsiveness

So far in this chapter, we have presented the CST as it was administered during our project—a low-stakes classroom-based summative measure of learning for individual students in a PBL-APGOV course. We were driven by teachers' requests for a valid and efficient (easy-to-administer and score) end-of-course test that aligned with the course outcomes. We were also driven by our desire to have a common assessment across teachers and classrooms that would promote collegial conversation about teaching for deeper civic learning. Furthermore, we were driven, as mentioned above, by our need to achieve a moderate correlation of scores on the CST with scores on the AP test. Within these constraints, we aimed for an assessment and a test shell that would be responsive to the cultural, experiential, and educational diversity of the students in our study. Although we attended, to some extent, to reading and task difficulty, topical and cultural relevance, and student engagement, we believe that substantially more attention to issues of cultural diversity and equitable assessment is warranted in the next iterations of the CST.

Similarly, we believe that the potential of the CST as a formative classroom assessment needs further exploration (Wiliam, 2010). Formatively, it may allow for more cultural responsiveness by integrating a CST into instruction after each unit (instead of at the end of the course) and by fostering student–teacher and student–student interactions. For example, using scenarios specific to a unit (e.g., Founders Intent, Elections), students might be encouraged to discuss and debate responses, work collaboratively, or offer examples similar to the scenarios from their own experience as they work through the assessment while teachers observe and provide feedback.

In the paragraphs below, we draw on the literature of culturally relevant education (CRE) (Stembridge, 2020), culturally responsive assessment (Evans, 2021, 2023), socioculturally responsive assessment (Bennett, 2023), equitable assessment (Gordon, 1995), and assessment in an equity-focused learning culture (Shepard et al., 2020) to present what we believe are some possibilities for the CST shell (used either formatively or summatively) to be more responsive to the experiences and cultures of students than the one that was administered during the project. We organize our thinking using the six themes of Evans's (2023) Culturally Responsive Classroom Assessment Framework, clustered into three groups, to explore possible adaptations and enhancements to the CST shell.

Student Engagement and Relationships

From their inception, the PBL-APGOV course and the CST aimed to be an authentic performance assessment of deeper understanding. However, assessing competence and problem-solving alone will not necessarily address cultural diversity; instead, it is vital for an authentic assessment to also consider the different contexts of student experiences (Gordon, 1995). In addition, Stembridge (2020) points out that engagement is vital to learning: students' achievement is enhanced when they can make connections between classroom learning and their lived experience. In an effort to capitalize on authentic engagement, the CST utilizes relevant, real-world problems. However, without directly attending to the cultural diversity of students, the prompt may be more relevant to some and less relevant to others. By design, the CST shell provides enough flexibility to be adapted for diversity in students' interests, proclivities, and cultural experiences. For example, the prompt on federalism could ask students to provide their own examples of how the federal, state, and local governments interact (or not) together as part of providing advice to the interest group, which allows students to incorporate their own experiences and understandings as part of the response. To be sure, there are limits to how much any assessment can do to recognize the wide-ranging interests and experiences of students while staying aligned with the tested curriculum, but Bennett's (2023) work suggests that it is possible to have prompts that draw on/from multiple experiences, cultures, and identities.

At the same time, constructing the CST around both core disciplinary *concepts* and *reasoning strategies* provides options for creating more engaging tasks because the response can showcase different ways of student thinking that draw on their own experiences. New versions of the CST might draw on different examples of the key concepts (rather than eliciting just one correct answer). Moreover, if the CST is used formatively, teachers would have opportunities to build on their relationships with students and offer different options for how students demonstrate their understanding (e.g., written, oral, performance). Students could be encouraged to openly discuss the kinds of scenarios that are relevant to them and how they might advise others by leveraging their cultural identities, background knowledge, and disciplinary knowledge. This process would not only help make the CST more responsive to students' diverse backgrounds but could also encourage teachers to think more deeply about what and how they are teaching, since assessments often reflect what is taught and how it is taught (Gordon, 1995).

Additionally, one can imagine a version of the CST where students respond to a scenario collaboratively, as a group, deliberating their different perspectives in the advice-giving task, thus building understandings of cultural differences and relationships among their peers while focused on the course content (Evans, 2021). This would align more with the ways they engage with one another throughout the course, integrating curriculum instruction, and assessment in a more seamless way so that their experience on the assessment aligns with their instructional and curricular experiences (Shepard et al., 2020).

Cultural Identity and Assets

In order for an assessment to engage students, it should recognize and address their cultural identities (Montenegro & Jankowski, 2020). Because culture and cultural identity are complex and multifaceted, this is a particular challenge for an on-demand group-administered assessment. Many large-scale, high-stakes assessments tend to be decontextualized to avoid this complexity; however, Randall (2021) argues that context-less assessments reinforce dominant ways of knowing. In the case of the CST, the implemented version presented above is not decontextualized in the ways that Randall described since it was not a high-stakes assessment; however, the examples and contexts privileged certain ways of understanding the world, because it relied on moot court cases for its scenarios. To design for more cultural diversity, a classroom assessment version of the CST, either formative or summative, could provide different scenarios, beyond just a moot court format, that leverages students' unique cultural identities, especially if results are used along with other ongoing formative assessment opportunities, such as those built into the PBL curriculum.

For example, because the existing CST shell allows for different scenarios, documents, critical incidents, and formats, future topic selections could be more closely aligned with students' cultural identities. A task designed to assess students' understanding of the core concept of *federalism*, for instance, could draw on a range of topics (i.e., the Navajo Nation's water rights, Georgia's Election Law, Abortion Pill), reflecting students' lived experiences or interests. Going further, we can imagine a set of parallel CSTs, used formatively after each curriculum unit, that includes a range of community issues from which students might choose. To create these parallel CSTs, designers would take into account the transferable content/skill that students are expected to learn from the curriculum and select present-day scenarios that would make the information relevant for students.

Imagine students who are completing a U.S. History unit on factory conditions of American laborers in the early 20th century. Since they would likely be learning about laws that were developed to improve working conditions, governmental agencies in charge of overseeing labor, and ways that workers overcame inhumane conditions, formative CSTs that provide different scenarios could give students opportunities to transfer learning from each lesson into relevant scenarios. Parallel CSTs might ask students to take on roles as advisors to the U.S. Department of Labor and provide advice on modern-day working condition complaints (i.e., accusations of meat processing plants hiring child labor to clean their facilities, Amazon warehouse working conditions, or even wage disputes that had arisen in the students' community).

Instead of asking about the constitutionality of the issue as in the existing CST, the items on these formative CSTs would be broader, so students could practice reasoning about them in different scenarios. For example, (1) What is the issue at hand? (2) What makes this a complex scenario (i.e., multiple perspectives on this issue)? (3) Which stakeholders and agencies might need to be involved to investigate and solve the problem? (4) What advice would you give to the U.S. Department of Labor as logical and reasonable next steps in this scenario? With broader items of this sort, the rubric could focus on students' ability to provide accurate information, reasoning based on that information, and an explanation of their reasoning. Rubrics would still assess students' RWC and showcase how they are thinking about the issue. Similarly, the advice-giving task on the CST could be adapted to encourage students to draw on their community, work, and family experiences as they provide advice to the U.S. Department of Labor. One of us has experimented with some success on upper-elementary versions of the CST with this more personal framing on the advice-giving task (Siegel-Stechler, et al., 2025).

Culturally responsive assessments also need to be asset-based (Stembridge, 2020). Rather than only elucidating what students do not know (i.e., what they get wrong on a test), assessments need to allow students to present what they do know (Evans, 2023). Several of the suggestions above capitalize on the assets students bring to the classroom. These include adapting future CST scenarios to students' lives, offering alternative response modes, adjusting "clients" to be more personal and meaningful (e.g., community, family), and adjusting the rubric criteria. The dichotomous tree rubric could also be constructed deliberatively with students, as they are tasked with exploring various reasoning pathways and content evidence. This work would be highly contextualized (not context-neutral) and best suited for formative classroom assessments because the work is iterative and depends on discussions around content, warrants, and arguments. The rubric could also be adapted to account for differences in students' cultural identities by weighing their rationales differently based on earlier class discussions about the course concepts and ways of thinking about evidence. As long as the arguments are grounded in disciplinary knowledge and reasoning, the rubric should produce similar scores even if students have different perspectives and opinions.

Rigor and Vulnerability

While we presented our notion of rigor (complex and adaptive) in the AP context above, much of what we believe about deeper learning and rigor applies outside of the college prep context. Specifically, by focusing on how students respond to a novel scenario and apply reasoning to its particular content, the CST is first and foremost concerned with how students engage in cognitive tasks that require higher-order thinking—regardless of setting (Darling-Hammond & Adamson, 2014). This does not mean that the CST should be contextless; instead, following Stembridge's (2020) lead, we believe rigor (in the form of higher-order thinking) can increase engagement when paired with student experiences. This means that the content taught in the course should better incorporate students' lived experiences so that they can leverage their assets and knowledge on the CST when it prompts them to reason with what they learned through the course.

At the same time, this level of rigor can be challenging. Students may be unprepared, whether because of academic preparation (course-specific or general) or cultural and linguistic incompatibilities. The final version of the CST addressed some of these challenges by minimizing reading difficulties (e.g., abridged reading passages, directions read aloud by the teacher, scoring that prioritizes ideas rather than spelling and grammar) and by adding scaffolds within the task structure to support student performance. In addition, students' sense of vulnerability (embarrassment, shame) was reduced because the CST problem-solving tasks are similar to classroom projects that are central to the PBL curriculum. However, more could be done in terms of the types of scenarios introduced to the students. Furthermore, the final version of the CST did not account for various language translations or contextual information needed to address the cultural diversity of students. But we can imagine future versions of the CST in which documents, artifacts, or readings, thanks to advances in technology, would be indexed with a glossary, translations, or read-aloud functions to facilitate accessibility and engagement with the assessment and yet still retain the rigor of reasoning with the content provided.

Limitations

We have presented the CST as an assessment of deeper civic learning and some ways that it does and can support CRE. Although we had multiple years to work on the CST, the samples of students and teachers shifted over time (as did the versions of the CST); consequently, we were unable to compare findings on the CST over time and cannot generalize to other samples. Similarly, we were unable to investigate students' thinking about their responses with think-alouds on the final version of the CST. Even with these limitations, the CST as a summative classroom assessment provides insights into how one might assess deeper civic learning that takes authenticity into account.

At the same time, as suggested above, we believe that the CST could be adapted both to address cultural responsiveness and for formative assessment. Using a redesigned version of this assessment that is more focused on cultural diversity in a formative way could support more equity and fairness when assessing deeper civic learning. Specifically, CRE requires critical reflection and cultural competence (Aronson & Laughter, 2016), both of which cannot be adequately tackled by a static assessment, no matter how flexible. Nevertheless, designers, implementers, and graders should consider aspects of CRE at every stage of assessment development, both summative and formative. To incorporate a more culturally relevant approach, we believe that the CST structure is robust enough to assess students' reasoning, even if some of the evidence provided comes from personal experience. The point is to negotiate what counts as sound reasoning, which requires a deliberative process. As Montenegro and Jankowski (2020) argue in their call for more embedded equity in assessments, "equity work is not someone else's responsibility" (p. 14). We do not claim that the CST as developed is sufficiently culturally relevant; however, we believe a future version of the CST, as a summative classroom assessment and a flexible formative assessment, could support CRE when it is designed, implemented, and interpreted with students' cultural identities and vulnerabilities in mind.

Conclusion

This chapter has focused on deeper learning of a common high school subject, U.S. Government and Politics, which is the most durable site of civic education in the country. We argue that a deeper understanding of political knowledge is worth measuring, especially in an era where democracy is in decline. Specifically, if we want students to be able to navigate the complexities of our particular brand of democracy, which requires both faith in democracy and a healthy dose of skepticism about what they read, they will need both to know how our system of government works and be able to apply that knowledge in actual political scenarios. We characterize deeper learning as complex and adaptive (nuanced and transferable), and our multi-year DBIR study has resulted in both a course and an assessment that approach this target. The chapter has provided, we hope, sufficient course description—the four design principles and the core concepts and reasoning strategies—so that readers can examine and make sense of the assessment, the CST. The test asks students to apply the course's concepts and reasoning to a novel problem and to give smart advice to an interest group that wants to advance its policy agenda.

Over seven years and multiple school settings, we iteratively designed and revised the CST. Positioned as a summative, end-of-course, classroom-based assessment, the CST is a tool to assess individual students' long-term learning across the course *and* to provide evidence to us and our teacher collaborators that can inform revisions to the course (both curriculum and instruction) across time, schools, and states. Our goal was to design an assessment of deeper learning that could be administered in one class period, reliably and efficiently scored by teachers, and used alongside students' performance in the collaborative projects (political simulations) that were the spine of the course. Through its iterations, the CST stayed true to its complex scenario format, challenging students to think deeply about, and to apply, the concepts and reasoning strategies they had learned.

Our study occurred during the "AP for all" movement, which has not ended. This means that nontraditional, underserved students were (are) entering AP courses at an unprecedented rate. Our goal was to ensure that the newcomers would not only enroll but also feel welcome and then learn, enjoy, and succeed on the breadth-oriented AP test that culminates the course but also succeed on the CST, demonstrating that their understandings of core ideas and skills were, indeed, complex and adaptive. Efforts were made to address the academic and cultural backgrounds and experiences of the diverse students enrolled in the course and to minimize construct-irrelevant variance on the CST. Reading difficulty was controlled, the test tasks were scaffolded, the rubric considered RWC, and the scenarios were constructed to be engaging, relevant, and meaningful to high school students.

Additional efforts can extend the CST's responsiveness to the everyday sociocultural realities of students' lives, most especially if the CST itself and new scenarios are used formatively during instruction. Here is where we can leverage the shell's flexibility along with a curriculum based on core concepts and strategies rather than mere coverage. Going forward, we will add CRE as the fifth design principle for future iterations of both the course and the assessment. This inclusion will require a more intentional deliberative process during every stage of assessment development to ensure that RWC can encompass both disciplinary knowledge and culturally relevant tasks.

Notes

1 This chapter draws extensively on previously published works on the CST (Parker & Lo, 2016; Parker et al., 2013, 2017; Valencia et al., 2023). Here we expand on the CST's potential to incorporate tenets of culturally responsive assessments.
2 Across the schools, the percentage of students eligible for free and reduced-price lunch ranged from 50% to 100%.
3 The original research study is detailed elsewhere (Parker et al., 2013, 2017). In this chapter, we highlight key points about the research study that may be useful for readers to better understand the CST.
4 There are nearly 40 AP courses, and they are offered in many high schools across the United States. Participation in these courses and passing the summative test can influence students' college admissions, and, once admitted, they often may skip the matching introductory courses, hence "advanced placement."
5 See Parker and Lo (2016) for a detailed account of how curricular decisions were made to incorporate looping.
6 See Ercikan and Seixas (2015) for a discerning treatment of the interaction of content and reasoning in assessment.
7 Our thanks to developers Barry Stein and Ada Hynes for their advice.
8 Our thanks to Soa-Jin Sher, who designed this weighted scoring procedure.
9 See http://www.pmean.com/definitions/kappa.htm

References

American Educational Research Association, American Psychological Association, & National Council on Measurement in Education. (2014). *Standards for educational and psychological testing*. Washington, DC: American Educational Research Association. https://www.testingstandards.net/uploads/7/6/6/4/76643089/standards_2014edition.pdf

Aronson, B., & Laughter, J. (2016). The theory and practice of culturally relevant education: A synthesis of research across content areas. *Review of Educational Research, 86*(1), 163–206. https://doi.org/10.3102/0034654315582066

Bennett, R. E. (2023). Toward a theory of socioculturally responsive assessment. *Educational Assessment, 28*(2), 83–104. https://doi.org/10.1080/10627197.2023.2202312

Black, P., & Wiliam, D. (1998). Assessment and classroom learning. *Assessment in Education, 5*(1), 7–74.

Bransford, J., Vye, N. J., Stevens, R., Kuhl, P., Schwartz, D. L., Bell, P., Meltzoff, A., Barron, B., Pea, R., Reeves, B., Roschelle, J., & Sabelli, N. (2006). Learning theories and education: Toward a decade of synergy. In P. A. Alexander & P. H. Winne (Eds.), *Handbook of educational psychology* (2nd ed., pp. 209–244). Erlbaum.

Bransford, J. D., & Schwartz, D. L. (2000). Rethinking transfer: A simple proposal with multiple implications. In A. Iran-Nejad & P. D. Pearson (Eds.), *Review of research in education* (Vol. 24, pp. 61–100). American Educational Research Association.

Darling-Hammond, L., & Adamson, F. (2014). *Beyond the bubble test: How performance assessments support 21st century learning.* John Wiley & Sons.

Ercikan, K., & Seixas, P. (Eds.). (2015). *New direction in assessing historical thinking.* Routledge.

Evans, C. (2021, November 3). *Creating culturally responsive assessment.* Center for Assessment. https://www.nciea.org/blog/culturally-sensitive-relevant-responsive-and-sustaining-assessment/

Evans, C. M. (2023). Applying a culturally responsive pedagogical framework to design and evaluate classroom performance-based assessments in Hawai'i. *Applied Measurement in Education, 36*(3), 269–285. https://doi.org/10.1080/08957347.2023.2214655

Gordon, E. W. (1995). Toward an equitable system of educational assessment. *The Journal of Negro Education, 64*(3), 360–372. https://doi.org/10.2307/2967215

Haladyna, T. M., & Downing, S. M. (2004). Construct-irrelevant variance in high-stakes testing. *Educational Measurement: Issues and Practice, 23*(1), 17–27.

Hansen, M., Levesque, E., Valant, J., & Quintero, D. (2018). *The 2018 Brown Center report on American education.* Brown Center on Education Policy at Brookings.

Hatano, G., & Inagaki, K. (1986). Two courses of expertise. In H. Stevenson, H. Azuma, & K. Hakuta (Eds.), *Child development and education in Japan* (pp. 262–272). Freeman.

Heritage, M., Kim, J., Vendlinski, T., & Herman, J. (2009). From evidence to action: A seamless process in formative assessment? *Educational Measurement: Issues & Practice, 28*(3), 24–31.

Hewlett Foundation. (2013). *Deeper learning defined.* Author. Retrieved September 8, 2018 from http:www.hewlett.orglibrarydeeperlearningdefined

Lacey, T. (2010). Access, rigor, and revenue in the history of the advanced placement program. In P. M. Sadler, G. Sonnert, R. H. Tai, & K. Klopfenstein (Eds.), *AP: A critical examination of the Advanced Placement program* (pp. 17–48). Harvard Education Press.

Levitsky, S., & Ziblatt, D. (2018). *How democracies die.* Crown.

Messick, S. (1994). The interplay of evidence and consequences in the validation of performance assessments. *Educational Researcher, 23*(2), 13–23. https://doi.org/10.3102/0013189X023002013

Miller, M. D., & Linn, R. L. (2000). Validation of performance-based assessments. *Applied Psychological Measurement, 24*(4), 367–378.

Mislevy, R. J., & Haertel, G. D. (2006). Implications of evidence-centered design for educational testing. *Educational Measurement, Issues and Practice, 25*(4), 6–20. https://doi.org/10.1111/j.1745-3992.2006.00075.x

Montenegro, E., & Jankowski, N. A. (2020, January). *A new decade for assessment: Embedding equity into assessment praxis* (Occasional Paper No. 42). University of Illinois and Indiana University, National Institute for Learning Outcomes Assessment (NILOA.

National Research Council. (2000). *How people learn: Brain, mind, experience, and school.* National Academies Press.

National Research Council. (2001). *Knowing what students know: The science and design of educational assessment.* National Academies Press.

National Research Council. (2012). *Education for life and work: Developing transferable knowledge and skills in the 21st century.* National Academies Press.

Newmann, F., & Associates. (1996). *Authentic achievement: Restructuring schools for intellectual quality.* Jossey-Bass.

Niemi, D., Baker, E. L., & Sylvester, R. M. (2007). Scaling up, scaling down: Seven years of performance assessment development in the nation's second largest school district. *Educational Assessment, 12*(3 & 4), 195–214.

Norris, P. (2022). *In praise of skepticism: Trust but verify.* Oxford University Press.

OECD. (2018). *The future of education and skills: Education 2030.* OECD.

Onuch, O. (2022). Why Ukrainians are rallying around democracy. *Journal of Democracy, 33*(4), 37–46.

Parker, W. C., Lo, J., Yeo, A. J., Valencia, S., Nguyen, D., Abbott, R. D., Bransford, J. D., & Vye, N. J. (2013). Beyond breadth-speed-test: Toward deeper knowing and engagement in an advanced placement course. *American Educational Research Journal, 50*(6), 1424–1459.

Parker, W. C., & Lo, J. C. (2016). Content selection in advanced courses. *Curriculum Inquiry, 46*(2), 196–219. https://doi.org/10.1080/03626784.2016.1144466

Parker, W. C., Valencia, S. W., & Lo, J. C. (2017). Teaching for deeper political learning: A design experiment. *Journal of Curriculum Studies, 50*(2), 252–277.

Pellegrino, J., Chudowsky, N., & Glaser, R. (2001). *Knowing what students know: the science and design of educational assessment.* National Research Council of the National Academy of Sciences.

Pressley, M., & Afflerbach, P. (1995). *Verbal protocols of reading: The nature of constructively responsive reading*. Lawrence Erlbaum Associates.

Randall, J. (2021). "Color-neutral" is not a thing: Redefining construct definition and representation through a justice-oriented critical antiracist lens. *Educational Measurement: Issues & Practice, 40*(4), 82–90. https://doi-org.offcampus.lib.washington.edu/10.1111/emip.12429

Resnick, L. B., & Klopfer, L. E. (1989). *Toward the thinking curriculum: Current cognitive research*. Association for Supervision and Curriculum Development.

Schwab, J. J. (1970). *The practical: A language for curriculum*. National Education Association.

Schwartz, D. L., & Bransford, J. D. (1998). A time for telling. *Cognition and Instruction, 16*(4), 475522.

Schwartz, M. S., Sadler, P. M., Sonnert, G., & Tai, R. H. (2008). Depth versus breadth: How content coverage in high school science courses relates to later success in college science coursework. *Science Education, 93*(5), 798–826. https://doi.org/10.1002/sce.20328

Shavelson, R. J., Baxter, G. P., & Pine, J. (1992). Performance assessments: Political rhetoric and measurement reality. *Educational Researcher, 21*(4), 22–27.

Shavelson, R. J., Baxter, G. P., & Gao, X. (1993). Sample variability of performance assessments. *Journal of Educational Measurement, 30*, 215–232.

Sheehan, K. M., Kostin, I., Napolitano, D., & Flor, M. (2014). The TextEvaluator tool: Helping teachers and test developers select texts for use in instruction and assessment. *The Elementary School Journal, 115*(2), 184–209. https://doi.org/10.1086/678294

Shepard, L. A., Diaz-Bilello, E., Penuel, W. R., & Marion, S. F. (2020). *Classroom assessment principles to support teaching and learning*. Center for Assessment, Design, Research and Evaluation, University of Colorado Boulder.

Siegel-Stechler, K., Lo, J. C., & Burham, S. (2025). *Complex scenarios for elementary grades: Performance-based assessment of social studies thinking and skills* [Manuscript in preparation]. Center for Information and Research on Civic Learning and Engagement: Tufts University.

Solano-Flores, G., & Shavelson, R. J. (1997). Development of performance assessments in science: Conceptual, practical, and logistical issues. *Educational Measurement: Issues and Practice, 16*(3), 13–22.

Stembridge, A. (2020). *Culturally responsive education in the classroom: An equity framework for pedagogy*. Routledge.

Stenner, A. J., Burdick, H., Sanford, E., & Burdick, D. (2006). How accurate are Lexile text measures? *Journal of Applied Measurement, 7*(3), 307–322.

Valencia, S., Parker, W., & Lo, J. (2023). Assessing deeper learning of high school civics. *JSSE – Journal of Social Science Education, 22*(4), Article 4. https://doi.org/10.11576/jsse-5918

Valencia, S. W., Wixson, K. K., & Pearson, P. D. (2014). Putting text complexity in context: Refocusing on comprehension of complex text. *Elementary School Journal, 115*(2), 270–289.

Wiliam, D. (2010). An integrative summary of the research literature and implications for a new theory of formative assessment. In H.L. Andre & G.J. Cizek (Eds.), *Handbook of formative assessment* (pp.18–40). New York: Routledge.

14
Developing Civic Competencies through Scenario-Based Learning and Assessment Tasks

Alli Brettschneider, Greg Vafis, and Caroline Wylie

Strong democracies require educated citizens. To participate effectively in their own democracy, citizens must know how government works, must have the skills to make informed decisions about policies and political candidates, and must be disposed to engage in civic activities—listening to candidates' speeches and debates, analyzing referenda, discussing issues thoughtfully with fellow citizens, voting, and maybe even running for office themselves. Historically, K-12 schools in the United States have been tasked with developing students' civic competencies (Dewey, 1900; Jamieson, 2013), but recent evidence suggests that many schools have fallen short on this goal.

Signs of a civic crisis in the United States abound. A 2018 RAND Corporation study describes the disturbing current phenomenon of "truth decay" in American public life, which it defines as "increasing disagreement about facts and analytical interpretations of facts and data; a blurring of the line between opinion and fact; the increasing relative volume, and resulting influence, of opinion and personal experience over fact; and declining trust in formerly respected sources of factual information" (Kavanagh & Rich, 2018, pp. x–xi). Researchers at Tufts University's Center for Information & Research on Civic Learning and Engagement (CIRCLE) have raised an alarm about a related phenomenon: "civic deserts," or areas where people have a dearth of opportunities for civic engagement, such as those offered in the past by religious congregations, unions, local political parties, local daily newspapers, and other civic institutions (Atwell et al., 2017). CIRCLE's studies have concluded that 60% of rural young people and 30% of people in urban and suburban communities see themselves as living in civic deserts, a status that contributes to alienation from government agencies and community organizations and even distrust of their neighbors (Kawashima-Ginsberg & Sullivan, 2017). Together, these trends point to a politically polarized population that seems ill-equipped and unmotivated to replace incendiary rhetoric with deliberation on important policy questions. While American K-12 civic education does not bear the full responsibility for this crisis, it does have the potential to contribute to a solution.

In 2011, the Campaign for the Civic Mission of Schools (Gould et al., 2011), in partnership with other civic education organizations, engaged in an extensive literature review to identify six educational "proven practices" that each had empirical support for having a positive impact on some

DOI: 10.4324/9781003476825-17
This chapter has been made available under a CC BY-NC-ND license.

aspect of students' civic knowledge, skills, and dispositions. The Campaign's report calls for a more systematic approach to civic education that would combine these practices in deliberate ways:

1) instruction in government, history, law, and democracy
2) discussion of current local, national, and international events, especially those students view as relevant to their lives
3) service-learning programs
4) extracurricular involvement in students' schools or communities
5) participation in school governance
6) simulations of democratic processes and procedures

In 2017, researchers at CIRCLE (Levine & Kawashima-Ginsberg, 2017) followed up on the Campaign's (2011) report, adding four additional "promising" practices:

7) news media literacy education
8) action civics
9) social and emotional learning
10) school climate reform

Hansen and colleagues at the Brown Center on Education Policy at the Brookings Institution then studied the prevalence of these ten practices in K-12 schools, based on state social studies standards, curriculum frameworks, and high school course requirements (Hansen et al., 2018). They demonstrated that, as of 2018, three of these practices—#1, #2, and #7—were widely represented–on paper, at least. Forty-two states and Washington, DC, required students to complete at least one civics course before graduation. In their social studies standards or curriculum frameworks, all 50 states and Washington, DC, called for discussion of current events, and 39 states and Washington, DC, included news media literacy. A fourth practice (#6) was somewhat well represented, with 26 states and Washington, DC, incorporating simulations of democratic processes and procedures into their standards or curriculum frameworks. To provide some evidence of students' actual experience of these practices in the classroom, the Brown Center report includes a separate analysis of 2010 NAEP survey data from 12th-grade students; it suggests that roughly 45% of students participated at least a few times a year in "role playing, mock trials, or dramas" related to civics (practice #6) and 92% engaged in discussions of current events (practice #2) at least a few times a year, with 63% reporting weekly current events discussions.

The Brown Center report indicates that most US students are being exposed to civics content—including discussions of current events and media literacy—at some point in their K-12 years, and that roughly half of students participate in some kind of civics-related simulation, such as a trial or a congressional hearing. However, simply incorporating these practices into standards and curricula does not guarantee their effective use. The most recent NAEP civics assessment, from 2022, identifies just 22% of eighth-grade students as proficient, 3% fewer than in the previous assessment in 2018 (U.S. Department of Education, 2022). The most recent 12th-grade results, from 2010, are similarly concerning: only 24% scored at or above proficiency level (U.S. Department of Education, 2010). This pattern of poor NAEP performance cannot be explained as a simple mismatch between this assessment and states' learning goals for civics. The content included in the NAEP civics assessments seems well aligned with the four most commonly used practices identified in the Brown report. For instance, based on the NAEP's achievement level details, eighth-grade students who are classified as proficient can "analyze the responsibilities and purposes of government," content that would be expected in any civics course (#1); "examine ways in which the United States influences other countries," content that should surface in classroom discussions of current events (#2); "describe how the media can play a role in elections and the democratic process," a topic that should appear in media literacy education (#7); and "apply the Bill of Rights to real-world scenarios," a skill that should develop both through civics instruction and through effective simulations of democratic processes (#6) (U.S. Department of Education, 2022). Together, the NAEP results suggest teachers may need more support in translating these four "proven" and "promising" practices (Gould et al., 2011; Levine & Kawashima-Ginsberg, 2017) into effective learning, although studies involving direct classroom observation would be helpful to better understand what is happening. In high-poverty schools—with fewer experienced social studies teachers compared to low-poverty schools (Hansen et al., 2018)—and in rural schools, where more than half of K-12 social studies teachers report having received no training on how to foster students' civic knowledge and dispositions (Hamilton et al., 2020)—the need for support seems especially acute.

This chapter describes the development and preliminary pilot of a learning and assessment prototype designed to help address this need. Incorporating the four most commonly used practices above (Hansen et al., 2018), the prototype uses digital-scenario-based tasks (SBTs) and a culminating face-to-face group performance to develop students' civics competencies, providing actionable assessment data to teachers in the process. A teacher guide contains resources for supporting and assessing students' learning, along with preparation and extension activities to help connect learning to their local communities and experiences. Preliminary findings suggest this could be a worthwhile approach for helping middle school social studies teachers—even those with limited expertise and experience—to support students' civic development.

Prototype Design

In a 2021 symposium on the assessment of civic learning jointly hosted by Educational Testing Service (ETS) and the Educating for American Democracy (EAD) initiative, panelists discussed the need for assessment developers to "provide educators more formative assessment tools and performance assessments that can serve as learning experiences" (Hamilton & Parsi, 2022). Our team sought to meet this challenge by designing an eighth-grade learning and assessment prototype that was developed with teacher support and piloted in 2022. The prototype follows a hybrid learning structure with three main components: two digital SBTs with embedded assessment questions, followed by a face-to-face group performance task.

The SBTs contain several design elements consistent with scenario-based assessments, such as the Global Integrated Scenario-Based Assessment (GISA (Sabatini et al., 2020)). These elements include the following:

- An overarching purpose for reading, viewing, and listening to sources
- A variety of source types, including those in digital formats
- A sequencing of activities from less to more complex
- Simulated peers to provide guidance and anticipate misunderstandings or errors

For the civics prototype, the overarching purpose is outlined at the beginning of the first SBT (Task 1): It's 2033, and students have been selected as youth ambassadors to the White House, tasked with contributing to a kids' website on presidential power and helping the president research options for establishing a new mining policy that could lower the cost of electric vehicles (EVs).

After meeting a simulated peer—a fellow youth ambassador named Amy—and a simulated mentor—a presidential aide named Mr. Ruiz (Figure 14.1)—students engage with written, graphic, and video sources to gather information on presidential power and its limits that can help them build a web page for the site and make a recommendation about the policy proposal. Ultimately, they need to decide whether the president should issue an executive order to allow the mining or work with Congress to pass a law.

The second SBT (Task 2) picks up where the first one left off: the president decides to work with Congress to try to pass a mining law, and Mr. Ruiz and the youth ambassadors are asked

Developing Civic Competencies through Scenario-Based Tasks • 223

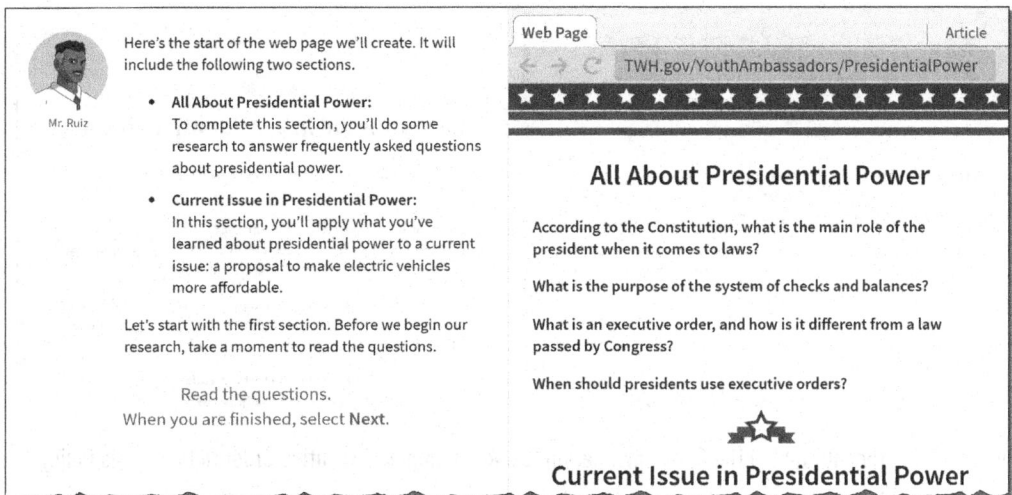

Figure 14.1 Simulated Mentor Mr. Ruiz Introduces the Purpose for SBT 1.

to help draft a bill that could become that law. In the process, students evaluate several claims about the impact of the proposed mining—using different sources to check their accuracy—and weigh possible revisions to the bill to try to win the support of an opponent.

Both SBTs build gradually from less complex to more complex activities. For instance, the first SBT begins with a straightforward knowledge-building activity, identifying the president's role as executor of laws, information that is explicitly stated in a text. Later, it requires students to synthesize information from a text and a video to compare laws and executive orders (Figure 14.2); interpret an excerpt from a historical Supreme Court opinion to consider how the constitutionality of an executive order is likely to be determined by the present (hypothetical) Supreme Court; apply what they've learned to determine whether a proposed

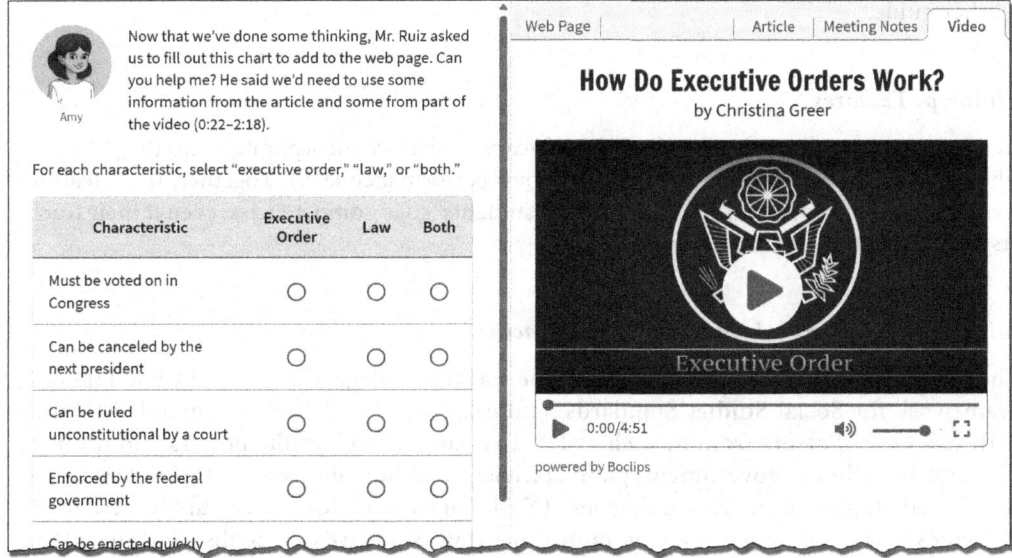

Figure 14.2 Simulated Peer Asks Students to Synthesize Information from Multiple Sources.

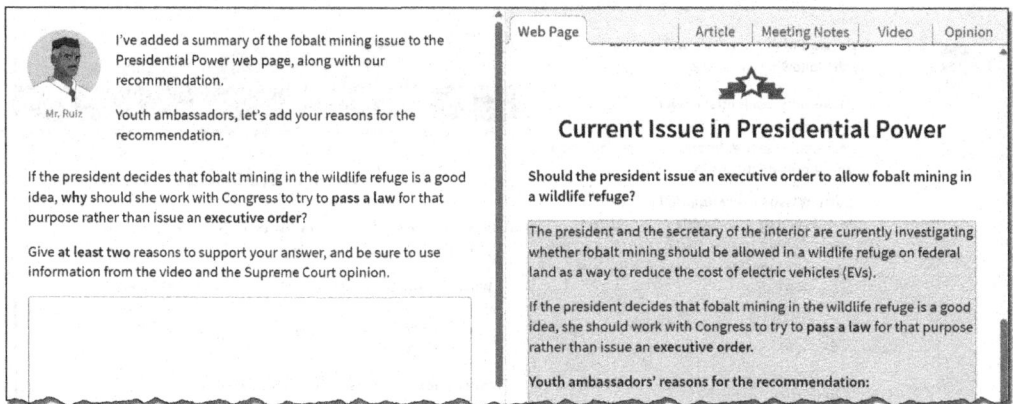

Figure 14.3 Students Justify the Recommendation to Avoid Using an Executive Order to Enact this Policy Proposal.

executive order allowing mining of a fictional EV battery component ("fobalt") in a wildlife refuge may be constitutional; and finally, use evidence from the sources they have analyzed to explain why, in this circumstance, the president should work with Congress to try to pass a mining law, rather than issuing an executive order (Figure 14.3).

After completing both SBTs, students are told that the fobalt mining bill has passed the House, but the Senate version of the bill does not yet have the votes needed to pass. Students' charge for Task 3—a face-to-face performance task—is to work in a small group to produce and present an information packet, or press kit, written from the perspective of a special interest group that either supports or opposes the bill. Each information packet must draw on evidence and arguments presented in Tasks 1 and 2 to try to persuade senators to support or reject the bill. Packets should contain social media content such as a post or video; talking points; a graph, chart, or table; and an image. Detailed lesson plans, rubrics, and student support materials for this group performance task are included in the teacher guide.

Prototype Features

In this section, we detail four research-based features that we incorporated into the prototype (the two digital SBTs and the face-to-face group performance task). Together, these features were intended to support the development of students' civic competencies, even if their teachers have limited experience teaching civics.

Alignment to Framework, Standards, and Practices

The main conceptual guide for the prototype was the College, Career, and Civic Life (C3) Framework for Social Studies Standards, and each task's activities are intended to align with specific indicators from it, such as D2. Civ.4.6–8: "Explain the powers and limits of the three branches of government, public officials, and bureaucracies at different levels in the United States and in other countries" (National Council for the Social Studies, 2017). Activities also align to specific Common Core State Standards in English Language Arts and Literacy in History/Social Studies, such as RH.6–8.7: "Integrate visual information (e.g., in charts, graphs, photographs, videos, or maps) with other information in print and digital texts" (National Governors Association Center for Best Practices; Council of Chief State School Officers, 2010).

The prototype was developed primarily to begin exploring whether a hybrid civics learning experience that relies heavily on standardized digital interactions could help teachers, especially those with limited social studies expertise and experience, translate four "proven" and "promising" civics development practices into effective learning (Gould et al., 2011; Levine & Kawashima-Ginsberg, 2017).

The first practice—instruction in government, history, law, and democracy (Gould et al., 2011)—is the backbone of the two SBTs, which include activities to develop and assess students' understanding of the president's role as an executor of laws, checks, and balances among the three branches of government, the differences between laws and executive orders, the role of the courts in interpreting ambiguous constitutional questions, and how a bill becomes a law.

The second practice—discussion of local, national, and international current events relevant to students' lives (Gould et al., 2011)—is the inspiration for the hypothetical but realistic policy dilemma. Rather than choosing a real policy debate—which could quickly become outdated and could easily lead students down predictable party lines based on opinions they might have heard from parents or other trusted adults—we tried to design a novel policy dilemma that cut across party lines. We also wanted an issue that was relevant to students' lives and would allow them to think about the US in relation to other countries. These goals were the basis for the hypothetical proposal in the first SBT to make EVs more affordable by opening up a federally protected wildlife refuge to the mining of a fictional mineral ("fobalt") critical for EV battery production, reducing the country's reliance on foreign fobalt producers.

The third practice—simulations of democratic processes and procedures (Gould et al., 2011)—makes an appearance in both the second SBT and the face-to-face group performance task. In the second SBT, students must practice political compromise when they analyze the reasons a member of Congress opposes the mining bill and consider how to revise the bill to enlist the member's support while still achieving its main goals. In the group performance task, students act as members of an interest group who must try to persuade US senators to support or reject the bill, marshaling evidence from the sources they have analyzed, and making their case through social media posts, talking points, graphs, and images.

The second SBT also incorporates the fourth practice, news media literacy education (Levine & Kawashima-Ginsberg, 2017), when students are enlisted as fact checkers of claims made about the fobalt mining proposal. They must analyze fictional vetted sources for evidence to confirm or refute the claims, and when some claims are refuted, students must revise them to fit the evidence.

Constrained Inquiry

In addition to the C3 framework (National Council for the Social Studies, 2017), the prototype design was influenced by EAD's Roadmap to EAD (Educating for American Democracy, 2021). Both of these frameworks endorse the inquiry-based approach to civics and social studies education favored by a broad consensus of educators. Referencing the research of Torney-Purta, Hahn, and Amadeo (Torney-Purta et al., 2001), the authors of the C3 Framework describe this approach as providing students with "opportunities to ask questions, pursue answers to those questions under the tutelage of expert teachers who can show them how to discipline their thinking processes, and take part in opportunities to communicate and act on their understandings" (National Council for the Social Studies, 2017, p. 83).

Although we recognized the great potential of inquiry-based learning to stimulate student engagement and learning (Barron & Darling-Hammond, 2008; Lazonder & Harmsen, 2016), we also knew that teachers with little to no training in civics education—part of our target audience—were not likely to be able to provide the kind of "expert tutelage" required to guide students effectively through an open-ended inquiry process. As Barron and Darling-Hammond point out in a research review, successful inquiry-based instruction requires not only deep content knowledge but "careful planning and the development of strategies for collaboration, classroom interaction, and assessment" (Barron & Darling-Hammond, 2008, p. 8).

Our solution was to design a learning experience that simulated a more open-ended inquiry process for students while relying mainly on digital scaffolds, rather than teachers, to provide formative assessment feedback and expert guidance. The key to this solution is employing "constrained choice activities" to structure the inquiry process for students (Sibley et al., 2023). These activities present a concrete, real-world situation, or problem, provide relevant information to analyze, and then call for a decision to be made based on this information. Our approach to constrained choice activities immerses students in a fictional but realistic public policy dilemma and supports them in analyzing texts and multimedia resources as they attempt to resolve it. Embedded assessment questions track their progress, and students' responses trigger feedback to address errors or misconceptions as they move through each activity.

In the constrained inquiry process used in the prototype, teachers, even those with limited civics teaching experience, still play an important role in facilitating learning and acting on formative assessment evidence, with support from a written teacher guide. They select, implement, and adapt preparation and extension activities based on the best fit for their students; share learning goals with students before each task; track students' progress throughout the experience with the help of a digital reporting dashboard; and evaluate students' written responses and group performance tasks using rubrics, sample responses, and other tools in the teacher guide. Teachers with more civics experience and expertise, of course, can play a much more active role in shaping their students' learning experience.

Embedded Formative Assessment Probes and Support

There is a strong research base that supports the importance of students and teachers engaging in formative assessment (e.g., Black & Wiliam, 1998; Hattie & Timperley, 2007). We drew on this research to incorporate numerous formative assessment practices into the prototype.

In the teacher guide, the learning goals for each SBT and the performance task are provided. Ensuring that students understand what they will be learning and why is a foundational aspect of formative assessment (Wylie & Heritage, 2024). The teacher guide provides recommendations for when and how to communicate the learning goals to students before starting each SBT and the performance task.

As students progress through each SBT, they receive feedback from simulated mentor Mr. Ruiz after submitting their responses (Figure 14.4). This ensures that any misconceptions are corrected before students move to the next activity. At the same time, their responses are captured and scored in real-time so that teachers can track their progress and intervene if needed. The only activity for which they do not receive automatic feedback is the final activity in each SBT (Figure 14.3 for the first SBT), a short, written response that teachers can grade using the rubrics and sample responses in the teacher guide.

Students also help each other to process the information they are encountering. At two points during each SBT, the digital interaction pauses so that students can engage in a real-time conversation with one or more peers about what they are learning (Figure 14.5). These "think and

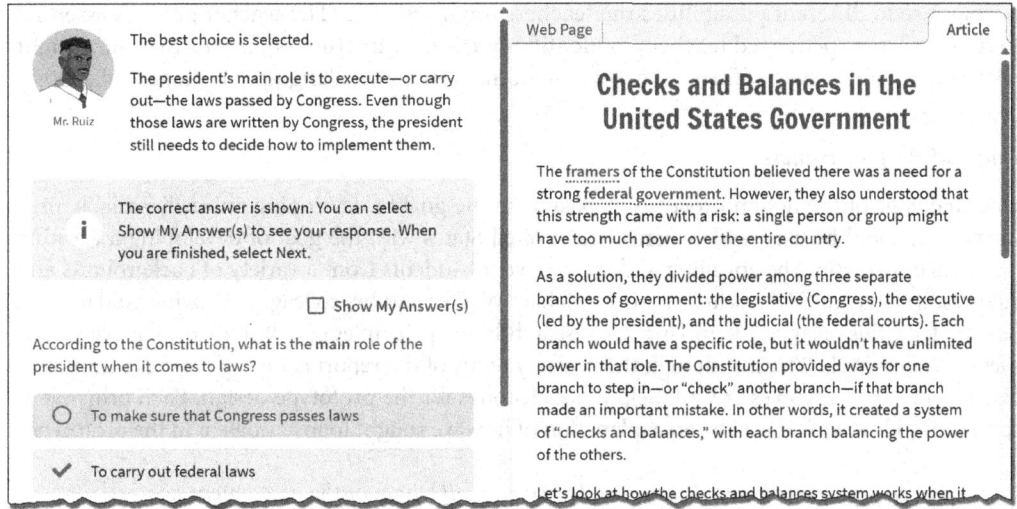

Figure 14.4 An Example of the Automatic Feedback Provided within the SBT.

discuss" activities, a departure from the typical scenario-based assessment structure, allow students to help each other work through challenging content and provide teachers an opportunity to listen to student discussions, another form of evidence of their students' learning.

Altogether, teachers are able to gather evidence of student learning from student responses within the SBTs, the multiple embedded "Think and Discuss" interactions with peers in the classroom, exit tickets (short questions that students respond to on a sticky note or small piece of paper as their "ticket out the door" that gives the teacher insight into student learning during the lesson), and student responses to the performance task. The teacher guide provides observation guidelines and possible follow-ups for student-pair and whole-class discussions

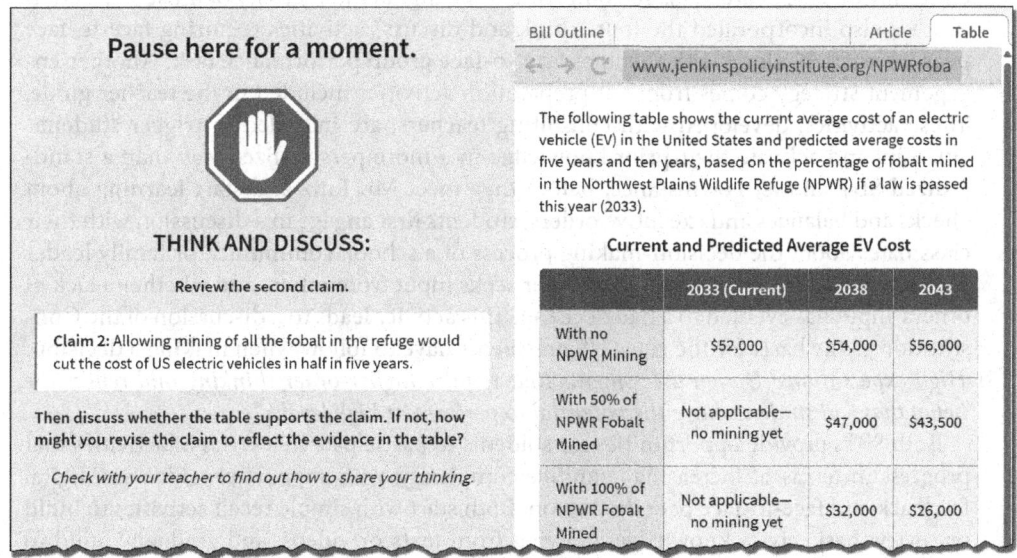

Figure 14.5 This "Think and Discuss" Activity in SBT 2 Allows Students to Work Through Challenging Content with their Peers.

in response to different possibilities the teachers might observe. The teacher guide is essential to support less experienced teachers in identifying the next instructional steps that they might take, as this is the aspect of formative assessment that is most challenging (Heritage et al., 2009).

Cultural Responsiveness

One challenge of the design process was balancing the goal of developing an easily scalable prototype that could be used widely across the United States with the goal of developing a learning experience that would be engaging and responsive to students from a variety of backgrounds and cultures. In a recent ETS research report, Michael Walker and his colleagues provide guidance on how to strike this balance, identifying five research-based principles of culturally responsive assessment (Walker et al., 2023). Although the primary focus of the report is on high-stakes summative assessments, the principles are still helpful touchstones for the prototype design. Each principle is summarized below, followed by an explanation of how we sought to instantiate it in the prototype.

1) *Shared power: Include all concerned parties in all stages of the assessment process.*

    We enlisted educators from geographically, politically, economically, and ethnically diverse communities to participate in the development and piloting of the prototype. One member of the educator review panel was a social studies teacher educator at a Northeastern university. The others were middle school social studies teachers from five schools described in Table 14.1. Three of the five teachers also participated in the pilot of SBT 1, and one provided feedback on SBT 2. (Three of the original five were no longer in the classroom when SBT 2 was developed.) All teachers had at least three years of experience teaching civics so that they could provide informed feedback on the design and content. In a future pilot, we plan to enlist teachers with less civics teaching experience to determine whether this model provides the necessary support for their instruction.

2) *Engagement: Design assessments to "foster active participation, use of productive cognitive strategies (e.g., self-regulation), and feelings of belonging."*

    We designed the SBTs to be engaging and context-rich and to include visually and culturally diverse characters. To complement the digital interactivity of most SBT activities, we also incorporated the four "think and discuss" activities requiring face-to-face peer interaction, along with the final face-to-face group performance task. Another engagement strategy comes from the preparation activities included in the teacher guide. These activities, developed with consulting teachers, are intended to trigger students' curiosity and activate their prior knowledge in a more personalized way than a standardized SBT allows. For instance, before they meet Mr. Ruiz and start learning about checks and balances and executive orders, students first engage in a discussion with their classmates about the decision-making process of a school, community, or family leader they know—considering when this leader seeks input from others and whether a lack of others' input has ever led to a bad decision. This activity leads to a discussion of the Constitution as the basis for the rules US presidents have to follow when making a decision.

3) *High expectations: Design assessments that require higher-order thinking and reflect the belief that "all students have the potential to perform at high levels."*

    Both SBTs provide opportunities for students to participate in a series of activities that progress in terms of increasing cognitive complexity, with support provided via digital feedback and face-to-face peer discussion. Both start with simple recall activities to build or review basic civics knowledge, drawing from texts or videos, and gradually build to synthesis, analysis, and writing activities. The ultimate expectation is that, after completing the two SBTs, all students will have the knowledge and skills needed to engage successfully with the final performance task, which requires strategic thinking to apply the knowledge and skills in a new format.

4) *Flexibility: Maximize flexibility in both context and content to match student preferences and/or needs, accounting for individual differences in culture, interests, and identities.*

There are two main sources of flexibility in the prototype. First, during the third task—the group performance to create and present a press kit for an interest group—students can choose their mode of expression and/or perspective on the bill. Next, teachers have the flexibility to choose among the optional preparation and extension activities in the teacher guide, based on student interest and cultural relevance. For instance, in one optional extension activity after the first SBT, students explore how important decisions are made in their town, city, or community. They are asked to think about whether they have a mayor, a city council, a school board, or a tribal leader and what checks and balances exist in their local government to prevent one powerful person from making bad decisions. Students are asked to create graphics that demonstrate this power relationship and to share them in a class discussion.

5) *Asset-Based: Measure what students know and can do, drawing on individual and cultural assets.*

The group press kit task provides the best opportunity to draw on students' individual assets. Students with a knack for expressing themselves effectively via text on social media might gravitate to that mode of expression during the press kit task, while other students with a talent for visual expression might create the graphic for their group's kit. Whatever the mode of expression, students are still tasked with using evidence from the SBTs to persuade fictional policymakers to adopt their position. As for cultural assets, many of the preparation and extension activities encourage students to interact with members of their community beyond their own classroom. For instance, one extension activity after the first SBT invites students to build understanding of a concept from the SBT by explaining it to a younger audience in a picture book.

Table 14.1 Demographics of Middle Schools Whose Teachers Participated in the Prototype Development

Location	Ethnic Representation of School	Students Receiving Free or Reduced-Price Lunch (%)	Political Leaning of Community*
New York, NY	54% white 16% Latinx 10% Asian American 9% African American 9% Multiracial 2% other	22	Liberal
Van Buren County, MI	60% white 36% Latinx 4% other	59	Mixed
Whitehouse Station, NJ	81% white 10% Latinx 6% Asian American 3% other	8	Conservative
Sheboygan Falls, WI	85% white 8% Latinx 3% Asian American 4% other	32	Conservative
Flagstaff, AZ	89% Native American 5% Latinx 4% multiracial 2% white	53	Mixed

*as described by participating teachers

Evaluation of the Prototype

Validity evidence for the assessment prototype was collected iteratively (American Educational Research Association (AERA) et al., 2014). Initial evidence in terms of *test content* was obtained from the development process (described in the section Alignment to Framework, Standards, and Practices), in which the C3 Framework for Social Studies Standards was used to inform and guide development of the tasks. Following that process, internal feedback was solicited from content and assessment experts at ETS. Only then was the prototype shared with social studies educators in the field for external feedback. As will be described in this section, feedback from the mini-pilot provided some additional validity evidence in terms of *student response processes*, specifically information on timing, engagement, and depth of understanding about civics content (e.g., differences between executive orders and laws and the reasons a president should not use an executive order to carry out all policy goals, but rather work with Congress to pass a law). For this classroom assessment prototype, which blends learning with assessment, the other relevant type of validity evidence is information related to teachers' *interpretation and use of assessment evidence*, to begin the process of understanding how teachers used the prototype.

Educator feedback was gathered on an early draft of the first SBT and an early draft of the teacher guide. Student and educator feedback was gathered during and after a mini-pilot of the first SBT, which was used in conjunction with the teacher guide.

Feedback on First SBT

In May 2021, a social studies education professor from the Northeast and five middle school social studies teachers from geographically, demographically, and politically diverse communities were recruited to review an early draft of the first SBT and provide written and oral feedback via interviews and focus groups. (See Table 14.1 for the schools represented by these teachers.) These educators supported the general approach in the first SBT but suggested providing additional supports to help students engage with and comprehend the content and help teachers quickly understand how to make the best use of the SBT with their students. The educators' feedback inspired two major decisions related to the overall prototype. First was the decision to develop a supporting teacher guide with preparation and extension activities for students, among other resources. The teacher guide was a significant addition to the prototype, as it not only provided a pathway to making the SBT content more engaging and relevant to students but also served as a toolkit to strengthen teachers' own civics knowledge and formative assessment practices.

The second decision was to incorporate student supports when developing the second SBT to reduce students' reading load—specifically, the use of videos to provide summary information and an audio recording, rather than a written speech, from the Congressional representative who opposes the mining bill. The incorporation of video and audio to reduce the reading load in the second SBT also allowed us to keep the focus on civics knowledge, skills, and dispositions rather than reading comprehension.

Feedback on Teacher Guide

In March 2022, we gathered written feedback from the five social studies teachers on the newly developed teacher guide and followed up with a virtual focus group to gather more detailed suggestions. With the focus group, we shared our two main goals in developing the teacher guide:

- To support teachers in deepening students' engagement in and understanding of the concepts in SBT 1, in part through helping them to make local and personal connections to these concepts.

- To help teachers—including teachers with limited experience teaching civics—understand quickly and easily how to make the best use of SBT 1 with their students, so that it is a valuable teaching and learning experience.

The group generally agreed that the Guide accomplished each goal, and made several suggestions for summarizing the content and rearranging and synthesizing information for easier navigation. The group also reacted very positively to the preparation and extension activities. One wrote, "I found the 'before the module' activity to be extremely helpful for engaging students ... very cross-cultural." Another said, "Honestly, I could see myself using all three of the [after the module] extension activities." The group provided ideas for graphic organizers to support the two "Think and Discuss" screens in SBT 1 and several additional extension activities, most of which contributed to the goal of increasing students' local and personal connections to the concepts introduced in SBT 1. They also suggested several questions that might come up for students as they complete the module.

Based on feedback from the focus group, we revised the teacher guide to add a "Frequently Asked Questions" section intended to help teachers anticipate and respond to student questions during the SBT, additional extension activities, a sample student response for the final constructed response prompt, and new graphic organizers to support student engagement with the Think and Discuss activities. We also rearranged some content to make the flow of information more intuitive. Eventually, we expanded the teacher guide to include support for all three tasks: the two SBTs and the face-to-face performance task.

Focus group participants made two suggestions we chose not to implement: adding links to background civics information and general information on formative assessment practices for new teachers. In the first case, we wanted to avoid concerns about copyright permission and datedness, and we decided that the new "Frequently Asked Questions" sections would provide the most critical background information teachers needed to support student learning goals. In the second, we decided to avoid drifting away from our focus on activities and practices specific to the civics content in SBT 1, especially since information about formative assessment practices is readily accessible in other places.

Student Mini-Pilot of First SBT

In May 2022, we conducted small-scale virtual pilot testing of the first SBT with three of the original teachers across six eighth-grade classrooms. The three schools represented a politically, socio-economically, and geographically diverse group. Teachers 1 and 2 taught SBT 1 once, and Teacher 3 taught it to four classes, stretching into a second day, which included an extension activity. At the time of the virtual pilot, an external delivery platform for the SBT was not yet available, so a member of our research team shared the SBT from our internal platform over Zoom, and this content was then projected by the teacher. Students followed along with the teacher's screen projections, completing the SBT questions and additional feedback on a separate digital survey form, rather than progressing through the task at their own pace. Students were also given PDFs of all stimuli used in the prototype, so they could review them as needed. In the classrooms of Teachers 2 and 3, we could hear most or all of the teacher's comments during the pilot, and for Teacher 3, we could hear roughly a third of the student comments as well. In the classroom of Teacher 1, we were able to hear very little of the teacher's comments and no student comments. In addition to the student survey information and observation notes, we gathered feedback from two of the teachers (Teachers 2 and 3) in a focus group after the tryouts. Teacher 1 was not able to join the focus group.

The pilot provided some useful information about timing and content. However, because the constraints on delivery required more active teacher facilitation, it provided little information about how SBT 1 would function as a self-paced learning and assessment experience with limited teacher facilitation. Furthermore, all three of the teachers recruited for the pilot were experienced civics teachers, so the pilot shed more light on how the module could work in the hands of veteran teachers than how it might support student learning in the hands of new or less experienced civics teachers.

Timing

The teachers' class periods ranged from 45 to 60 minutes, with time on task for SBT 1 ranging from 36 to 42 minutes. All three teachers seemed a bit rushed in this time frame, and the third teacher chose to extend the final SBT 1 activities into a second day, combining them with an extension activity about recent executive orders. It is not clear how well these timing observations can help us to predict the length of time the module will take for average students when they can access it on their own screens and move at their own pace. On the one hand, the feedback from more advanced students suggests that they would move through the module more quickly; on the other hand, the framing and support provided by the teachers' facilitation during the pilot may have prevented confusion for other students who otherwise might have needed more time to process the content. Both teachers who were able to participate in the debrief agreed that without the technical challenges caused by the delivery constraints, the module could fit comfortably in a 40–50-minute class. However, more time would allow teachers to incorporate the recommended preparation and extension activities and provide targeted support for students, drawing on the formative assessment and discussion resources in the teacher guide.

Engagement

Both teachers in the debrief reported that student engagement with the module was comparable to or better than it usually is in their classes. Many student comments from the survey bore this out: One from Teacher 2's class wrote, "It was actually kind of fun and it was interactive. I liked this better than a regular lesson." Another from Teacher 3's class wrote, "I liked the activity because … the scenario was believable. I like that there was a relevant issue being discussed and that there was a female president." Several students commented on how they enjoyed the whole-class experience necessitated by the technical limitations (e.g., "I like working with the entire class to see their perspectives and to work together"). However, a handful of students commented on aspects of the design that they found less engaging: One wrote that the avatars seemed "childish." (The avatar styling has since been updated for a more mature look.) Several also complained that the use of a fictional mineral was confusing. (Choosing a name less similar to "cobalt" might help to alleviate this confusion, although teachers have the latitude–and tips provided from the teacher guide–to clarify any student confusion.)

The teachers also reported that some more advanced students were a bit bored by the pace required because the whole class had to move through the module at the same time, and several student survey responses echoed this feedback. Along the same lines, a few students in Teacher 3's classes mentioned that they disliked the Think and Discuss screens because they slowed down the momentum of the task (e.g., "remove please waits. allow students to move at their own pace"). (Please see "Differentiation" and "Think and Discuss Screens" for more information on these issues.) When the self-paced version of the module is available for external delivery, teachers will have some options for addressing this concern. For instance, they might choose to pair students who move at a similar pace, allowing those who move more quickly to finish the Think and Discuss screens and the rest of the SBT before others in the class and engage in an extension activity with their additional time. Alternatively, they might pair students who move at different paces to provide collaborative learning opportunities.

Student Understanding

The vast majority of selected-response answers entered by students on the survey were correct, but because these individual responses were completed in the context of class discussion, we should be cautious not to infer too much about individual student understanding from this information alone. However, based on the portions of class discussion that were audible, the final written responses, and the teachers' comments during the debrief, it did seem as if most students completed the module with a basic understanding of the differences between executive orders and laws and the reasons a president should not use an executive order to carry out all policy goals.

The final written responses of students in Teacher 1's class, which moved most quickly through the module, demonstrated the weakest understanding of the content. Roughly half of the students supplied responses that did not clearly articulate two valid reasons why the president should work with Congress to pass a law allowing fobalt mining in the wildlife refuge, rather than issuing an executive order. For a handful of these students, language skills may have been an issue. For instance, one response reads only "needs the houses to vote on it the president needs to sign it." Time pressure seemed to be a factor for a few other students in this class; the following response articulates one accurate reason but then ends abruptly in the middle of the second reason: "It would be unconstitutional and an abuse of power to override the decicions [sic] and laws already made by congress. It would be more agreeable and reflect the views and oppinions [sic] of more people if it was also."

In Teacher 2's class, about two-thirds of the students provided two appropriate reasons, although many reasons needed a clearer or more complete explanation (e.g., "Because Congress would last longer than the executive order and the Congress. Also has more people to bring in unlike the executive order"). The rest either wrote nothing (6 of 27) or supplied only one accurate reason.

Responses by students in Teacher 3's four classes showed the strongest command of the content. The majority of the responses provided two accurate reasons that were adequately explained, although some were so similar that they may have been entered after class discussion and therefore used ideas articulated by other students—or the teacher—during the discussion. Most responses provided at least one reason drawn from the module content (e.g., "Because the next president could cancel it and we'd have much less fobalt - It's unconstitutional to do an EO"), while others made logical inferences that drew more on common sense and background knowledge about the national political climate than strictly on the information presented in the module (e.g., "1. If president Walker tried to work out a solution with Congress, it would build a healthy relationship. 2. Congress might help president Walker come up with a better idea than if she tried to solve the problem herself").

Think and Discuss Screens

Teachers 2 and 3 both treated the Think and Discuss screens as opportunities for full-class discussion rather than think–pair–share configurations with students. One teacher mentioned in the debrief that this decision was based partly on Covid social distancing rules, which made it difficult to pair students and have them all engaged in discussion at the same time. All three teachers spent no more than a minute on the first Think and Discuss screen, but several minutes on the second Think and Discuss screen. Those who were audible (Teachers 2 and 3) used the first Think and Discuss screen as a brief introduction to a class discussion of the grid item that followed it, and the second Think and Discuss screen as an opportunity for more in-depth discussion. Based on the post-pilot debrief, this decision was a consequence partly of teachers' perceived concern about limited time to complete the module and partly of their perception that the first Think and Discuss screen served as more of a quick formative check of understanding (since it is at a lower Depth of Knowledge level) than the second one, which required more sophisticated synthesis of ideas and could support a deeper discussion and multiple perspectives. This observation suggests that we may want to focus future Think and Discuss screens on more cognitively complex questions. As for the concerns raised in some student feedback that Think and Discuss screens slowed down the pace of the module, these were balanced somewhat by feedback like the following: "I liked how it said wait for your teacher to answer the next question so us students didn't get lost." Overall, observations related to the effectiveness of the Think and Discuss screens are inconclusive at this point because of the limited time spent on them and the fact that they were used only in a whole-class discussion format, rather than in the smaller peer-to-peer formats suggested in the teacher guide.

Differentiation

Both teachers in the debrief mentioned that the self-paced version of the module will allow for significantly more differentiation compared to the teacher-facilitated approach used for the pilot. They saw a real need for self-pacing for their more advanced students, who seemed bored by the slow pace of class progress. For students who move through the module quickly and successfully, the teachers suggested either providing them with advanced extension activities from (or based on those in) the teacher guide or having us build an additional advanced learning path as part of the digital experience of SBT 1. The teachers also suggested that self-pacing would allow them to provide more targeted support to small groups of students who need it.

Preparation and Extension Activities

Both teachers in the debrief reported having used the preparation activity in the teacher guide, in which students explored the decision-making styles of leaders in their community. They agreed that this was a useful entry point for their students to learn about constraints on presidential decision-making and connect this topic to their own lives. Teacher 3 also included an extension activity after SBT 1 that was based on one in the teacher guide, in which students researched and evaluated recent executive orders from the past three presidents. Based on the comments audible during the mini-pilot, students seemed engaged in this activity, and the teacher was able to use it to lead a brief discussion with them about principles that should guide the use of executive orders.

Stand-Alone vs. Embedded Use

In the debrief, both teachers agreed that SBT 1 would be most useful as part of a larger unit, either one focused on civics or on history. Teacher 3 had incorporated it into a unit on the Civil War as a way to deepen students' understanding of Lincoln's Emancipation Proclamation, one of the most famous executive orders in American history; in the following year, Teacher 3 planned to incorporate it into a larger civics unit about political decision-making. The teachers also expressed interest in the development of Tasks 2 and 3, and Teacher 3, who is charged with creating a new semester-long civics course for next year, expressed interest in further collaboration on new content for this course.

Guidance for New Teachers

In the post-pilot debrief, both teachers agreed that the teacher guide would help teachers with limited experience teaching civics to use SBT 1 effectively with their students. When asked for additional guidance that might be helpful for new teachers in implementing SBT 1, one teacher suggested adding a warning that teachers should not use this activity as an opportunity to dictate their personal beliefs to students but should be reminded to act more as a moderator. The other teacher suggested a warning to stay focused on the SBT 1 learning goals (as stated in the teacher guide) and not get bogged down in tangential topics.

Discussion

The data gathered from students and teachers during the mini-pilot provided useful food for thought, although it was too limited to draw definitive conclusions about the viability of the model. Validity evidence based on test content was strongest, given the design process, which drew heavily on existing civics learning frameworks. Some validity evidence based on response processes came from the mini-pilot with students, but more extensive piloting is needed. Finally, evidence from the teachers' use of the SBTs and reflections in the focus group provided some preliminary evidence of how these assessments and the associated teacher guide can support teachers' interpretation and use of evidence of student learning. Overall, the survey responses and teacher feedback indicated that most students were engaged by and demonstrated a basic understanding of the content of the first SBT. The teacher guide–especially its preparation and extension activities–also seemed to be a useful resource for supporting student learning. Both teachers who incorporated the preparation activity on local leadership styles reported that it was a helpful way to connect the content to students' own lives and communities. Teacher 3's successful integration of the extension activity on recent executive orders also suggested that the teacher guide could help teachers to deepen students' understanding of the SBT content through application in new contexts. Based on this initial exploration, combining the "constrained inquiry" of the standardized SBT—including its embedded formative assessment probes and learning supports—with more flexible, teacher-selected wraparound activities to generate interest and extend learning seems like a design worth further investigation.

The disparate performance of Teacher 1's students compared to those of Teachers 2 and 3 raises several questions that are difficult to answer without more data. For instance, if students had been able to move through the content at their own pace, would Teacher 1 have been able to use the support materials in the teacher guide to differentiate the learning experience effectively for her students who needed more support? Or did the multilingual students in her class actually need a version of the SBT with embedded language supports to access the content in a meaningful way?

Finally, we should note that given the 2024 Supreme Court ruling on presidential immunity and the flurry of executive actions early in 2025, the assumptions about presidential power that underlie the content of the prototype are in flux. Future iterations of the prototype may need to be revised to account for these changes.

Key Takeaways

The preliminary evaluation data suggest the following key takeaways:

- SBTs could be a worthwhile way to bring a version of inquiry learning to social studies classrooms that might not otherwise be able to experience it.
- Combining standardized SBTs with teacher-facilitated and selected preparation and extension activities can help to make the learning experience responsive to students and their cultures while providing embedded formative assessment probes and content expertise.
- The teacher guide may provide an educative structure that both supports teacher use of the taskset and greater use of formative assessment practices more broadly.

Recommendations for Future Work

The full civics prototype—with all three tasks—is still awaiting a larger-scale pilot with a fully functional delivery platform and in-person classroom observations. Such a pilot will allow a more comprehensive study of how students engage with and learn from both SBTs and the final face-to-face performance task, as well as selected preparation and extension activities from the teacher guide. An especially important area to investigate is whether the prototype can support students in having productive and safe conversations about difficult and controversial topics, even with novice civics teachers. Another important area of study would be the impact of the prototype on teacher learning—especially the learning of teachers with little to no experience teaching civics. Longer term, triangulation with other data sources (e.g., student surveys focused on civic interests and understandings) could help to elucidate whether and how the prototype supports the development of students' civic competencies more broadly.

References

American Educational Research Association (AERA), American Psychological Association (APA), National Council on Measurement in Education (NCME), & Joint Committee on Standards for Educational and Psychological Testing (U.S.). (2014). *Standards for Educational and Psychological Testing*. AERA.

Atwell, M., Bridgeland, J., & Levine, P. (2017). Civic Deserts: America's Civic Health Challenge. In M. Jonathan (Eds.), *National Conference on Citizenship*. Tisch College of Civic Life at Tufts University, and Civic Enterprises.

Barron, B., & Darling-Hammond, L. (2008). Teaching for meaningful learning: A review of research on inquiry-based and cooperative learning. *Edutopia*. The George Lucas Foundation.

Black, P., & Wiliam, D. (1998). Assessment and classroom learning. *Assessment in Education: Principles, Policy & Practice, 5*(1), 7–74.

Dewey, J. (1900). *The School and Society*. University of Chicago Press.

Educating for American Democracy. (2021). *Roadmap to Educating for American Democracy: Excellence in History and Civics for All Learners*. iCivics. Retrieved from www.educatingforamericandemocracy.org

Gould, J., Jamieson, K., Levine, P., McConnell, T., and Smith, D., eds. (2011). *Guardian of Democracy: The Civic Mission of Schools*. Leonore Annenberg Institute for Civics of the Annenberg Public Policy Center at the University of Pennsylvania and the Campaign for the Civic Mission of Schools.

Hamilton, L., Kaufman, J., & Hu, L. (2020). *Preparing Children and Youth for Civic Life in the Era of Truth Decay: Insights from the American Teacher Panel*. RAND Corporation.

Hamilton, L., & Parsi, A. (2022). *Monitoring Civic Learning Opportunities and Outcomes: Lessons from a Symposium Sponsored by ETS and Educating for American Democracy*. ETS Research Notes, ETS.

Hansen, M., Levesque, E., Valant, J., & Quintero, D. (2018). *The 2018 Brown Center Report on American Education: How Well Are American Students Learning?* Brookings Institution.

Hattie, J., & Timperley, H. (2007). The power of feedback. *Review of Educational Research, 77*(1), 81–112.

Heritage, M., Kim, J., Vendlinski, T., & Herman, J. (2009). From evidence to action: A seamless process in formative assessment? *Educational Measurement: Issues and Practice, 28*(3), 24–31.

Jamieson, K. (2013). The challenge facing civic education in the 21st century. *Daedalus, 142*(2), 65–83.

Kavanagh, J., & Rich, M. D. (2018). *Truth Decay: An Initial Exploration of the Diminishing Role of Facts and Analysis in American Public Life*. RAND Corporation.

Kawashima-Ginsberg, K., & Sullivan, F. (2017). Study: 60 percent of rural millenials lack access to a political life. *The Conversation*. Retrieved from https://theconversation.com/study-60-percent-of-rural-millennials-lack-access-to-a-political-life-74513

Lazonder, A., & Harmsen, R. (2016). Meta-analysis of inquiry-based learning: Effects of guidance. *Review of Educational Research, 86*(3), 681–718.

Levine, P., & Kawashima-Ginsberg, K. (2017). *The Republic is (Still) at Risk–and Civics Is Part of the Solution*. Jonathan M. Tisch College of Civic Life, Tufts University.

National Council for the Social Studies. (2017). *The College, Career, and Civic Life (C3) Framework for Social Studies State Standards: Guidance for Enhancing the Rigor of K-12 Civics, Economics, Geography, and History*. National Council for the Social Studies.

National Governors Association Center for Best Practices & the Council of Chief State School Officers. (2010). *Common Core State Standards for English language arts & literacy in history/social studies, science, and technical subjects*. Author.

Sabatini, J., O'Reilly, T., Weeks, J., & Wang, Z. (2020). Engineering a twenty-first century reading comprehension assessment system utilizing scenario-based assessment techniques. *International Journal of Testing, 20*(1), 1–23.

Sibley, J., Roberson, B., & O'Dwyer, B. (2023, January 11). Constrained choice activities: A simple way to improve critical thinking. *Educause*.

Torney-Purta, J., Hahn, C., & Amadeo, J. (2001). Principles of Subject-Specific Instruction in Education for Citizenship. In J. Brophy (Eds.), *Subject-Specific Instructional Methods and Activities* (pp. 373–410). Elsevier Science.

U.S. Department of Education. (2010). *National Assessment of Educational Progress (NAEP), 2010 Civics Assessment*. Institute of Education Sciences, National Center for Education Statistics.

U.S. Department of Education. (2022). *National Assessment of Educational Progress (NAEP), 2022 Civics Assessment*. Institute of Education Science, National Center for Education Statistics.

Walker, M., Olivera-Aguilar, M., Lehman, B., Laitusis, C., Guzman-Orth, D., & Gholson, M. (2023). *Culturally Responsive Assessment: Provisional Principles*. ETS.

Wylie, E. C., & Heritage, M. (2024). Assessment Literacy and Professional Learning. In S. F. Marion, J. W. Pellegrino, & A. I. Berman (Eds.), *Reimagining Balanced Assessment Systems*. The National of Education Press.

15
Exploring Implications of Transformative SEL for Civic Measurement in Diverse K-12 School Communities

Robert J. Jagers, Brittney V. Williams, Johari Harris, and Briana Coleman

Over the past 30 years, a substantial body of evidence has been generated indicating that well-resourced and well-implemented classroom-based social and emotional learning (SEL) programs contribute to desirable academic, social, and emotional outcomes among children (e.g., Cipriano et al., 2023; Durlak et al., 2011; Greenberg, 2023). Importantly, compared with their peers, young people in certain SEL programs experience their classrooms as more democratic, have more participatory citizenship beliefs, and report increased prosocial behavior (Domitrovich et al., 2022). While encouraging, the role of context in influencing the local readiness, adoption, adaptations, refinements, and sustainability of SEL in diverse school communities represents an important consideration as the field continues to evolve. This includes whether and in what ways various SEL programs and approaches meaningfully address the developmental needs and aspirations of underserved children, youth, and adults from diverse backgrounds (Camangian & Cariaga, 2022; Cipriano et al., 2023; Jagers et al., 2019, 2021, 2024).

We offered the notion of transformative SEL (*tSEL*) to better articulate and pursue educational equity and excellence in diverse school communities (Jagers et al., 2019, 2021, 2024). tSEL is the process whereby young people and adults build strong, respectful, and lasting relationships that facilitate co-learning to critically examine root causes of inequity and to develop collaborative solutions that lead to personal, community, and societal well-being (CASEL, n.d.a). tSEL is grounded in the Collaborative for Academic, Social, and Emotional Learning (CASEL) framework and is anchored in informed, engaged citizenship in tSEL processes and outcomes, one of the framework's expressed long-term outcomes (CASEL, n.d.b). The centering of citizenship is essential because an informed and engaged populace is vital to individuals *and* groups exercising the rights and responsibilities required for well-functioning, healthy democratic societies (Flanagan & Levine, 2010; Hart et al., 2014; Zimmerman, 2016). In this sense, tSEL can be understood as part of the civic socialization process that reflects and fosters developmentally appropriate civic engagement – the range of knowledge, values, attitudes, and behaviors related to constructive involvement in one's local community and broader society.

This chapter continues our efforts to advance tSEL action research by identifying assessments that support young people and adults in diverse school communities in their efforts to

DOI: 10.4324/9781003476825-18
This chapter has been made available under a CC BY-NC-ND license.

imagine, build, and sustain fertile local learning ecosystems. As such, we attempt to craft and clarify connections and alignment between concepts related to a tSEL continuous improvement (CI) model, participatory action research approaches, and civic learning and development. We view collaborative problem-solving (CPS) as an essential component of this work, as it reflects a developmental comtepency that undergirds engagement in the types of democratic and civic practices and processes while also cultivating individual and group competencies that are central to authentic school-family-community partnerships. The goal of tSEL is to promote and leverage the knowledge, attitudes, and skills of youth and adults so that they can actively engage in critical examination and collaborative action to address root causes of inequities they experience. Such partnerships reflect an equity focus, as they can position stakeholders to enact their rights and responsibilities to craft developmental relationships and learning experiences that foster personal, interpersonal, and community-level excellence and thriving (Jagers et al., 2019). The process of developing authentic partnerships, and ultimately CPS, requires a level of civic competence and engagement among those involved.

In the pages that follow, we first highlight the opportunity for assessments that can help give insight into community and school-level processes and outcomes associated with efforts to co-construct, implement, and evaluate local educational change initiatives. Examples of recent and ongoing work are brought forth from the perspectives of caregivers, educators, and youth as researchers. Indeed, the processes behind how one determines what measurements to utilize to determine efficacy or feasibility are incredibly important to ensuring the scholarship generated is grounded in democratic principles of equity and collaboration, yet process is often overlooked in the pursuit of methodology. We then consider a few models and assessments of developmental competencies that are relevant to youth and adults who might engage in building such vibrant learning environments.

School Family Community Partnerships – Assessing the Co-Creation of a Local Learning Ecosystems

Since the mid-1990s, SEL has been construed as "processes through which children and adults acquire and effectively apply the knowledge, attitudes, and skills necessary to understand and manage emotions, set and achieve positive goals, feel and show empathy for others, establish and maintain positive relationships, and make responsible decisions" (National Center on Safe Supportive Learning Environments, n.d.). Recently, the CASEL has defined SEL as an "integral part of education and human development. SEL is the process through which all young people and adults acquire and apply the knowledge, skills, and attitudes to develop healthy identities, manage emotions and achieve personal and collective goals, feel and show empathy for others, establish and maintain supportive relationships, and make responsible and caring decisions." Further, the CASEL definition asserts that SEL can advance educational equity and excellence through authentic school-family-community partnerships to establish learning environments and experiences that feature trusting and collaborative relationships, rigorous and meaningful curriculum and instruction, and ongoing evaluation. The inclusion of school-family-partnerships also empowers young people and adults to co-create thriving schools which have the potential to dismantle various forms of inequity and contribute to safe, healthy, and just communities.

The elevation of school-family-community partnerships is consistent with the meaningful, intergenerational relationships that empower young people and adults to engage in collective action and collaborative solutions offered in the tSEL approach. This appropriately shifts the field's attention beyond a narrow focus on pre-packaged classroom-based SEL programs that help form the extant evidence of efficacy. It also recognizes that students and adults model, learn, and practice their SEL competencies across key settings: classrooms, schools, homes, and communities (CASEL, n.d.b). By embedding SEL systemically into the policies, practices, and culture of the local learning ecosystem, SEL can support long-term, meaningful changes that promote student and adult academic, social, and emotional learning and development within and across settings.

Civic socialization processes occur through various social institutions, including families, schools, and communities, and involve learning about civic responsibilities, political systems, social norms, and collective decision-making. This situates systemic tSEL and school-family-community partnerships clear channels for developing the knowledge, skills, values, and dispositions necessary for active participation in civic and democratic life.

CASEL currently promotes a Theory of Action for implementing school, district, and statewide SEL efforts include four focus areas: (1) building foundational support and planning among stakeholders, (2) strengthening adult SEL competencies and capacity, (3) promoting SEL for students, and (4) reflecting on data for CI aligning with tSEL emphasis on the key role of adults in the civic socialization process (https://schoolguide.casel.org/what-is-sel/indicators-of-schoolwide-sel/). For example, the *Comer School Development Program (SDP)* represents one of the seminal school-based relational approaches that supports learning and well-being of low-income Black children and youth (Comer, 1989) and is foundational to the SEL field. Likewise, Community Schools (Blank et al., 2023; Dryfoos, 2002; Learning Policy Institute, 2021) are contextualized to address local priorities and leverage local assets. Both of these approaches leverage CPS in their processes to ensure optimal outcomes for youth and adults. For example, local capacity for collaborative problem-solving is a key impact area for Community Schools (Oakes et al., 2023) as local stakeholders "collaboratively identify, track and make progress toward local goals and outcomes for both the school and community." This includes the gathering of process and outcome data that is accessible and actionable, self-organizing to implement indicated processes and practices, and using rapid cycle CI data to monitor progress toward articulated goals. Corollary impact areas to such collaborations are (1) transformed schools, (2) students and families that are engaged, healthy and empowered, and (3) confident, well-prepared students.

Building School Communities Through Community-Based Participatory Action Research

Oakes and colleagues (2023) point to useful indicators and outcomes of developing a Community School. However, we believe there is benefit to leveraging insights from community-based participatory action research (CBPR) to investigating school-family community partnerships through a tSEL lens. This suggests that SEL implementation is an opportunity to engage in an iterative process that meaningfully involves a range of stakeholders such that their expertise, experience, and perspectives are employed to ensure that school communities support all young people and adults in realizing their fullest potential (see Figure 15.1).

Within this framing for SEL implementation, CI is a critical component of any effort to launch a new district- or school-based initiative. Yet too often CI is not inclusive of all stakeholders or is treated as an afterthought being pursued after the initiative or implementation is underway. It then becomes detached from the planning, implementation, and evaluation processes.

Since tSEL explicitly promotes a CPS process (solving for educational excellence for local children and youth), we see benefit in framing CI as a CBPR initiative. CI and CBPR participatory action research share several principles and practices. Both participatory action research and CI emphasize the empowerment and agency of stakeholder participants (Creswell, 2013). By empowering stakeholder participants, they are positioned to offer their voice and ideas in

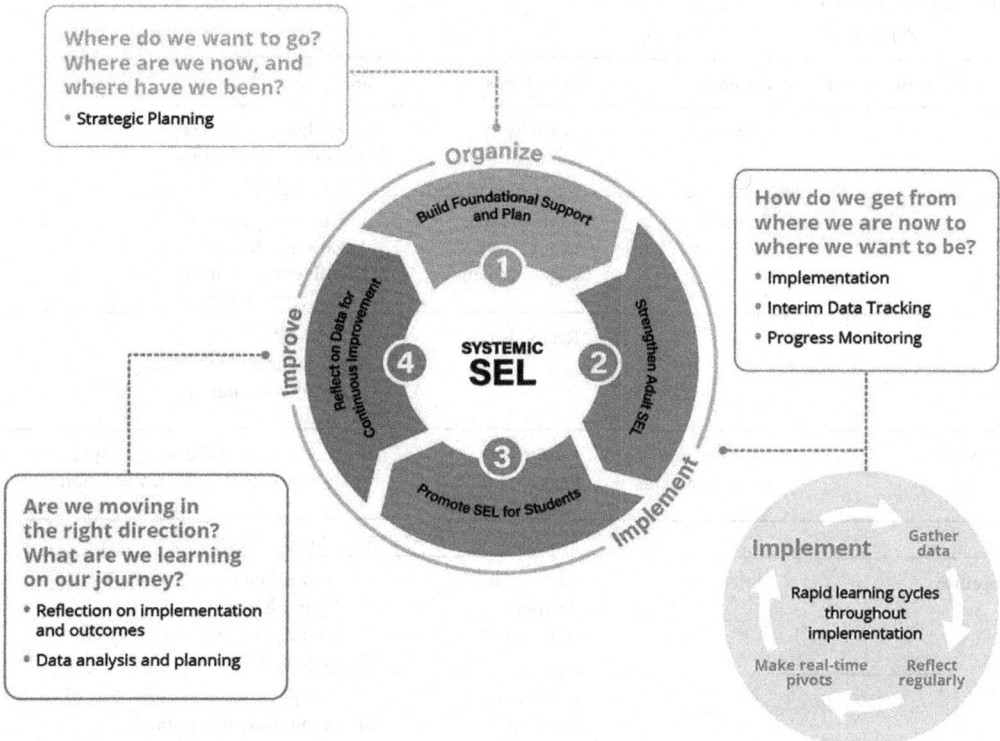

Figure 15.1 Continuous Improvement Model and SEL Implementation Cycle.

decision-making in all phases of an initiative. CBPR actively involves community members at-large in identifying research questions, collecting data, and co-creating solutions that address issues that would serve the community as a whole. In like manner, CI engages stakeholders, in the case of SEL – students, educators, and caregivers, in identifying a problem of practice (root cause analysis) and implementing changes to the process or system as a solution. With a shared emphasis on empowerment from participants, solutions are informed by the knowledge, experience, and perspectives of those being directly impacted by the issue at hand.

Over the past 25 years, community-engaged research and community-based participatory research (CBPR) have become more widely accepted by public health practitioners and academic researchers as an effective approach to health promotion in underserved communities (Oetzel et al., 2018). Wallerstein and colleagues have helped to advance the science of CBPR by offering a conceptual model and measures that articulate and assess CBPR processes and outcomes. These and other tools were developed as part of the Engage for Equity project (see Wallerstein et al., 2019). The model contains four domains: (1) context, (2) group dynamics and equitable partnerships, (3) intervention and research, and (4) outcomes. Briefly, contextual factors inform the background for group dynamics. Group dynamics include the structural as well as the intergroup and interpersonal aspects of partnership relations which guide programming and learning processes. This collaborative action research approach helps generate process data that aid with refinements and subsequent individual and collective outcomes.

Importantly, Boursaw and colleagues (2021) reported on efforts to develop and test psychometrically sound scales and associated subscales (see Table 15.1).

The Organize dimension of the tSEL CI model encompasses and could be operationalized through the capacity, commitment to collective empowerment and relationship constructs.

Table 15.1 Caption: Alignment of Continuous Improvement Model and Community-Based Participatory Research Processes and Assessment Scales

tSEL Implementation	Domain	Scale Constructs	Subscales
Organize	Context	Capacity	a) Bridging differences b) Community history c) Partnership capacity
	Partnership processes	Commitment to collective empowerment	a) Partnering principles b) Community fit c) Influence in partnership d) Collective reflection
		Relationships	a) Leadership b) Dialogue and listening c) Conflict resolution d) Trust
Implement	Intervention/research actions	Community engagement in research actions	a) Background and design analysis and dissemination community action
		Synergy	No subscale
Improve	Outcomes	Partner and partnership transformation	a) Personal benefits b) Agency benefits c) Community power in research d) Sustainability
		Projected outcomes	a) Policy b) Community integration into research social transformation health improvement

The Implement dimension of the tSEL CI model is reflected in the community engagement in research actions and the synergy constructs. Finally, the Improve dimension of the CI model includes developmental outcomes for individuals and groups as well as the degree to which specified shared goals and objectives are achieved. Importantly, Lucero and others (2020) examined the role of trust and synergy in CBPR. Trust and synergy are foundational to collaborative efforts. Trust is essential to create synergy, which reflects the generation of unique and valuable (research) insights through the effective integration of the perspectives, resources, and skills of diverse stakeholders. They constructed a quantitative forced-choice measure to place trust types on a continuum. Trust types include (1) trust deficit (suspicion), (2) role-based trust (based on title), (3) functional trust (purposed focused), (4) proxy trust (representative of a trusted other), and (5) reflective trust (allows for mistakes and constructive reconciliation). They confirmed that CBPR principles and processes correspond most with reflective trust. This type of assessment is thought to be useful since establishing and maintaining reflective trust is a dynamic feature of partnerships that requires monitoring and ongoing cultivation.

The Engage for Equity measures were recently developed in collaboration with diverse stakeholder groups that comprised a network of community-engaged health promotion research initiatives (Boursaw et al., 2021). While their work on these measures continues, they impress us as potentially useful to our fledgling work aimed at using data to support the building of vibrant, inclusive learning ecosystems. Assessing the evolution of relational processes, especially power sharing and trust, is essential to our emerging research agenda. We also see value in including observational measures to assess participatory action research processes with youth (Ozer & Douglas, 2013). Such measures provide insights into the following: (1)

training and practice of research skills, (2) promotion of strategic thinking, (3) group work, (4) opportunities for networking, (5) communication skills, (6) power sharing over major decisions, (7) power sharing over group structures. In the sections below we describe our nascent work, primarily in the Organize dimension of the tSEL CI model. These efforts have been aimed at helping us to learn how to identify and nurture capacities of caregivers, educators, and young people to generate and leverage research data to co-construct, refine, and sustain authentic partnership initiatives.

Caregivers as Researchers

We resonate positively and actively support the broader social sentiment that parents and caregivers should have greater participation and informed input into the K-12 schooling process (Pittman & Irby, 2024). Indeed, we strive to ensure that all caregivers, especially those from under-resourced backgrounds, have equitable voice and choice in shaping the educational opportunities for their young people. We utilize the Dual Capacity framework which recognizes the "funds of knowledge" that parents and other community members hold, viewing the expertise for promoting academic, social, emotional, and civic learning of young people and adults as a collective responsibility (Mapp & Kuttner, 2013). Caregivers are seen as leaders, advocates, co-constructors, and decision-makers capable of making meaningful impact in their child's learning. Their engagement necessitates a focus on reciprocity – a shared understanding among caregivers, educators, and young people of roles, goals, strategies, and desires for educational change that is representative of the needs and imperatives of all local stakeholder groups. Measurement of the Dual Capacity framework processes and skills being supported represents the type of assessment that we are calling into focus.

There is some evidence that capacity-building efforts can aid caregivers in informed engagement with schools and educators. For example, Fuentes (2009) used qualitative methods to document the ways in which three parent-led community organizations conducted their own mixed method research and organized themselves to improve learning conditions for Black and Latino students at one high school. Likewise, Minneapolis Public Schools (MPS) developed parent-participatory and youth-participatory evaluation teams to ensure that these stakeholders could help inform the vision, programs, and practices enacted in the district and local schools. MPS began meeting with families early in the redesign process through district-sponsored parent programs to co-identify how SEL should look, feel, and sound in their schools. The MPS Achievement, Research, and Equity (ARE) division then partnered with parents to determine research methods, deciding upon a parent participatory evaluation process, to better capture parent and family voice around issues of school climate and culture. A recent report describes the work of 51 parent evaluators from five cultural groups (Black, Native American, Hmong, Somali, Latinx) who worked with the ARE division to design data (survey, focus group, and other participatory methods) collection and analysis processes (Richards-Schuster et al., 2021).

Finally, Village of Wisdom (VoW), a parent-focused support organization, equips Black parents to be empowered and support Black students in schools through four main areas: (1) organizing and advocacy, (2) consulting and evaluation; (3) research and tool creation; and (4) by uplifting the Black Genius Brand. VoW seeks to democratize the research process by using community-based participatory research (CBPR) as a collective inquiry approach with parents. Black parents lead the research process including idea generation, data interpretation, and dissemination. VoW utilizes an approach called a *Dream Assessment* which is an inquiry method grounded in principles of racial justice, equity, and empowerment. Then parents used collected data to create the *Dreamandments*, which are the conditions required to be in place to receive Black learners that were developed from the study's findings. The Dream Assessment and Dreamandments provide the basis for Keep Dreaming reports that are disseminated to interested school and community stakeholders (https://villageofwisdom.org/).

Driven by these and other examples, we have recently developed a caregiver dialogue series and caregiver SEL ambassadorship program with the goal of fostering caregiving coalitions who use their knowledge of tSEL to partner with educators to improve learning environments. These efforts resulted in caregivers reporting an increased capacity to advocate for change within their children's school. Upon the request of caregivers desiring more action-oriented training to develop and implement school-level change, the Caregiver SEL Ambassadorship included the parent-PAR (PPAR) framework. The Caregiver Ambassadorship is intended to (1) strengthen and define the ambassadorship's role as an educator and leader, (2) encourage caregiver agency and curiosity as they examine school-level problems and develop recommendations for change, (3) promote CPS among caregivers and school staff, and (4) empower parents to build coalitions as an accountability measure for school personnel to meet the needs of diverse students and families.

Through the ambassadorship, we implemented a mixed methods design to measure caregivers' capacity for identifying and co-constructing change initiatives through tSEL-rooted partnerships with youth, parents, and educators. Caregivers' capacity is defined as necessary "skills, knowledge, confidence and belief systems" that empower authentic partnerships among caregivers and educators (Mapp & Kuttner, 2013, p. 5). The framework identifies (1) *connection* between school staff and families, (2) *capabilities* through access to knowledge about classroom and school structures, (3) *confidence* to work across cultural differences to co-construct partnerships, and (4) *cognition* to assume a diverse set of roles, as indicators of caregivers capacity to co-construct, implement, and evaluate school change initiatives. Civic engagement empowered through tSEL has led to positive outcomes related to caregivers capacity for partnership in prior CASEL initiatives (Coleman & Martinez-Black, in press). The addition of PPAR adds an opportunity to assess caregiver capacity outcomes, particularly related to collaborative problem-solving, relative to their interactions with school-level processes and staff.

Educator as Researcher

Much of the recent work on adult SEL is concerned with assessing the impacts of teacher self-care – minimizing professional stress and burn-out and promoting well-being and job satisfaction (e.g., Jennings et al., 2022). School climate data frequently serves as the primary tool for educators to gain insight into the extent and nature of family engagement as active partners in shaping their children's educational experiences (Osher et al., 2025). While the vast majority of surveyed high school staff expressed an interest in school climate data from their schools, less than one-third of participants reported seeing or utilizing the data to plan and enact improvements in educational experiences for young people or adults (Debnam et al., 2021). Attention has been paid to teacher collective efficacy and its contributions to student achievement (Tschannen-Moran & Barr, 2004), innovating teaching practices through collaboration (Goddard et al., 2004). Given the limited research on educators' participatory and civic socialization processes in collaboration with students, caregivers, and other invested adults, we contend that greater scholarly and practical attention is warranted toward assessing these processes from the perspective of educators as researchers.

Transformative SEL Implementation Tools

CASEL has offered SEL implementation tools, such as the School-based Staff SEL Implementation Survey and Schoolwide SEL Walkthrough Protocol (CASEL, n.d.c), that assist in planning, setting goals, progress monitoring, and continuously improving Schoolwide SEL implementation. These formative, CI assessments were derived from the ten Indicators of Schoolwide SEL (CASEL, n.d.d), which are also in alignment with the Theory of Action. The resulting data from these implementation tools are intended to support school-based SEL teams in collecting data on staff SEL implementation practices and perceptions mainly for the purposes of CI (CASEL, 2022).

Through the development and use of these tools, CASEL has learned that without formative assessment instruments, schools lack insight into the implementation process. This gap creates a "black box" effect, making it difficult to identify which strategies and practices are effective and how they can be improved in classrooms and other learning settings. Employing both the staff survey and walkthrough protocol allows schools to assess SEL implementation from multiple perspectives, allowing for calibration and corroboration that was sorely needed for schools to build a deeper understanding of their SEL practices. The use of multiple tools offers valuable implications for capturing the full complexity of implementation or conditions that accelerate or hinder progress. Being inclusive of multiple assessment tools provides a more comprehensive picture of implementation fidelity and effectiveness. It also signals an investment in engaging in multiple stakeholder perspectives, which aid in more collaborative processing.

The continued evolution of these tools will include items that measure the very types of participatory concepts we proposed in this chapter should be assessed. For example, the current *adult SEL* indicators could also lend themselves to staff reflections regarding their readiness, skills, and mindsets related to a more participatory approach. The *youth voice and engagement* indicator could be expanded to examine perceptions around staff willingness to empower students positioned as leaders, problem-solvers, and decision-makers of their learning experience could present valuable solutions to increasing student engagement and development.

Additionally, adding items to *authentic family partnerships* indicator would assess staff ability to foster understanding and appreciation for the expertise, diverse cultures, and perspectives of families. We believe these additions will enable both staff and families to align around a shared vision of student and community success and well-being (Kelly et al., 2023). *Aligned community partnerships items* would benefit from the inclusion of items assessing how staff and community partners came together to build collaborative relationships or to align their support for student academic, social, and emotional learning.

Further, our recent research-practice partnership work positioned CASEL staff, district leaders, and school-based staff to engage in rapid learning cycles using student reports of classroom experiences to improve academic content and student-teacher relationships by centering students' assessment of the classroom environment. The collaboration featured the Elevate Tool (PERTS, 2024), which collected real-time student feedback and experience of six learning conditions. Each learning condition was reflective of student perceptions of the degree to which classroom experiences affirmed their identities, built community and belonging, fostered a growth mindset, and honored their lived experience (see PERTS Elevate, https://www.perts.net/elevate).

In this pilot, educators across four secondary schools were invited to employ Elevate as a job-embedded CI and action research opportunity. Where teams of educators (i.e., teachers, counselors, and instructional coaches) in each school participated in mini professional learning communities to collectively elect a learning condition they would concentrate on as a school as well as the best practices to leverage and impact the growth and positive movement in the student experience. The focus of the pilot was to improve equitable practices in classrooms to improve student experiences and a good deal of adult support was provided during the process. Some educators extended the collaboration to their students, engaging in data reflection with students, empowering and inviting them to a more participatory role. Although there was a lack of documentation of that collective CI and action research process those educators engaged in. However, it was clear that an adult growth mindset and a positive learning culture were necessary for educators to reflect meaningfully on improvements based on student experience data (Nwafor et al., 2023). As a result, we launched a tSEL adult learning series to support educator readiness for utilizing student data for collaborative dialogue, exploration, and problem-solving (Nwafor et al., 2023).

Transformative (tSEL) Adult Learning Series

The CASEL team, along with educational consultants and a high school administrative team, collaboratively developed and piloted the tSEL Adult Learning Series. The series consisted of six interactive workshops designed to provide adult educators with opportunities to enhance their self-awareness and explore strategies for fostering equitable learning environments for young people. The pilot was intended to examine and assess which conditions, strategies, and activities are the most successful in shifting mindsets and ultimately influencing educator classroom- and school-level behaviors. The teams co-developed research and learning questions to serve as the foundation for their inquiry around the impact of the series on educator mindset and will to implement equitable practices in classrooms.

A mixed methods approach to research design and analysis was used to include end-of-session feedback surveys and focus group interviews in this project. Survey data included the following:

1) Session-specific items assessing participants' perspective regarding whether the session's objectives were met.
2) Catalyze (PERTS, 2023a, 2023b) offered a way to measure six organizational conditions: collective vision, inclusive empowerment, learning culture, supportive leadership, transformative equity, and trusting community.
3) CASEL SEL Implementation Survey captured educators' SEL beliefs and attitudes, as well as perceptions around relevant working conditions.

Preliminary findings of the tSEL Adult Learning Series pilot confirm that specific conditions of collective visioning and trust are necessary to support educator agency at the district level (Williams et al., 2024). Pilot findings at the school level found that inclusive empowerment and learning culture were additional conditions that were assessed along with community trust to grow significantly over the course of the series. The inclusion of these findings related to organizational conditions is leading us to acknowledge the mindsets and perceptions that lead to the skills needed for participatory and collaborative approaches to problem-solving. Here we bring attention to how key organizational conditions are intimately connected to agency and action for educators, illuminating what conditions need to be assessed to cultivate critical self-reflection in educators and promote reflective, equitable practices and processes in classroom settings where civic socialization is taking place. This acknowledges the promise, that if fostered, conditions could better position educators to engage in transformational work.

Youth as Researchers

In previous work, we have highlighted classroom-based approaches and programs that employ collaborative inquiry and contribute to civic development (Jagers et al., 2024). Our working assumption is that young people and adults who participate in these programs and practices are better prepared to actively engage in youth participatory action research (YPAR), a youth-focused version of CBPR, which positions young people of all ages as experts – critical consumers and producers of knowledge relevant to the launch, refinement, and sustainability of local tSEL initiatives (Ozer et al., 2020, 2021; Skoog-Hoffman et al., 2024). Consistent with tenets of CI, the research process is understood to be an iterative problem identification/analysis-design-action-reflection cycle. YPAR requires youth-adult power sharing and has been successfully conducted with elementary and secondary school-aged young people with a range of adult partners (i.e., trained educators, school staff, and/or external university research partners). YPAR is often conducted in youth-serving community organizations. Educators and youth workers in these settings are typically more attuned to youth and community assets and aspirations but may have less access to professional development opportunities that allow them to consistently enact rigorous community-relevant content and pedagogy (Baldridge, 2020).

To explore how best to collaborate with such organizations, a CASEL team recently partnered with the BlackSEL, a community-based, youth-serving organization, that has focused on supporting youth engaging in participatory action research in their school community. The overarching goal of this work was to help build staff capacity to build Black youth's social emotional competencies, with a particular focus on civic competencies such as critical awareness and action. We sought to understand the processes that promoted or hindered the Black youth engagement and how these processes contributed to the civic competencies of interest. All adolescents who were leading YPAR participated in a co-designed five-week seminar in which they learned the principles of YPAR and the possibilities of YPAR in their communities. While participants were learning YPAR research processes, adult facilitators were simultaneously collecting data on their experiences of *the* process.

In collaboration with the BlackSEL organization, we identified what tSEL constructs we were interested in exploring over the processes of this programming, deciding upon the following: civic competencies, critical consciousness (CC), agency, identity, belonging, collaborative problem-solving, and curiosity and determined a mixed method approach was the best way to gain a deeper understanding of how these constructs in youth are molded over the course of this program. By engaging in meaningful collaboration with BlackSEL we centered collaborative problem-solving in our own research process (Syvertsen et al., 2015).

Over a period of four months we collected pre- and post-programming surveys measuring these constructs within youth participants, while conducting focus groups, to probe these constructs qualitatively. Utilizing both surveys and focus groups over the course of implementation allowed us to gain a deeper understanding of how these processes contribute to youth's civic socialization and development. Results from this work are currently being analyzed. Ultimately, by shifting the focus to process, we not only align methodology with the goals of citizenship, but we can also better understand where to intervene to support the development of youth's civic competencies.

We anticipate leveraging mixed method data to further develop our capacity-building efforts. Since tSEL implementation is an intergenerational undertaking, we find the work of Wilhelm et al. (2021) instructive for the next phases of these efforts. They describe lessons learned from project TRUST, a multisite, multicomponent participatory research initiative that brought together youth, parents, community members, and academics to surface and advance practices and policies that improve the school environment and experiences for Somali, Hmong, Latino, Indigenous, and Black youth. Impact logs and interviews were used to evaluate variations in implementation across school community settings (Hawe et al., 2004). Impact logs allowed for the recording of, for example, meeting objectives and outcomes, reflections on challenges, successes, and next steps for implementation activities. Logs were supplemented and expanded on by semi-structured interviews (in-person or virtual). The cadence for interviews varied from weekly to monthly. Four lessons emerged from these data: (1) experiential learning opportunities strengthened PAR researcher's skills and maintained high levels of engagement; (2) building a sense of community supported PAR processes; (3) PAR requires consistent support from facilitators with diverse skill sets; and (4) individuals with bridging roles helped position PAR researchers for success within institutions.

Key Individual Level Competencies

tSEL is anchored in informed, engaged citizenship and includes constructs from each of the five core competence domains (self-awareness, self-management, social awareness, relationship skills, and responsible decision-making) of the CASEL framework. We have highlighted the development of individual level competencies (i.e., knowledge, attitudes/beliefs, and behaviors) of identity (self-awareness), agency (self-management), belonging (social awareness), CPS (relationship skills), and curiosity (responsible decision-making) for young people *and* adults. The development of competencies both influences and is influenced by the extent to which young people and adults are willing and able to actively participate in the collaborative efforts required to build and maintain a thriving local learning ecosystem.

Collaborative Problem-Solving (CPS)

CPS is defined as the capacity of an individual to effectively engage in a process whereby two or more agents attempt to solve a problem by sharing the understanding and effort required to come to a solution and pooling their knowledge, skills, and efforts to reach that solution (Jagers et al., 2021) and is central to engaged citizenship. Most frameworks distinguish between (1) problem-solving processes – exploring and understanding, representing and formulating planning and executing, and monitoring and reflecting; and (2) collaborative (relational) processes – establishing and maintaining shared understanding, taking appropriate actions to solve the problem, establishing and maintaining group organization (Hao et al., 2019). The community engagement in research scale of the Engage for Equity measure (mentioned earlier in the chapter) seems useful to assess CPS as well (Boursaw et al., 2021).

There are ongoing efforts to develop scalable reliable measures of CPS using computer-supported collaborations (Hao et al., 2019, 2024). It is not clear whether and in what ways the inputs and outputs of these assessments are transferable or generalizable to real-world problem-solving efforts. We agree with Flanagan et al. (2007) that assessing active participation in CPS includes – engaging in creating a plan to address a problem, getting other people to care about a problem, expressing views to others, forming attitudes after listening to conflicting viewpoints, summarizing what another person has said, contacting relevant others (peers or leadership) about a problem are assessable behaviors that aid in organizing and enacting effective problem-solving activities.

Identity

Identity is an individual difference variable that connotes who one is or aspires to be. Identity has long been the focus of social science research and has come to encompass how young people and adults view themselves both in terms of personal identity (e.g., interests, sense of one's talents, weaknesses, and purpose) and with regard to social group identity components (e.g., family roles, ability status, race/ethnicity group membership, socioeconomic status, gender, religion, and political party). From a structural perspective, each dimension has a level of importance (centrality) and emotional tenor (positive/negative public and private regard), and situational (salience). There is a substantial and evolving body of research on ethnic/racial identity with measures that examine its structure (e.g., Sellers et al., 1997) and developmental processes (see Syed & Westberg, 2024; Umaña-Taylor, 2024). A more systematic study of racial ideologies (assimilation, humanism, oppressed minority, and nationalism) may be warranted in this connection. Ideologies reflect notions of what racial/ethnic groups "should" do regarding intra- and intergroup, institutional, and international relations (Sellers et al., 1997), which has an impact on civic development and engagement. We have also highlighted the perceived economic status as an important consideration in relational dynamics (Jagers et al., 2024). However, it appears that assessments of this construct are limited.

Agency

Exercising one's rights and responsibilities implies a sense of agency. Agency refers to the perceived and actual capacity of individuals and groups to effect change through purposeful action (Bandura, 1989). Measures need to reflect the reality that young people and adults can have a voice and make choices within specific life domains. In the present case, we are concerned with a sense of efficacy around learning and career goals to pursue and engage in CPS with others to create a local learning ecosystem - holding the assumption that local learning ecosystems provide opportunities for personal and collective growth and development. Relevant measures to consider are community self-efficacy, which connotes one's beliefs about their ability to work with others to make a positive contribution to the community (Flanagan et al., 2007), and civic efficacy, which refers to confidence that personal knowledge can be used to solve real-life problems in one's community (Metzger et al., 2018). Agency also includes collective agency/efficacy and connotes coordinated actions among adolescents and adults that contribute positively to shared activities and common responsibilities (e.g., Flanagan et al., 2023; Nagaoka et al., 2015; Sampson et al., 2005). The synergy scale of the Engage for Equity measure seems relevant in this regard.

Belonging

Belonging signifies being aware of experiences of acceptance, respect, and inclusion within a group, school, or community. It implies not only feeling recognized but also being connected and fully involved in and co-creating relational and learning processes while meaningfully contributing to developmental outcomes for oneself and for others. Having and creating a sense of belonging is critical to students' and adults' cognitive, social, and emotional well-being, as well as school and work satisfaction; and academic motivation and achievement (e.g., Healey & Stroman, 2020).

There are several indicators of positive classroom and school community that can be utilized (see Domitrovich et al., 2022 for examples). In our view, it would be useful to develop a more nuanced understanding of constructive peer relations in school and community contexts. Rivas-Drake et al. (2017) employed social network analysis (e.g., popularity, reciprocity, propinquity, heterogeneity) to document improvements in cross-race peer relations in the context of a school-wide SEL initiative. Oosterhoff et al. (2021) used social network analysis to examine civic development within the peer context, finding that various aspects of peer relations were associated with civic efficacy, political engagement, and behaviors. The Contextual Capacity and Commitment to Collective Empowerment Scale of the Engage for Equity measure reflect important aspects of belonging as well.

Curiosity

Curiosity can animate academic, social, and emotional exploration and action. Curiosity has both cognitive and affective elements that contribute to an enduring tendency to pursue knowledge and new experiences. As such, it appears to be essential to attention, engagement, and learning. Curiosity is understood to be a multidimensional construct though the research is somewhat fragmented. In their scoping review, Yow et al. (2022) suggested that the literature includes three broad approaches and related measures in the study of curiosity. There is the following: (1) interest-type curiosity that reflects the volition to seek knowledge for the joy of learning, (2) deprivation-type curiosity which reflects anxiety due to a lack of knowledge, and (3) social curiosity, which reflects a desire for information about other people and oneself.

The first two constructs seem most germane to academic learning, while the third construct seems relevant to relational aspects of CPS.

Clark and Seider (2020) focus on social curiosity, utilizing the curiosity subscale of the Values in Action Inventory of Character Strengths for Youth (Park & Peterson, 2006), which is an eight item measure designed to assess curiosity as one of 24 character strengths. The curiosity subscale includes statements such as, "I am always curious about people, places, or things I am not familiar with." Findings from Clark and Seider's study reported growth in curiosity over four years was positively linked to increased social analysis and societal involvement confirming links to civic engagement.

Related Civic Competency Assessments

In addition to the connections to the Engage for Equity measure we allude to above, tSEL focal constructs can be found in several frameworks in the psychology and education fields. Summarized in Table 15.2 is a crosswalk of tSEL focal constructs with dimensions and elements of the Civic Readiness Map (Institute for Citizens and Scholars, 2023; see Chapter 4 in this volume) and with CC/sociopolitical development (SPD) (Diemer et al., 2017; Heberle et al., 2020).

The Civic Readiness Map (Institute for Citizens and Scholars, 2023; Gallos et al., this volume) was offered recently as a means for organizing extant models and measures of civic engagement. Civic engagement is generally understood to be a multidimensional construct concerned with social and political functioning thereby including various types of civic knowledge and reflection, civic attitudes, values and motivations, and civic behaviors. Civic readiness refers to an individual's preparedness to engage actively and responsibly in civic life through "1) *what individuals understand, 2) what or how they participate, 3) how they connect with organizations and others, and 4) what they believe influences their engagement as citizens*" (Institute for Citizens and Scholars, 2023, p. 13). These dimensions encompass what are referred to as elements and specific coordinates that encourage assessments of civic

Table 15.2 Crosswalk of tSEL Focal Constructs with Civic Readiness Map Dimensions and Critical Consciousness/Sociopolitical Development

tSEL Focal Constructs	Civic Readiness Map	Critical Consciousness
Collaborative problem-solving	Participate • Collaborative problem-solving • Effective communication	Critical action
Identity	Connect • Civic identity	Critical reflection (self)
Agency	Believe • Agency • Trust	Critical efficacy
Belonging	Connect • Belonging	Critical reflection (social)
Curiosity	Understand • Critical thinking	Critical reflection (self and social)

knowledge, complex skills, dispositions, and capacities necessary for informed, ethical, and sustained civic engagement.

In our view, some of the more pertinent aspects of civic readiness include the following:

- **Connect** dimension and the civic identity, community building, and inclusion and empathy elements and coordinates of belonging, interpersonal skills and negotiation, which align with tSEL focal constructs of **identity** and **belonging.**
- **Believe** dimension which aligns with the tSEL focal construct of **agency**.
- **Participate** dimension and the elements of CPS and public decision-making and coordinates relevant to effective communication (e.g., teamwork, listening, speaking up, facilitation skills) which align with the tSEL focal construct of CPS.
- **Understand** dimension and the element of critical thinking and coordinates of fact-finding, analytic skills, and ethical reasoning which align with the tSEL focal construct of **curiosity**.

tSEL focal constructs are also consistent with aspects of CC/SPD, which both reflect a more justice-oriented approach to civic engagement (Deimer et al., 2011; Herberle et al., 2020; Watts & Flanagan, 2007). CC/SPD models entail critical reflection, critical efficacy, and critical action.

- **Critical reflection** refers to the examination of individual, group, and/or institutional contributions to inequities and aligns with tSEL focal constructs of **identity**, **belonging**, and **curiosity**.
- **Critical efficacy** implies a belief in personal or group capacity to help correct inequities and aligns with the tSEL focal construct of **agency**.
- **Critical action** (CPS) refers to becoming actively involved in actions intended to address and modify circumstances or behaviors that are unfair or contribute to inequities. What constitutes relevant/appropriate critical action should be understood as problem, situation, or context dependent. It is noteworthy that the SPD model includes opportunity structure as an important contextual consideration. Thus, informal helping, volunteering in local institutions like schools, joining the school board and/or engaging in group study, contacting politicians, and participating in protests can all be viable ways to enact local social change efforts.

Competency development has been a major focus of SEL assessment efforts.[1] There has been less systematic attention to tSEL focal competencies, however, even in the context of aligned programs and practices. We have begun to identify and compile useful indicators, we see promise in recent reviews of relevant measures for the Civic Readiness Map and for CC. Part of ongoing work is to critically examine the psychometric qualities and developmentally appropriateness of the various assessments in order to make informed recommendations to partners.

Brief Synopsis and Research Directions

In this chapter, we are calling the field's attention to an opportunity to construct a collaborative process that can be monitored and refined to get closer to providing youth and adults with settings that facilitate them solving local problems that prevent or limit thriving. We offer tSEL as a systemic approach, grounded in democratic processes, with strong alignment to CI and participatory research models as one possible vehicle to this end. The processes and competencies we point to are intended to invite and position adults and young people from diverse school communities to exercise their rights and responsibilities to co-create a relationally rich, rigorous, and relevant local learning ecosystem in order to realize their conceptions of individual and collective well-being and thriving. We suggest that developing authentic school-family-community partnerships as a means to achieve this and such partnerships require civic skills. All stakeholders who have a vested interest in contributing to the collective flourishing of these dynamic partnerships have a responsibility to monitor processes and hold themselves as stakeholders accountable through assessment.

We seek to support such endeavors by building individual skills and capacities of stakeholders to gather, curate, make meaning, and utilize various forms of data to intentionally pursue the collective goals and CPS endeavors set out for them. Toward this end, we are laboring to leverage a CBPR approach to organize and operationalize this work. This approach supports careful attention to context from an asset perspective and recognizes the power and expertise each stakeholder brings to the collective, the learning ecosystem, and the school-family-community partnership. It requires the use of mixed methods to adequately capture common features as well as more subtle and complex contours and textures of settings, relationships, and aspirations that inform the utility and applications of the co-constructed knowledge regarding processes and outcomes.

This chapter encourages the next phase of work to continue the development, psychometric testing, and validation of various assessment tools – such as those highlighted from Engage for Equity and others – to deepen our understanding of the relevant processes and critical skills discussed above. Deepening this work will advance efforts to assess and explore individual competencies that reflect different developmental stages and experiences stakeholders bring to collaborative processes. Assessments must be sensitive enough to capture relational dynamics and should include observational and qualitative data collection methods to reflect the nuances of civic development and collective action at play. Furthermore, assessments of relevant skills and processes must maintain enough flexibility that honors the nature of formative assessment for CI and progress monitoring. This flexibility allows for rapid learning to occur as well as the use of research designs capable of capturing both nonlinear movement and long-term growth.

Note

1 See, for example, the EdInstruments student well-being measures database (https://edinstruments.org/topics/student-well-being) and the EASEL Lab at Harvard (https://easel.gse.harvard.edu/)

References

Baldridge, B. J. (2020). The youthwork paradox: A case for studying the complexity of community-based youth work in education research. *Educational Researcher*, 49(8), 618–625. https://doi.org/10.3102/0013189X20937300

Bandura, A. (1989). Human agency in social cognitive theory. *American Psychologist*, 44(9), 1175–1184.

Blank, M., Harkavy, I., Quinn, J., Villareal, L., & Goodman, D. (2023). *The community schools revolution: Building partnerships, transforming lives, advancing democracy*. Collaborative Communications Group. https://www.communityschoolsrevolution.org/

Boursaw, B., Oetzel, J. G., Dickson, E., Thein, T. S., Sanchez-Youngman, S., Peña, J., Parker, M., Magarati, M., Littledeer, L., Duran, B., & Wallerstein, N. (2021). Scales of practices and outcomes for community-engaged research. *American Journal of Community Psychology*, 67(3–4), 256–270. https://doi.org/10.1002/ajcp.12503

Camangian, P., & Cariaga, S. (2022). Social and emotional learning is hegemonic miseducation: Students deserve humanization instead. *Race Ethnicity and Education*, 25(7), 901–921.

CASEL (n.d.a). *What is transformative SEL?* https://casel.org/fundamentals-of-sel/how-does-sel-support-educational-equity-and-excellence/transformative-sel/#what-is-transformative-sel

CASEL. (n.d.b). *What is the CASEL framework?* https://casel.org/fundamentals-of-sel/what-is-the-casel-framework/

CASEL. (n.d.c). *Track progress*. CASEL Guide to Schoolwide SEL. https://schoolguide.casel.org/track-progress/

CASEL. (n.d.d). *Indicators of schoolwide SEL*. https://schoolguide.casel.org/what-is-sel/indicators-of-schoolwide-sel/

CASEL. (2022). *School-based staff survey research snapshot*. https://schoolguide.casel.org/resource/school-based-staff-survey-research-snapshot/

Cipriano, C., Strambler, M. J., Naples, L. H., Ha, C., Kirk, M., Wood, M., Sehgal, K., Zieher, A. K., Eveleigh, A., McCarthy, M., Funaro, M., Ponnock, A., Chow, J. C., & Durlak, J. (2023). The state of evidence for social and emotional learning: A contemporary meta-analysis of universal school-based SEL interventions. *Child Development, 94*(5), 1181–1204. https://doi.org/10.1111/cdev.13968

Clark, S., & Seider, S. (2020). The role of curiosity in the sociopolitical development of black and Latinx adolescents. *Journal of Research on Adolescence, 30*(1), 189–202. https://doi.org/10.1111/jora.12511

Coleman, B., & Martinez-Black, T. (in press). Transformative SEL: Building capacity for authentic caregiver-school partnerships. In T. Lewis & D. Hiatt-Michael (Eds.), Promising practice of engaging families and communities around mental health in schools: A volume in Family-School-Community Partnership Issues. Emerald Publishing.

Comer, J. P. (1989). Racism and the education of young children. *Teachers College Record, 90*(3), 352–361. https://doi.org/10.1177/016146818909000312

Creswell, J. W. (2013). *Qualitative inquiry and research design: Choosing among five approaches.* SAGE.

Debnam, K. J., Edwards, K., Maeng, J. L., & Cornell, D. (2021). Educational leaders' perceptions and uses of school climate data. *Journal of School Leadership, 32*(4), 362–383. https://doi.org/10.1177/10526846211001878

Diemer, M. A., & Li, C. (2011). Critical consciousness development and political participation among marginalized youth. *Child Development, 82*(6), 1815–1833.

Diemer, M. A., Rapa, L. J., Park, C. J., & Perry, J. C. (2017). Development and validation of the critical consciousness scale. *Youth & Society, 49*(4), 461–483.

Domitrovich, C. E., Harris, A. R., Syvertsen, A. K., Morgan, N., Jacobson, L., Cleveland, M., & Greenberg, M. T. (2022). Promoting social and emotional learning in middle school: Intervention effects of facing history and ourselves. *Journal of Youth and Adolescence, 51*(7), 1426–1441.

Dryfoos, J. (2002). Partnering full-service community schools: Creating new institutions. *Phi Delta Kappan, 83*(5), 393–399. https://doi.org/10.1177/003172170208300515

Durlak, J. A., Weissberg, R. P., Dymnicki, A. B., Taylor, R. D., & Schellinger, K. B. (2011). The impact of enhancing students' social and emotional learning: A meta-analysis of school-based universal interventions. *Child Development, 82*(1), 405–432. https://doi.org/10.1111/j.1467-8624.2010.01564.x.

Flanagan, C., & Levine, P. (2010). Civic engagement and the transition to adulthood. *The Future of Children, 20*(1), 159–179.

Flanagan, C. A., Syverstsen, A. K., & Stout, M. D. (2007). *Civic measurement models: Tapping adolescents' civic engagement.* Center for Information and Research on Civic Learning and Engagement.

Flanagan, T., Wong, G., & Kushnir, T. (2023). The minds of machines: Children's beliefs about the experiences, thoughts, and morals of familiar interactive technologies. *Developmental Psychology, 59*(6), 1017–1031. https://doi.org/10.1037/dev0001524

Fuentes, E. (2009). Learning power and building community: Parent-initiated participatory action research as a tool for organizing community. *Social Justice, 36*(4 (118)), 69–83.

Goddard, R. D., Hoy, W. K., & Hoy, A. W. (2004). Collective efficacy beliefs: theoretical developments, empirical evidence, and future directions. *Educational Researcher, 33*(3), 3–13. https://doi.org/10.3102/0013189X033003003

Greenberg, M. T. (2023). *Evidence for social and emotional learning in schools.* Learning Policy Institute. https://doi.org/10.54300/928.269

Hao, J., Cui, W., Kyllonen, P., Kerzabi, E., Liu, L., & Flor, M. (2024). Scaling up the evaluation of collaborative problem solving: Promises and challenges of coding chat data with ChatGPT. *arXiv preprint arXiv:2411.10246.* https://arxiv.org/pdf/2411.10246

Hao, J., Liu, L., Kyllonen, P., Flor, M., & von Davier, A. A. (2019). *Psychometric considerations and a general scoring strategy for assessments of collaborative problem solving* (Research Report No. RR-19-41). Educational Testing Service. https://doi.org/10.1002/ets2.12276

Hart, D., Matsuba, K., & Atkins, R. (2014). Civic engagement and child and adolescent well-being. In *Handbook of child well-being* (pp. 957–975). Springer.

Hawe, P., Shiell, A., Riley, T., & Gold, L. (2004). Methods for exploring implementation variation and local context within a cluster randomised community intervention trial. *Journal of Epidemiology and Community Health, 58*(9), 788–793. https://doi.org/10.1136/jech.2003.014415

Heberle, A. E., Rapa, L. J., & Farago, F. (2020). Critical consciousness in children and adolescents: A systematic review, critical assessment, and recommendations for future research. *Psychological Bulletin, 146*(6), 525–551. https://doi.org/10.1037/bul0000230

Healey, K., & Stroman, C. (2020). *Structures for belonging: A synthesis of research on belonging-supportive learning environments.* Student Experience Research Network. https://studentexperiencenetwork.org/research_library/structures-for-belonging-a-synthesis-of-research-on-belonging-supportive-learning-environments/

Institute for Citizens and Scholars. (2023). *Mapping civic measurement: How are we assessing readiness and opportunities for an engaged citizenry?* https://citizensandscholars.org/wp-content/uploads/2023/02/Citizens-Scholars-Mapping-Civic-Measurement-1.pdfcivic-learning/what-is-civic-learning/.

Jagers, R. J., Gilchrist, A. G., Skoog-Hoffman, A., & Jagers, J. P. (2024). At the intersections of moral education and social and emotional learning: Some reflections and directions for transformative social and emotional learning. In *Handbook of moral and character education* (pp. 148–164). Routledge.

Jagers, R. J., Rivas-Drake, D., & Williams, B. (2019). Transformative social and emotional learning (SEL): Toward SEL in service of educational equity and excellence. *Educational Psychologist, 54*(3), 162–184. https://doi.org/10.1080/00461520.2019.1623032

Jagers, R. J., Skoog-Hoffman, A., Barthelus, B., & Schlund, J. (2021). *Transformative social and emotional learning: In pursuit of educational equity and excellence*. American Educator. https://www.aft.org/ae/summer2021/jagers_skoog-hoffman_barthelus_schlund

Jennings, R. E., Lanaj, K., & Kim, Y. J. (2022). Self-Compassion at work: A self-regulation perspective on its beneficial effects for work performance and wellbeing. *Personnel Psychology, 31*(4), 665–699. https://doi.org/10.1111/peps.12504

Kelly, O. A., Skoog-Hoffman, A., & Jagers, R. J. (2023). *Collaborating with communities and caregivers: Conditions for building authentic partnerships*. Collaborative for Academic, Social, and Emotional Learning. https://library.belenetwork.org/wp-content/uploads/2023/07/EA-2-Learning-Brief_-4__.pdf

Learning Policy Institute. (2021). *How can states and districts use federal recovery funds strategically? Investing in community schools*. https://learningpolicyinstitute.org/product/federal-funds-cs-factsheet#:~:text=State%20Support%20for%20Community%20Schools,through%20regional%20technical%20assistance%20centers%20.

Lucero, J. E., Boursaw, B., Eder, M. M., Greene-Moton, E., Wallerstein, N., & Oetzel, J. G. (2020). Engage for equity: The role of trust and synergy in community-based participatory research. *Health Education & Behavior, 47*(3), 372–379. https://doi.org/10.1177/1090198120918838

Mapp, K. L., & Kuttner, P. J. (2013). Partners in education: A dual capacity-building framework for family–school partnerships parents. *Sedl*, 1–30. https://eric.ed.gov/?id=ED593896

Metzger, A., Alvis, L. M., Oosterhoff, B., Babskie, E., Syvertsen, A., & Wray-Lake, L. (2018). The intersection of emotional and sociocognitive competencies with civic engagement in middle childhood and adolescence. *Journal of Youth and Adolescence, 47*(8), 1663–1683. https://doi.org/10.1007/s10964-018-0842-5

Nagaoka, J., Farrington, C. A., Ehrlich, S. B., & Heath, R. D. (2015). *Foundations for young adult success: A developmental framework. Concept paper for research and practice*. University of Chicago Consortium on Chicago School Research. https://files.eric.ed.gov/fulltext/ED559970.pdf

National Center on Safe Supportive Learning Environments. (n.d.). *Social emotional learning*. https://safesupportivelearning.ed.gov/hot-topics/social-emotional-learning

Nwafor, E., Kelly, O., Skoog-Hoffman, A., & Kroshinsky, F. (2023). *Using student experience data to co-design learning environments*. Collaborative for Academic, Social, and Emotional Learning. https://library.belenetwork.org/wp-content/uploads/2023/02/BELE-Using-Student-Experience-Data-2.pdf

Oakes, J., Germain, E., & Maier, A. (2023). *Outcomes and indicators for community schools: A guide for implementers and evaluators*. Community schools forward project series. Learning Policy Institute. https://learningpolicyinstitute.org/project/community-schools-forward

Oetzel, J. G., Wallerstein, N., Duran, B., Sanchez-Youngman, S., Nguyen, T., Woo, K., Wang, J., Schulz, A., Keawe'aimoku Kaholokula, J., Israel, B., & Alegria, M. (2018). Impact of participatory health research: A test of the community-based participatory research conceptual model. *BioMed Research International, 2018*, 7281405. https://doi.org/10.1155/2018/7281405

Oosterhoff, B., Poppler, A., Hill, R. M., Fitzgerald, H., & Shook, N. J. (2021). Understanding the costs and benefits of politics among adolescents within a sociocultural context. *Infant and Child Development, 31*(2), e2280.

Osher, D., Jones, W., & Jagers, R. (2025). *Building supportive conditions and comprehensive supports to enhance student and educator well-being and thriving: National academy of education committee on addressing educational inequities in the wake of the COVID-19 pandemic*. National Academy of Education.

Ozer, E. J., Abraczinskas, M., Duarte, C., Mathur, R., Ballard, P. J., Gibbs, L., Olivas, E. T., Bewa, M. J., & Afifi, R. (2020). Youth participatory approaches and health equity: Conceptualization and integrative review. *American Journal of Community Psychology, 66*(3–4), 267–278.

Ozer, E. J., & Douglas, L. (2013). The impact of participatory research on urban teens: An experimental evaluation. *American Journal of Community Psychology, 51*, 66–75. https://doi.org/10.1007/s10464-012-9546-2

Ozer, E. J., Shapiro, V., & Duarte, C. (2021). Opportunities to strengthen SEL impact through youth-led participatory action research (YPAR). *Innovations for Youth (I4Y) Center*. https://prevention.psu.edu/wp-content/uploads/2022/09/PSU-Youth-Empowerment-Brief-REV.pdf

Park, N., & Peterson, C. (2006). Values in Action (VIA) inventory of character strengths for youth. *Adolescent & Family Health, 4*(1), 35–40.

PERTS. (2023a, June 21). *What are organizational conditions?* (Catalyze). About Catalyze. https://catalyzesupport.perts.net/support/solutions/articles/67000570152-what-are-organizational-conditions-catalyze

PERTS. (2023b, May 31). *Catalyze: Measures summary & changes*. https://docs.google.com/document/d/1Pklku6LyXlP6CqcpynzSiWpPixGtP32p45WvLOx8RLw/edit?tab=t.0

PERTS. (2024). *Elevate*. https://www.perts.net/elevate

Pittman, K., & Irby, M. (2024). *Too essential to fail: Why our big bet on public education needs a bold national response*. Education Reimagined. https://thebigidea.education-reimagined.org/wp-content/uploads/2024/02/Too-Essential-to-Fail-FINAL.pdf

Richards-Schuster, K., Wernick, L. J., Henderson, M., Bakko, M., Rodriguez, M. A., & Moore, E. (2021). Engaging youth voices to address racial disproportionality in schools: Exploring the practice and potential of youth participatory action research in an urban district. *Children and Youth Services Review, 122*. https://doi.org/10.1016/j.childyouth.2020.105715

Rivas-Drake, D., Umaña-Taylor, A. J., Schaefer, D. R., & Medina, M. (2017). Ethnic-racial identity and friendships in early adolescence. *Child Development, 88*(3), 710–724. https://doi.org/10.1111/cdev.12790

Sampson, R. J., Morenoff, J. D., & Raudenbush, S. (2005). Social anatomy of racial and ethnic disparities in violence. *American Journal of Public Health, 95*(2), 224–232.

Sellers, R. M., Rowley, S. A. J., Chavous, T. M., Shelton, J. N., & Smith, M. A. (1997). Multidimensional Inventory of Black Identity: A preliminary investigation of reliability and constuct validity. *Journal of Personality and Social Psychology, 73*(4), 805–815. https://doi.org/10.1037/0022-3514.73.4.805

Skoog-Hoffman, A., Miller, A. A., Plate, R. C., Meyers, D. C., Tucker, A. S., Meyers, G., ..., & Schlund, J. (2024). *Social and emotional learning in US schools: Findings from CASEL's nationwide policy scan and the American teacher panel and American school leader panel surveys* (Research Report No. RR-A1822-2). RAND Corporation. https://www.rand.org/content/dam/rand/pubs/research_reports/RRA1800/RRA1822-2/RAND_RRA1822-2.pdf

Syed, M., & Westberg, D. W. (2024). Building better models of racial/ethnic identity development: A commentary on Satterthwaite-Freiman and Umaña-Taylor. *Human Development, 68*(3), 139–146.

Syvertsen, A. K., Wray-Lake, L., & Metzger, A. (2015). *Youth civic and character measures toolkit*. Search Institute.

Tschannen-Moran, M., & Barr, M. (2004). Fostering student learning: The relationship of collective teacher efficacy and student achievement. *Leadership and Policy in Schools, 3*(3), 189–209. https://doi.org/10.1080/15700760490503706

Umaña-Taylor, A. J. (2024). Revisiting the conceptualization and measurement of ethnic-racial identity affect: Recommendations for future directions. *Child Development Perspectives, 18*(4), 215–220. https://doi.org/10.1111/cdep.12517

Wallerstein, N., Muhammad, M., Sanchez-Youngman, S., Rodriguez Espinosa, P., Avila, M., Baker, E. A., Barnett, S., Belone, L., Golub, M., Lucero, J., Mahdi, I., Noyes, E., Nguyen, T., Roubideaux, Y., Sigo, R., & Duran, B. (2019). Power dynamics in community-based participatory research: A multiple-case study analysis of partnering contexts, histories, and practices. *Health Education & Behavior: The Official Publication of the Society for Public Health Education, 46*(1_suppl), 19S–32S. https://doi.org/10.1177/1090198119852998

Watts, R. J., & Flanagan, C. (2007). Pushing the envelope on youth civic engagement: A developmental and liberation psychology perspective. *Journal of Community Psychology, 35*(6), 779–792. https://doi.org/10.1002/jcop.20178

Wilhelm, A.K., Pergament, S., Cavin, A., Bates, N., Hang, M., Ortega, L.E., ... Allen, M.L. (2021). Lessons Learned in Implementing Youth and Parent Participatory Action Research in a School-Based Intervention. *Progress in Community Health Partnerships: Research, Education, and Action, 15*(1), 15–36. https://dx.doi.org/10.1353/cpr.2021.0002.

Williams, B. V., Skoog-Hoffman, A., Jagers, R., & Barthelus, B. (2024). *Educator well-being as a pathway toward investing in education staff: Insights from the transformative SEL (TSEL) adult learning series pilot*. The BELE learning series. Collaborative for Academic, Social, and Emotional Learning. https://library.belenetwork.org/wp-content/uploads/2024/02/EA-2-Learning-Brief_5_CASEL.pdf

Yow, Y. J., Ramsay, J. E., Lin, P. K. F., & Marsh, N. V. (2022). Dimensions, measures, and contexts in psychological investigations of curiosity: a scoping review. *Behavioral Sciences, 12*(12), 493. https://doi.org/10.3390/bs12120493

Zimmerman, A. (2016). Transmedia testimonio: Examining undocumented youth's political activism in the digital age. *International Journal of Communication, 10*, 1886–1906.

16
CIRCLE's Civic Data Tool
Connecting Practitioners with Measures and Data for Impact

Abby Kiesa and Alberto Medina

Introduction

A wide range of stakeholders need access to measures and data of youth civic engagement that can inform their efforts and guide decision-making. Policymakers, community organizers, librarians, local leaders, political campaigns, concerned community members, and young people themselves all play a role in the diverse ecosystems that shape whether, and how, young people participate in U.S. democracy. Many of these individuals and organizations have limited capacity to collect and analyze data or to conduct rigorous formal evaluations. Therefore, the potential to derive insights from high-quality measures that can inform policies and programming goes largely unfulfilled and limits the ability of evaluation and measurement to serve those who could benefit from it the most.

For more than two decades, the Center for Information & Research on Civic Learning and Engagement (CIRCLE), part of Tufts University's Jonathan M. Tisch College of Civic Life, has endeavored to bridge that gap by providing accessible and digestible data on youth civic engagement. Our research has focused on a central question: what factors help or hinder young people's civic participation and are therefore levers of change that can be pulled to improve youth engagement in our communities and in our democracy? Our research output has been intentionally practitioner-facing, with the goal of empowering stakeholders and decision-makers with data that they may not otherwise be able to find or interpret.

Our scholarship on youth civic learning and engagement, and our partnerships with leaders and organizations in various youth-serving fields, have illuminated a series of complex answers to the question of what can shape youth civic engagement. Election laws, community support, historical inequities, socioeconomic conditions, educational opportunities, partisan politics, and more—all can influence, directly and indirectly, whether young people have the access and support they need for civic and political participation. These conclusions reaffirm the need to put accessible data in the hands of the stakeholders from these diverse fields, who have immense local and practical knowledge that can be combined with data to inform youth civic engagement efforts.

To that end, our organization created the Youth Voting and Civic Engagement in America (or the "CIRCLE Data Tool", for short) accessible at https://youthdata.circle.tufts.edu. The tool,

DOI: 10.4324/9781003476825-19
This chapter has been made available under a CC BY-NC-ND license.

which is primarily designed for non-academic audiences, provides measures and resulting data on more than 30 different conditions or outcomes related to young people's civic participation at multiple geographic levels. The tool allows and encourages users to look beyond individual indicators to understand how multiple factors may shape young people's civic opportunities and engagement. And it allows for easy use and sharing, so that the measures, data, and insights can be communicated with various audiences.

The CIRCLE data tool is a direct response to the needs of community leaders, educators, policymakers, and practitioners. For years, CIRCLE has regularly fielded inquiries from these and other non-researchers about the state of youth civic engagement and what might engage a broader group of young people. However, the impact of these responses was previously limited by our capacity and by the nature of the inquiries themselves. Leaders, organizations, and community members can only ask about what they already know, or at least suspect, is relevant to their work. These ad hoc inquiries preclude exploration and inquiry that can expand the breadth of stakeholders' knowledge of what is being or could be measured and limit their agency to explore new questions and find solutions.

This chapter describes the development, content, and use cases of the CIRCLE data tool: a project to expand the accessibility and field-level impact of youth civic engagement measures and data for non-researcher stakeholders. We describe the key steps and considerations involved in building a data tool that is based on high-quality measurement (often from federal datasets), addresses the above challenges, and serves the data needs of various fields. Driven by CIRCLE's foundational commitment to be a partner to practitioners and policymakers, including youth, we discuss the opportunities and challenges in building a research product that is user-friendly for people who don't regularly implement while still providing valuable and actionable information.

Background

Our work was guided by the literature on the use of research and evidence, as well as an understanding, informed by decades of research and partnerships, about the type of information needed to support building more civic learning and engagement opportunities for all young people:

- **Serving as a guide:** Being an information broker to those who don't have access to the information that we do and supporting an inquiry mindset among practitioners (Cooper et al., 2009; Earl & Katz, 2006; Shaxson & Bielak, 2012).
- **Context- and community-specific data:** What works to promote stronger and more equitable youth engagement varies widely for different youth, in different communities, with different social, political, economic, and civic contexts (Wray-Lake & Ballard, 2023).
- **A focus on structures and systems:** Young people's ability to participate in civic life is shaped by structures and systems, so interventions to increase participation must be oriented toward transforming those structures (United States Department of Education, 2022).
- **Centering inequality and marginalization:** Improving youth civic participation cannot mean merely increasing the overall total of youth who volunteer or vote. It must mean eliminating long-standing historical inequities by education, geography, socioeconomic status, and other factors—so data must explicitly surface those sources of inequality (Siegel-Stechler & Kawashima-Ginsberg, 2024).
- **An assets and challenges approach:** While it's easy to focus on the problems and inequities that plague communities and serve as barriers to engagement, there are also extraordinary civic assets in many communities that can serve as a source of strength and action in engaging youth (Nel, 2018; Perkins et al., 2004).

Our goal is to democratize access to measures, data, and analysis for various stakeholders. That data does not necessarily represent causality or directly lead to ironclad inferences. But it allows stakeholders to ask questions about the factors that potentially influence youth civic engagement outcomes and to consider how the data may connect with what they see and experience in their communities. That exploration can empower them to identify where action may be needed, potential levers for change, and how they can fit in. That reflects a core belief in the importance of local leaders, including youth themselves, as the people who are best positioned to make decisions about their own communities and address systemic barriers to youth engagement that are currently preventing us from having a fully representative electorate and an equitable multiracial democracy.

We also contend that the data exploration and awareness this tool allows and encourages can result in valuable forms of measurement which may not have occurred otherwise, and at the local level in diverse contexts. The conversations, data-driven decisions, and assessments enabled by our tool may not always meet the standards of highly rigorous evaluations, but they are often what is accessible, relevant, and necessary within the organizational limitations and contexts of youth civic engagement stakeholders.

Design

Like the data in the tool itself, the process behind its development also reflects some of the assets we relied on and the challenges we faced as an organization trying to create a tool for civic learning and exploration. By briefly detailing that process and key considerations, we hope to inform the efforts of researchers, educators, and other leaders who share our mission of filling and building capacity with data—whatever form those efforts might take.

The development of the CIRCLE Civic Data Tool was co-led by the authors, who combined their experience and expertise in the youth civic engagement field writ large and with communicating research to wide audiences of diverse stakeholders. We were deeply informed by countless inquiries and conversations with those stakeholders, over many years, that shaped our understanding of their data needs. We also drew on the deep knowledge of our full team, which brought both theoretical (e.g., what does the research literature say about the relationship between socioeconomic status and youth civic engagement?) and practical (e.g., which features would be useful for teachers wanting to use this tool in their classrooms?) expertise to bear on the project. Throughout the process, we shared data and design updates with team members and with key partners to receive feedback that helped refine the tool and keep us on the right track.

The tool's development was supported by university-level fundraising that allowed us to assign an adequate budget to the project and contract with a web development firm. During the firm selection process, we prioritized vendors with extensive experience in data visualizations and, especially, in creating user-friendly designs and functionality for non-researchers. The insights and recommendations from the web developers were invaluable and shaped the final product. The timeline and budget served as constraints but also opportunities to streamline and focus the tool so it would meet its goals.

The full data tool development team focused the process on these key questions:

1) Big picture: What do people want and need to know in order to support higher and more equitable youth participation in their communities and in democracy?
2) What structures and dynamics do we know, from our own research and from other existing scholarship, have an impact on youth civic engagement?
3) What specific data captures the above structures and dynamics and is publicly available and shareable at multiple geographical levels?
4) How can we structure and format the data to guide non-research users, encourage exploration, and inspire ideas for action?

Our team's experience with inquiries from various fields made it abundantly clear that multiple types of stakeholders were interested in and moved by data about youth civic engagement. In a given week, we might receive requests for data from a state legislator, a nonprofit leader, a college student, and a middle-school civics teacher. They were often interested in data specific to their state or their community, which they felt was most relevant to guiding action. But they also wanted to be able to see how their state or community compared to others.

If they were among the top states for youth voter turnout or creating volunteering opportunities for young people, they could assess which efforts or policies in their communities were potentially contributing to positive outcomes. That information can be valuable, for example, for a local leader working to secure support for scaling their activities. Conversely, if their community ranked poorly on a measure like youth voter turnout compared to others, stakeholders could make a research-informed case for more attention and resources or for policy changes.

This understanding drove our commitment to making data available at multiple geographical levels and allowing for comparisons—e.g., displaying a county's youth voter turnout compared to the entire state's youth turnout, or a map of volunteering rate by state. It also informed our commitment to provide data that could be wielded by a range of local actors and practitioners. For this diverse audience, we concluded that it was less important whether the data indicated statistically significant relationships that allowed for causal inference and more important that they could understand it and communicate it effectively to meet their needs and goals.

Our experience over time had also revealed that many stakeholders, including some young people themselves, made oversimplified and situational assessments based on a single data point or on what they perceived as young people's attitudes toward participation. They did not spend as much time on what our research revealed was far more influential: the settings and opportunity structures of support available (or not) to young people in different communities. This concern informed one of the main organizing and design principles of the tool: civic engagement outcomes on one "side", context and conditions that shape civic engagement on the other, and the ability to visualize multiple indicators on both "sides" in order to encourage drawing connections within and between both kinds of data.

Which Measures and Data Were Relevant and Available?

The list of factors that can shape youth civic participation is nearly endless and decision-making on what to include was challenging. Some previous decisions helped begin to narrow it down: the focus on data at various geographic levels, and specifically our interest in county-level data that would be most useful to local actors, narrowed our options considerably. The desire for ease of use, and the constraints of a design that was within our means, helped us limit the number of indicators and home in on those that would be understandable and accessible to a broad range of audiences.

We were primarily guided by a research-backed understanding of which factors and dynamics might support or serve as barriers to youth engagement and by our intersecting areas of long-standing expertise: youth civic development, K-12 civic education, and youth voting. But this also created a difficult conceptual and design question that has always bedeviled CIRCLE's work: how should we define "youth"?

Data on youth voting from sources like the Census, exit polls, and voter files often utilizes the 18–29 age group. The conditions that shape youth development certainly have an impact before young people reach voting age, and teens are already engaging in activities like helping neighbors and talking about politics. Data on K-12 civic education, like the National Assessment of Educational Progress, captured a younger age group but is not available at the

Congressional district or county level. Because sharing local data was a core element of the tool, we decided not to include data specifically on K-12 civics.

Ultimately, it proved impossible to use a single age group to capture the breadth of data that we felt was important to include. The tool would include data on youth of various age ranges—properly sourced and labeled—depending on what was available for any given indicator.

For data on youth civic engagement beyond elections, we looked to the Census Current Population Survey (CPS). Historically, the survey had focused on volunteering; after feedback from scholars and practitioners, that portion was expanded and combined with other instruments into a Civic Engagement and Volunteering Supplement that asks about a much wider range of civic engagement activities. These included actions that focus on whether community members interact and are in discussion with each other—which can be both a measure of engagement and a building block to other forms of participation. This data is collected every two years and was only available at the state and national level, not the county level. But it does include 16- and 17-year-olds, which allowed us to report on young people's civic development and engagement even before reaching voting age.

While the CPS also asks about registration and voting, CIRCLE regularly pays for access to a national aggregate voter file, which allows for more disaggregation and which we believe produces more accurate estimates of youth voter turnout. Unlike much of the other data in our tool, the source voter file data is not publicly available but is well-understood and valued in the field of voter engagement.

We had many difficult choices to make regarding which data to include about the conditions that shape youth civic engagement. Again, we went back to our key goals and principles. What factors has the research literature documented have an influence on more equitable youth development or engagement? What are stakeholders in various fields looking for, and what do they need to do their work? For example, we are often asked about the size of the youth electorate or of the youth population nationally or in a particular state. While that number by itself may not reveal much about youth civic participation, it is a key data point for the media and other stakeholders who want to highlight that young people are numerous and powerful in order to garner attention or resources for youth engagement.

The other key consideration was including domains that illuminated some of the major sources of inequity in individual or aggregate youth civic participation. These included educational experience (Campbell, 2009; Flanagan & Levine, 2010; Maskara, 2024; Mayer, 2011); socioeconomic inequalities that can shape access to civic learning and engagement opportunities (United States Department of Education, 2022; Rubin et al., 2021); and a political landscape that creates geographic inequity between states with more or less facilitative election laws (Booth, 2025; Siegel-Stechler & Kawashima-Ginsberg, 2024), and more or less competitive elections (Ainsworth et al., 2024; Divounguy et al., 2024; University of Florida Election Lab, 2023). The major challenge was narrowing it all down to a number of indicators that our team, including web developers, believed would be feasible and user-friendly given practical constraints (i.e., timeline and budget) as well as other data and design priorities.

Structure and Format

Two of the central design principles of this tool (context specific and widely accessible for action) played out in the structure of the tool. Since our primary audience was non-researchers, there was a desire to have a more guided experience with a tool based on our lessons from translating data, and away from a tool where a user needs to understand lots of jargon to figure out or requires a primer in how to produce the desired data. This goal and the budget shaped the amount of data in the tool.

The entry point to the tool emphasized the central design principle and message: that general context matters. Since the tool was being designed for those focused on specific geographies, that's where the user had to go next, by choosing a geographic level. After doing so, both sides (i.e., behavior data and conditions) are always present, emphasizing that point. Additional features helped with the translation and sense-making processes to ensure wider accessibility. Each data point has a "tooltip" (the tiny "i" next to each indicator) that can easily be rolled over for a definition. Additionally, when the desired geographic data was shown, there is always a comparison point to the national data to help users put their data into perspective.

Because we ultimately want this to be a tool for action, we also ensured that various features supported that goal. Each "view" of the data—meaning, any screen in which a specific combination of data points is displayed—has a unique URL so it can be embedded on a website or shared on social media. They can also be easily downloaded as images for use in presentations, educational materials, or funding proposals. Other features, like state-level summaries, are meant to help with synthesize data or serve as initial prompts for exploration. In additional materials that accompany the data tool, we provide concrete ideas for what stakeholder groups like educators, journalists, and community organizers can do with the tool.

Results: Measurement for Learning and Action

The CIRCLE Civic Data Tool includes 37 indicators that are related in some way to young people's civic engagement. (See Figure 16.1, which shows how users can select data.) Each of these data points is available for at least two of four different geographic levels: national, state, county, and Congressional district level.

Voting and Elections

Voting is not the only form of civic engagement or necessarily the most important. But it is a critical type of participation that is, in theory, accessible to all American citizens—and to non-citizens and those in their teens who can participate in elections in other ways, like volunteering and elevating conversations about key issues. There is local infrastructure for electoral engagement in every county in the United States, and it is connected to major outcomes for American democracy.

Elections are also major national events elicit extraordinary attention and in which youth can have meaningful impact. They can be an entry point to get a wide range of stakeholders thinking about young people, how elections operate, and how inclusive (or not) they are for young people. But not all of that attention is good: the focus on young voters, especially during times of rancorous partisan and political discussion, can lead to oversimplified narratives and misconceptions. For example, the fact that young people generally vote at lower rates than older adults is often taken a sign that youth are innately apathetic about politics. Those ideas can ignore and prevent action on the systemic challenges to youth electoral participation.

One reason why youth electoral participation garners such attention, both positive and negative, is because voting is measurable and easily understandable. Those measurements are imperfect; every data point on any population's youth voter turnout is ultimately an estimate. But the ability to produce such estimates at various geographical levels and for various subgroups makes them valuable for highlighting which young people, and where, may be neglected or underserved by the structures that are supposed to be supporting their participation.

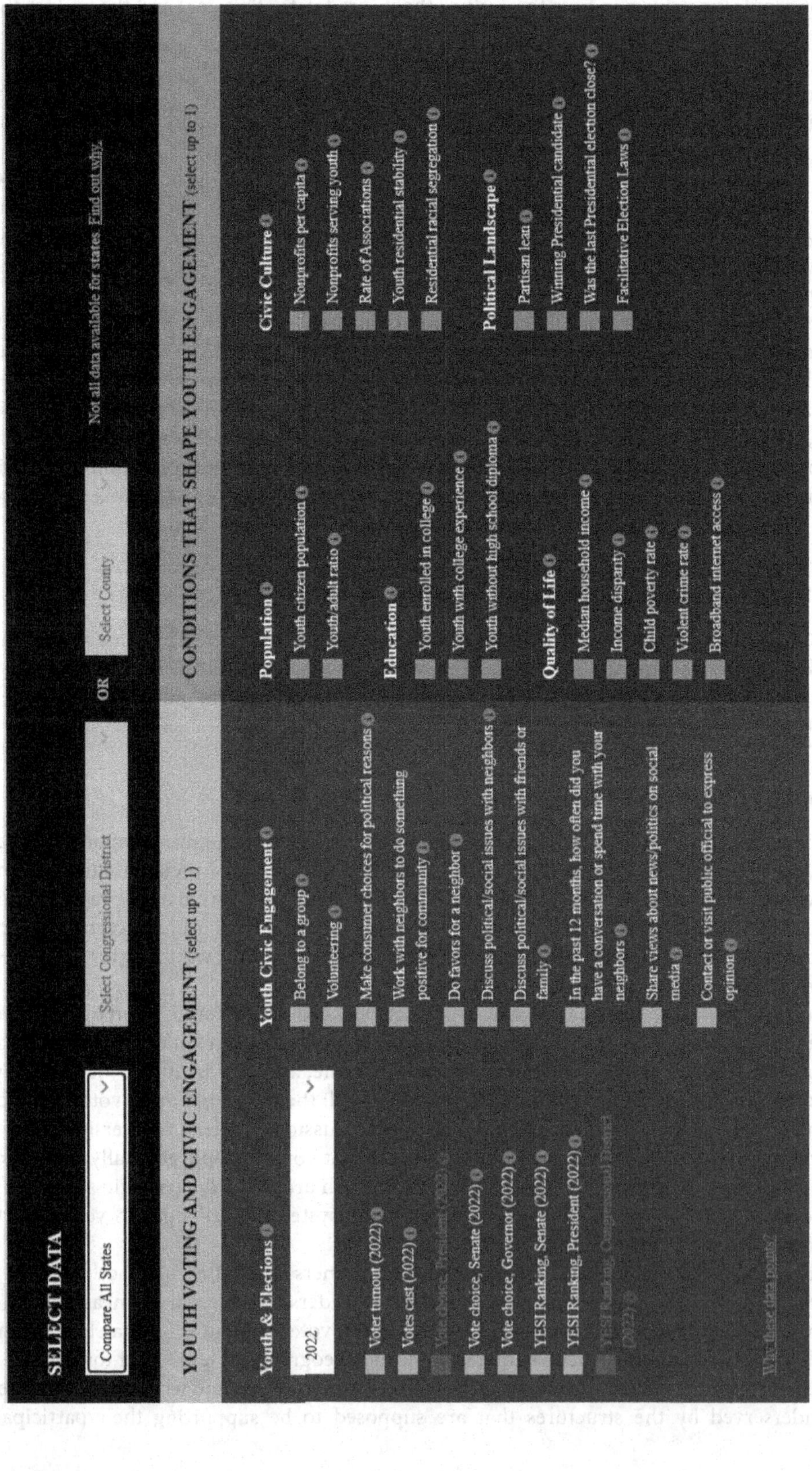

Figure 16.1 Screen Capture of the Main Data Selection Screen in the CIRCLE Data Tool.

Those inequities, both between different groups of youth and between youth and older adults, have a massive impact on the representativeness of our democracy. They must be tracked, understood, and addressed.

The CIRCLE Civic Data Tool includes estimates for youth voter turnout and an estimated count of youth votes cast for four different federal election cycles (2016–2022). The inclusion of both turnout (the percentage of youth eligible to vote who cast ballots) and of total votes cast is intentional, given the extraordinary difference in population size between states. For example, in 2020, "only" 110,000 young people voted in Maine—but the state had one the highest turnout rates in the country: 61%. In Texas, just 41% of youth voted—well below the national rate of 50%. But that still meant nearly 1.8 million young Texans cast ballots, which provides a different sense of the scale of the youth vote and the significant role young people are playing in elections and democracy.

We also include young people's vote choice preference, by party, in the presidential, Senate, and/or governor races in any given election cycle. While CIRCLE is a nonpartisan research center that is primarily concerned with whether young people vote, not who they vote for, we know that many organizations and stakeholders approach the issue of youth electoral participation from a partisan lens and with particular electoral goals. The inclusion of these data points highlights the power of young people to shape election results. We also include ratings, including at the Congressional district level, from CIRCLE's Youth Electoral Significance Index, another tool which estimates the likelihood that young adults will affect the outcomes of elections.

Other Forms of Civic Engagement

Election data alone does not tell a full and holistic story about youth civic engagement; there are many other valuable ways for young people to contribute to their communities and to our democracy. As a result, the data tool also includes biennial Census data on ten different indicators of non-voting forms of civic engagement like volunteering, working with neighbors, and discussing political issues.

These are other important manifestations of engagement in civic life, of healthy civic development for young people, and of thriving communities. Those forms of action, which range from group membership to sharing news, are both other outcomes that are shaped by the socioeconomic and community conditions discussed in the next section, as well as "conditions" themselves that are often associated with whether young people vote. These indicators also speak to the collective "readiness" of youth to participate in communities and in democracy, and to whether the existing culture in a community is conducive to youth participation. For example, being a part of discussions about various community or neighborhood issues with family or neighbors can build awareness/knowledge and further motivation to engage in political action.

The data in this section comes from the Census CPS Civic Engagement and Volunteering Supplement. The CPS is a massive rigorous survey designed to provide information at the national and state levels about all people living in the United States. This supplement of the Survey is published every two years and has a respondent sample of over 40,000 in each iteration. At the time of writing, CIRCLE's data tool includes the 2021 data from this supplement.

The theoretical framework for this data collection is based on a definition of civic engagement used by AmeriCorps, the independent U.S. agency that enrolls millions of young Americans in volunteering opportunities. That definition reads, "the constellation of activities individuals engage in to make a difference in their communities and promote the common good" (AmeriCorps & US Census Bureau, 2024, p. 2). This framework includes forms of civic engagement and questions from two separate supplements on volunteering and civic engagement that were reviewed by scholars and combined starting in 2017 (AmeriCorps & US Census Bureau, 2024; Habermann et al., 2014).

Some of the data points in this section are more directly political or action-oriented; for example, making consumer choices for political reasons (e.g., boycotts) or contacting public officials to express their opinion. These highlight the other forms of valuable civic participation that millions of young people in the country are engaged in—in Oregon, a full third of young people say they have made politically influenced consumer decisions. Others speak to the ways in which young people develop civic competencies like understanding information and talking about issues; experience and contribute to community belonging; or take action to directly support communities beyond the ballot box.

When visualized and considered together, these data points can illuminate valuable insights about youth civic engagement and underscore potential connections that can be leveraged for action. Young people in Oregon do not just express themselves politically through their consumer choices: the state also had one of the top-five youth voter turnout rates in the country in 2018, 2020, and 2022. The five states where young people are least likely to talk politics with their friends and family are Oklahoma, Alabama, West Virginia, New Mexico, and South Carolina. All have been in the bottom half of states with the highest youth voter turnout in recent election cycles; in 2020, West Virginia, New Mexico, and Oklahoma were among the bottom five. These data points may not represent direct causality, but they can highlight the interconnectedness of different forms of civic action, all of which happen within a community context in which different factors may influence each other. They also represent potential entry points to strengthening youth civic engagement for different types of stakeholders.

Context and Conditions that Shape Youth Engagement

The other "half" of the tool is dedicated to various factors that, according to extant scholarship and our own research over the past two-plus decades, affect young people's civic development and whether they can participate in their communities and our democracy. In total, there are 19 indicators broadly categorized as providing information about a state or county's population, educational attainment, quality of life, civic culture, and political landscape. Except where specifically noted, much of this data is about communities as a whole, not just about youth. That is intentional: the conditions and dynamics that make up a community's civic ecosystem and culture affect people of all ages, including the adults who are therefore more or less able to support youth engagement efforts.

The data in this section promotes discovering and understanding potential associations between various conditions and youth civic engagement. In some cases, that association may be bidirectional; for example, research has found a positive association between voting and population-level health outcomes (Kelly et al., 2021). In addition to highlighting the interconnectedness of civic participation with a range of socioeconomic and community-level factors, these links can also prompt interest and action from additional stakeholders (e.g., public health professionals) who might not otherwise pay attention to youth civic engagement.

We briefly describe each type of data and its connection to youth civic engagement below:

> **Population:** At a very basic level, the more young people there are in a given community, the more youth need information about elections and support for participation; the more youth can come together to build political homes and take political action; and the more they can impact major outcomes like election results.

We also include the youth/adult ratio in a community, which can also point to the potential for electoral impact. In most places in the country, young people vote differently than older adults, so where they make up a higher share of the electorate their impact can be magnified. At the same time, the youth/adult ratio can point to potential challenges. In communities where young people make up a relatively small percentage of the population, they may be more "invisible" and be neglected by organizations and efforts that don't take them into account. Where there are many young people to serve in proportion to the number of older adults who can serve and support them, organizations may be stretched thin and youth may end up underserved.

> **Educational attainment:** Educational attainment has historically been one of the biggest drivers of inequality in youth voting and civic engagement. In 2020, for example, we estimated that the national voter turnout of young people with at least a bachelor's degree was 75%. Among youth whose highest level of education was a high school diploma, turnout was 39%; among youth who didn't finish high school it was an even lower 24% (Maskara, 2024).

There are multiple reasons for this strong association. Educational attainment is often a proxy for socioeconomic status, which is itself linked to inequities in civic participation. Colleges and universities also serve as institutions where civic learning takes place both in and out of the classroom, allowing youth to continue developing the knowledge, skills, and efficacy they need to vote and otherwise engage in their communities (Campbell, 2009; Flanagan & Levine, 2010; Mayer, 2011). Higher education institutions can additionally serve as political homes where young people connect with others to make sense of politics and take civic action together.

The data in this section can have major implications for stakeholders trying to reach and support young people. Electoral outreach and engagement efforts, especially, tend to focus on college campuses—that strategy will likely be ineffective in places where relatively few youth are enrolled in schools. In communities with a high rate of young people without a high school diploma, there may be deeper challenges to youth participation that must be addressed, and that are partly explored in the following sections.

> **Quality of life:** Research has long shown a connection between the daily struggles and challenges people face, resources available in a community, and civic engagement. We consider this to be quality of life, and the CIRCLE team initially used this construct in the development of our RAYSE Index (Center for Information & Research on Civic Learning and Engagement (CIRCLE), 2017), another CIRCLE tool that gives stakeholders the opportunity to examine civic assets and engagement at the county level. These assets include well-funded schools that can provide effective and equitable civic education; time to participate in extracurricular or volunteer activities that build community connections and foster civic development; access to digital infrastructure for news and information about civic issues; transportation to the polls on Election Day, among others. These were all included in the quality of life index developed for our RAYSE tool, and they are directly or indirectly considered here.

Inequality (especially in income) is linked to lower participation of some forms of civic action (Gaby, 2017). Among other things, it harms a sense of community connection and social cohesion, which can be associated with civic engagement (Collins & Guidry, 2018; Yang & Konrath, 2023). Notably, research has shown that income inequality is related to lower voting rates at both the highest and lowest extremes of the income scale—though for different reasons (Anderson & Beramendi, 2008). By including median household income, childhood poverty rate, and income inequality in our tool, we allow stakeholders to explore where these and other issues may be contextual contributors to lower participation.

There has also been scholarship on crime and safety in relation to civic engagement (Collins & Guidry, 2018). Particularly, research on urban youth of color has found that safety concerns can cause some young people to have differing responses: some retreat from community and others take action (Wray-Lake & Abrams, 2020). Finally, we include data on broadband access, which CIRCLE research has shown is a key element of civic infrastructure and of a strong media ecosystem that supports participation.

Civic culture: The presence of social associations and nonprofit organizations in a community—particularly those that explicitly serve youth—can help create a strong culture that promotes civic participation and serve as a support system for young people who want to engage in democracy (Sintos et al., 2024). Nonprofits and other community organizations can provide information, resources, and direct support to their members; think of a local group that organizes an advocacy day, has voter registration forms available, or holds educational sessions about ballot initiatives. As with higher education institutions, they can also serve as political homes for learning, connection, and action and in fact are especially valuable for young people who did not attend college. Sintos et al. find that participation in civil society organizations can reduce a community's income inequality.

Nonprofits and social associations, while relevant to all youth, appear to be especially valuable to some youth of color. A CIRCLE analysis focused on youth of color showed that young Black men were more likely to be contacted by community organizations than by any political party in the last month before the 2020 election (Lam & Suzuki, 2022). It also showed that youth of color who were contacted by community organizations were more likely to pay attention to local and statewide elections, and more likely to be civically engaged than those who were not contacted. According to Jimenez et al. (2024), groups and nonprofits may also support youth of color in an additional way: by creating spaces for the emotional and relational labor that young people of color need to develop their voice.

The transience of a community also affects its civic culture and, in turn, its civic participation (Schoppa, 2013). The effect of residential stability on voter turnout is well-known. It can take time for newcomers to a state or community to learn about local issues and politics, build connections, find a support system for participation, and potentially reregister to vote (Vallbé & Ferran, 2017). The fact that young people are much more likely to move than older adults, and therefore are more susceptible to these barriers, is often cited as one of the primary reasons for their lower rates of voter turnout.

Less discussed, but also critical, is the level of residential racial segregation, which we include in the CIRCLE Civic Data Tool by using a measure from the Robert Wood Johnson Foundation. Studies have highlighted that residential racial segregation is one of the main drivers of racial inequality in the United States; of particular interest, Schwartz et al. (2022) find particularly negative impacts on long-term outcomes for Black young adults.

Political Landscape

The final set of data highlights the partisan political landscape and electoral laws at the state level. We include data on election results and a state's electoral competitiveness as measured by the Cook Political Report. CIRCLE's research in recent election cycles has found that, on aggregate, youth voter turnout is higher in battleground states than in those that are less electorally competitive. There is often much more electoral information, outreach, and resources devoted to engaging voters in communities with highly contested races, and the ability to cast a potentially decisive vote can serve as a major motivating factor.

Figure 16.2 Screen Capture of the CIRCLE Data Tool Displaying a Choropleth Map of State-by-State Facilitative Election Law Scores.

Election laws and policies can make it easier or harder to register to vote and to cast a ballot, and many of these policies are especially influential on youth participation. Pre-registration at age 16, for example, allows young people to sign up to be registered, often while in high school, and have their registration be automatically activated when they turn 18. Same-day registration can ensure that missing a registration deadline weeks before Election Day is not a barrier that prevents youth from participating. See Figure 16.2 for an example of how the tool helps users visualize where many such policies are in place.

CIRCLE research has long focused on how these and other policies affect youth participation. The effect of the individual impact of each policy is not always straightforward—for example, they may increase the voter registration rate of white youth but not youth of color, or improve voter registration rates but not voter turnout.

To illustrate that dynamic, we calculate and include in the data tool a Facilitative Election Law Score that takes into account whether a state has four laws that help participation (Automatic Voter Registration, Same-Day Voter Registration, Pre-Registration at Age 16, and Online Voter Registration) and one that may help hinder it: voter ID laws. This data is drawn from a policy scan periodically conducted by our team by consulting the laws in each state. The score goes from 0 to 10; a higher number means it's easier to vote in a given state. In the 2022 midterm election, the five states with the highest youth voter turnout had an average Facilitative Election Score of 6.6. The five states with the lowest youth turnout had an average score of 2.6.

The data on facilitative election laws underscores how the CIRCLE Civic Data Tool can be a tool for critical education. By focusing on the policies, socioeconomic conditions, settings, and opportunity structures that support or serve as barriers to youth voting, we can begin to challenge myths about young people's relatively lower voting rates being solely due to their behavior or to apathetic attitudes. It also gives multiple stakeholders new questions to investigate with the goal of improving youth civic participation. State legislators can start to glean information about how voting laws may be connected to youth voter turnout in their community and how that compares to others. Community foundations can explore the potential role of critical infrastructure like broadband or youth-serving nonprofits. Political campaigns or voter registration organizations can examine potential opportunities to reach youth by tapping into existing strengths in a community or identify potential challenges to their strategies.

In the next section, we detail some examples of how various stakeholders can engage with the tool to inform their efforts.

Discussion: Using the Measures and Data

According to website analytics data, the CIRCLE Civic Data Tool is being widely used by a broad range of stakeholders. Since the start of 2023 until the time of writing (July 2025), more than 6,000 users have visited the site and triggered more than 40,000 "events": instances in which users are viewing data based on their selections. This average of more than six events per visitor demonstrates that, as intended, many users are exploring multiple layers of data rather than honing in on a single indicator.

In addition to this above data, messages and inquiries from educators, organizational leaders, and community members who are using the tool in these and other ways have allowed us to develop use cases that highlight the CIRCLE Civic Data Tool's utility for diverse stakeholders and purposes. We present several examples below.

Building a Local Political Home

Many local organizations need data about their communities to make decisions and set goals, as well as to describe the need for their work to funders and other external stakeholders. These groups sometimes do not have research teams or evaluation capacity; their ability to know where to look for data is mixed. But by homing in on their county in our tool, they can have more than 30 data indicators about their local community at their fingertips.

The CIRCLE data allows local leaders and organizers to build a profile of their community: what are its civic strengths, challenges, and needs? Which parts of its civic engagement or youth-serving ecosystem are different organizations well-situated to improve? Community leaders can use their own deep knowledge and understanding of their community to drive their inquiries and to draw additional insights and conclusions from the data. At the same time, the data can serve as another type of evidence of what they have observed about their communities. Organizational leaders often tell us that having such data is key, especially when making the case to external stakeholders for more attention or resources.

The breadth of data available can be especially helpful to organizations that want to go beyond episodic engagement and want to become political homes for young people. CIRCLE defines political homes as spaces, physical or digital, where young people can learn about issues in their communities, discuss and process what they learn, take action with others, and enjoy support for their civic participation. Those spaces are harder to build in the face of residential instability or segregation, crime and income inequality, or lack of broadband access to communicate and coordinate. Understanding how these factors may be serving as barriers to organizing and belonging is essential.

Focusing Resources and Fine-Tuning Strategies Across a State

Statewide and even national organizations can also use the CIRCLE Civic Data Tool to understand regional differences and to use different tactics or strategies accordingly.

Take, for example, a voter registration and education organization in New Mexico that is primarily focused on digital outreach and on reaching youth in college campuses. That may work in Los Alamos County, where 37% of youth are enrolled in college (3 percentage points above the state's average) and 92% of residents have fixed or mobile broadband internet access (14 points above the state's average). But it may be less effective in San Juan County, where 24% of youth are enrolled in college (10 percentage points below the state's average) and 66% of residents have broadband access (13 points below the state's average). See Figure 16.3 for an example of how users can see all of that data at a glance.

A statewide organization in Missouri may be seeking to partner with local groups and nonprofits on a series of educational and advocacy events to engage young people. That may be a promising strategy in Jackson County, which has a nonprofit per capita rate (15.6/10 k) well above the state and national average, and an above-average percentage of them serve youth. But in St. Charles County, where the rate of nonprofits and social associations per capita is well below-average, other efforts may be better at reaching young people.

Notably, despite having an above-average percentage of youth enrolled in college and a very high median household income, St. Charles County's youth voter turnout in 2020 was 32%, which was well below Missouri's turnout rate of 46% and the national rate of 50%. That defies the usual association between socioeconomic status and youth voter turnout and may prompt stakeholders to explore, through the tool and through conversations in their community, which other conditions could be influencing below-average participation. Being able to

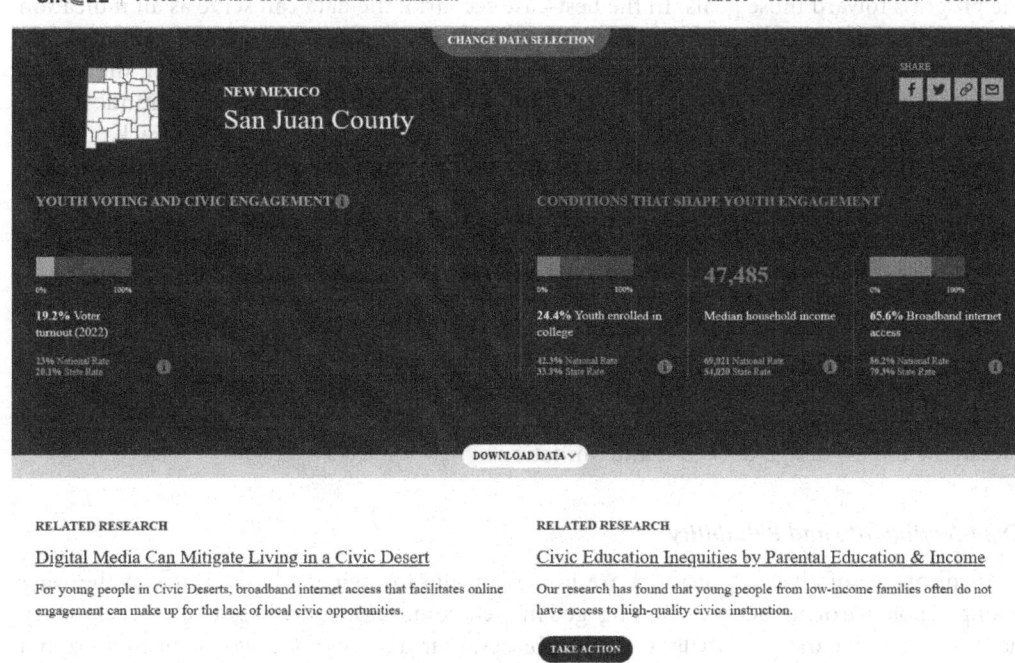

Figure 16.3 Screen Capture of the CIRCLE Data Tool Displaying User-selected Data Points for San Juan County, New Mexico.

see multiple data points on a single screen, and to share it with others with a single click, can reveal issues and dynamics that could otherwise bewilder practitioners who are focused on a single variable of explanation for low or high youth engagement.

Benchmarking and Storytelling

When used in combination with local information and experiences, the data tool is also useful for setting goals, tracking progress, and telling stories about what may be working to improve youth civic engagement—and what remains to be done.

The "Compare all data" functionality, which displays a shaded map of the United States with the statewide data for any single data point, can be a powerful visualization of some of the country's biggest problems—and of which places are struggling most. We have had, for example, state legislators and other policymakers from some of the states with the lowest youth voter turnout tell us they were surprised, disappointed, and moved to take action by seeing their state shaded the lightest color on the map or at the very bottom of the table.

That ability to easily compare any state-level data point to the national rate or average, and county-level data points to state and national data, can also help leaders and organizations set medium- to long-term goals. It may not be reasonable, in the short term, to aspire for a county with severe socioeconomic and structural challenges to have one of the highest voter turnout rates in the country. But community leaders can aim to bring it in line with the rest of state, or at least with other counties in the state that face similar challenges but manage to have higher participation. This data can serve as an organizational tool to craft goals that are both aspirational and attainable. Additional research that specifically evaluates interventions within the community's context can then help illuminate whether efforts toward meeting those goals are being effective.

Finally, the ability to track youth voting data over multiple election cycles can help evaluate the progress toward those goals. In the best-case scenario, the data can serve as an indication of what's worked and therefore validate strategies and efforts. Alternatively, in communities or states where youth civic engagement doesn't appear to be showing improvement, the data is an invitation to go back to the drawing board and try other strategies. As we continue to add data to the tool for the most recent and subsequent election cycles, the ability to track progress and identify trends (beyond just a couple of presidential or midterm election cycles) will only increase.

Challenges, Limitations, and Future Work

We acknowledge various challenges and limitations of the CIRCLE Civic Data Tool, due to both the nature of the data and to various practical considerations, which we share as areas for continued improvement and future work in various fields. These limitations fit into three categories which sometimes overlap: (1) data availability reliability; (2) framework and interpretation; and (3) design decisions and limitations.

Data Availability and Reliability

Most measures of civic engagement are imperfect due to their methods. Data on the ways young people are or are not civically engaged in their communities are based on surveys, which have both known and potentially unknown biases. Our data on youth voter turnout are not based on self-reported voting in surveys; they are instead calculated using aggregated voter file data and Census population data. But they remain estimates, and they are not reliably available for every state. Our tool includes youth voting estimates for 40 states; our analyses have determined that, in the remaining states, the data by age is too incomplete to allow for accurate estimates.

As stated earlier, not all data included in the tool is available at every geographic level of interest. Most notably, the current iteration of the data tool does not include data on non-voting forms of youth civic engagement by county, and it includes very little data by Congressional district—which we were further limited in adding by the post-2020 Census redistricting. There are other availability limitations due to sample size and other issues with the data. For example, data on all ten indicators of non-voting forms of civic engagement are available for California, but only six are available for West Virginia. Users may wish to take that into account when exploring the data and the strength of conclusions they might reach based on more or fewer data points. We also chose to omit data when the county-level sample of young people was deemed too small for reliable calculations.

We also acknowledge that, even within a county, there can be significant differences by town, by school district, and by even smaller communities that profoundly shape young people's civic learning, development, and participation. However, it would have been impossible or impractical to share data at those more granular levels.

Most of the data in the tool comes from external sources which only produce or share it annually, biennially, or create multi-year estimates. That means the data is often a snapshot in time from a recent year in which relatively new data was available, which we specify in the tooltips and source documentation. But it does mean that what people find as they explore the tool may not always represent the conditions on the ground as they are experiencing them today—another reason why using the tool with local knowledge is critical.

Finally, we recognize that some data challenges will arise and evolve with time. We already faced one such challenge after Congressional redistricting following the 2020 Census. Because our election data allows users to explore some election data by Congressional district for years before and after redistricting, we were forced to partially rework the tool so it could accommodate both sets of data. In addition, as new data sources become available and others are potentially eliminated, we expect to frequently reevaluate the best data to include. The desire for constant updates with the most relevant data that can serve the needs of our audience is in tension with some of the practical limitations of changing and maintaining the tool.

Framework and Interpretation

The data included in the tool is not meant to, and could not possibly, be exhaustive of all the ways young people can engage in civic life or the factors that influence engagement. As detailed in the earlier section about our process, we made choices guided by our team's extensive knowledge and experience of youth civic engagement. That means, even as we seek to challenge common assumptions about young people's civic participation, we have made our own judgments about what matters most. Those judgments are also informed by our interpretation of the decades-long work of many scholars in the field, but many of the dynamics we seek to highlight remain poorly understood and largely unaddressed in the literature.

We also acknowledge that data, even when presented thoughtfully, can sometimes be a blunt tool for understanding the nuanced experiences of individuals and communities. Our tool should not be a substitute for seeking local knowledge and understanding by engaging directly with residents—and especially with young people themselves—in any given community. Moreover, while we were guided by relevant scholarship when deciding which indicators to include, we do not claim that there are straightforward causal relationships between any or all the community conditions in the tool and youth civic engagement outcomes like voting in every community. These are highly complex and often changing dynamics that merit more national research and local, context-specific investigation.

Design Decisions and Limitations

Other challenges stem from the design of the tool and from practical limitations on our team's resources and capacity.

The tool does not include data by race, gender, or other dimensions of diversity within youth. We know that these dimensions are often some of the biggest drivers of inequality among young people and in our democracy, and we explore them at length throughout the rest of CIRCLE's work. But in addition to issues with data availability and soundness for various subgroups of youth below the national level, we were concerned that adding such data would have introduced additional layers of complexity that would have negatively impacted the tool's design usability. We continue to explore ways to add such data while mitigating those negative impacts in the future and by adding links to that data when on the CIRCLE site.

Design and usability also shaped our decision to cap the number of data points a user could select and visualize at one time. This facilitates some forms of exploration and analysis, but we acknowledge that it also forces users who may want to look at many different combinations of data points to continuously reselect them. Similarly, comparing states in a map or table is currently capped at one data point at a time, and it is not possible to directly compare counties within a state in a single view. We will consider adding these and other features in the future.

Conclusion and Takeaways: The Challenge Ahead

The CIRCLE Civic Data Tool is one of the few sources of data on young people's civic engagement that explicitly combines outcomes with a diverse set of systemic and structural conditions that shape youth participation. It empowers practitioners working directly with young people and other stakeholders to wield data as a tool for impact, so that their efforts are informed by accurate and actionable measurements. It encourages them to explore how they are best positioned to take action supporting the work of improving youth engagement in democracy.

The tool is also a call for researchers producing measurements, data, and evaluation tools related to youth civic engagement to consider the public accessibility and impact of their work. It is one example of how to center usability and self-guided data exploration that centers what users may consider most relevant to their own civic learning or engagement initiatives. Our own takeaways and reflections from the data tool, and from the many hours spent working on it, underscore the importance of that mission. The data tool is massive (tens of thousands of individual data points) because the efforts needed to transform how we grow voters and educate young people for civic participation are just as enormous. It is an ambitious project to put that amount of data in the hands of practitioners and other non-researchers. The result is sometimes complicated and messy, as is the work to strengthen democracy.

The old saying that all politics is local also applies to the work of preparing young people for political and other forms of civic engagement. Any given national Election Day in the United States is really thousands of elections happening across the country. They have different laws that shape how and when young people can participate, and they occur in vastly different political contexts that shape whether youth feel their vote matters. They are conducted by election administrators in more than 3,000 counties, and voting may require driving miles to go register to vote or to pick up a form or ballot in a P.O. Box or walking to cast a ballot in a neighborhood that residents may not feel is safe. And the young people who we hope participate will have learned about elections and politics—or not—in one of over 12,000 school districts in the country, which may have more or fewer resources to provide equitable civic learning opportunities and to educate them for democracy.

With that scale and diversity comes extraordinary inequality. Youth voter turnout in the 2022 midterm elections ranged from 36% in Michigan to 13% in Tennessee. Seventy-seven percent of young people are having conversations and spending time with neighbors in Delaware, and only 38% in New Mexico. The child poverty rate is 8% in Utah and 26% in Mississippi.

Our data tool captures the enormous challenges and complexity of those dynamics and inequities. We hope that it serves as a call to collaboration and action, so that we may build together a more representative electorate and a robust and equitable American democracy in our increasingly multiracial society.

References

Ainsworth, R., Munoz, E. G., & Gomez, A. M. (2024). District competitiveness increases voter turnout: Evidence from repeated redistricting in North Carolina. *Quarterly Journal of Political Science, 19*(4), 387–432. http://dx.doi.org/10.1561/100.00022114

AmeriCorps & US Census Bureau. (2024). *Current population survey civic engagement and volunteering supplement frequently asked questions.* https://americorps.gov/sites/default/files/document/CEV_FAQs_11012024_508_final.pdf

Anderson, C. J., & Beramendi, P. (2008). Income, inequality, and electoral participation. Anderson, C.J. and Beramendi, P. *Democracy, inequality, and representation.* (pp. 278–311).

Booth, R. B. (2025). *Race and rurality shape the impact of facilitative election laws.* Center for Information and Research on Civic Learning and Engagement at Tufts University. https://circle.tufts.edu/latest-research/race-and-rurality-shape-impact-facilitative-election-laws

Campbell, D. E. (2009). Civic engagement and education: An empirical test of the sorting model. *American Journal of Political Science, 53*(4), 771–786. https://doi.org/10.1111/j.1540-5907.2009.00400.x

Center for Information & Research on Civic Learning and Engagement (CIRCLE). (2017). *The RAYSE index: Detailed sources and methodology.* https://circle.tufts.edu/sites/default/files/2020-01/rayse_index_sources_methodology.pdf

Collins, C. R., & Guidry, S. (2018). What effect does inequality have on residents' sense of safety? Exploring the mediating processes of social capital and civic engagement. *Journal of Urban Affairs, 40*(7), 1009–1026. https://doi.org/10.1080/07352166.2018.1439338

Cooper, A., Levin, B., & Campbell, C. (2009). The growing (but still limited) importance of evidence in education policy and practice. *Journal of Educational Change, 10*(2), 159–171. https://doi.org/10.1007/s10833-009-9107-0

Divounguy, O., Josko, J., & Schuster, A. *Competitive elections raise voter participation, uncontested elections hinder democracy.* Illinois Policy. https://www.illinoispolicy.org/reports/competitive-elections-raise-voter-participation-uncontested-elections-hinder-democracy/. Accessed 1 July 2025.

Earl, L. M., & Katz, S. (2006). *Leading schools in a data-rich world.* Corwin Press.

Flanagan, C., & Levine, P. (2010). Civic engagement and the transition to adulthood. *The Future of Children, 20*(1), 159–179. http://www.jstor.org/stable/27795064

Gaby, S. (2017). The civic engagement gap(s): Youth participation and inequality from 1976 to 2009. *Youth & Society, 49*(7), 923–946. https://doi.org/10.1177/0044118X16678155

Habermann, H., Mackie, C. D., & Prewitt, K. (Eds.). (2014). *Civic engagement and social cohesion: Measuring dimensions of social capital to inform policy.* National Academies Press.

Jimenez, C., Schofield Clark, L., & Ramirez, J. (2024). "We know about things too": Exploring the labors of love involved in cultivating youth voice in online youth civic engagement programs with youth of color. *Youth & Society, 56*(4), 734–753. https://doi.org/10.1177/0044118X231207973

Kelly, G., Pennington, J., Segev, Y., Brokamp, C., Jones, M. N., Camara, S., Henize, A. W., Kahn, R. S., & Beck, A. F. (2021). Voter participation is associated with child health outcomes at the population level. *The Journal of Pediatrics, 235,* 277–280. https://doi.org/10.1016/j.jpeds.2021.04.027

Lam, M., & Suzuki, S. (2022). *Outreach from community organizations is key to engaging youth of color.* Center for Information and Research on Civic Learning and Engagement at Tufts University. https://circle.tufts.edu/latest-research/outreach-community-organizations-key-engaging-youth-color

Maskara, S. (2024). *Non-college youth need information and opportunities to engage in civic life.* Center for Information and Research on Civic Learning and Engagement at Tufts University. https://circle.tufts.edu/latest-research/non-college-youth-need-information-and-opportunities-engage-civic-life

Mayer, A. (2011). Does education increase political participation? *The Journal of Politics, 73,* 633–645. https://doi.org/10.1017/S002238161100034X

Nel, H. (2018). A comparison between the asset-oriented and needs-based community development approaches in terms of systems changes. *Practice, 30*(1), 33–52. https://doi.org/10.1080/09503153.2017.1360474

Perkins, D. D., Crim, B., Silberman, P., & Brown, B. B. (2004). Community development as a response to community-level adversity: Ecological theory and research and strengths-based policy. In K. I. Maton, C. J. Schellenbach, B. J. Leadbeater, & A. L. Solarz (Eds.), *Investing in children, youth, families, and communities: Strengths-based research and policy* (pp. 321–340). American Psychological Association. https://doi.org/10.1037/10660-018

Rubin, B. C., El-Haj, T. R. A., Bellino, M. J., Banks, J. A., Dryden-Peterson, S., Freedman, S. W., & Gonzales, R. G. (2021). Civic reasoning and discourse amid structural inequality, migration, and conflict. In C. Lee, G. White, & D. Dong (Eds.), *Educating for civic reasoning and discourse* (pp. 245–272). National Academy of Education.

Schoppa, L. (2013). Residential mobility and local civic engagement in Japan and the United States: Divergent paths to school. *Comparative Political Studies, 46*(9), 1058–1081. https://doi.org/10.1177/0010414012463896

Schwartz, G. L., Wang, G., Kershaw, K. N., McGowan, C., Kim, M. H., & Hamad, R. (2022). The long shadow of residential racial segregation: Associations between childhood residential segregation trajectories and young adult health among Black US Americans. *Health & Place, 77*, 102904. https://doi.org/10.1016/j.healthplace.2022.102904

Shaxson, L., Bielak, A., Ahmed, I., Brien, D., Conant, B., Fisher, C., & Phipps, D. (2012, April). Expanding our understanding of K*(Kt, KE, Ktt, KMb, KB, KM, etc.). In *A concept paper emerging from the K* conference held in UNU-INWEH Hamilton*, Ontario, Canada, April 2012.

Siegel-Stechler, K., & Kawashima-Ginsberg, K. (2024). *Voter registration policy: Impact and potential for increasing electoral equity*. Center for Information & Research on Civic Learning and Engagement at Tufts University. https://circle.tufts.edu/sites/default/files/2024-10/voter_registration_policy_study.pdf

Sintos, A., Chletsos, M., & Kontos, K. (2024). The political process in nations: Civil society participation and income inequality. *Kyklos, 77*(3), 471–495. https://doi.org/10.1111/kykl.12375

United States Department of Education, Institute of Education Sciences, National Center for Education Statistics. (2023). *NAEP report card: 2022 NAEP civics assessment highlighted results at grade 8 for the nation*. https://www.nationsreportcard.gov/highlights/civics/2022/#student-group-performance

University of Florida Election Lab. (2023). *Voter turnout rates among metropolitan statistical areas in the 2016 and 2020 presidential elections*. https://election.lab.ufl.edu/content/MSA_turnout_report.pdf

Vallbé, J. J., & Ferran, J. M. (2017). The road not taken. Effects of residential mobility on local electoral turnout. *Political Geography, 60*, 86–99. https://doi.org/10.1016/j.polgeo.2017.04.010

Wray-Lake, L., & Abrams, L. S. (2020). Pathways to civic engagement among urban youth of color. *Monographs of the Society for Research in Child Development, 85*(2), 7–154. https://doi.org/10.1111/mono.12415

Wray-Lake, L., & Ballard, P. J. (2023). Civic engagement across adolescence and early adulthood. In L. J. Crockett, G. Carlo, & J. E. Schulenberg (Eds.), *APA handbook of adolescent and young adult development* (pp. 573–593). American Psychological Association. https://doi.org/10.1037/0000298-035

Yang, Y., & Konrath, S. (2023). A systematic review and meta-analysis of the relationship between economic inequality and prosocial behaviour. *Nature Human Behaviour, 7*(11), 1899–1916. https://doi.org/10.1038/s41562-023-01681-y

Index

Note: Page references in *italics* denote figures, in **bold** tables and with "n" endnotes.

accountability 17, 35, 113–114, 116, 118–120, 152, 154, 244
Advanced Placement in US Government and Politics 18
agency 58, 75, 153, 155, 157, 240, 244, 246–248, 249, 251, 257, 263
Alaska Department of Education and Early Development (DEED) 115–116
Alaska History Workgroup (AHWG) 115–116
"American Creed" (Myrdal) 16
American Dream 13
American Educational Research Association 138
American Government (Magruder) 15
American Historical Association 10, 14
American Institutes for Research (AIR) 109, 112, 114, 116, 118, 188
Americanization 13–14
American Political Behavior 17
American Political Science Association 10
American Psychological Association 138
"American Way of Life" (Herberg) 16
"AP for all" movement 217
artificial intelligence (AI) 22, 170; and assessments 29; and civic skills 25–31; defined 36n1; and educational assessment 23; emerging approaches 26; fairness in testing 31; generative 22, 25–26, 29–30, 32–33, 35–36, 161; ratings and related methods 27; scoring of tasks and essays 30; situational judgment tests (SJTs) 27; working examples of performance tasks with 31–34
assessment: authentic 14, 213; digital literacy as civic skill in K-12 classrooms 187–199; educational 23; in equity-focused learning culture 213
authentic assessments 14, 213
automatic item generation (AIG) 29
average inter-item correlation (AIC) 144

balanced assessment systems 3
belonging 45, 81, 169–170, 228, 245, 247–251, 264, 268
benchmarking 35, 66, 84, 270
blended approach 191–192

Campaign for the Civic Mission of Schools 220–221
Caregiver Ambassadorship 244
caregivers 239, 241; capacity 244; capacity-building efforts 243; as researchers 243–244
Census Current Population Survey (CPS) 260
Center for Information & Research on Civic Learning and Engagement (CIRCLE), Tufts University 220, 256
citizenship 7–9, 11–19, 25–26, 35, 42, 49, 56–57, 65, 70–72, 76, 81–82, 84, 87, 100–102, 108, 139, 141, 151, 168–180, 238, 247–248
citizenship education and assessment 12–15; ILSAs on 80–82
Citizenship Education Project 16–17
citizenship self-efficacy 84–87, **85–86**
Citizenship Self-Efficacy and Internal Political Efficacy 139
CIVED 80–82
civic and citizenship education (CCE): cross-national assessment 100–101; school and classroom contexts 93–100; young people's views of political system 90–93
civic competencies 2–4, 151–152, 155, 160, 163, 164n1, 220–236; critical 22; essential 34; future 24; scenario-based learning and assessment tasks 220–236
civic competency assessments 250–252
civic culture 264, 266–268
civic dispositions 14, 56, 68, 71, 111, 159

civic education and assessment 74; in the 20th and 21st centuries 15–18; defined 9; foundations in the US 9–12; ILSAs on 80–82; questions 8

civic engagement 2–3, 15, 19, 24–25, 28, 30, 33, 43, 55, 58, 70–72, 76, 82, 119, 140–142, 146, 156, 159, 187, 198, 220, 238, 244, 250–251, 256–261, 263–266, 268, 270–272

civic identity 137–148; development 137–138; empirical studies 142–144; evidence based on content 139–141; evidence based on internal structure 142–146; evidence based on relations with other variables 146–148; evidence based on response processes 141–142

civic learning 1, 44, 151–164; classroom- and teacher-level indicators 156–158; CLO indicator system 160–163; CLO monitoring 154–155; defining 2; game-based approaches 26–27; importance of monitoring CLO 154; innovative measures for 28; large-scale assessments 65–77; measurement opportunities in 73–74; multimodal measures of 27–28; opportunities 152–155; overview 151–152; performance measures in 26; robust systems of assessment for 3–4; school-level indicators 158–160; skills 23–24; system of CLO indicators 155–160

civic learning opportunities (CLO) 152; alternate approaches to measurement 161–162; classroom- and teacher-level indicators 156–158; conditions supporting indicator system 160–163; connecting indicators to data on civic readiness 162–163; courses and curricula 158–159; current state of CLO monitoring 154–155; data from multiple sources 160–161; defined 152; importance of monitoring 154; indicators 155–160; instructional activities and content 156–157; instructional materials and assessments 157–158; instructional quality 157; longitudinal monitoring 163; opportunity to learn (OTL) 152–154; policy relevance of 152–154; positive school climate 159–160; prioritize measurement quality 162; school-level indicators 158–160; service learning 159; staffing supports 160; student voice opportunities 159; teacher capacity 158; teachers' attitudes and beliefs 158

civic measurement 44; conceptual framework 43–44; defined 41; definitions for good citizenship 56–57; gaps in the availability of tools 54–55; implications for promoting equity in 59; map 44–47, **46–47**, 57–58; map interactions 52; mapping 41–60; methodology 42–43; themes 52–57; tools 42–43, 57; voting dominates 55, 55–56

civic online reasoning (COR) 193

civic opportunities 41, 44; map 48–49, **49–51**, *54*; measured more civic readiness 52–53

civic participation 8, 13, 15, 23, 25, 70, 81, 84, 139–141, 256–257, 259–260

civic principles 70, 83, 107–121; accountability 116; civics standards and assessment indicators 120–121; civics standards revision process 109–113; civility 117–118; lessons learned 120–121; measurable civics assessment indicators 119–120; overview 107–109; plurality 117; representation 114–116; social studies team 109; for standards revision 113–118; transparency 113–114

civic readiness 41, 44, 155; map 52, *53*; measured more civic opportunities 52–53

Civic Readiness Map 44–47, *45*, **46–47**, 250

civic reciprocity 140–141, 143, 145, 147–148

civics assessment indicators 119–120

civic self-care 139–141, 143, 146, 148

civic self-confidence 139–143, 145–148

civic skills: and artificial intelligence 25–31; complex, difficult-to-measure 25; and technology 24–25

civics standards revision process 109–113; implement 111–113; preparation phase 110; revision 110–111

civic values 9, 120, 137–148

civic values questionnaire (CVQ) 137, 138–139, 140, 141, 143–145, **145**

civility 113, 117–118, 119

co-creation of local learning ecosystems 239–240

Collaborative for Academic, Social, and Emotional Learning (CASEL) 238–240, 244–248

collaborative problem-solving (CPS) 239–240, 244, 248–252, 260, 263

College, Career, and Civic Life (C3) Framework for Social Studies Standards 224–225

Collegiate Learning Assessment (CLA+) 198

common school movement 10

community-based participatory action research 240–247

community-based participatory research (CBPR) 240–241, 243, 246, 252

community civics 11–12

complex scenarios as performance assessments 203–217

Complex Scenario Test (CST) 3, 203; addressing cultural responsiveness 212–216; cultural identity and assets 214–215; design and scoring rubric 207–209; design principles 205–206; development 207; PBL-APGOV course 206–207; potential of 212–216; rigor and vulnerability 215–216; rubric design 208–209; student engagement and relationships 213–214; test shell 207–208; validity and reliability evidence 209–210; working with content and constructs 211–212; working with reading and writing difficulty 210; working with scoring 212; working with tasks and questions 210–211

constrained inquiry 225–226, 235
construct cousins 169, 173–174
constructed-response COR items 194–195
Council of Chief State School Officers 112
Council of State Social Studies Specialists 112–113
COVID-19 pandemic 1, 29, 102, 170, 176, 178, 180
cultural identity and assets 214–215
culturally relevant education (CRE) 213
culturally responsive assessments (CRAs) 31, 213
cultural responsiveness 228–229; potential of CST to address 212–216
culture wars 13, 15–18
curiosity 26–27, 228, 244, 247–250

DARPA's Warrior Simulation program 29
deeper learning 203–208, 210–212, 215–217
Democratic Knowledge Project (DKP) 137–139, 143, 148
democratic recession 102
Department of Defense Education Activity (DoDEA) 113
design and scoring rubric 207–209
differentiation 12, 234
Digital Inquiry Group (DIG) 193, 195, 199n2
digital literacy 25, 198, 199n1; assessing as civic skill in K–12 classrooms 187–199
digital literacy assessments 189–197; blended approach 191–192; constructed-response COR items 194; evaluating headlines 189–193; Evaluating Live Sources approach 193–196; Evaluating Real Headlines approach 190; Evaluating Simulated Headlines approach 190–191; multiple-choice 194–195; self-report surveys 196–197
discrete-choice measures (DCMs) 168, 177–178, 179
Dreamandments 243–244
Dream Assessment 243–244

Educating for American Democracy (EAD) initiative 76, 222
educational assessment 12; and artificial intelligence 23; understanding 23
educational attainment 7, 87, 264
Educational Testing Service (ETS) 24–25, 28–29, 222, 228, 230
Education for Life and Work: Developing Transferable Knowledge and Skills in 21st Century Skills 204
educator as researcher 244–246
Educator Workgroup (EWG) 115–116
Emancipation Proclamation 17, 234
embedded formative assessment 226–228
emerging approaches 26, 28
Engage for Equity measures 242

equitable assessment 213
equity-focused learning culture 213
ETS Human Progress Report 24
Evaluating Live Sources approach 193–196
Evaluating Real Headlines approach 190
Evaluating Simulated Headlines approach 190–191
Every Student Succeeds Act 154
Evidence Centered Design (ECD) 31

game-based approaches 26–27
generative AI 22, 25–26, 29–30, 32–33, 35–36, 161
Global AI Debates 33–35
global citizenship education (GCE) 168–180; conceptual barriers 173–175; consensus definition 170; discrete-choice measures (DCMs) 177–178; measurement 170–172; methodological barriers 175–176; multidimensionality 173–174; overview 168–170; political barriers 176–177; potential for cultural universality 174–175; situational-judgment tests (SJTs) 178–180
Global Integrated Scenario-Based Assessment (GISA) 222
Goals 2000: Educate America Act 153
good citizenship 7, 11–13, 19, 71; civic measurement 56–57; definitions for 56–57
Guiding Principles Workgroup (GPWG) 115–116

high-demand skills 24–25
high-quality instructional materials (HQIMs) 112

identity 13, 30, 44–45, 49, 55, 107–108, 111, 129, 137–139, 143, 147, 176, 191–192, 214–215, 247–249, 251
implementation study 143
Institute for Citizens & Scholars 153, 155
Internal Political Efficacy 140
International Association for the Evaluation of Educational Achievement (IEA) 80–84, 101
International Civic and Citizenship Education Study (ICCS) 2–3, 65, 81–82, 139; affective behavioral framework 71; civic knowledge proficiency scale 84; cognitive framework 70–71; framework 70; frameworks *vs.* NAEP 72; framing the assessment of 82–83; instruments used in **83**; learning context framework 71; students' civic knowledge and citizenship self-efficacy 84–87, **85–86**; U.S. participation in 76
international large-scale assessments (ILSAs): on citizenship education 80–82; on civic education 80–82
Internet Research Agency 188
An Introduction to Problems of American Culture (Rugg) 15

jack-knife repeated replication (JRR) 103n2
Jim Crow laws 11
justice-oriented citizenship 139

K-12 classrooms: digital literacy as civic skill in 187–199; digital literacy assessments 189–197; future directions 197–198; overview 189
K-12 school communities: agency 249; belonging 249; brief synopsis and research directions 251–252; collaborative problem-solving (CPS) 248; curiosity 249–250; identity 248–249; key individual level competencies 248–250; related civic competency assessments 250–252; transformative SEL for civic measurement in diverse 238–252
Kentucky Department of Education (KDE) 114

"Laboratory Practices in Citizenship" 17
large language models (LLMs) 29–30, 161
large-scale assessments (LSAs): civic learning and engagement 65–77; construct frameworks in 67–68; data 75; defining 66–67; to support and improve teaching 74–75
lateral reading 193, 196–197
learning ecosystems 60, 239–240, 242, 248–249, 251–252
local learning ecosystems 239–240, 248–249, 251

Maslow's hierarchy of needs 177, *177*
media literacy 1, 24, 26, 52, 55, 73–74, 119, 141, 143, 145–147, 188, 221, 225
Minneapolis Public Schools (MPS) 243
Misinformation Susceptibility Test (MIST) 191–192
mock civic advocacy 32–33, 35
Monitoring Educational Equity report 154
MPS Achievement, Research, and Equity (ARE) 243
multimodal measures of civic learning 27–28
multiple-choice 8, 14, 17–18, 30, 71, 193–195

National Academies of Sciences, Engineering, and Medicine (NASEM) 154, 188
National Academy of Education 152
National Assessment of Educational Progress (NAEP) 2, 18, 65, 108, 154–155; civics exam 8; content framework 68–69; *vs.* ICCS frameworks 72; reading scores 66; survey questionnaires 69–70
National Council for the Social Studies 107
National Council on Measurement in Education 138
National Defense Education Act 16
National Education Association (NEA): *Cardinal Principles of Secondary Education* 12; Committee of Ten 10; Committee on Social Studies 11

National Science Foundation 17
National Standards for Civics and Government 68
A Nation at Risk 17
natural language processing (NLP) 28
Nebraska Department of Education (NDE) 110
Nebraska State Board of Education (NSBE) 110
New Mexico 109, 111, 116, 121, 125, 264, 269, 273
New Mexico Public Education Department (NMPED) 116
New York Times 16, 191
non-formal learning 103n11

online adult study 143–144, 146–147
online youth study 142–143, 145–147
"Open Classroom" movement 17
opportunity to learn (OTL) 3, 66, 152–154
Organisation for Economic Co-operation and Development (OECD) 175

participatory action research: community-based 240–247
PBL-APGOV course 206–207, 209–210
performance assessments 3, 198, 203–217, 222
performance tasks: AI scoring 30; face-to-face 224–225, 228, 231, 236; working examples of 31–34; working examples with artificial intelligence 31–34
A Plain Political Catechism (Winchester) 9–10
Pledge of Allegiance 14–15
plurality 113, 117, 119–120, 125
political landscape 260, 264, 266–268, *267*
political system: students' expected active political participation 92; students' satisfaction with 92, **93, 94**; young people's views of 90–93
population 11, 13, 43, 59, 65–66, 70, 82, 110, 112, 117, 121, 125, 139, 162–163, 173, 192, 220, 260–261, 263–265, 270
preparation and extension activities 222, 226, 229–232, 234–236
professional development (PD) 108–109, 112
Programme for International Student Assessment (PISA) 173, 175
project-based learning (PBL) 137, 151, 159, 203

quality of life 264, 265–266

Rasch Partial Credit Model 103n5
reasoning with content (RWC) 203–217; assessment 207–212; context 205–207; design principles 205–206; limitations 216; PBL-APGOV course 206–207; potential of CST to address cultural responsiveness 212–216
representation in civics standards revision 114–116
rubric design 208–209

scenario-based learning and assessment tasks: developing civic competencies through 220–236; evaluation of the prototype 230–235; prototype design 222–224; prototype features 224–229
school communities: caregivers as researchers 243–244; community-based participatory action research 240–247; educator as researcher 244–246; youth as researchers 246–247
school family community partnerships 239–240
school quality and student success (SQSS) 154
self-efficacy 102, 139, 146, 156, 210, 249: citizenship 84–87, **85–86**; defined 84
self-report surveys 196–197; reporting behaviors 196; reporting understanding 196–197
situational-judgment tests (SJTs) 27, 161, 168, 178–180
social and emotional learning (SEL) 74; transformative (tSEL) adult learning series 246; transformative SEL implementation tools 244–246
socioculturally responsive assessment 213
South Dakota Department of Education (SD DOE) 118
Standards for Educational and Psychological Testing 162, 204
Stanford History Education Group (SHEG) 193, 199n2
State Education Agencies (SEAs) 109–112
The State of State Standards for Civics and U.S. History 108
storytelling 10, 270
student engagement 123–133; classroom observation coding **128**; classroom observations 126, 132; conceptualized 123–124; data analysis 127–128; data collection 126–127; implications 132–133; methods 125–128; multidimensional construct of 131–132; overview 123; and relationships 213–214; results 128–131; sample population and context 125; self-report surveys 132; survey 126–127, **128**
Student Mini-Pilot of First SBT 231–235; differentiation 234; engagement 232; guidance for new teachers 234–235; preparation and extension activities 234; stand-alone *vs.* embedded use 234; student understanding 233; Think and Discuss screens 233–234; timing 232

teacher guide 222, 224, 226–232, 234–236
technology and civic skills 24–25
Tennessee Technological University for the Critical-Thinking Assessment Test 208
Texas Education Administration 109
Think and Discuss screens 233–234
timing 73, 126, 230–232
transformative (tSEL) adult learning series 246
transformative SEL: for civic measurement in diverse K-12 school communities 238–252; exploring implications of 238–252; implementation tools 244–246
transformative social-emotional learning (tSEL) 3
transparency 22, 35, 93, 113–114, 118–120

urban debate leagues (UDLs) 33–34
US Citizenship and Immigration Services (USCIS) 7–8; Naturalization Test 7–8, 13–14, 19
U.S. Citizenship and Immigration Services department 108
U.S. History Through Inquiry: Beginning to 1877 125
U.S. Virgin Islands (USVI) 109, 112, 117

Village of Wisdom (VoW) 243
Virtual Cultural Awareness Trainer (VCAT) 179
voting 58, 81, 147, 158, 220, 256, 259–260, 264–265, 267–268, 270–272; cluster 55; dominates civic measurement 55, 55–56; and elections 261–263

World Values Survey 173, 175

youth as researchers 239, 246–247
youth civic engagement: civic culture 266–268; context and conditions shaping 264–266; educational attainment 265; political landscape 266–268, *267*; population 264–265; quality of life 265–266
youth participatory action research (YPAR) 246–247
Youth Voting and Civic Engagement in America (CIRCLE Data Tool) 3, 256–273; background 257–258; benchmarking and storytelling 270; challenge ahead 272–273; challenges 270–272; civic engagement 263–264; context/conditions shaping youth engagement 264–266; data availability and reliability 270–271; design 258–261; design decisions and limitations 272; framework and interpretation 271; future work 270–272; limitations 270–272; local political home, building 268; measurement for learning and action 261–268; political landscape 266–268; resources and fine-tuning strategies 269–270; voting and elections 261–263

Printed in the United States
by Baker & Taylor Publisher Services